# ADVERTISING AND THE MARKETPLACE

*In Memory of Helen Marie Pepall*

# ADVERTISING AND THE MARKETPLACE

## AN ECONOMICS PERSPECTIVE

LYNNE PEPALL

*Professor of Economics, Department of Economics, Tufts University, USA*

DAN RICHARDS

*Professor of Economics, Department of Economics, Tufts University, USA*

Cheltenham, UK • Northampton, MA, USA

Published by
Edward Elgar Publishing Limited
The Lypiatts
15 Lansdown Road
Cheltenham
Glos GL50 2JA
UK

Edward Elgar Publishing, Inc.
William Pratt House
9 Dewey Court
Northampton
Massachusetts 01060
USA

A catalogue record for this book
is available from the British Library

Library of Congress Control Number: 2021938669

ISBN 978 1 78897 811 8 (cased)
ISBN 978 1 78897 813 2 (paperback)
ISBN 978 1 78897 812 5 (eBook)

Printed and bound in Great Britain by TJ Books Limited, Padstow, Cornwall

# CONTENTS IN BRIEF

# FULL CONTENTS

# TABLES

# INTRODUCTION TO *ADVERTISING AND THE MARKETPLACE*

This book investigates the role of advertising in modern market economies. We examine the role through the lens of economic analysis—both theoretical and empirical. Our experience is that few economics classes cover this material. Our aim is therefore two-fold: to make the case that advertising is an important topic in economics, and to provide a coherent and accessible treatment of the economics literature on the topic of advertising.

Those familiar with Bagwell's (2005) well-known article on the economics of advertising will recognize some of the material cited there in the early chapters of our book. We find it useful to adopt his three-type categorization—informative, persuasive, or complementary—of the ways that advertising can affect consumer demand. This frames our review of the material in Chapters 3, 4, and 5, where we work through in considerable detail microeconomic models of each type of advertising.

Subsequent chapters include a variety of topics that, to our knowledge, have not been systematically reviewed in a single text elsewhere. These include reviews of some recent empirical studies on the impact of advertising, deceptive advertising and regulation, signaling, and the twenty-first-century interplay between advertising and two-sided platforms. The many aspects of this last important topic are the focus of the final three chapters of the book.

Because we review a number of empirical studies, we have included in Chapters 6 and 7 a brief synopsis of basic econometric techniques. The problem of identifying true causal relationships, as distinct from those relationships that reflect a correlation, is a critical but much underappreciated issue in social sciences and beyond. It is a challenging problem and it is difficult to comprehend it unless there is first an understanding of basic empirical methods and the pitfalls that those methods, such as linear regression, often encounter. Fortunately, economists have made much progress in the past 20 years in addressing this challenge. We believe that the empirical advertising studies that we have chosen to review demonstrate in a clear and important way the challenge of making accurate statistical inferences and the ways economists have been able to meet those challenges.

Our detailed discussion of empirical studies is matched throughout the book with an equally detailed presentation of various models of advertising. These models capture the ways by which advertising affects consumer and firm behavior and the impact advertising has on market outcomes. We believe that our approach will be helpful to policy-makers and to those involved in marketing analyses, as well as to economists. Our presentations are designed to be accessible to a wide audience across these groups.

Advertising is an important phenomenon and makes up a non-trivial part of the nation's gross domestic product. It affects consumers' welfare, the nature of business competition, and firms' profits; in each case raising substantive issues for public policy. Advertising also serves as a principal way in which we finance news and other kinds of public goods. We very much hope that readers of this text will come away with an appreciation for the roles that advertising plays in a market economy and the complexities these entail.

Our choice to view advertising through an economic lens reflects an additional goal. Specifically, we hope that readers will take away from this text an appreciation for economic modeling and careful empirical work. Viewed in this light, the book is about more than the phenomenon of advertising. It makes a broader statement that, notwithstanding the complaints of excessive mathematics and unrealistic assumptions, there is a case to be made for rigorous modeling and data analysis. Indeed, it is the only way to get good answers to important questions.

We owe a great deal to a number of institutions and people. We thank the Institute for New Economic Thinking (INET) at Cambridge University and Clare Hall College for the hospitality and support they provided during our time as visitors there in the winter and spring of 2019. We also thank the Advertising Education Foundation for its support. Among the many individuals from whose comments we have benefited are: Simon Anderson, Jeremy Edwards, Silke Forbes, Christos Genakos, John Kwoka, Sheilagh Ogilvie, Christopher Snyder, and Flavio Toxvaerd. We would also like to thank Emily Ehrnschwender, Vivian Kim, and Shahen Hagen for excellent research assistance and Dr. Diego Álvarez for his careful and thoughtful reading of the manuscript. Finally, we owe a special thanks to those students at Tufts who passed through the Economics 174 class on Advertising and Imperfect Information. Their feedback on the issues they wanted to cover and the need for accessible presentations of economic modeling and econometrics were invaluable to us in the development of this book.

# 1
# Foundations

## 1.1 INTRODUCTION

Advertising is something of a paradox—often disparaged as intrusive, annoying, deceptive, and manipulative, yet at the same time lauded as artful, humorous and socially
provocative. Advertising is also omnipresent in our culture—it's on television networks,
YouTube, Google, Facebook, newspapers, radio, magazines—it dots the landscape
and cityscape with billboards, and even shows up on our T-shirts and headbands.
The magnitude of the advertising phenomenon, in terms of total dollars spent, is also
significant. Total expenditure on advertising in the US was over $200 billion in 2017,[1]
roughly three times what was spent on tuition at state and community colleges.[2] As
much as we might be critical of advertising, it seems that contemporary society can
hardly live without it.

The advertising phenomenon poses a challenge for both the consumer side of the
market and the producer side. How (and whether) advertising works on the consumer
side is far from clear. Does it really generate additional sales? If it does, is this because
it alerts consumers to the existence of products at attractive prices? Or, is its impact
instead due to the fact that it somehow persuades consumers to believe they need something they previously thought was unnecessary? Perhaps, advertising itself is something
that people like and they can show their enjoyment by buying those brands whose
advertising they most appreciate.

As we will see, understanding precisely how (and how well) advertising works can be
difficult. For instance, if advertising works because it gives consumers information about
the availability and prices of different products, why then are so many well-established
firms such as Coca-Cola, GM, and McDonald's among the largest advertising spenders?
Surely most, if not all, consumers know of the availability of the goods and services of
these major firms. Moreover, if knowing the price is important, why is it that advertising
by these and other well-known firms typically makes no mention of price? Indeed, the
heavily viewed and very expensive Super Bowl ads for example seem to have telling a
story or building an image as their main purpose—not notifying consumers of a low
price.

If advertising does not generally provide clear and concrete information about products, then its objective may well be to persuade consumers that they want goods that
they knew were available but had previously thought they would not buy, potentially

because they thought they preferred to spend their money on something else. This line of reasoning though carries the unpleasant suggestion that consumers can be "tricked" or cajoled into buying items that they really do not want, in a way similar to the consumer victims of the nineteenth-century promoters of "snake oil." Yet while one can imagine this happening in the nineteenth century, it is more difficult to believe that today's consumers can be tricked repeatedly into buying a good that they do not want.

In addition to whatever uncertainty there is about the mechanism by which advertising affects consumer decisions, there remains the further uncertainty firms must have about the efficacy of their advertising expenditures. Whether advertising works by providing information or by persuading consumers or in some other way, a firm can find it difficult to isolate the impact of its advertising from other factors affecting consumers in the marketplace. For example, many companies advertise heavily in the month leading up to the Christmas holiday and sales may be correspondingly high. Yet a lot of those sales would have likely happened anyway. It may be that the holiday season and the prospect of high sales induces the firm to advertise rather than the other way around. Moreover, the effect of one firm's advertising may depend critically on whether its rivals advertise as well. So, again, working out the net incremental effect on one's own sales is likely to be difficult for a firm. Yet if a firm cannot determine the effect of its advertising, it cannot determine the optimal amount of advertising funds to spend.

In sum, it is a challenge to develop an economic understanding of how advertising affects consumer behavior and, consequently, how firms should choose their advertising strategies. Such difficulties were recognized very early on by marketing pioneers and were reflected in the famous remark of John Wanamaker, an entrepreneur of the late nineteenth and early twentieth centuries who is often credited with inventing both the price tag and the "money-back" guarantee. Wanamaker said, "Half the money I spend on advertising is wasted; the trouble is I don't know which half."

There is a further complication in understanding how advertising works. This is that most advertising takes place on media platforms such as television, radio, newspapers, magazines, and of course, the Internet, and these platforms simultaneously serve two markets. Print media sell content to readers while at the same time selling print space to advertisers. Cable viewers pay a fee for access to the programs, but firms pay often bigger fees to the cable firm to air their commercials. The advertising market has in fact three sets of players—the firms that want to advertise, the consumers that view those ads, and the platform that acts as an intermediate between. In turn, this means that the pricing and content of the platforms and their ability to attract viewers and advertisers are important determinants of how advertising works, and this introduces new complications into how we understand advertising.

Our goal in this book is to present from an economics perspective the analytical approaches and empirical evidence on advertising that economists have developed to answer many of the questions about advertising raised above. That means we will review economic models and empirical studies to work out how advertising affects consumer demand, competition, and market performance. In the case of media platforms, this requires analyzing both sides of the market, the advertisers, the viewers and what attracts them to each other. We will be interested in such questions as: Does advertising lead to lower or higher prices? Does it encourage or inhibit entry into markets? Does advertising foster more or less concentrated industries? What are the effects of advertising for consumers and, more generally, does advertising lead to a more or less efficient allocation of resources?

The text is divided into several parts. The first part reviews basic economic models of competition and the role that advertising may play in this competition. These models investigate the different mechanisms by which advertising affects consumer demand. They also explore what economic theory may be able to reveal about the impact of advertising on social welfare. Subsequently, we explore empirical evidence regarding the impact of advertising and the mechanisms by which that impact may be transmitted. Lastly, in the final three chapters, we turn our attention to media platforms and their role as intermediaries bringing firms' advertising to their potential consumers.

In today's digital age, media platforms are notably better at gathering and compiling data on consumers' habits. This data can be used by the platforms and the firms they serve so that advertising to consumers may be better targeted. In addition to shedding light on the role of advertising in product markets, our investigation into media platforms, such as Facebook, permits exploration of a number of challenges and opportunities that will shape media competition for years to come.

Before we begin, a basic grounding in economic foundations is needed. In the remainder of this chapter, we review some basic models of market competition. These provide a framework in which to consider the potential roles that advertising may play in the marketplace and to evaluate its impact on market performance.

## 1.2 PERFECT COMPETITION VERSUS PERFECT MONOPOLY[3]

We begin with the two polar cases of perfect competition and pure monopoly. An understanding of these two cases will make it easier to investigate the more complex but more realistic world of imperfect competition, specifically, monopolistic competition and oligopoly.

### 1.2.1 A Perfectly Competitive Market

Every market whether competitive, monopolized, or something in between has two sides—the consumer side (demand) and the producer side (supply). Our review starts with the description of consumer demand for a particular product, say ice skates or blue jeans or household detergent, that defines the market of interest. Utility maximization by consumers, who are each subject to a budget constraint, leads to the demand for the product being inversely related to the product price. The demand curve for any product describes this inverse relation by expressing the total quantity of the good that all consumers in the market will buy at each price.

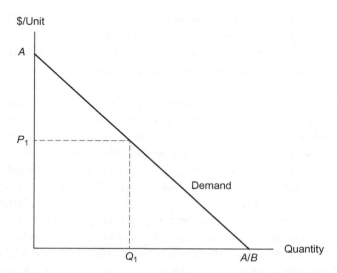

*Note:* At price $P_1$ all consumer purchases combined will sum to $Q_1$ units. Alternatively, when $Q_1$ units are sold, $P_1$ is the marginal valuation of the $Q_1^{\text{th}}$ unit.

**Figure 1.1  Consumer demand**

Figure 1.1 shows an example of a market demand curve—more specifically, a linear market demand curve, which can be described by the equation $P = A - BQ$.[4] Observe that the demand curve intersects the vertical or price axis at the point A. The value A describes the maximum amount that any consumer in the market is willing to pay to have this good. It is called the maximum reservation demand price. At prices greater than A, no consumer in this market wants to buy the product—there is no demand for this product. At prices less than A there is positive demand for the product. For example, if the good sells at a price $P_1$ then each consumer's preferences are such that taken as a group, all consumers want to purchase quantity $Q_1$ of the good at this price. The price $P_1$ is in fact the reservation demand price for the $Q_1$th unit of the good and describes consumer willingness to pay at that margin.

When we say that a demand curve represents consumer demand for a good it is important to understand that the quantities of the good being purchased at any particular price are the quantities bought over some specified interval of time during which the good is consumed, e.g., per week, per month, per quarter, or per year. Similarly, when we talk about firms producing the good, we want to consider their production quantities as correspondingly those quantities produced over the same weekly, monthly, quarterly, or annual production period. If we are interested in consumer demand for the product during a quarter, then the production and marketing possibilities available to firms are more constrained than if we consider consumer demand over the year. The shorter the time period, the fewer options that any firm has for hiring more inputs and increasing production of the good.

Following the tradition in microeconomics, we distinguish between two general time periods: the short run and the long run. The short run is a sufficiently short time period so that no new production facilities—no new plant and equipment—can be brought into production. In the short run, neither the number of firms nor the fixed capital at each firm can be changed. Only labor and raw materials can be varied. By contrast, the long run is a production period sufficiently long so that both established firms and new entrants can build new production facilities to meet market demand or exit.

For both the short run and the long run economists are interested in understanding when a given market is in "equilibrium." By this we mean a market outcome in which no consumer and no firm in the market has an incentive to change its decision regarding how much to buy or how much to sell. Equilibrium is a state in which no one could benefit by changing his or her trading decision unilaterally.

Consumer behavior is described by the market demand curve and the constrained utility maximization underlying it. What is the analogous description of firm behavior that determines how much firms want to supply and sell?

To understand a firm's behavior in the market it is helpful to first think about the firm's size relative to the entire market. Suppose for example that a firm's potential supply of the good is "small" relative to the market. Think of an apple farmer in Massachusetts or, alternatively, a broker on the New York Stock Exchange trading Apple stock. Each is so small that any change in how much they sell would have essentially no impact on the price of apples or on the price of Apple stock. Neither the "small" farmer nor the "small" broker can affect the price at which he or she trades. In other words, the farmer or the broker is a "price taker." The price of the product is not something that they can affect by their decision to sell.

In a perfectly competitive market, each firm is small relative to the market and cannot influence the price. Each firm is a "price taker." Because a perfectly competitive firm cannot influence the market price at which the good trades, the firm can sell as much, or as little, as it wants at that price. If the firm was not able to sell as much as it wants at the market price, then the implication would be that to sell more to consumers the firm must lower its price to induce consumers to buy. But then the firm would not be a "price taker" because its selling decision would affect the market price. Moreover, if the firm tried to raise its price it would sell nothing, as its consumers would switch to other firms selling the same product at a lower price. The products sold by perfectly competitive firms are, in the eyes of consumers, perfect substitutes.

Being a "price taker" is the fundamental reason why advertising does not play a role in perfectly competitive markets—a perfectly competitive firm is selling as much as it wants at the current price—it does not need to advertise to sell more.

The "price taking" feature of the perfectly competitive firm can be represented by distinguishing between the demand curve faced by the individual firm and the demand curve for the entire market. The market demand curve is the one already described. It shows the total amount bought by all consumers from all firms at any particular price. However, the individual perfectly competitive firm does not observe that demand curve. All the competitive firm sees is the current price and it believes (correctly) that it can sell as much or as little as it wants at that price. Graphically, this means that the individual competitive firm perceives the demand curve it faces as a horizontal line at the current market price. Again, the overall market demand curve is downward sloping. If *all* the firms in the market increased their output, the price would have to fall. However, each individual firm is so tiny relative to the overall market, that any increase (or decrease) in its output leaves the price unaffected. This is why the demand curve facing the individual competitive firm is a horizontal line at the current price.[5]

The perfectly competitive firm, like all the firms that we will study, is a profit maximizer. It will choose to sell the precise amount of output that maximizes its profit. Profit is the difference between the firm's revenue and its total costs. Firm revenue $R(q)$ is equal to the market price times the firm's entire output. Marginal revenue $MR(q)$ is the revenue associated with the last or $q$th unit of the product sold by the firm. Mathematically, $MR(q)$ is the derivative of $R(q)$ with respect to $q$, i.e., $MR(q) = q\dfrac{dP(Q)}{dq} + P(Q)$. Because the perfectly competitive firm's choice of $q$ has no effect on the market price, the first term in this expression is zero implying that $MR(q) = P$. This is of course just another way to say that such a firm faces a horizontal demand curve at the current market price $P$. Each additional unit that it produces raises revenue by that price $P$. Likewise, it loses revenue $P$ for each unit that it reduces its output.

The firm's cost of producing output in a given time period is described by a total cost function, $C(q)$. The cost function measures how much it costs the firm, in terms of what it must pay for inputs, to produce any given output level $q$. To produce more output $q$ requires more input. So, $C(q)$ rises with an increase in the output level $q$.

In order to hire inputs for production, the firm must pay an amount that is at least as high as what that input could earn in its next best alternative employment. This is true for the capital employed by the firm as much as it is true for the labor and raw materials that the firm uses in production. The opportunity cost for the firm's capital is measured as the rate of return that the capital could earn if it was invested in other industries. It is helpful to define a condition in which the firm earns just enough revenue to cover all of its costs so that at the current market price and production decision $Pq = C(q)$, the firm earns zero or no *economic* profit. It is important to recognize that such a condition does not mean that its stockholders go away empty-handed or that the firm is a bust. When the revenue is covering *all* the costs, then there is enough to pay investors their opportunity cost. When a firm earns zero economic profit, stockholders do not earn zero returns. They simply earn the same return on their investment that they would have received if they had invested in other companies.

Analogous to marginal revenue $MR(q)$, we define a firm's marginal cost denoted by $MC(q)$. Marginal cost measures the cost incurred by the firm to produce the last or the $q$th unit of output. Mathematically, it is the derivative of $C(q)$ with respect to $q$, or

$$MC(q) = \frac{dC(q)}{dq}.$$

Profit $\pi(q)$ is the difference between revenue and costs, i.e., $\pi(q) = R(q) - C(q)$. For a firm to choose an output level to maximize its profit, it is necessary that the following condition is satisfied:

$$\frac{d\pi(q)}{dq} = \frac{dR(q)}{dq} - \frac{dC(q)}{q} = MR(q) - MC(q) = 0$$

Or
$$MR(q) = MC(q) \tag{1.1}$$

For the perfectly competitive firm we know that $MR(q) = P$. So, for each firm in a perfectly competitive market, equation (1.1) becomes:

$$P = MC(q) \tag{1.2}$$

The profit-maximizing perfectly competitive firm produces an output level $q$ where $P = MC(q)$ in equilibrium. The firm is maximizing profit and has no reason to change its output decision.

Diagrams like those shown in Figures 1.2(a) and 1.2(b), respectively, illustrate the standard textbook model of the perfectly competitive firm and the perfectly competitive market. The initial market demand curve is $D_1$ and the market price is $P_C$. A profit-maximizing firm produces output $q_C$ and incurs a marginal cost of $MC(q_C)$, which is simply equal to that price. Producing one more unit would incur an extra cost that exceeds the price at which that unit would sell. Conversely, producing less than $q_C$ would save less in cost than it would sacrifice in revenue. Hence, when the firm produces $q_C$ and sells it at market price $P_C$, it maximizes profit. Note however that, as drawn, at this price, the firm also just covers its average cost. It is therefore earning zero economic profit.

The total market supply is defined as the sum of each firm's profit-maximizing output, $q$, at a given market price. Because for each output decision a firm is maximizing profit, the condition $P = MC(q)$ will hold for each firm. If demand for the product increases to say curve $D_2$ and the market price rises to say $P_1$, each firm will revise its production decision and increase output to $q_1$ where $P_1 = MC(q_1)$. This will increase total production to $Q_1$. Because the firms' production decisions are governed by costs at the margin, the marginal cost curve of each firm provides the basis for determining the total supply at any given market price. To be precise, the supply curve is generated using the $P = MC$ rule to determine the amount produced by each competitive firm and then summing these production levels across all the firms.[6] The initial market supply function is illustrated by the curve $S_1$ in Figure 1.2(b).

In Figures 1.2(a) and 1.2(b), the market always clears, i.e., supply always equals demand and each firm always produces at a point where $P = MC$. Initially, with demand given by $D_1$ the number of firms is such that this occurs at price $P_C$, with each firm producing at minimum average cost and each just breaking even. If, however, demand shifts to $D_2$ then, in the short run, the price will rise as each of the existing firms follow the $P = MC$ rule to produce at $q_1$ and the market supply increases steadily along $S_1$ to $Q_1$. Note though that this can only be a short-run equilibrium as each firm is selling at a price above its average cost and therefore earning a positive economic profit. Over time, that profit will persuade more firms to enter this market. The supply curve will

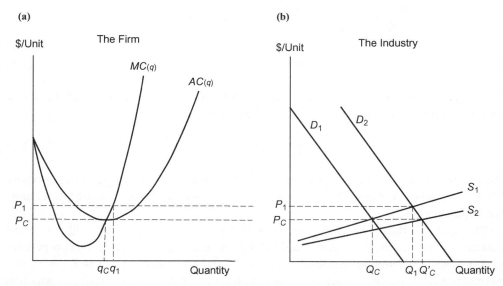

**(a)**

$/Unit    The Firm

$MC(q)$

$AC(q)$

$P_1$
$P_C$

$q_C q_1$    Quantity

**(b)**

$/Unit    The Industry

$D_1$    $D_2$

$S_1$
$S_2$

$P_1$
$P_C$

$Q_C$    $Q_1 Q'_C$    Quantity

*Note:* Price $P_1$ is consistent with a short-run equilibrium in which each firm produces at a point where its marginal cost is equal to $P_1$. However, at $P_1$ price exceeds average cost and each firm earns a positive economic profit. This will encourage entry by new firms, shifting out the supply curve as shown in (b). The long-run competitive equilibrium occurs as price $P_C$ in which each firm produces output level $q_C$ and price equals both average and marginal cost.

**Figure 1.2** Competitive equilibrium

consequently shift out to $S_2$, and a long-run equilibrium will be restored with $P = MC(q) = AC(q)$. Each firm will again be producing $q_C$ units at the minimum average cost. Total market output though will have increased to $Q'_C$ because there are more firms.

The fact that the long-run competitive equilibrium is characterized by each firm producing an output at which average cost is minimized is worth emphasizing. This means that any scale economies have been fully exploited. This illustrates another reason why perfectly competitive firms are not incentivized to sell more output. In a long-run equilibrium, no firm enjoys any potential cost savings or profit gain from expanding (or contracting) its production.

## 1.2.2 A Pure Monopoly Market

A monopoly firm, by definition, is the only supplier of the good, and is therefore, likely to be large relative to the market. Specifically, the monopolist's demand curve is identical with the market demand curve. In complete contrast to the competitive firm, the monopolist's output decision *will* in fact determine the market-clearing price. The monopoly firm has market power or is a "price-maker." This is illustrated in Figure 1.3.

Because the monopolist's demand curve is the market demand curve, it must be downward sloping. Hence, selling more means selling at a lower price. A monopolist who is

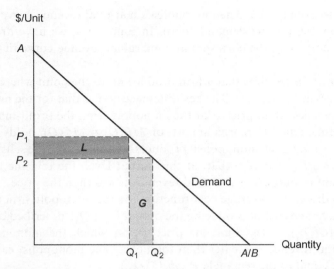

*Note:* A small increase in production from $Q_1$ to $Q_2$ causes price to fall from $P_1$ to $P_2$. The monopolist gains additional revenue $P_2(Q_2 - Q_1)$ equal to area $G$. However, it loses revenue $Q_1(P_1 - P_2)$ equal to area $L$. The net marginal revenue from the increased output is $G - L$, which is always less than the initial price $P_1$.

**Figure 1.3** Monopoly marginal revenue

currently selling $Q_1$ units at price $P_1$ will find that to sell $Q_2 > Q_1$ units requires that the market price must fall from $P_1$ to some lower level $P_2$[7] for *all* of its production. Selling the additional output earns additional revenue of $P_2$ on each of the $Q_2 - Q_1$ additional units of output. This is the area $G$ in Figure 1.3. Yet because the price for the first $Q_1$ units produced must also fall to $P_2$, that revenue gain is somewhat offset by the loss of revenue on these units equal to $(P_1 - P_2)Q_1$—the area $L$ in Figure 1.3. It follows that for a monopolist, the effective marginal revenue from an additional unit sold is not the current market price (as it is for the perfect competitor) but something less.[8] The effective marginal revenue is the difference between the gain and the loss or $G - L$ in Figure 1.3.

More formally, total revenue for the monopolist $= R(Q) = (A - BQ)Q = AQ - BQ^2$. As before, $MR(Q) = \dfrac{dR(Q)}{dQ}$, which yields:

$$MR(Q) = \frac{dR(Q)}{dQ} = A - 2BQ \tag{1.3}$$

Remember that price is given by $P = A - BQ$. So, equation (1.3) makes it clear that for the monopolist, marginal revenue is less than the price for any positive level of output $Q$. This is clearly different from the case of the perfectly competitive firm, for whom marginal revenue and market price are identical. Specifically, in the case of a linear demand curve such as $P = A - BQ$ the equation for the monopolist's marginal revenue function, $MR(Q) = A - 2BQ$, has the same price intercept A as the monopolist's demand curve but twice the slope, $-2B$. The monopolist's marginal revenue curve therefore lies everywhere below the inverse demand curve. In Figure 1.4, we have drawn both the market demand curve and the corresponding marginal revenue curve that the monopolist faces.

Profit maximization requires that a firm produce up to the point where the marginal revenue just covers marginal cost. The key difference here is that for the monopoly firm, marginal revenue is less than price. For the monopoly firm, the profit-maximizing rule of marginal revenue equal to marginal cost, or $MR(Q) = MC(Q)$, holds at the output $Q_M$. The profit-maximizing monopolist produces at this level and sells each unit of output at the price $P_M$. Observe that, at this output level, the revenue received from selling the last unit of output, or marginal revenue, is less than the price.

We have also drawn the average cost function for the monopoly firm in Figure 1.4. The per unit or average cost of producing the output level $Q_M$, described on the average cost curve by $AC(Q_M)$, is less than the price $P_M$ at which the monopolist sells the good. Hence, total revenue is greater than total cost. The monopolist earns a positive economic profit, equal to the rectangle $P_M abAC(Q_M)$.

If entry by new firms is blocked, say, because the monopolist has a patent or for some other reasons, this is a long-run equilibrium outcome. Each consumer buys as much as

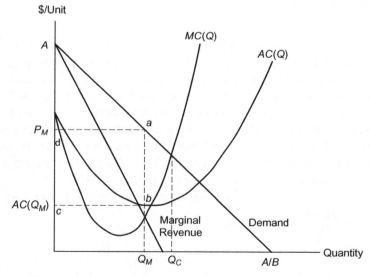

*Note:* The monopolist maximizes profit by choosing the output $Q_M$ at which marginal revenue equals marginal cost. This output then sells at price $P_M$, which exceeds marginal cost. Profit is the rectangle *abcd*. In the short run, the competitive industry produces $Q_C$, at which point price equals marginal cost. In the long run, it produces at minimum average cost at which point average cost and marginal cost are the same, implying that $P = MC = AC$, so that no economic profit is earned.

**Figure 1.4** The monopoly equilibrium

is desired at price $Q_M$. Still, the monopolist has no profit incentive to sell more or to sell less. As we have drawn the diagram, the monopolist is operating at minimal average cost. However, this need not (and may well not) be the case.

In order to compare perfect competition to pure monopoly it is useful to define the concept of the price elasticity of demand that a firm faces. We denote the price elasticity of demand by $\varepsilon$, where $\varepsilon$ is the proportional change in the quantity demanded in response to a proportional change in price, i.e.,

$$\varepsilon = -\frac{dQ/Q}{dP/P} = -\frac{P}{Q}\frac{dQ}{dP} \tag{1.4}$$

Note that we have inserted a negative sign so that the elasticity measure is positive as $dQ/dP < 0$. The monopolist's marginal revenue $MR(Q) = \frac{d[P(Q)Q]}{dQ} = Q\frac{dP}{dQ} + P$. Hence, we can write:

$$MR(Q) = P\left(1 - \frac{1}{\varepsilon}\right) \tag{1.5}$$

Substitution into the profit-maximizing condition $MR(Q) = MC(Q)$ yields:

$$MR(Q) = P\left(1 - \frac{1}{\varepsilon}\right) = MC(Q) \Rightarrow \frac{(P - MC)}{P} = \frac{1}{\varepsilon} \tag{1.6}$$

The term $\frac{(P - MC)}{P}$ is commonly referred to as the Lerner Index of Monopoly Power, due to the popularization of this measure by the inventive economist, Abba Lerner. It indicates the degree by which a firm raises its price above marginal cost and it is inversely proportional to the price elasticity of demand.

Recall that a perfectly competitive firm can sell all it wants at the current price. If it charges a higher price, it loses all of its customers, and if it charges a lower price it gains an infinite number. This is a way of saying that the competitive firm faces an infinitely elastic demand, which by equation (1.6) indicates its price will equal marginal cost, since $\varepsilon \to \infty$. For a monopolist however, the price elasticity of demand is considerably less than infinite. Hence, its price is above marginal cost.[9]

A numerical example may be helpful. Suppose the total cost function for a firm is $C(q) = 10q$, so that average cost and marginal cost are both constant and equal $\frac{C(q)}{q} = \frac{dC(q)}{dq} = 10$. In addition, suppose that the market inverse demand curve is: $P = 100 - Q$, where $Q$ is total market output. In a perfectly competitive market, the equilibrium price will be driven to marginal cost or $P = 10$. Market output will be $Q = 90$ and each of the competitive firms will just break even, producing $q = 10$.

In contrast, a monopoly firm (created, say, in Rockefeller style by buying up all the competitive firms) would instead recognize its market power in facing the entire market demand curve and work out that its marginal revenue curve is: $MR(Q) = 100 - 2Q$. Equating this with its marginal cost of 10 yields the monopolist's profit-maximizing output of $Q = 45$, implying a price of 55, and a considerable economic profit of \$2025.

The monopoly firm restricts output in order to keep prices and profits high. Note too that at $Q = 45$, the price elasticity of demand is $-\dfrac{P}{Q}\dfrac{dQ}{dP} = -\dfrac{55}{45}(-1) = 1.222$, so that $\dfrac{P-MC}{P} = \dfrac{45}{55} = \dfrac{1}{1.222} = \dfrac{1}{\varepsilon}$, as in equation (1.6).

The extreme cases of both perfect competition and pure monopoly are somewhat rare. Few firms feel they have absolutely no power over the price they charge. Similarly, neither Standard Oil of the early twentieth century nor Google of the early twenty-first century have control over *all* of their respective markets. Most markets are characterized by firms having some but not complete market power. Firms' decisions can impact market prices, yet they also have at least a few competitors. We now turn to modeling these messier but generally more realistic cases.

## 1.3 IMPERFECTLY COMPETITIVE MARKETS

Imperfectly competitive firms have some monopoly power in so far as they face downward-sloping demand curves. However, they are not without rivals—sometimes facing many competitors in a given market. The source of their power over price is two-fold. Very often, it reflects some product differentiation because consumers do not, as in the case of perfect competition, regard the products of different firms to be perfect substitutes. In the eyes of consumers, McDonald's is a somewhat different fast food experience than Burger King, and even more distinct from Pizza Hut. Likewise, a car made by BMW is not considered a perfect substitute for either an Audi or Toyota's Lexus model. Each firm has some market or monopoly power over its own product lines, but the firm still faces constraints on its pricing in that it will lose many but not all of its customers if it raises its price by a substantial amount.

The other source of market power for imperfectly competitive firms is simply their size relative to the market. For example, consider the passenger aircraft industry. For various reasons, including significant scale economies, this market is dominated by two large firms, Boeing and Airbus. It is true of course that their aircrafts are not identical. Yet even if they were, each would still face a downward-sloping demand in that any significant increase in production by say, Boeing, would be a significant increase in the output of the industry and therefore lead to lower aircraft prices overall.

Two different kinds of models represent imperfect competition, each reflecting the two different sources of market power just described. One is the model of monopolistic competition in which there are many firms each offering a differentiated product so that each brand corresponds to a different version of some basic good or service, e.g., fast food establishments. The other is oligopoly in which there are just a few, large firms whose products may or may not exhibit much differentiation but in which each firm is sufficiently large that its actions affect the entire market environment. The two models do overlap. Even when there are just a few firms they may each put considerable effort into differentiating their products, e.g., Coca-Cola and Pepsi. Similarly, even when there are many monopolistically competitive firms, such as grocery stores, the relevant arena of competition may be a town or urban area in which only two or three of these firms compete directly with each other.

## 1.3.1 Monopolistic Competition

A firm with market power can potentially earn more profit than a perfect competitor who loses all its customers if it tries to raise price. A firm has a strong profit incentive to seek market power, and one way to do this is for the firm to differentiate its product from rival products so that they are no longer perfect substitutes. If the firm can do this then the firm may lose some customers when it raises its price but not all. That is what it means to have market power.

Products and services may be differentiated in many ways. Location is one way. In the consumer's eyes, there is a difference between a dry cleaner across the street and one five miles away. Physical attributes also differentiate products. Some restaurants specialize in serving hot and spicy foods. Some may emphasize vegetarian meals. In a small town with two hotels, one may specialize in luxury service while the other focuses on providing low-cost, no-frills service. Note though that the vegetarian restaurant will not sell much to beef eaters and the luxury hotels will not attract price-conscious consumers on a tight budget. The quest for market power may lead a firm to be in a smaller market niche and its limited market may mean that it has not exhausted all the scale economies in production, i.e., the firm does not produce at minimum average cost. This was an important insight of Edward Chamberlin described in his classic 1933 book, *The Theory of Monopolistic Competition.*[10]

There are many ways to model monopolistically competitive markets and we will make use of a number of these throughout the text. Here, we use a relatively simple numerical example to illustrate some of the basic insights of models of monopolistic competition. Suppose then that there are $n$ firms in a market and each firm offers a different variety of a good, say ice cream or running shoes. If each charges the same price, $p_i$, then we will assume that the firms split the market evenly, and each has a market share of $1/n$. However, any firm can raise (lower) its market share above (below) this share by setting a relatively lower (higher) price.

The following is the assumed demand curve for firm $i$:

$$q_i = \frac{A}{n} - \frac{\bar{P}}{n} + \gamma(\bar{P} - p_i) \qquad with \ \gamma > \frac{1}{n}, \tag{1.7}$$

where $\bar{P} = \dfrac{\sum_{i=1}^{n} p_i}{n}$ is the average price set, $A$ is the maximum amount consumed, i.e., when each firm sets a zero price, and the parameter with $\gamma > \dfrac{1}{n}$ measures how price sensitive are consumers in this market.

Suppose that the number of firms $n$ is sufficiently large such that each firm reasonably believes that changing its price $p_i$ has negligible or no effect on the overall average price $\bar{P}$. In other words, each firm takes $\bar{P}$ as given. In this case we can write firm $i$'s inverse demand as:

$$p_i = \frac{A}{n\gamma} + \left(1 - \frac{1}{n\gamma}\right)\bar{P} - \frac{q_i}{\gamma} \tag{1.8}$$

Let's work through a numerical example and assign values to the parameters $n$, $A$, and $\gamma$. Let $A = 18$; $\gamma = \frac{1}{4}$; and $n = 100$. Firm $i$'s inverse demand curve is rewritten as:

$$p_i = 16.72 + 0.96\,\bar{P} - 4q_i \tag{1.9}$$

The corresponding marginal revenue curve has a slope that is twice as steep and is:

$$MR(q_i) = 16.72 + 0.96\,\bar{P} - 8q_i \tag{1.10}$$

Suppose that each firm has the same costs of production, which can be represented by a total cost function $C(q_i)$, given by:

$$C(q_i) = q_i^3 - 12q_i^2 + 50q_i \tag{1.11}$$

Hence, each firm has a marginal cost function of $MC(q_i) = 3q_i^2 - 24q_i + 50$, and an average cost given by: $AC(q_i) = q_i^2 - 12q_i + 50$.

To solve for firm $i$'s profit-maximizing output we set marginal revenue equal to marginal cost and solve for $q_i^*$:

$$MR(q_i^*) = 16.72 + 0.96\,\bar{P} - 8q_i^* = 3q_i^{*2} - 24q_i^* + 50 = MC(q_i^*) \tag{1.12}$$

We can solve this quadratic equation and find:

$$q_i^*(\bar{P}) = \frac{8 + \sqrt{2.88\bar{P} - 35.84}}{3} \tag{1.13}$$

Now we want to find a price $p_i$ for each firm $i$ and hence an average price $\bar{P}$ such that the market is in equilibrium and each firm $i$ can sell as much output as it produces. Since the firms are symmetric, each firm in equilibrium will expect to sell at the same price $p$, and hence $\bar{P} = p$. Therefore, when we substitute the profit-maximizing output $q_i^*$ in (1.13) into the firm $i$'s demand function and by symmetry set $p_i = p^*$ it must be the case that:

$$p_i = 16.72 + 0.96\,\bar{P} - 4q_i^*(\bar{P}) \rightarrow p^* = 16.72 + .96p^* - 4\left(\frac{8 + \sqrt{2.88p^* - 35.84}}{3}\right) \tag{1.14}$$

Solving (1.14) we find that $p^* = 18$, which is consistent with each firm $i$ selling $q_i^* = 4$. This implies a total output for the $n = 100$ firms equal to $Q^* = 400$. By producing $q_i^* = 4$ each firm is maximizing its profit based on accurate expectations of price, and each firm's market, as well as the overall market, clears.

What about the long run when new firms can come into an industry and others exit? A long-run equilibrium requires that no firm wants to change its decision unilaterally. With this in mind, note that if each firm produces at $q_i = 4$, each firm has an average cost $AC(q_i) = q_i^2 - 12q_i + 50 = 18$. As this is exactly equal to price, each firm is just breaking even. While each firm has market power and each is setting $MR_i = MC_i$, each is earning zero economic profit. So, there is no reason for any one firm to change its output or for any new firms to enter or any existing firms to exit. This market *is* in long-run equilibrium.

Figure 1.5 shows the canonical graph of a monopolistically competitive firm in long-run equilibrium. Product differentiation permits it to have market power and face a downward-sloping demand curve. However, there are so many rivals producing similar (but not identical) products that the firm's demand curve is pushed in far enough that even when it sets the profit-maximizing price $p^*$, it earns no economic profit. That price is merely enough to cover the firm's average cost. Note that this means the long-run equilibrium must occur at a point of tangency between the firm's demand curve and its average cost curve. In turn, this means that the firm must be operating on the downward-sloping portion of its average cost curve implying that average cost would be lower if it expanded its production.

Our numerical example is consistent with this view. Each firm faces a downward-sloping demand curve and produces at the profit-maximizing level where $MR_i = MC_i$,

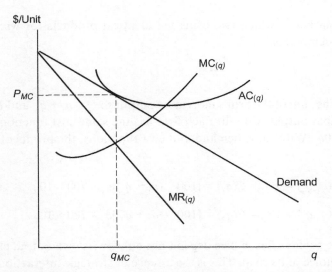

*Note:* The monopolistically competitive firm faces a downward-sloping demand curve. Profit maximization requires that $MR(q) = MC(q)$ implying $P > MC(q)$ at production level $q_{MC}$. The large number of differentiated product rivals is so large that the firm's demand curve is pushed inward so far that all scale economies cannot be exploited. The profit-maximizing price $P_{MC}$ just covers average cost.

**Figure 1.5 Monopolistic competition**

yet each firm just breaks even. It is true that each firm's effort to carve out a market niche where it has some market power has been successful. Yet it is also true that such success comes at a cost, namely, that each market niche is so small that scale economies are not fully exploited, and average cost is not minimized.

In our numerical example, each firm produces $q_i^* = 4$, where average cost = 18. However, the average cost minimum occurs where $q_i = 6$ and average cost = 14. Each firm is therefore operating at two-thirds of the efficient scale and each has an average cost that is nearly 30 percent above the minimum.

## 1.3.2 Oligopoly

We typically distinguish between monopolistically competitive and oligopolistic markets. The primary difference is the nature of the strategic interaction of a firm with its rivals. Under monopolistic competition, a firm has numerous rivals. So, we can largely regard its actions as having little effect on the market overall. This is equivalent to each firm regarding their own price as having no effect on the average market price $\bar{P}$. In contrast, firms in an oligopoly market face only a few rivals, and each firm knows that its actions *will* affect the overall market. As a result, any action that a firm takes can be expected to induce a reaction from its rivals and that reaction must be considered before any action is taken. While there are many ways to model this strategic interaction, a common one is the Cournot-Nash duopoly model to which we now turn.

Consider a market in which two firms sell identical products for which the overall market inverse demand is:

$$P = 100 - Q \tag{1.15}$$

As before, $Q$ = the sum of the firm's individual output so $Q = q_1 + q_2$, and $P$ is the market price at which that output will sell. Each firm has the same cost function described by: $C(q_i) = 700 + 10q_i$. With these demand and cost functions, the profits of the two firms are:

$$\pi_1(q_1, q_2) = Pq_1 - C(q_1) = [100 - (q_1 + q_2)]q_1 - 700 - 10q_1$$
$$\pi_2(q_1, q_2) = Pq_2 - C(q_2) = [100 - (q_1 + q_2)]q_2 - 700 - 10q_2 \tag{1.16}$$

Observe that the profits of each firm depend not only on its own output choice, but also on the output choice of its rival. This is the essence of strategic interaction. Neither firm has complete control of the market, but each is large enough that its actions affect the market environment that both firms face.

How does either firm choosing its profit-maximizing choice proceed in this case? Let's begin by working out firm 1's profit-maximizing choice for $q_1$ given any particular choice of $q_2$ by its rival. To do this, we maximize $\pi_1$ with respect to $q_1$ taking $q_2$ as given. Solving for $q_1^*$ yields:

$$q_1^* = \frac{90 - q_2}{2} \tag{1.17}$$

Doing the same for firm 2 yields a symmetric result.

$$q_2^* = \frac{90 - q_1}{2} \tag{1.18}$$

Equations (1.17) and (1.18) are typically referred to as "best response" functions for firm 1 and firm 2, respectively. The reason should be clear. Equation (1.17) describes the best or profit-maximizing choice of $q_1^*$ that firm 1 should choose in response to any output choice $q_2$ by its rival. Likewise, equation (1.18) describes the analogous choice for firm 2 given $q_2$. A graph combining each of these two best response functions is shown in Figure 1.6.

Where is the equilibrium? It will likely not surprise you to learn that it lies at the intersection of the two best response functions shown in Figure 1.6; that is, where each firm is producing 30 units. Let's think about why that is the equilibrium. An equilibrium outcome is one where neither firm has an incentive to change its production unilaterally. At the intersection point, setting $q_1^* = 30$ is firm 1's profit-maximizing choice given that firm 2 has chosen $q_2 = 30$. There is no reason for firm 1 to change that choice unless firm 2 changes. But, firm 2 has no incentive to change either. Its choice of $q_2^* = 30$ is its profit-maximizing response to firm 1's setting $q_1 = 30$.

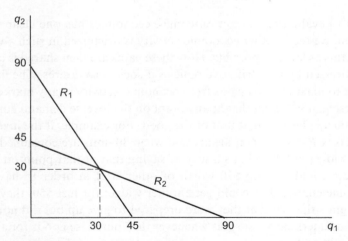

Note: Oligopolistic firms engage in strategic interaction as illustrated by the Cournot example. The Best Response curve $R_1$ gives firm 1's best choice of output for any choice of output by firm 2. Likewise, the Best Response curve $R_2$ gives firm 2's best choice of output for any choice of output by firm 1. Equilibrium occurs at the intersection of the two best response curves so that each firm is choosing its profit-maximizing output given what the other firm is doing and neither wants to change.

**Figure 1.6** Cournot-Nash equilibrium numerical example

Observe that these output choices lead to a price of 40, and therefore a profit to each firm of $(40 - 10) \times 30 - 700 = 200$. Recall too that the marginal cost as for each firm is just 20. The fact that competition is imperfect has allowed these firms to earn a profit and survive. Pricing at marginal cost would leave each firm unable to cover its fixed cost of 700.

The essence of this model was developed long ago by Augustin Cournot (1838). However, because its equilibrium is in fact completely consistent with the equilibrium concept developed a century later by Nash (1951) for all non-cooperative games, it is often now referred to as the Cournot-Nash equilibrium.

## 1.4 OUTSTANDING ISSUES—EVALUATING MARKET OUTCOMES AND THE ROLE OF ADVERTISING

Our review of economic foundations has generated four possible outcomes. These are the polar cases of perfect competition and perfect monopoly, and two models of imperfect competition, monopolistic competition and Cournot oligopoly. Two questions naturally arise at this point. The first is how do we compare the performance of these different markets? How good or bad is the monopoly outcome relative to the competitive one? The second question is: What role for advertising do these models suggest?

### 1.4.1 Evaluating Market Outcomes—Economic Efficiency

When it comes to evaluating market outcomes, economics has one clear standard. In its simplest form, we see whether economic activity is organized in such a way to make the economic gains as large as possible. How these gains are then shared is a matter that can then be addressed by redistributive policies if society so desires. The first objective though must be to maximize the gains from economic activity in any market.

What are these gains? Recall that at any point on the inverse demand curve we know the value consumers place on that unit of the good. For example, if the inverse demand curve for widgets is $P = 100 - Q$ it means that when 30 units are consumed, consumers value the 30th widget at $70. That's a way of saying that at that point on the demand curve, consumers could give up $70 worth of other stuff in order to have one more widget. If by some chance they could get another widget for just $50, they would gain $20 at this margin—the $20 that they were prepared to give up but did not have to. In other words, consumers earn a surplus whenever they purchase goods for a price below what they were willing to pay.

Similarly, the marginal cost curve for any widget producer indicates what the producer has to pay to attract labor and capital inputs away from other activities to widget production. Ultimately, what the firm has to pay for inputs is the value of what they could produce in other sectors of the economy. Hence, the firm earns a surplus on any widget sold to consumers for a price greater than what the firm pays those inputs, i.e., greater than the value of their production elsewhere.

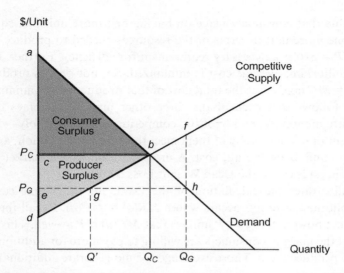

*Note:* All market trades take place at price $P_C$. Consumers therefore earn a surplus equal to the dark-shaded area $abP_C$. Competitive producers earn surplus equal to the light-shaded area $bdP_C$. An efficient market outcome maximizes the total surplus—the sum of consumer and producer surplus. As shown above, a perfectly competitive market achieves this efficient outcome.

**Figure 1.7** **Maximizing the surplus from economic activity**

Maximizing the economic gains from a market's activities means maximizing the total surplus—the surplus of consumers and the surplus of producers combined. When this is achieved, economists call the market outcome efficient. How far the market outcome falls short of this standard is then a measure of market inefficiency. An attractive feature of the efficiency standard is that it is, in principle, measurable.

Figure 1.7 shows the equilibrium for a perfectly competitive market. Again, the demand curve traces out consumer valuations at the margin, while the supply curve traces out the marginal cost of each unit. (Recall the supply curve is the horizontal summation of the firms' marginal cost curves). In a market equilibrium, all transactions take place at the equilibrium price $P_C$. Consumers enjoy a total surplus equal to the triangle *abc*. Similarly, producers enjoy a total surplus equal to triangle *cbd*.

This is an efficient outcome because there is no way to make the total surplus achievable in the market larger. Producing less than the equilibrium amount $Q_C$ would forgo some of the surplus earned by both consumers and producers on the last few units short of that total. Producing more than $Q_C$ requires either forcing consumers to pay more than they value for additional goods (and moving up along the supply curve) or forcing producers to accept less than it costs them to produce the goods (and moving down along the demand curve).

Perfectly competitive markets tend to yield efficient outcomes where the sum of producer and consumer surplus is maximized because, at a competitive equilibrium, price is equal to marginal cost. At such a point, there are no further gains from exchange because the value that consumers place on having one more unit just equals the cost of producing one more unit in terms of the resources needed to produce other goods. The condition $P = MC$ is a necessary requirement for efficiency. Further, in a long-run competitive equilibrium, average cost is minimized. So, not only is production at the point where $P = MC$ holds, but the total cost of that production is minimized.

It therefore follows that each of the three other market outcomes that we have considered—pure monopoly, monopolistic competition, and oligopoly—do not generally yield efficient outcomes. None of them meet the $P = MC$ condition, and they often do not result in minimizing average cost. A measure of how far a market falls short of the efficiency criteria is called the Dead Weight Loss (DWL).

Figure 1.8 illustrates the calculation of the DWL for the simple case of a pure monopoly. Profit maximization occurs where $MR(q) = MC(q)$. Recall though that for firms with market power, $MR(q) < P$ implies that $MC(q) < P$ as well. This is the source of the DWL. At the margin, consumers are willing to pay more for additional units than it truly costs to produce them. Those exchanges would generate additional surplus, but

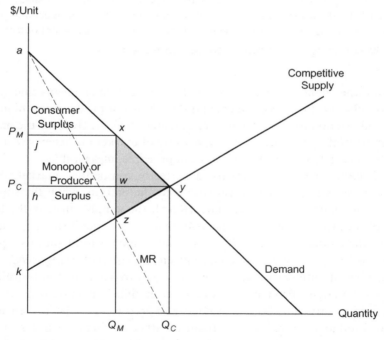

*Note:* The monopolist maximizes profit by setting $MR(q) = MC(q)$ and producing output $Q_M$. This output sells at $P_M$, allowing the monopolist to transfer area *jxwh* from consumer surplus and increasing producer surplus to area *jxzk*. Because $P_M > MC(q)$ monopoly output $Q_M$ is less than the competitive output $Q_C$. Therefore, the potential surplus on units $Q_C - Q_M$ or triangle *xyz* is not realized. This is the Dead Weight Loss.

**Figure 1.8 Measuring the dead weight loss**

firms with market power prevent them from happening because to make them happen, would require lowering the price to all.

A further inefficiency can occur when the average cost is not minimized. This is a loss in the case of monopolistic competition. However, it may well happen under monopoly and oligopoly. On the other hand, monopolistically competitive industries do introduce a wider variety of products. This increase in the menu of product choices that are available to consumers can at least partially offset the other inefficiencies to some extent.

Our primary goal here, however, is not to rank the different market outcomes. Rather, it is to make clear the usefulness of the DWL measure. Given demand and cost estimates, we can then determine the value of any DWL. This is important because while many markets will exhibit some inefficiency, so will many policy interventions. Having a clear measure of market performance allows us to determine whether such government interventions generate net efficiency gains and, if so, whether these gains are large enough given the costs of an intervention.

## 1.4.2 The Role of Advertising

At long last, we are ready to return to the main topic of this book, advertising. What role is there for advertising in the market models discussed above? How does the market structure affect the amount firms spend on advertising? How are a firm's pricing strategies affected by its advertising decisions? Will advertising make the market outcome more or less efficient? How does advertising reach consumers?

We hope to answer many of these questions in the subsequent chapters. Before we begin that more complicated analysis though, we can gain some insight on the answers by thinking first about the perfectly competitive firm. How much advertising will a perfectly competitive firm wish to do? None! Why? Because the perfectly competitive firm can sell as much as it wants at the current price. The reason it does not sell more is because to produce more output would incur a cost (MC) greater than the valuation (P) consumers put on the good.

Does this mean there is no benefit to advertising in a perfectly competitive market? At the level of the individual firm the answer is yes. However, all the firms together could potentially benefit from advertising. Suppose for example there is new research on the health benefits of some foodstuff, say quinoa, which is sold in a perfectly competitive market. If consumers are informed of this new evidence, they would demand more quinoa, and the demand curve would shift out. In the short run, firms would expand their production to the point where $P = MC(q)$ but where $P >$ average cost and makes some economic profit.

However, no individual firm has an incentive to pay for such advertising. Other firms would just free ride on its efforts and enjoy the short-run profit at no cost. Yet if each individual firm refrains from doing any advertising, how would consumers become informed of this newly found quinoa benefit? As this example illustrates, perfectly competitive markets may undersupply valuable product information to consumers.

There is evidence to suggest that this problem holds in markets for many unprocessed or natural food products. This is why producers of many agricultural products often join together in generic advertising that promotes the industry product in general, e.g., the "Got Milk" or "Beef: It's What's for Dinner" campaigns. Whether such efforts are worth the cost and raise efficiency are questions that economists continue to investigate.[11]

How would the outcomes for production, price, and advertising be different under an imperfectly competitive market structure? Suppose, for example, all the perfectly competitive firms in a market suddenly become consolidated into one seller, that is, into a monopoly. In general, firms with market power will have some incentive to advertise. The basic intuition is straightforward. Firms with market power sell at a point where price exceeds marginal cost. If they could sell more at that same price, they gladly would do so. They cannot, of course, because they face a downward-sloping demand curve. If they could somehow shift that curve out to the right though, then more sales with a markup of $P > MC(q)$ would be possible. Advertising may be a means of achieving this shift of demand.

In imperfectly competitive markets, there is a further potential benefit from advertising. Recall for example that the monopolistically competitive firm operates on too small a level and therefore does not fully exploit all scale economies. So, here again if advertising can induce an outward shift of the demand curve it will help to lower the firm's average cost and again increase its profitability.

The advertising that an imperfectly competitive firm engages in could benefit or harm its rivals in the market. A producer of a non-aspirin pain reliever may advertise the benefits of non-aspirin drugs and that advertising could raise the demand for some of its competitors' non-aspirin products, as well. Or the non-aspirin pain reliever producer may have a unique delivery and advertising feature that could adversely affect the demand of its rivals.

We often say advertising works by shifting the demand curve outward. Advertising could in fact rotate the demand curve making it either steeper (which would warrant charging a higher price) or flatter (which would induce an output expansion). This is just a way of saying that we need to consider how advertising works fairly carefully in order to understand why firms advertise in the ways and as much as they do. Again, this is what this book is all about.

## 1.5 SUMMARY

Advertising is a widespread phenomenon in modern economies. In the US, it annually accounts for 1.5 to 2.0 percent of gross domestic product. In the digital age, laptops, tablets, and smart phones are all potential platforms for advertising messages. So, understanding how advertising works and how it affects market outcomes has become increasingly important.

This book presents an analysis of advertising from an economics perspective. Over the last 50 years or longer, economists have developed considerable theory and evidence regarding the impact of advertising on markets and market performance. The economics approach has the advantage that it has a clear standard by which to evaluate market outcomes—namely, efficiency. This gives us a framework for investigating the economics of advertising.

Moreover, because advertising is likely to occur in markets where competition is less than perfect, we need an understanding of imperfect competition. Further, the role of advertising may well depend on the nature of such imperfect competition and so it should not be surprising that, as we will see, the various economic models and empirical studies on advertising do not always point to the same conclusions.

One should therefore not expect this book to provide clear-cut answers to all our questions about advertising. Instead, our hope is that it will help one think about such questions in a productive way. Understanding why the different approaches to advertising differ forces one to recognize the different assumptions underlying each of these methods—both what they leave in and what they leave out. This permits us to recognize that any specific approach may be right for some cases and not for others.

## NOTES

1 https://www.adweek.com/agencies/18-bullish-stats-about-the-state-of-u-s-advertising/ (accessed March 23, 2021).

2 http://www.slate.com/blogs/moneybox/2015/01/14/free_college_here_s_how_much_public_college_stu dents_pay_in_tuition.html (accessed March 23, 2021) gives expenditure for 2013 which adjusted for growth in tuition of roughly 4% per year gives a rough estimate of expenditure for 2017.

3 A more complete review of the material in sections 1.2.1 through 1.4 can be found in Pepall et al. (2014).

4 When price is on the left-hand side of the equation it is often called an inverse demand curve. The reason for this terminology is that traditionally in microeconomics, we think of quantity demanded as being the dependent variable (left-hand side of the equation), and price, the independent variable (right-hand side of the equation). However, when firms choose quantities and price adjusts to clear the market, it is preferable to put market price on the left-hand side, hence, the inverse demand function. Our discussion should make clear that the market demand curve is the horizontal summation of each consumer's individual demand curve.

5 This follows from the definition of a perfect competitor. One may wonder how each firm can face a horizontal demand curve while industry demand is downward sloped. The answer is that the demand curve facing the industry reflects the summation of the individual demand presented by each consumer—not the individual demand facing each firm.

6 We should also note that if the price falls below the minimum average variable cost, the firm will shut down even in the short run.

7 Under perfect competition, firm output is different from industry output. So, we use a lower case $q$ to refer to firm output and an upper case $Q$ for industry output. Under monopoly, firm output is the market output and so we use $Q$ to describe both.

8 For now, we assume that the monopolist cannot charge the first $Q_1$ customers a high price and the next $Q_2 - Q_1$ customers a lower price for the same commodity. The fact that such price discrimination is ruled

out means that the monopolist must sell at the market-clearing price to all consumers and, therefore, that increases in the monopolist's total output and will reduce the equilibrium market price.

9  Note that the monopoly firm will never operate where $\varepsilon < 1$. If it did, a price increase would raise revenue because the gain in price would more than offset the decline in units sold. However, that decline would imply lower production costs meaning that if $\varepsilon < 1$, a price increase would raise revenue, lower costs, and therefore raise profit. Therefore, the monopolist will always raise price to a point where $\varepsilon > 1$.

10  Joan Robinson's book, *The Economics of Imperfect Competition* (1933) was also a major contribution to this development. Hotelling's (1929) model of spatial competition provided a tractable approach to product differentiation.

11  See Messer et al. (2008).

# 1.6 REFERENCES

Chamberlin, E. H. 1933. *The Theory of Monopolistic Competition*. Cambridge, MA: Harvard University Press.

Cournot, A. 1838. *Recherches sur les Principes Mathématiques de la Théorie des Richesses*. Paris: Hachette.

Hotelling, H. 1929. "Stability in Competition." *Economic Journal* 39 (March), 41–57.

Messer, K. D., H. M. Kaiser, and W. D. Schulze. 2008. "The Problem of Free Riding in Voluntary Generic Advertising: Parallelism and Possible Solutions from the Lab." *American Journal of Agricultural Economics* 90, 540–52.

Nash, J. 1951. "Non-Cooperative Games." *Annals of Mathematics* 54 (September), 286–95.

Pepall, L., D. Richards, and G. Norman. 2014. *Industrial Organization: Contemporary Theory and Empirical Applications*. Hoboken, NJ: Wiley.

Robinson, J. 1933. *The Economics of Imperfect Competition*. Cambridge: Cambridge University Press.

# 2
# The Rise of Advertising and the Economics of Advertising

## 2.1 INTRODUCTION

Advertising is a common and widespread feature of modern economies. In the US, it regularly accounts for anywhere from 1.5 percent to 2.0 percent of annual gross domestic product. In this chapter, we briefly review how this phenomenon emerged: how advertising became an integral part of the modern economy and the business thinking behind advertising that contributed to this development. We also show how those business attitudes mirror, to a large extent, the major approaches to advertising that economists have adopted and what these approaches suggest for market outcomes and efficiency.

## 2.2 THE RISE OF NATIONAL MARKETS AND BRANDS

In the late nineteenth century, a combination of technology and market forces combined to transform the American economy. Generally regarded as the second Industrial Revolution, the 50 years after the American Civil War saw per capita GDP double, as new inventions and patents flowed rapidly. Whole new industries including meatpacking, steel, automobiles and many others emerged—each relying on large factories to organize production. Local markets became regional ones, and regional markets grew into national ones. Large firms with national brands emerged and with them came an expanded role for advertising.

### 2.2.1 The Rise of National Markets

Railroads were critical to the industrial transformation of the American economy after the Civil War. The development of locomotive transport was a major breakthrough that for the first time made possible the transportation of large volumes of freight over great distances. This became dramatically clear during the Civil War, as reflected in Union general William Sherman's comment that "the Atlanta campaign was an impossibility without these railroads." Sherman's recognition of the importance of the railways was made even clearer by the fact that he took great efforts to destroy the railroad lines supplying Confederate forces.[1]

In the years following the war, the railroads quickly grew and spread. While the first transcontinental railroad was completed in 1869, four more were added in the next 30 years. The total miles of track increased five-fold from slightly over 40,000 to 215,000. This rapid expansion helped transform the American economy. It gave producers in one region reasonably quick access to consumers in many other, distant regions. Donaldson and Hornbeck (2016) argue that without the railroads providing such access, the value of US farmland would have fallen by over 60 percent during this time.

Of course, farmers were not the only ones benefiting from this transportation revolution. In the first half of the nineteenth century, most manufacturing took place in small artisan shops with less than five employees including the owner/manager. Over the second half of that century this changed as factories employing many more workers became dominant. To a significant extent, the rise of factories reflected a combination of labor-saving technical change (James, 1983) and a fall in capital prices (Atack et al., 2005). However, railroads and access to markets were an important contributing factor, as well.

The larger market access that railroads made possible enabled manufacturing firms to realize scale economies. Factory production, which employed large numbers of workers specializing in different aspects of production, was a natural way to do this. Improved access to markets also made it less necessary for firms to hold inventories. Funds formerly invested in those activities could now be used to finance productive capital investments further enhancing productivity and the capital intensity of production. It is also likely that the reduction in work stoppages due to more continuous access to supplies made employees of factories more willing to accept lower wages in exchange for more hours, further expanding employment and the scale of operations.[2]

In rail transport there are significant scale economies due to the large sunk costs of track investment. So, it is not surprising that accompanying the extensive railroad growth was the rise of large regional dominant firms, such as the New York Central system, the Illinois Central group in the Midwest, the Union Pacific group in the south and southwest, and the Great Northern railway of the northwest. It is estimated that just seven systems accounted for 85 percent of all railroad revenues by 1906.[3]

The revolution in transportation that the railroads embodied had a parallel in communication. Complementing the spread of the railroads was the spread of the telegraph (and much later, the telephone). Telegraph communication allowed the railroads to coordinate trains moving in different directions and became a centralized means of dispatching trains and reporting arrivals and departures throughout a railroad's system.

However, the impact of the telegraph extended far beyond the railroad industry. Telegraph communication meant that businesses in one region could take orders from consumers in another region far away. Moreover, because capital markets could also operate on a more national scale, local businesses in one region—say the East coast—could grow to serve larger regional, or ultimately, national markets. Indeed, for many years, several telegraph companies reported that their New York and Philadelphia offices generated as much as two-thirds of revenue even though they accounted for less than 20 percent of their system's stations (DuBoff, 1980).

The introduction of Edison's "universal stock printer" in the early 1870s intensified the use of the telegraph for transmitting business—especially finance and stock market—information.[4] By 1874, Western Union supplied financial information on its ticker service to customers in 116 cities outside New York. Regional asset price differences could now be eliminated by arbitrageurs relatively quickly because by 1887 transactions anywhere in the US could be completed within 1.5 minutes or less. By 1894, even transactions across the Atlantic could be completed within four minutes (Field, 1998). Indeed, it is arguable that it was the spread of the telegraph and the associated financial links that made it possible to raise the funding needed for railroad growth. Perhaps more importantly for our purpose, the innovations in transportation and communication led the trend toward a decidedly more imperfectly competitive structure. By 1906, Western Union controlled roughly 90 percent of the telegraph market (Goldin, 1947).

## 2.2.2 From National Markets to National Brands

At the end of the American Civil War, roughly 20 percent of the population lived in urban areas. The vast majority of Americans lived in rural small towns, and more often than not households themselves made the final goods they consumed—such as bread, jams, soap, and even clothing. The stores they went to sold local flour, locally grown fruit, local wool, and supplies—products that were typically sold generically in bulk. Local farmers would bring their fruit, vegetables, and produce to the town general store or butcher or fabric shop, and the shop would put the apples in one bin, the potatoes in another, and so on, letting customers examine these and then make their choice.

There were as well many artisan shops. Again, these were small local operations typically producing customized goods to order. A consumer who needed a new pair of shoes would go to the local cobbler who would take measurements and modest style requests and turn out a pair of custom made shoes. Those needing home furniture would turn to the local cabinet-maker for tables, chairs, storage chests, and cupboards. The local blacksmith would provide metal tools, wagon wheels, metal cookware, and horseshoes. There was no shoe store or furniture store or kitchen supply store selling multiple brands of manufactured goods (see, e.g., Atack and Margo, 2017).

However, all of this changed dramatically over the 50 years following the Civil War as the railroad and telegraph united the country, permitting large-scale factory production of many of these products. By 1910, the American population more than doubled from 38 million to 92 million and nearly 50 percent were now living in cities. Low transportation costs and large-scale mass production in factories made it possible for new emerging corporations to provide household products more cheaply than local artisans. At the same time, they needed to find ways to ensure that consumers would buy their products, and not those of a rival. A role for the branding and marketing of a manufacturer's product emerged.

Interestingly there were other technological breakthroughs in communication that increased the scope of advertising. Specifically, the 1871 development of the perfecting press, which made it possible to print both sides of a single role of paper, and the 1886 invention of the Linotype machine by Ottmer Mergenthaler, which mechanized type-setting, made newspaper and magazine printing much less costly. When Congress passed the Postal Act of 1879 that allowed magazines to be delivered at the lower, second-class rate, a new low-cost means of transmitting information—including advertising—was assured.[5]

Admittedly, advertising in newspapers had been going on for many decades. Benjamin Day's *New York Sun* and James Bennet's *New York Herald* began using ad sales as a source of finance in the 1830s. Rival so-called "penny papers" soon followed. The entre-preneurial publishers of these and similar papers were quick to realize that increasing circulation by means of keeping the price low (1 cent) made the paper attractive as a medium for advertising. Day made this explicit in the prospectus he issued with the launch of *The Sun*:

> The object of this paper is to lay before the public, at a price within the means of everyone, ALL THE NEWS OF THE DAY, and at the same time afford an advantageous medium for advertising.[6]

However, the penny newspaper ads were primarily issued by local firms and customers interested in help wanted ads, marriage announcements, death notices, and so on. The use of advertising to market trademarked brands had not yet begun.

Mail-order catalogs such as those issued by Montgomery Ward (and later Sears) were an early start. To a considerable extent, these catalogs simply listed products in various categories without brand names—dry goods, silverware, toiletries and drugs, harnesses and saddlery, boots and shoes, ladies wear, crockery and glassware, and the like. Occasionally, manufacturer names, e.g., Goodyear Rubber Products or Cline's Steam Washer, did appear, but for the most part, the catalogs sold private label goods. Their success in reaching consumers outside the urban markets was, however, undeniable.

Montgomery Ward's first mail-order solicitation in 1872 went out on just a few pages and listed 163 items. Four years later, it had grown to 152 pages and 3,000 items. By 1897, it was one thousand pages long with well over 20,000 items listed (Latham, 1972). That success gave testament to the growing dominance of production in large, cost-efficient factories. Small rural retailers found it difficult to compete with the price and product quality offered by the catalogs. Many small establishments went out of business. More importantly perhaps, the success of mail-order showed that there was a potentially large consumer demand that the right kind of marketing could reach.

With the railroads and the telegraph uniting an increasingly urbanized country, a market for national periodicals also emerged. Daily newspapers were, by design, focused on local events, whereas magazines like *Harper's Monthly* and *The Atlantic Monthly* had both a broader audience and more diverse content, including authors such as Mark Twain, Thomas Hardy, and Oliver Wendell Holmes and featuring artwork by such luminaries as Frederick Remington and Winslow Homer. Not only were these magazines gaining a national readership, but others such as *The Ladies Home Journal* with targeted audiences and content also began to reach a national scale.

At the start, some magazines were reluctant to run advertising pages with the view that it diminished their quality. In the very early 1870s, *Harper's Monthly* famously rejected an offer from the Howe Sewing Machine Company to run ads for a year in return for the then-generous fee of $18,000.[7] However, the combined lessons of the newspapers and mail-order catalogs, along with the financial pressure exerted by the very serious recession of 1873, soon persuaded magazine publishers that advertising was a critical source of revenue. In the early 1880s, a typical issue of *Harper's Monthly* had about seven pages devoted to advertising. By the end of the nineteenth century, that number had grown to 92.[8] Along with advertising in newspapers, billboards, and other media, advertising expenditures grew roughly ten-fold over the 40 years after 1875 (Pope, 1983).

The concept of brand identity became more tangible with the development of modern packaging. Glued paper packaging for coffee, tobacco, and other products was cheaper than cotton sacks and an easy surface on which to print branded labels. A production change that whipped more air into Procter & Gamble's very white soap bars enabled these bars to float. In turn this was a novel feature that consumers seemed to value. By 1880, the company was selling large amounts of this new soap, packaged in paper with the name of Ivory Soap in bold letters, Procter & Gamble in smaller ones, and "It Floats" printed along the side. The brand was born. A similar story may be told for many consumer goods.

Before the 1870s, customers would buy oats for hot cereal by scooping them from 180-pound barrels in which the oats of different manufacturers were mixed. In 1877, Quaker Oats became the first trademarked breakfast cereal in the US, and soon started offering its oats in 2-pound paper boxes adorned with its trademarked logo of a smiling eighteenth-century Quaker. Nor did it stop there. The American Cereal Company, as Quaker's parent came to be known, recognized that their market would be larger if there were more uses for oats than just making oatmeal. So, they soon started printing recipes on the box for oatmeal bread and, yes, oatmeal cookies.[9] It would not be long before Kellogg's and other ready-to-eat cereal makers would replace their glued paper bag containers with light cardboard boxes—again permitting more printing and branding.

Metal packaging—most ubiquitously in tin (steel tinplate) cans—also emerged. In 1898, Campbell's famously devised a way to condense soup, thereby making it much lighter and much cheaper to ship. The considerable cost advantage quickly allowed Campbell's soup tins and their iconic label to dominate the market. Another successful use of tin packaging was made by Patrick Towle, a small Minnesota grocer who produced a maple syrup product that he sold in a tin package shaped like a log cabin and which he aptly named Log Cabin Maple Syrup.

Perhaps the best-known story of this era from both an advertising and branding perspective is the case of the National Biscuit Company (Nabisco) and its *Uneeda* cracker. Nabisco was created in 1898 from the merger of the Chicago American Bakeries with the New York Biscuit Company. As a result, Nabisco had 114 bakeries throughout the US to serve the growing American market. Shortly thereafter, the company switched its packaging to a new, tray-style paper carton with a waxed paper liner. The wax paper kept the cracker fresh for a considerable time in comparison with the older way of selling crackers in open barrels, and the wax paper packaging and design made transportation much easier.

For marketing advice, Nabisco turned to one of the very first advertising firms, N. W. Ayer & Son. Advertising firms like Ayer and J. W. Thompson had by then existed for some time. However, until the late 1890s, these firms mainly played the role of a broker—matching firms looking to list their product with newspapers or magazines that had advertising space available. It was only near the end of the nineteenth century that such firms began to design campaigns and write advertising copy for brand products.

Ayer's agency recommended to Nabisco that it sell its crackers under the brand name "Uneeda" (you need a). Further, Ayer recommended that the package carry the picture of a young boy carrying a *Uneeda* biscuit package in a hat and raincoat to emphasize the water-resistant packaging, accompanied by the slogan, "Lest you forget, we say it yet, *Uneeda* biscuit." Ayer also launched a national advertising campaign in magazines and newspapers. Success was immediate. Within a year, Nabisco was selling 10 million boxes of *Uneeda* crackers every month (Batchelor, 2002). Many other firms adopted a similar approach to using familiar, everyday characters for branded packaging, including the Dutch Cleanser housekeeper, the Morton Salt girl, Planter's Mr. Peanut and Nipper the RCA dog.

Companies such as Campbell's, American Cereal, and Nabisco were large relative to their respective markets. The new factory production system enabled the creation of mega-firms through mergers and consolidations. Indeed, a huge merger wave swept through American industry in the last two years of the nineteenth century and the first two years of the twentieth. Over the years 1898 to 1902, 2,653 independent firms combined to form just 300 or so.

Strikingly, most of the mergers of this era involved many firms rather than just two. Many were mergers of three or five or ten or sometimes numerous firms. The American Can Merger of 1901 reflected a combination of 120 firms, leaving the new company with an 80 percent share of the tin can market. Most famous of all was the $1.4 billion merger creating the US Steel Corporation from Carnegie Steel, National Steel, and Federal Steel companies who were themselves the result of mergers of 170 smaller firms. US Steel then became the largest corporation in the world controlling 65 percent of the steel market.

There was also an accompanying revolution in the retail sector in the early part of the twentieth century. As a few brand name products and firms came to dominate several industries, a new kind of retailer emerged selling the leading brands of many different products. These were the chain retail stores, such as the Great Atlantic & Pacific Tea Company, Woolworths Stores and J. C. Penney. They too had an interest in advertising and in getting consumers to know the products and services they had to offer.

In short, by the early 1900s, the modern era of large brand name firms with market power that, in turn, were enabled and promoted by media advertising, had arrived.

## 2.3 TWENTIETH-CENTURY ADVERTISING IN PRACTICE AND THEORY

If the emergence of large national firms with market power created a role for advertising and brand promotion, many questions remained about how to use this new strategic tool and what effects it had on consumer behavior. John Wanamaker's prescient comment regarding the uncertainty over which half of his advertising expense is wasted colorfully reflects the challenge facing advertisers to determine how advertising can best be used to increase profit.

Early advertising efforts by large brand name firms were largely designed to be content-oriented, i.e., to provide information about the product being advertised. The importance of informative content was most obvious in the Montgomery & Ward and Sears mail-order catalogs, in which item listings, e.g., those for pocket watches, would describe the metal used in the watch frame (usually either nickel plate, pure nickel, or silver), whether the watch face included a calendar, whether the frame included a closing cover, the nature of the movement mechanism, and of course, the price.

This focus became common among many of the new, national marketing firms. Typical Ford Motor Company ads of the early twentieth century would show a picture of the car and describe key features such as seating capacity, availability of a roll-up top or roof, whether the car had a horn and possibly, a speedometer, and the price.[10] Nabisco focused attention on the wax paper wrapping inside the *Uneeda* box that kept the crackers fresh. Coca-Cola openly advertised the caffeine and cocaine ingredients that gave its beverage "rejuvenating" power. The manufacturer of the new gelatin product, Jell-O, used advertising to explain how Jell-O could be used, including numerous recipes.[11]

In part, the focus on informative product content in advertising might have been a reaction to the recognized excesses of the "snake-oil" traveling salesman of the late nineteenth century.[12] This was evident in the writings of *Printers' Ink*, the first and dominant trade journal to provide a forum for advertising ideas. Its editor, George Rowell, had made a career of forcing newspapers to report their circulation accurately so as to prevent them from inflating their advertising fees. His journal carried this view into its prescriptions for business advertising in general. While visual and other enhancements to catch the consumer's eye were legitimate, *Printers' Ink* insisted that the best approach was to present product facts honestly—"Making the Truth 'Sound True'" (Lears, 1994, p. 286).

Yet the need to solve Wanamaker's proverbial problem and find out how advertising affected consumers persisted. It was not long before early advertising agencies such as N. J. Ayer and J. Walter Thompson began to conduct research for their client firms that looked at customers' income, residence location, ethnicity, and other demographic characteristics. Thompson's Chicago office also solicited and collected magazine reader reactions to full-page advertisements that were released in 25 national magazines. They received over 30,000 responses suggesting that, among other insights, consumers did not like ads without illustrations (Strasser, 1989). It is perhaps not surprising that alternative views on how to best design one's advertising slowly but surely emerged.

In 1908, Walter Dill Scott, a psychology professor at Northwestern University's School of Commerce (now the Kellogg School of Management), published a book titled *The Psychology of Advertising*. It was his second book on this topic, and it was soon followed by many similar ones by other authors. In the view of Scott and these other writers, advertising had to do something besides inform consumers about a product. In Scott's view, a focus on product content might be warranted if the product was relatively inexpensive and frequently purchased, e.g., soap, cigarettes, and toothpaste, but not if it was a more expensive durable good purchased only sporadically. This new view argued that it was crucial to create in consumers an interest in the product and, more importantly, an interest that translated into a desire for the product and willingness to pay for it.

It was not long before this psychological approach became widespread in advertising. The emphasis began to be less on educating a consumer and more on suggesting how much pleasure a consumer could get from buying the product. A classic example of this was the ad for Cadillac that appeared in *The Saturday Evening Post* on January 2, 1915. The ad had no illustration of a car; in fact, there was no mention of the special features of a Cadillac car or its price. The advertisement simply read, "In every field of human endeavor, he that is first must perpetually live in the white light of publicity."[13] This tension between advertising that is informative about a product's key features, availability, and price versus advertising that eschews these points and, instead, focuses on creating a psychological attraction has continued to the present day, although the media carrying those messages has changed over time.

The advent of radio and television opened up new possibilities for messages in both style and content. These platforms offered companies a scale of reach, engagement with viewers, and demographic targeting that were not possible with the more traditional print media. The potential scale economies in advertising reach in these new media were also significant. Once a signal is transmitted, the broadcast firm incurs no additional cost regardless of whether one consumer tunes in or one million consumers do. Moreover, it was plausible to assume that a large number would hear or watch a program because anyone could generally access radio and television programming for free.

As became readily apparent, radio (and later television) allowed for more narrative content in advertising. A 1942 advertisement for AT&T (then the monopoly provider of long-distance telephone service), portrayed a young woman placing a long-distance call, which was a somewhat complicated procedure at the time with pay telephones and no direct dialing. The commercial dramatized how the consumer can with the operator place a call and concludes with an explicit price quote as the operator instructs the caller to deposit $3.85 for the first three minutes. Other ads were more dramatic. Lever Brothers, for instance, began marketing its *Lifebuoy* soap with "ministories" such as one where a loving father helps resolve his married daughter's domestic dispute by getting her to adopt *Lifebuoy* soap for a natural, healthy scent and cleanliness.

By the 1950s and 1960s, the narrative story-telling ads made possible by radio and television media had begun incorporating so-called motivational research, a term coined by Ernest Dichter, into their messaging. Dichter stressed that successful advertising had to address *why* consumers make the purchases they do, rather than focus on *what* function a product might serve. It was Dichter who developed the use of "focus groups" where marketers bring together small groups of representative consumers to interview them, or sometimes just watch them, to uncover their desires and attractions.

Among other successes, Dichter is credited with the marketing success of Mattel's *Barbie* doll. Prior to *Barbie*, dolls were sold as small babies that permitted little girls to mimic motherhood. In contrast, the *Barbie* doll was a curvaceous young woman. Dichter's argument, based on research, was that much of young girls' play was not about mothering, but about growing up. To overcome parental reluctance to purchase a "sexy" young woman doll, Dichter recommended that *Barbie* be marketed as a role model that would help parents guide their daughters to become "poised young ladies."[14] To that end, the first *Barbie* TV commercial showed a line-up of *Barbies* in different outfits from a swimsuit to more formal wear, culminating with a wedding gown, while a woman sang in the background, "Someday, I'm gonna be exactly like you."

Using motivational research in advertising to tap into consumers' psychological desires is quite different than providing product and price information. Whether it is Mattel's early *Barbie* campaign or the more recent *Dos Equis* "most interesting man in the world" commercials, much advertising does seem designed to persuade consumers that buying a particular product will yield happiness rather than designed to let consumers know about the products' main features.

The history of radio, television, and more recently, Internet advertising, also suggests another possible way that advertising may work on consumers. It may simply be that consumers *like* advertising—that it enhances their enjoyment of consuming the product. For example, it may be that while drinking *Dos Equis* beer, two friends recall the "most interesting man in the world" commercial and share a laugh over it. Similarly, consumers may find the iconic Coca-Cola commercial based on the song "I'd Like to Teach the World to Sing" enjoyable to recall while sipping a glass of Coke.

There is another issue that the evolution of advertising practice reveals. Advertising may not only reflect the strategic choices of the firms advertising their products. Whether an ad is transmitted via print media, radio, television, or, today, the Internet, the media platform that hosts the advertisement has a role to play as well. The media platform is engaged in selling in two different markets at the same time. To consumers of media, the platform sells content such as news, opinion pieces, and entertainment by way of music and drama. To advertisers, the platform sells space or airtime that allows these firms a way to reach potential consumers.

For most of the twentieth century economists focused on how advertising affects consumer behavior—whether it informed, persuaded, or simply entertained consumers. With the advent of the digital revolution and the growth of online platforms, traditional media economists have started to focus more on the two-sided nature of media plat-forms in the digital age.

## 2.4 ECONOMICS AND ADVERTISING

As noted earlier, advertising is largely a phenomenon of imperfectly competitive markets. Remember a perfectly competitive firm can sell as much as it wants at the going price, obviating the need to advertise. Not surprisingly, the economics of advertising really begins in the early twentieth century when economists Chamberlin (1933) and Robinson (1933) began to develop models of imperfect competition.[15] This is not to say that advertising had not been considered at all. Alfred Marshall of the University of Cambridge was a dominant figure in the discipline. Indeed, his 1890 textbook, *The Principles of Economics*, is widely thought to be the first text to present formalized models illustrating the basic principles and concepts of supply and demand, perfect competition, monopolies and related topics as part of an organized vision.

However, Marshall (1919) did subsequently offer some brief thoughts on advertising that anticipated later analyses. Specifically, he wrote about two types of advertising—one type called *constructive* because it helped markets to perform better by providing con-sumers with information about the existence of products, their functionality and where they can be bought. The other type of advertising Marshall labeled as *combative* and this he deemed potentially wasteful as it often contained no new information and only served the purpose of shifting consumers from one rival to another. As A. C. Pigou, a student of Marshall, wrote in 1920:

> It may happen that expenditures on advertisement made by competing monopo-lists [that is, what we now call monopolistic competitors] will simply neutralize one another and leave the industrial position exactly as it would have been if neither had expended anything. For, clearly, if each of two rivals makes equal efforts to attract the favor of the public away from the other, the total result is the same as it would have been if neither had made any effort at all (p. 197).[16]

Such an outcome increases selling costs with little benefit to consumers. Yet while the work of Marshall, Pigou, and other early writers suggested interesting questions about how advertising might alter the basic competitive model of Marshall's textbook, it was not until Chamberlin's (1933) work on monopolistic competition that advertising started to become an integral part of how firms sell in the marketplace.

Chamberlin (1933) was the first to explore product differentiation in a competitive-type market setting. Advertising was part of a firm's effort to differentiate its product. Moreover, Chamberlin's discussion of how advertising affects consumers and the firm's demand reflects much of what was then happening in actual advertising practice. In particular, Chamberlin recognized that there was a difference between advertising that is informative about a product's features and advertising that is designed to change consumer tastes in a way to make them want only that product.

Together the insights of Marshall (1919), Pigou (1920), Robinson (1933), and Chamberlin (1933) map out two of the main issues that the economics of advertising must address. One of these is the question of economic efficiency. Specifically, is there reason to believe that the amount of advertising that firms engage in will be too little, too much, or just right from the perspective of maximizing the total (consumer plus producer) surplus? The second and related issue concerns the impact of advertising on market outcomes and whether, in particular, advertising pushes imperfectly competitive markets either closer to or further from the competitive ideal.

Chamberlin did address these questions to some extent. He noted that informative advertising could shift out a firm's demand curve and at the same time make it more elastic. The consequent output expansion would allow scale economies to be more fully exploited, and any increase in elasticity would imply a lower markup over costs.[17] Both effects imply a pro-competitive effect of advertising on the market outcome. However, Chamberlin also recognized that advertising was itself a cost that firms must cover and therefore more advertising could lead to higher prices. His conclusion was that the ultimate effect "depends on the fact of the case" (Chamberlin, 1933, p. 167).

Building on Chamberlin's work, economists have recognized that advertising may impact consumer demand and market outcomes in, broadly speaking, three ways. Two of these ways reflect Chamberlin's dichotomy. Advertising may inform consumers of product availability and prices. Alternatively, advertising may alter consumer tastes by convincing consumers that they need or want a particular product. Since the 1970s, a third way has emerged from the work of Stigler and Becker (1977) and Becker and Murphy (1993).[18] This is based on the view that advertising may be a good in itself—one that serves as a complement to the advertised product—as when Coca-Cola drinkers enjoy it more when they see several young people each holding a bottle of Coke, singing "I'd Like to Teach the World to Sing." Following Bagwell (2005), we refer to these three views of advertising as the *informative view*, the *persuasive view*, and the *complementary view*, respectively.

It should be clear than any economic analysis of advertising will depend upon which underlying view of advertising is assumed. As Chamberlin surmised, informative advertising may be pro-competitive. If advertising makes consumers better informed about what products are available and at what price, it lowers their search costs and makes comparative shopping much easier. This, in turn, forces firms to be more price-competitive. Such a positive view of advertising is often associated with the "Chicago School" of economics that has historically defended the free-market choices of profit-maximizing firms.

If, however, advertising works by persuading people and altering their tastes, then the economic analysis becomes more complicated. To begin with, such persuasion could create brand loyalty, making consumers less likely to switch brands even in response to significant price differentials. This would suggest that advertising softens price competition among existing firms. Such persuasive advertising could also act as a barrier to entry to new firms who must somehow overcome the consumer loyalty to incumbent firms that has been built up by their extensive advertising over the years. It also makes Marshall's and Pigou's combative advertising scenario more likely, implying further inefficiency due to the excessive advertising efforts that largely cancel each other out.

More fundamentally, the view that advertising can be a persuasive tool used to manipulate consumers' behavior[19] poses something of a problem for traditional economic analysis based on rational consumer decision-making by consumers who know what they like. This is because it becomes difficult to talk about the impact of advertising on consumer surplus if the demand curve after advertising differs from the demand curve before viewing that message. Unlike the informative approach, the persuasive view makes it difficult to evaluate whether there is too much or too little advertising by looking at how advertising affects total welfare—which demand curve should we use? However, to the extent that the persuasive approach suggests that advertising enhances market power, it also suggests that concern about advertising by large firms is warranted.

The complementary view calls attention to the fact that advertising is consumed for free by the consumers of print media, of the airwaves, and of the Internet. That is, these consumers receive ads without paying for them. Because these consumers value these ads, firms can recover the cost of advertising through a higher price for the advertised good. Accordingly, higher prices emerge with advertising. However, because advertising is both costly and valued by consumers, such price increases do not imply a transfer of surplus from consumers to producers. Indeed, it is quite possible that prices may not rise sufficiently high to compensate producers for the advertising cost, and that therefore, there will be inefficiently too *little* advertising. The complementary view thus permits the informative as well as the non-informative advertising to be valuable. In other words, advertising that may seem at first to be persuasive or manipulative may actually be truly valued.

Much of this book explores economic models and empirical studies related to the three ways advertising can affect consumer behavior. It is useful to note here a few of the difficulties that we will encounter. First, distinguishing between the three approaches is not always easy. For example, the fact that a firm is advertising may itself be informative even if the ads have little factual content, as argued by Nelson (1970, 1974) among others. Consumers might, for instance, reason that a firm that can afford to advertise must be a firm that knows it has a great product. Moreover, the lines dividing informative from persuasive from complementary advertising are not altogether clear. Is Jell-O's early advertising that provided recipes on how to use the Jell-O informative, persuasive, complementary, or a bit of all three?

Empirical work also quickly runs into difficulties. Early studies by Bain (1956) and Comanor and Wilson (1967, 1974) explore a positive link between profitability, on the one hand, and advertising intensity, on the other.[20] Recall though that perfectly competitive firms have little reason to advertise. Instead, it is precisely in cases of imperfect competition, where firms have a positive markup of price above cost, that the motivation to advertise is strongest so that more units may be sold that earn that markup. In turn, this implies that any positive link between advertising and profitability may be because a high markup leads to more advertising and not the other way around. While subsequent studies have tried to deal with such ambiguities in the direction of causation, the general point is clear. Our work in the next several chapters will need to proceed carefully on both the theoretical and empirical fronts as we deal with the complexities just raised.

The extensive economic research on advertising over the last several decades has also forced economists to recognize other issues beyond whether market forces generate the right amount of advertising and/or how advertising affects the efficiency of the market outcomes. As noted earlier, there is now greater recognition that much of what we observe in advertising reflects not only the choices of the advertising firms, but also the market behavior of media platforms—print media, radio and TV, Internet websites—that host advertising. Because these platforms market to two groups—potential consumers and advertising firms—their pricing strategies need to be factored in as well.

The *New York Times*, for instance, sells subscriptions (both print and Internet) to readers while simultaneously selling advertising space to firms trying to reach those readers. A higher subscription price will likely mean fewer subscribers. In turn, this will mean that the paper cannot charge advertisers as high a price for space as they could with a lower subscription price and more readers. The *Times* and other two-sided media platforms then have a difficult pricing problem to solve in their efforts to maximize profits in that they have to work out a pricing structure across both market sides. The platform may for example charge a low price or even a zero price to consumers as *Facebook* does while charging a higher price to advertisers. However, in other markets, we might consider a firm setting a low or zero price to be evidence of predatory behavior designed to eliminate rivals. Yet such a pricing structure is here a logical consequence of the balancing act that two-sided platforms must perform. Understanding the pricing strategies of modern, digital platforms and the impact this has on advertising and competition is the topic of the final three chapters of this text.

## 2.5 SUMMARY

The large-scale advertising of branded products is a relatively modern phenomenon. Its origins can be traced to the late nineteenth century as large, factory-based firms serving national markets grew to dominate many sectors in manufacturing. Prior to that time, most goods bought by consumers were largely undifferentiated, being sold in bins as unlabeled bulk products at town general stores.

As advertising grew to be more important in the twentieth century, different approaches to the practice of advertising emerged. Early advertising strategies emphasized promoting a product's key features and often touting its low price. Later, more psychological approaches based on motivational research replaced the factual content of advertising, associating consumption of a good with desired "role models" and status. Elements of both advertising strategies continue to this day.

Economic analysis of advertising also began in the early twentieth century, especially with the work of Chamberlin (1933), and it has mirrored to some extent the development of actual advertising practice. Economists early on made a distinction between informative advertising and persuasive advertising. They also recognized that advertising may itself be a good that consumers value as a complement to the product being advertised.

Key economic questions regarding advertising include whether market forces generate the right or efficient amount of advertising and whether advertising promotes or inhibits healthy competition among firms. Answering these questions within an economic model requires an understanding of—or at least some explicit assumption about—how advertising affects consumer behavior, or more generally, whether it is informative, persuasive, or complementary. In turn, evaluating the evidence testing any of the models developed requires careful analysis of the data with particular care taken to differentiate between correlation and causation.

Finally, any economic analysis of advertising must also examine the nature and impact of the modern advertising infrastructure, namely, the two-sided platforms such as newspapers, television, and Internet sites. Firms compete on these platforms and the platforms compete with each other. In engaging in the latter, between-platform competition, each platform must adopt a *pricing structure* as it simultaneously sells to both consumers and to advertisers trying to reach those consumers. This in turn has implications for the advertising and competition that occurs within the platforms. We address all of the foregoing issues in the remainder of this book.

## NOTES

1  Sherman (2000, p. 734).

2  See Atack et al. (2008, 2010).

3  There was as well explicit cooperation between different freight on shipments across connecting lines, regarding rates and the apportionment of revenues from the completed transport to the participating railroads (Taylor and Neu, 2003).

4  E. A. Calahan invented the first "ticker machine" in 1867. Edison's much-improved version became standard by 1874.

5  Also important was the fact that the public school movement had led to widespread literacy. By 1880, 80 percent of the adult population was literate. By 1910, that number had climbed to over 90 percent. *Historical Statistics of the United States, Series H 407–411*, https://fraser.stlouisfed.org/files/docs/publica tions/histstatus/hstat_1957_cen_1957.pdf (accessed March 23, 2021).

6  Presbey (1929, p. 188).

7  Browne and Kreiser (2003, p. 43).

8  Ohmann (1996, p. 84).

9  In one of the wilder promotional schemes, Quaker partnered in 1902 with a real estate developer who had bought a 15-acre lot in the town of Milford, Connecticut. Hoping that he would then be hired by land-owners to build housing on this plot, he persuaded Quaker to promote their oats product for a considerable length of time by putting a deed in every box conveying ownership of a small portion—sometimes just 10×10 square feet—of this land. The deeds were entirely legal but very little was ever built. Over

time, the "oatmeal lots" were so tiny and their ownership so dispersed that collecting taxes on any of the 15 acres proved next to impossible for the town. It was not until the mid-1970s that Milford officials were able to devise legal action that foreclosed the property and made it available for commercial development. Milford Historical Society (1988).

10 Curiously, Ford itself rarely ran these ads, but instead supported the dealers who placed them.

11 See Lears (1994, pp. 156–60).

12 The Pure Food and Drug Act leading to the creation of the Food and Drug Administration was passed in 1906, partly as a result of a series of articles in *Collier's* by muckraker Samuel Hopkins Adams revealing that the "secret ingredients" in many "patent medicines" included large amounts of alcohol and opium.

13 *Ad Age*, September 15, 2003.

14 Handler (1994).

15 As also noted in Chapter 1, Cournot's (1838) oligopoly models had long been available to economists by the early twentieth century. However, the discipline by and large overlooked Cournot until many years later.

16 Pigou (1920). See also, Kaldor (1950), Galbraith (1958), and Solow (1967) for further expressions of this view.

17 Refer to the discussion of the Lerner Index in Chapter 1.

18 Telser (1964) offers an analysis that has elements of the complementary approach as well.

19 See Packard (1957) for an especially negative view of persuasive advertising.

20 The advertising–profitability link found in Bain's (1956) pioneering study was not direct. Bain (1956) links profitability to a measure of barriers to entry. He then offers interview evidence that advertising is the main source of entry barriers. See also Nichols (1951), Lambin (1976), and Geroski (1982). See Telser (1964) for an early opposing view.

# 2.6 REFERENCES

Atack, J., F. Bateman, and R. A. Margo. 2005. "Capital Deepening and the Rise of the Factory: The American Experience in the Nineteenth Century." *The Economic History Review* 58 (August), 586–95.

Atack, J., M. Haines, and R. Margo. 2008. "Railroads and the Rise of the Factory: Evidence from the United States, 1850–70." NBER Working Paper #14410.

Atack, J., M. Haines, and R. Margo. 2010. "Railroads and the Rise of the Factory: Evidence for the United States, 1850–1870." In *Economic Evolution and Revolution in Historical Time*, ed. P. Rhode, J. Rosenbloom, and D. Weiman (162–79). Stanford, CA: Stanford University Press.

Atack, J., and R. Margo. 2017. "Gallman Revisited: Blacksmithing and American Manufacturing, 1850–70." NBER Working Paper #23399.

Bagwell, K. 2005. "The Economic Analysis of Advertising." Columbia University, Department of Economics, Working Paper 0506-01.

Bain, J. S. 1956. *Barriers to New Competition*. Cambridge, MA: Harvard University Press.

Batchelor, B. 2002. *The 1900s*. Westport, CT: Greenwood Press.

Becker, G., and K. Murphy. 1993. "A Simple Theory of Advertising as a Good or Bad." *The Quarterly Journal of Economics* 108(4), 941–64.

Browne, R. B., and L. A. Kreiser, Jr. 2003. *The Civil War and Reconstruction*. Westport, CT: Greenwood Press.

Chamberlin, E. 1933. *The Theory of Monopolistic Competition*. Cambridge, MA: Harvard University Press.

Comanor, W. S., and T. A. Wilson. 1967. "Advertising, Market Structure and Performance." *The Review of Economics and Statistics* 49, 423–40.

Comanor, W. S., and T. A. Wilson. 1974. *Advertising and Market Power*. Cambridge, MA: Harvard University Press.

Donaldson, D., and R. Hornbeck. 2016. "Railroads and American Economic Growth: A 'Market Access' Approach." *The Quarterly Journal of Economics* 131 (May), 799–858.

DuBoff, R. D. 1980. "Business Demand and the Development of the Telegraph in the United States, 1844–1866." *The Business History Review* 80 (Winter), 459–79.

Field, A. J. 1998. "The Telegraphic Transmission of Financial Asset Prices and Orders to Trade: Implications for Economic Growth, Trading Volume, and Securities Market Regulation." *Research in Economic History* 18, 145–84.

Galbraith, J. K. 1958. *The Affluent Society*. Boston: Houghton Mifflin.

Geroski, P. 1982. "Simultaneous Equations Models of the Structure-Performance Paradigm." *European Economic Review* 19 (January, Special Issue), 145–58.

Goldin, H. H. 1947. "Governmental Policy and the Domestic Telegraph Industry." *Journal of Economic History* 7 (May), 53–68.

Handler, R. 1994. *Dream Doll: The Ruth Handler Story*. Stamford: Longmeadow Press.

James, J. 1983. "Structural Change in American Manufacturing, 1850–1890." *The Journal of Economic History* 43 (June), 433–59.

Kaldor, N. 1950. "The Economic Aspects of Advertising." *Review of Economic Studies* 18(1), 1–27.

Lambin, J. 1976. *Advertising, Competition, and Market Conduct in Oligopoly over Time*. Amsterdam: North Holland Publishing.

Latham, F. B. 1972. *1872–1972, A Century of Serving Consumers: The Story of Montgomery Ward*. Chicago: Montgomery Ward.

Lears, T. J. 1994. *Fables of Abundance: A Cultural History of Advertising in America*. New York: Basic Books.

Marshall, A. 1890. *Principles of Economics*. London: Macmillan.

Marshall, A. 1919. *Industry and Trade: A Study of Industrial Technique and Business Organization; and of Their Influences on the Conditions of Various Classes and Nations*. London: Macmillan.

Milford Historical Society. 1988. *Ten Minutes Ahead of the Rest of the World: A History of Milford*. Milford Historical Society Press, Milford, Connecticut.

Nelson, P. 1970. "Information and Consumer Behavior." *Journal of Political Economy* 78 (March/April), 311–29.

Nelson, P. 1974. "Advertising as Information." *Journal of Political Economy* 82 (July/August), 729–54.

Nichols, W. H. 1951. *Price Policy in the Cigarette Industry*. Nashville: Vanderbilt University Press.

Ohmann, R. 1996. *Selling Culture: Magazines, Markets, and Class at the Turn of the Century*. London: Verso Publishing.

Packard, V. 1957. *The Hidden Persuaders*. New York: David McKay Co.

Pigou, A. C. 1920. *The Economics of Welfare*. London: Macmillan.

Pope, D. 1983. *The Making of Modern Advertising*. New York: Basic Books.

Presbey, F. 1929. *The History and Development of Advertising*. New York: Doubleday.

Robinson, J. 1933. *The Economics of Imperfect Competition*. New York: Macmillan.

Scott, W. D. 1913. *The Psychology of Advertising*. Boston: Small, Maynard & Company.

Sherman, W. T. 2000. *Memoirs of General W. T. Sherman* (Reprint). New York: Penguin Putnam.

Solow, R. 1967. "The New Industrial State, or Son of Affluence." *Public Interest* 9, 100–108.

Stigler, G., and G. Becker. 1977. "De Gustibus Non Est Disputandum." *The American Economic Review* 67, 76–90.

Strasser, S. 1989. *Satisfaction Guaranteed: The Making of the American Mass Market*. New York: Pantheon Books.

Taylor, G. R., and I. D. Neu. 2003. *The American Railroad Network, 1861–1890*. Champaign: University of Illinois Press.

Telser, L. 1964. "Advertising and Competition." *Journal of Political Economy* 72 (December), 537–62.

# 3
# Advertising and the Value of Information

## 3.1 INTRODUCTION

Since Alfred Marshall's work of the late nineteenth century, the textbook model of competitive supply and demand has been the starting point for most economic analyses. That is because it is a useful model, capable of generating a lot of insights regarding actual market outcomes. However, it is not the ending point. This is because like any model, the competitive supply and demand model is built on several simplifying assumptions. Such assumptions are useful in that they allow us to focus on some key features of the analysis, much as a roadmap allows a traveler to focus on the main ways of getting from point A to point B without showing every bump and turn in the road along the way. Yet such assumptions will not always reflect key aspects of reality. So, it is useful to ask what happens when these assumptions no longer hold.

In this chapter, we relax the assumption that consumers are "fully informed." That is, we stop assuming that consumers know what they want, i.e., their preferences, that they know which shops are selling what goods, and that they know the prices of the goods being sold. We relax this assumption partly because by comparing the market outcome when consumers are fully informed with what happens when they are not enables us to investigate the role and value of information. However, we also drop the assumption of fully informed consumers because in reality, it is a very strong assumption to make. Think about your last shopping experience. Did you know what design or brand you were going to buy and where to find that brand at the best price?

Far from being fully informed, many of us feel like freshly landed tourists in a new city when we go shopping. We are unsure about where to go to get the best deal. Later, we wonder whether we got a good deal or were "scammed." Both feelings help us understand the potential use of advertising to provide information. For any good or service that has value, there is always an incentive to provide more of it so long as the cost of doing so is less than the value that can be claimed. Information is no exception.[1]

We start by considering two cases of imperfectly informed consumers. In one case, consumers do not know the prices that different sellers are charging but do know that each seller offers the same product. In the other case, consumers are informed about the prices different sellers are charging but are unsure about whether the product is the same. That is, this last case is one in which the consumer is unsure about the quality of product that each seller offers.

In both cases there is an asymmetry between the buyer and the seller. In the first case, the seller knows whether the price charged is a relatively high or low price, but the consumer does not. In the second, the seller knows whether the product is of relatively high or low quality, but again, the consumer does not.[2] Models based on the first type of asymmetry fall under the category of "The Tourist Native Model." Those based on the second case of quality uncertainty fall under the category of "The Market for Lemons." Both cases illustrate how advertising can play a useful role in a competitive market once the assumption of fully informed consumers is relaxed.

## 3.2 THE TOURIST NATIVE MODEL[3]

Have you ever found yourself in a new city, hungry and tired, and looking for a place to eat? Rick Steves, the well-known travel guide writer, warns tourists of being ripped off by restaurants in places where there could be a double standard[4]—one for locals or natives and one for tourists. Such a double standard of course could not be practiced on a consumer in a perfectly competitive market because in such a world, all consumers are assumed to be "perfectly informed" about all restaurants. But when you arrive in a new city, you are unlikely to know which restaurants offer a good bargain and which ones are "rip-offs." A tourist is not fully informed, whereas the residents or natives of the city are—they know where to find a good deal.

In any product market there can be "tourists," that is, a proportion of consumers who are not well informed. Let's begin with an example of a market, say a restaurant market, in which *every* consumer is a tourist, that is, *every* consumer in this market is imperfectly informed about prices being charged by the firms in the market.

### 3.2.1 A "Knife-Edged" Single Price Equilibrium

Suppose that there are $L$ tourists imperfectly informed about the prices being charged by $n$ restaurants. The consumers do not know which of the restaurants offers a dining experience at a low price and which charge a high one. All other aspects of the market do satisfy, however, the conditions for perfect competition. There are lots of restaurants, none of the $n$ restaurants has any market power, and they all are selling the same kind and quality of dining experience.[5] The restaurants, unlike the consumers, do know the prices being set by other restaurants.

Each consumer or tourist demands only one unit of the good per period, e.g., meal per day, and each consumer obtains a utility equal to $V$ from consuming the product or meal. A consumer's demand function can be written as follows: buy one unit of the good if the price $p$ satisfies $p \leq V$, buy 0 otherwise. This demand function is drawn in Figure 3.1.

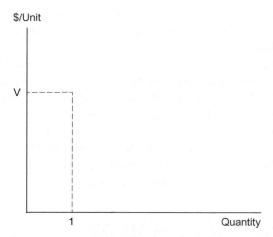

*Note:* Each consumer will buy at most one unit of the good if the price is $\leq V$.

**Figure 3.1** Consumer demand in the Tourist Native Model

Before choosing a restaurant, a tourist could spend time pounding the pavement and looking for deals or could buy a restaurant guide that informs them of prices. In taking the time to search or in buying a guide the consumer bears a search cost $s$. We will assume that without incurring this cost each consumer knows only: (1) the highest price any restaurant is charging; (2) the lowest price any is charging; and (3) the average of all prices. The question is whether it will be worthwhile for a tourist to incur the cost $s$ to become better informed. To answer that question, we need to examine more closely the behavior of the restaurants themselves.

We assume that each restaurant has a $U$-shaped average cost (AC) curve whose minimum occurs at the output level of $q_C$ meals served per day. The average cost at this output level is equal to $AC(q_C) = c$. When all consumers are perfectly informed then in equilibrium competition among restaurants will in the long run force each restaurant to produce at $q_C$, and to charge the break-even price $p = c$. We take this outcome as our starting point. Each restaurant is charging $p_C = c$ for a meal and serving $L/n = q_C$ consumers. Each restaurant is therefore just breaking even.

The question is whether this outcome is an equilibrium when we relax the assumption that all consumers are perfectly informed. Recall that the condition for an equilibrium is that no firm has an incentive to change its price unilaterally, i.e., given the price that all the other firms are charging. Would any firm have an incentive to change its price from $p = c$? Clearly, no firm would want to lower its price. With $p = c$, each firm is just breaking even, and average cost is minimized. Any lower price would be sure to lead to losses.

What about a possible increase in price by some amount $\Delta p$ to a new price $c + \Delta p$? Would any tourist buy at this higher price? In answering this question, recall that a tourist does have some information about the prices being charged. We assumed that a tourist knows the average price, the highest price and the lowest price being set in the market. In this thought experiment, where one restaurant raises its price, a tourist would know that the highest price is now $c + \Delta p$. The tourist also knows that the lowest price is $c$, and that the average price when one restaurant raises its price by $\Delta p$ is:

$$\overline{p} = \frac{n-1}{n}c + \frac{1}{n}(c + \Delta p) = c + \frac{\Delta p}{n} \tag{3.1}$$

From the tourist's perspective, equation (3.1) is the price the tourist can expect to pay. If, however, the tourist incurs the cost $s$, the tourist will know how to avoid the one high-priced seller and pay only $p = c$. Hence, the expected gain for a tourist to become informed is $\frac{\Delta p}{n}$. The cost of becoming informed is $s$. The answer as to whether a tourist will choose to become informed depends on whether the expected gains from doing so exceed the expected cost. In this case, a tourist will stay uninformed if the following condition is met:

$$\frac{\Delta p}{n} \leq s \tag{3.2}$$

It should be clear that whatever value $s$ has, there will be some positive value of $\Delta p$, or some increase in price that satisfies condition (3.2). In other words, there is some positive amount $\Delta p$ by which a restaurant could raise its price above the price $c$ that all others are charging. It will not lose any consumers because all of its consumers are tourists.

If at least one firm has the incentive to raise its price though, we no longer have an equilibrium. Indeed, if all restaurants raise their price above $c$ by the same amount $\Delta p$, then there is still no incentive for any tourist to become informed. And because each restaurant does not lose any customers each restaurant continues to serve $q_C = L/n$ meals at minimum average cost $c$. But now each restaurant is earning positive profit.

Of course, a little thought will quickly reveal that this price increasing will not stop here. If every restaurant is charging $p = c + \Delta p$, it again becomes profitable for any one bistro to raise its price by a further additional amount $\Delta p$ that satisfies condition (3.2). In fact, all restaurants will do this again. When will these rounds of price increases end?

Consider the case now in which each restaurant is charging the price $p = V$. Clearly, no restaurant will want to increase its price further. No consumer is willing to pay more than $V$. Faced with a higher price, consumers will simply exit from the market. What about a restaurant thinking about lowering its price by some amount $\Delta p$?

We must again now consider what the typical uninformed consumer knows. The consumer knows that the highest price any bistro is charging is $V$. The consumer will also know that the lowest price any restaurant is charging is now $V - \Delta p$. The average bistro price in this case is then:

$$\overline{p} = \frac{(n-1)}{n}V + \frac{(V - \Delta p)}{n} = V - \frac{\Delta p}{n} \tag{3.3}$$

Knowing that the lowest price is $p = V - \Delta p$, and so in this case the potential gain from search is

$$\bar{p} - (V - \Delta p) = \left(V - \frac{\Delta p}{n}\right) - (V - \Delta p) = \frac{(n-1)}{n}\Delta p \qquad (3.4)$$

As before, the cost of search is $s$. So, each consumer will not revise their plan and choose to remain uninformed so long as the following condition is now met:

$$\frac{(n-1)}{n}\Delta p \leq s \qquad (3.5)$$

When search costs are relatively high, condition (3.5) means the price cut would have to be relatively large, making such a deviation less likely to be profitable for the firm. Suppose for example that that $s > V - c$. Then it is clear that condition (3.5) will always be met for any $\Delta p \leq V - c$ and cutting price below $c$ would not be profitable. With no profitable price deviations each restaurant will charge $p = V$, and in this case, $p = V$ is a potential equilibrium outcome.[6]

We say that $p = V$ is a potential equilibrium because there is still one small issue. With each firm choosing $p = V$, each gets $L/n$ customers and therefore each has the minimum average cost of $c$. Hence, each is therefore earning a positive economic profit. Will this not attract entry? The answer is, "yes," but that does not change the equilibrium price condition $p = V$. As more restaurants enter, each serves a smaller pool of customers. Eventually enough restaurants will enter such that each one is serving a share of customers such that its daily output is $q_V$ where $AC(q_V) = V = p$. Hence, in the long run, we have an equilibrium outcome in which $p = V = AC(q_V)$, and restaurants are no longer operating at minimum average cost.

The foregoing result is really remarkable. We have simply replaced the assumption of fully informed consumers with the assumption that consumers are imperfectly informed but can become fully informed by incurring a search cost. Yet that small change has moved the market from a competitive equilibrium with $p = c$ to one where $p = V$, the same price set by a monopolist![7] This change in what we assume that consumers know balances the market on a knife-edge between an equilibrium price of $p = c$ when information is readily accessible to one where $p = V$ when it is not.

The lesson here is that information to consumers can be valuable. In turn, this implies a potentially useful role for informative advertising. If a firm can get the word out that it is a low-price seller, it can reduce consumer search costs making a price cut profitable. Advertising that informs can be beneficial for both consumers and the advertising firm.

## 3.2.2 Tourists and Natives Together—the Two-Price Equilibrium

We now return to our original setup in which while some consumers are uninformed (tourists) others (natives) are perfectly informed. This may be due to experience or simply to having received an excellent guide for free or just a real ability to sense a good deal. There are still $L$ consumers in total in the market. Now though, a proportion $\alpha$ of these are "natives" or informed, and a proportion $(1 - \alpha)$ are "tourists" (uninformed). Each consumer will buy at most one unit of the good if $p \le V$.

Uninformed consumers incur a cost $s$ to become informed. Informed consumers, however, will only buy a unit from a firm charging the lowest price. There are $n$ identical sellers, and again, each seller's production cost is represented by a $U$-shaped average cost function which is minimized at output $q_C$ and min $AC(q_C) = c$.

Let's begin with the outcome in which each seller is selling at a price $p = c$ and serving $q_C = \dfrac{L}{n}$ customers, where $\dfrac{\alpha L}{n}$ are informed consumers or natives, and $\dfrac{(1-\alpha)L}{n}$ are uninformed tourists. As $q_C = \dfrac{L}{n}$, the price just covers the average cost so that each firm breaks even. Can this be an equilibrium outcome?

Consider what happens to a seller who deviates and sets a higher price equal to $p' = c + \Delta p$, where $\Delta p < s$. This means that tourists will choose to remain uninformed and so the seller will retain its $\dfrac{(1-\alpha)L}{n}$ tourists. However, the $\dfrac{\alpha L}{n}$ natives know where to get a better deal and the restaurant will lose these customers. Its output therefore will fall to $q_V$ where $q_V = \dfrac{(1-\alpha)L}{n}$.

Remember that the price-raising firm was previously producing at an output $q_C$ that minimized average cost. So, by deviating the firm is now producing less ($q_V < q_C$), and as the average cost curve is U-shaped, its average cost will rise. Therefore, the profitability of this move will depend on whether the proportion of uninformed tourists that it serves, $\dfrac{(1-\alpha)L}{n}$, is sufficiently large that the price increase at least offsets the rise in average cost. This is our first lesson. If only a small fraction of consumers are uninformed, then such a deviation may not be possible, and the equilibrium is the competitive one with each firm selling at $p = c$ and each serving $L/n$ consumers.[8]

What happens if the proportion of tourists or uninformed consumers is not small? In that case, a two-price equilibrium outcome does become possible. Moreover, we can guess what it must look like. Some restaurants will sell at a high price of $p = V$, but will sell only to uninformed tourists. Other restaurants will sell at a low price of $p = c$ and they will sell to informed natives as well as to those lucky uninformed tourists who happen upon a low-priced restaurant. In the long run, each type of restaurant, low-priced and high-priced, must earn zero economic profit.

To fully characterize the two-price equilibrium we must do a bit more work and figure out the fraction of low-price and the fraction of high-price restaurants that sustains a long-run equilibrium. Let the fraction of low-price restaurants be $\beta$. This means that there are $\beta n$ low-price restaurants and $(1 - \beta)n$ high-price ones. In an equilibrium—each high-price restaurant charging $p = V$ and each low-price one charging $p = c$ has an equal share of the tourist market. Hence, every restaurant serves $\dfrac{(1-\alpha)L}{n}$ tourists. For a high-priced seller, this is all the demand that it serves. Informed natives will only buy from the low-price restaurants and there are $\beta n$ low-price restaurants. A low-price restaurant serves its share of informed natives, $\dfrac{\alpha L}{\beta n}$, in the market, along with its share of tourists, $\dfrac{(1-\alpha)L}{n}$. That is, in total, the low-price restaurant serves $\dfrac{\alpha L + (1-\alpha)\beta L}{\beta n}$ customers. A two-priced equilibrium is therefore characterized by the following:

High-Price Firms: Number: $(1 - \beta)n$; Price: $p = V$; Firm Output: $\dfrac{(1-\alpha)L}{n}$

$$\tag{3.6}$$

Low-Price Firms: Number: $\beta n$; Price: $p = c$; Firm Output $= \dfrac{\alpha L + (1-\alpha)\beta L}{\beta n}$

In a long-run equilibrium, both types of firms must earn zero profit. Hence, the output of each high-price firm must be such that the average cost of serving its customers is $V$. From before, we know that this output is $q_V$. Likewise, the output of each low-price firm must be such that its average cost is $c$. Again, we know from before that this is the perfectly competitive output $q_C$. Taking these two results together, we then have:

$$\frac{(1-\alpha)L}{n} = q_V \tag{3.7}$$

$$\frac{\alpha L + (1-\alpha)\beta L}{\beta n} = q_C \tag{3.8}$$

Given the production technology reflected in the average cost function and its corresponding values at $q_V$ and $q_C$, along with the total number of consumers $L$, and the fraction of those consumers who are informed $\alpha$, equations (3.7) and (3.8) are two independent equations with two unknowns—the equilibrium number of restaurants $n^*$ and the proportion $\beta^*$ of these setting a low price. We can therefore find a unique solution for each variable.

Denote the equilibrium number of sellers in total as $n^*$. Similarly, denote the equilibrium proportion of low-priced sellers that set $p = c$, as $\beta^*$. From equation (3.7) we have:

$$n^* = \frac{(1-\alpha)L}{q_V} \tag{3.9}$$

We may then substitute this expression for $n^*$ into equation (3.8) to obtain the equilibrium proportion of low-price firms yielding:

$$\beta^* = \frac{\alpha q_V}{(1-\alpha)(q_C - q_V)} \tag{3.10}$$

Observe that if all consumers are uninformed tourists (or $\alpha = 0$), then by equation (3.10), there are no low-price sellers. Every seller charges the monopoly price $p = V$, exactly as we had in our earlier knife-edged case.

Conversely, the proportion of low-price bistros $\beta^*$ will be equal to one and there will be no high-price sellers when the ratio of tourists (uninformed) to natives (informed)

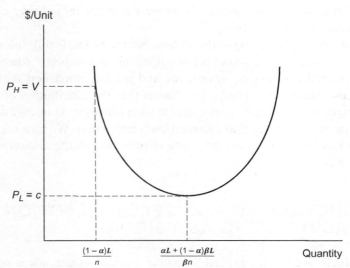

*Note:* A fraction $(1 - \beta)$ of firms charges the monopoly price $V$ and each serves $\frac{(1-\alpha)L}{n}$ customers. The remaining fraction $\beta$ of firms charges the competitive price and each serves $\frac{\alpha L + (1-\alpha)\beta L}{\beta n}$ customers. The smaller firms have higher average cost. In equilibrium, every firm earns zero economic profit.

**Figure 3.2  The two-price equilibrium in the Tourist Native Model**

or $\frac{(1-\alpha)}{\alpha}$ is equal to $\frac{q_V}{q_C - q_V}$. This again parallels our earlier result in that if there are sizable scale economies, reflecting the curvature of the Average Cost function so that $q_V$ is small relative to $q_C$, then the market will still reach the competitive equilibrium so long as the relative proportion of uninformed consumers or $\frac{(1-\alpha)}{\alpha}$ is comparably small. The two-priced equilibrium is described in Figure 3.2.

At this point, it may be worthwhile to pause for a moment and reflect on how you or others who you know behave as consumers when you either arrive in a new town or consider buying a product in a category with which you are unfamiliar, perhaps health insurance or a new computer. Do you know where to go for the best deal? Do you pore over guides and/or consumer websites and give close attention to advertised prices? Or, do you instead go out and take an offer from the first firm you find?

If time is an important element in acquiring information, then the value of time is an important contributor to the information cost $s$. In this light, we might expect that consumers with relatively high incomes, and therefore a relatively high opportunity cost for their time, will forgo the effort of search and learning more, and instead take their chances—especially if the good in question is relatively inexpensive such as a restaurant meal. However, when it comes to buying a dining table or an automobile, even a wealthy consumer might take the time to search and look for information about the best deal.

In short, the foregoing analysis points to where we might most likely observe firms providing information via advertising.

The potential role of advertising in the Tourist Native Model is thus informative, and we will return to this interpretation of retail advertising in Chapter 7 when we examine some of the empirical evidence on advertising and pricing in markets that come close to being perfectly competitive. The bottom line is that the distribution of information plays an important role in understanding any market outcome. How and whether firms choose to convey or not convey that information is important. We now turn to another important way in which consumers may lack information in the marketplace and the implications it may carry.

## 3.3 PRODUCT QUALITY, ADVERSE SELECTION, AND ADVERTISING AS A SIGNAL

For many products, such as a 10-speed bicycle or a cruise vacation it is not just information on price that consumers are seeking. In these and other cases, consumers are also typically concerned with a product's quality. That information, however, may not be readily available. A classic market where this lack of information confounds consumer decision-making is the used car market where there is the fear among buyers of purchasing a "lemon." This was brought to light in George Akerlof's (1970) seminal paper "The Market for Lemons."

Imagine yourself in the market to buy a used car. The market is a competitive one—there are many buyers, all of whom are like you, and also many sellers of used cars. However, we will assume that while sellers are also mostly alike they do differ in one critical dimension, namely, in the quality of the cars they sell. To be specific, there are two types of used car sellers: ones that sell a high-quality used car or a "peach," and ones that sell a low-quality one or a "lemon." A high-quality used car is more valuable and will provide the buyer with a value of services equal to $V_H$. A low-quality one will give a value equal to $V_L$, where $V_H > V_L$.

Once again, consumer information is imperfect. So, one cannot tell which seller is which. But you, like all consumers, do know the proportion of "lemons" that are for sale on the market. We denote this proportion as $\mu$. Not knowing in advance what kind of used car you will get, all you can do is work out your expected value of a car selected randomly from the pool of used cars available. This is: $\bar{V} = \mu V_L + (1 - \mu)V_H$. This expected value would be the maximum amount you would be willing to pay for a used car of unknown quality. By paying that price you expect to break even "on average" from the purchase of a used car.

As noted though, the imperfection in information is not symmetric. While buyers are somewhat uninformed, each seller of a used car knows exactly the type of car that is being offered—whether it is a peach or a lemon. Suppose that each seller has a slightly lower valuation of a used car than a buyer. Specifically, the seller puts a value $V_H - \Delta$ on a high-quality car and a value $V_L - \Delta$ on a low-quality one. This means that trades could and should happen. If buyer A values a peach at $V_H$ and if peach seller B values it at $V_H - \Delta$ then a deal that splits the difference leaves each better off by $\Delta/2$. The same is true if a lemon buyer pays a lemon seller an amount that splits the difference between their two separate reservation prices. Once again, both buyer and seller are better off by $\Delta/2$. Efficiency requires that these trades be consummated.

Recall however that for any buyer, the expected value of a randomly selected used car is $\bar{V} = \mu V_L + (1 - \mu)V_H$. Suppose then that $\Delta$ is sufficiently small that the following condition: $V_H - \Delta > \bar{V} > V_L - \Delta$ is satisfied. In that quite reasonable case, the market dilemma becomes readily apparent. As a buyer, you are only willing to pay $\bar{V}$ for a used car of unknown quality that is selected *randomly*. Yet an offer of $\bar{V}$ from you or any buyer offers a surplus only to someone selling a lemon. For someone selling a peach, the offer of $\bar{V}$ is below their reservation price, i.e., $V_H - \Delta > \bar{V}$. Accordingly, any car willingly sold at price $\bar{V}$ is not chosen randomly but, instead, is adversely "selected" to be a lemon.

Of course, not only you but every other buyer will recognize this selection issue. In turn, all buyers will change their strategy. Each will now realize that $\bar{V}$ is too much to pay. But at a lower price, only lemons are on offer. The market for peaches collapses and the maximum price a buyer will offer is the price $V_L$.

Again, this is not an efficient outcome. Some mutually beneficial trades that would generate a surplus for both parties, i.e., that are win–win, do not happen. Those trades would happen in the world of the perfectly competitive model where both buyers and sellers are perfectly informed about the quality of any used car. Once again, however, when we relax the assumption of fully informed buyers and assume instead that buyers face quality uncertainty in a way that sellers do not, that efficiency result no longer obtains.

The problem is that prices do more in this market than just work to balance the supply and demand of goods. They also sort or select which goods are traded. As just shown, this selection is in many cases biased so that only the low-quality used cars are traded. Indeed, economists refer to this as the adverse selection problem and it turns up in many places.[9]

### 3.3.1 Welfare Implications of Imperfect Quality Information

Advertising may be useful in solving the kind of imperfect information problem just described. In investigating that possibility, however, we need to address two issues. First, if advertising is to address the "lemons" problem of imperfect information, it must somehow be informative. Moreover, the method by which advertising informs must be more than a firm's simply announcing its type. After all, any used car seller can claim that she has a peach of a car for sale and no one will want to advertise that they are selling a lemon. Yet if all sellers make this claim—both those with peaches and those with lemons—such advertising provides no real information at all.

Second, the possible role for informative advertising depends very much on the structure of the imperfect information. Suppose for instance that there are 100 sellers and buyers each. Suppose as well that that $V_H = \$15,000$; $V_L = \$5,000$; and $\Delta = \$100$. There are then 100 potential buyer–seller exchanges each of which would generate a surplus of $100. Hence, the total potential surplus across the entire market is $10,000. Our discussion above implicitly assumed that the proportion $\mu$ of used cars that are lemons was fairly large. For instance, if $\mu = 0.5$, the buyer can expect that a car drawn at random from the population will have a value of $(0.5)\$5,000 + (1–0.5)\$15,000 = \$10,000$. As a result, each buyer will know that the only used cars willingly sold at that price will be lemons. No purchases of peaches will be possible.

However, the foregoing market outcome is not the only possibility. Suppose, for instance, that the proportion $\mu$ of lemons is very small—just under 1 percent. From any buyer's point of view, the expected value of a car drawn at random is now just a little over $0.01(\$5,000) + 0.99(\$15,000) = \$14,900$. In other words, a buyer would be willing to pay that price (or a bit more) for a car drawn at random from the pool of sellers. That sort of random draw though is precisely what they would now be facing. This is because the price $14,900 is just high enough to induce *all* sellers to sell—those with peaches as well as those with lemons. There would then be no adverse selection in this case. All 100 potential trades will take place.

Now consider a different scenario. In this instance we again assume that $V_H = \$15,000$; $V_L = \$5,000$; and $\Delta = \$100$. However, we now let the proportion $\mu$ of lemons revert to the earlier value of $\mu = 0.5$. To this though we add the further change that now *neither* buyers *nor* sellers know whether the car is a lemon or a peach. For each seller then, the expected value of the car is $0.5(\$15,000 – \$100) + 0.5(\$5,000 – \$100) = \$9,900$. Analogously, each buyer's expected value is $0.5(\$15,000) + 0.5(\$5,000) = \$10,000$. Here again, there will be no selection bias. The average buyer is willing to pay more than the average seller requires to induce a sale. All 100 potential trades will again be realized.

Of course, we would also observe all 100 cars being sold if all customers—buyers and sellers—were fully informed. Hence, in this and the two previous cases just described the total surplus of $10,000 is realized, unlike our first case in which $\mu$ was relatively large and the imperfect information was asymmetric. What is different among the three cases in which the maximum surplus of $10,000 is realized is the distribution of that surplus.

When all participants are fully informed, it is reasonable to expect that buyers and sellers will split the surplus evenly on any trade with each enjoying a surplus of $50. In the polar opposite case in which no one knows the value of the car until after the trade, each buyer is willing to pay $10,000 and each seller will accept a bid of $9,900 based on their *ex ante* expected values. Accordingly, we might again expect an even surplus split leading the price to settle at $9,950. This would again yield an *expected* $50 surplus to each buyer and seller individually. However, in this case, half the buyers will pay $9,950 for a peach worth $15,000 to them, while half will pay that same amount only to find subsequently that they have acquired a lemon that they only value at $5,000. Likewise, half the sellers will have sold a peach for $9,950 when its true value to them was $14,900 while the remaining half will have sold a lemon for that price that they only valued at $4,900. The gains expected *ex ante* are $50 for each buyer and each seller but the *ex post* realization will vary considerably across buyers and sellers.

The remaining case in which sellers have inside information but the proportion $\mu$ is just 1 percent is perhaps the most pernicious. As described above, we might expect the price in this case to be \$14,900—just enough to get the 99 sellers of peaches to sell. In each of these 99 trades the seller gets very little surplus while the buyer gets \$100. However, the one seller of a lemon knows who she is. She understands that she will earn a surplus of \$14,900 – \$4,900 = \$10,000. However, the one unlucky buyer of that car suffers a nearly offsetting loss of \$14,900 – \$5,000 = \$9,900.

Note that in this last case the presence of the one lemon seller affects the surplus distribution in two distinct ways. Clearly, it leads to a large *ex post* transfer to that seller from the one unlucky buyer. In addition, however, it forces all the other sellers who have peaches to lower their price to the point where they each earn virtually no surplus as opposed to the \$50 they earn on average in the other two scenarios. This is because no buyer wants to be the one who acquires the one lemon, and this leads them each to lower their willingness to pay to every seller in the market.

Simple as it is, the example just given provides further insights into a potential role for advertising as an informative tool. To begin with, it makes clear that this role will only be viable if there is a notable and recognized lack of information. When the extent of uncertainty $\mu$ is small, the full potential surplus of \$10,000 is nevertheless realized and the need for further information is much less compelling. This insight becomes all the more important when one recognizes that providing information—whether by advertising or otherwise—is itself costly. Even when $\mu$ is greater than say, 0.01, any gain from providing information must be weighed against its cost.

Second, note that it is not imperfect information by itself that leads to the adverse selection problem. It is instead the *asymmetry* of information that is key. It is the fact that buyers not only do not know product quality, but that they also realize that sellers do know that product quality. That is the key factor that leads buyers to be suspicious of those willing to sell at a relatively low price.

Finally, it is equally important to recognize that not only buyers, but high-quality sellers suffer from consumer uncertainty over product quality. That uncertainty leads consumers to be wary of *all* sellers as they cannot be sure *a priori* as to who is selling a peach and who is selling a lemon. This in turn suggests that if sellers do know their car's quality, the peach owners will have the strongest incentive to inform buyers of who they are.

## 3.3.2 Quality Signaling and Advertising

In some markets, there may be a straightforward solution to the adverse selection or "lemons" problem. In the used car market, for example, a "peach" seller could offer a form of third-party certification, i.e., a warranty that would solve the buyer's information problem. However, this will work only if the "lemon" seller, unlike the "peach" seller, cannot afford to offer a warranty as well. This seems likely because any warranty or guarantee for a used lemon car will be considerably more expensive given the much higher likelihood of breakdown and repair needs. This will permit what economists call a "separating equilibrium" in that the two types of cars will now be separately identified. "Peach" cars will come with extensive warranties and "lemons" will not.

However, there are many goods and services for which warranties or guarantees are not a practical solution. A fashion designer cannot guarantee that the styles offered at the start of the current season will be "cutting edge" or "in." Neither a drug nor a nutritional supplement firm can guarantee that its product will provide benefits for every patient or consumer. A ski resort cannot guarantee enough snow for good skiing conditions. To be sure, the fashion designer may be just as ill-informed as any buyer would be. So, this example may not be one in which adverse selection is a worry. Yet ski resorts likely do know more about their conditions on any given day than do potential skiers, and health products companies will very often know more about the efficacy of their product than will their consumers. Knowing this, consumers will be naturally wary that any price that is fair *on average* will be unfair to high-quality goods and therefore induce only low-quality goods to be offered for sale.

In short, the "lemons" information problem remains a real one for many products. Yet the insight that comes from markets in which meaningful warranties or guarantees do work is still insightful for markets in which they do not. For what makes the warranty successful is that consumers know that only a firm with a high-quality product can afford to commit to the substantial expense that an actual repair would entail. That potentially expensive commitment is what allows consumers to identify the high-quality firms and separate them from the low-quality ones. The question at hand then is whether advertising can somehow achieve this same identification.

Credibility is a key issue here. As the "snake-oil" salespeople of the late nineteenth century made abundantly clear, talk is cheap. Any product can claim to be a "miracle cure" or the highest possible quality. If the Federal Trade Commission (FTC) can prosecute firms that engage in deceptive advertising and if the legal consequences faced by a low-quality firm that falsely advertises are certain and significant, then the FTC's regulatory oversight could insure that high-quality products could be identified by advertising. However, the FTC's authority to contest incorrect product claims or false advertising may be limited. In fact, many advertising claims are simply difficult to verify or contest. We will discuss these limitations more fully along with issues related to deceptive advertising in Chapter 8.[10]

Clearly then, simply running ads that make unverifiable claims is unlikely to work. Yet there may still be other ways by which advertising can credibly establish the quality of a firm's products. We discuss these more formally in Chapter 9 but sketch out the intuitive argument based on the work of Nelson (1970, 1974) here.

Let us start by thinking about the kinds of consumer goods that are most prone to adverse selection problems. Clearly, they are products whose quality cannot easily be judged before purchase. Following Nelson (1974), we will classify those goods whose quality *can* be known before purchase as *Search Goods*. For these goods, there may still be an information problem as in the Tourist Native Model discussed earlier. However, the uncertainty here relates to price and not to product quality. Consumers likely know the high quality of Wedgwood china, for instance. What they do not know is where to get the best deal for a table setting.

In contrast to *Search Goods*, we have two other product types for which quality *is not* knowable before purchasing. These are *Experience Goods* and *Credence Goods*. For *Experience Goods*, e.g., films, books, hair stylists, and restaurant meals, among others, quality can only be ascertained *after* the consumer has purchased it and tried it. For *Credence Goods*, on the other hand, consumers lack the technical knowledge or other expertise needed to evaluate the quality of the good or service even after it has been purchased and used. Such goods may include legal, medical, and auto repair services, among others.

The potential for an adverse selection or "lemons" problem therefore seems to be greatest for *Experience* and *Credence* goods. The fact that a warranty or guarantee can work in some cases in turn suggests that any successful resolution of this problem requires some credible device by which a consumer can readily distinguish between a high-quality good and a low one before purchase. As noted above, simply claiming to be high quality is not likely to meet this credibility requirement.

Nelson's (1970, 1974) argument is based on the insight that repeat sales are valuable and that consumers are likely to return to a firm for repeat purchases so long as their experience with the firm's product has been a good one. Hence, it is the firms producing high-quality experience and credence goods that can likely count on such repeat sales once a consumer tries their product for the first time. Low-quality firms that produce these goods cannot. The consumer who goes to a hair stylist and ends up with a bad haircut, or the consumer who takes a car to a repair shop and finds out after paying the bill that the problem is still there, will be unlikely to return to those providers for further service.

The importance of repeat purchases means that, just as we saw in our numerical example, it is precisely those firms that know they have a high-quality product that have an incentive to make their superior quality known. Only a high-quality firm that attracts a first-time buyer can count on that buyer returning, which will generate additional profit for the firm in subsequent periods. Nelson's (1970, 1974) argument is that advertising can achieve this goal.

In Nelson's (1970, 1974) work, advertising can serve as a signal of quality precisely because it is expensive, and more advertising is more expensive. It is that expense that itself acts as the commitment mechanism by which a high-quality firm can credibly identify itself as such. Remember, repeat sales are important. They generate additional profits for a high-quality firm that cannot be obtained by a low-quality one. Hence, precisely because advertising is expensive, there will be a point where the expense of a commercial campaign will be more than a firm offering a low-quality product can afford but which one selling a high-quality product can as only the latter will have the profit from repeat sales to cover such expenses.

Nelson's (1970, 1974) insight is a valuable one. One of its key lessons is that advertising can signal quality even when it contains no explicit information or claims about the product. It is the expense of the advertising that serves to make a signal credible. This helps to explain why firms may hire famous athletes and film stars or advertise at peak times such as the Super Bowl and yet run ads that give very few details if any about the product's main features and price. It is that very expense that permits consumers to infer a product's quality. Note too the self-enforcing feature of this argument. Because consumers identify high-quality firms as those incurring a high advertising expense, high-quality firms have an incentive to identify themselves by making such expenses. In turn, precisely because high-quality product firms incur the heaviest advertising expense, consumers' belief that heavy advertising signals high quality is justified.

Economists now recognize that signaling quality is an important issue in product markets, labor markets, and other settings, e.g., political markets, as well. Nelson's (1970, 1974) advertising model was a critical step in this development. Like all models, it has its limitations. For example, it relies heavily on the value of repeat purchases. For large ticket items that consumers may only buy once or twice with considerable time before a repeat purchase, this argument may be less relevant. In addition, if it is significantly cheaper to produce a low-quality good or service relative to a high-quality one, then the profit from just one sale may be enough to ensure that a low-quality firm can afford expensive advertising. As mentioned earlier, we explore the signaling model more formally, including its associated caveats, in Chapter 9.

## 3.4 INFORMATION, CREDENCE GOODS, AND TWO-SIDED PLATFORMS

Besides the potentially informative role that advertising may play even when it does not include much explicit discussion of a product's features, the signaling model also calls our attention to the fact that other product characteristics may affect this information mechanism. For example, it probably makes sense to divide each of our three categories of goods, *Search, Experience, Credence*, into two further categories: *Convenience* goods and *Shop* goods. By *Convenience* goods we means ones that are purchased frequently and that are usually relatively inexpensive. In contrast, *Shop* goods are goods that are purchased infrequently and are fairly expensive. Milk, movies and haircuts are, in this sense, *Convenience* goods. Furniture, automobiles, and vacations qualify as *Shop* goods. Table 3.1 gives a possible taxonomy of how a sample of different goods might be categorized.

We know from our earlier discussion that advertising is unlikely to play a signaling role in the case of *Search Goods*, whether these fall into the *Convenience* category or

**Table 3.1** Plausible categorization of goods and services

|            | Convenience                | Shop                       |
|------------|----------------------------|----------------------------|
| **Search**     | Apples, milk, yogurt       | Furniture, clothing, shoes |
| **Experience** | Fast food, haircut, movie  | Vacation, dishwasher       |
| **Credence**   | Vitamins, anti-aging cream | Education, surgery         |

the *Shop* one. Turning to the *Experience Goods* category, the relatively low cost of *Convenience Experience Goods* suggests that for these goods, the benefits of spending a lot of time researching these products are small, implying that consumers will be less than well-informed. Here, advertising heavily may be quite important especially as repeat sales are frequent. In contrast, *Experience Shop* goods are "big ticket" expenses. In these cases, consumers might be willing to incur the cost of finding out about how well the good or service performs, diminishing the need for advertising to provide such information. In addition, these are also cases in which consumers may not make a repeat purchase for some time, dulling the importance of that later sale. So, if advertising works here, it likely will involve more than just a pure signaling mechanism. In particular, we may see firms marketing *Experience Shop* goods including considerable detail about their products' features, durability, and price in an effort to establish a well-recognized and long-lived brand name. In short, consideration of the signaling model of advertising has the further benefit of helping one think about the kinds of markets in which advertising will be heavy as well as how the kind of advertising we observe may differ across markets.

This brings us to the category of *Credence Goods* such as preventive surgery or a college degree. These are goods whose performance or quality cannot be easily assessed by the consumer even after consuming the product or service. Is an Ivy League degree really worth the tuition cost? What if one goes to a large state research university?[11]

*Credence* good purchases would be difficult to make if there were no information available to help consumers in making such choices. Even the signaling model breaks down when consumers cannot determine the quality of a good after purchasing it. One possibility, however, is that the views of others may matter. Indeed, one reason that an Ivy League degree may bring substantial benefits is that others view it as a high-quality degree. More generally, we can expect that while consumers do not necessarily trust the self-reporting of firms they may well place considerable weight on the experiences that other consumers report in regard to a school, or a medical practice, or a vacation spot, or similar goods and services. In these cases, advertising can again play an important, if somewhat indirect, role.

Consider the travel guide website *TripAdvisor*. If one clicks on its site, one will see a number of display ads posted by different, typically well-known companies, e.g., Guinness Stout or Singapore Airlines. *TripAdvisor* is paid for providing that space. If a traveler continues searching for a good place to stay in a town she is visiting, she will then be provided not only a list of possible hotels but, for each such hotel, a rating and a set of reviews from customers who have stayed there in the past. If a consumer clicks on one of the hotels listed and makes a booking, the hotel pays a fee to *TripAdvisor*.

Review sites and blogs have been greatly facilitated and expanded in the digital age, and for *Credence* goods they can be influential if not strictly informative for consumers. We explore the economics of these sites in our discussion of two-sided platforms in Chapters 10 through 12.[12]

## 3.5  SUMMARY

The standard model of perfect competition assumes that consumers are fully informed. They know which firms are selling which goods, the prices that each firm charges, and the quality of the product each provides. In the real world, markets with such perfectly informed consumers are likely to be rare. In this chapter, we have examined some of the possible roles that advertising may play in providing consumers with the missing information.

The Tourist Native Model is a way to describe what might happen when some consumers lack precise information about which sellers are setting low prices. In this case, it is quite possible that some firms will charge a high price and sell to uninformed consumers (tourists) while others will sell at a low price to informed ones (natives). However, because of competition, even the high-price firms earn zero economic profit because their customer base is sufficiently small that they cannot exploit available scale economies. In such a setting, advertising can play a useful role in providing price information to consumers. This can drive all firms to charge a lower price, expand demand, and encourage further exploitation of scale economies.

We also considered what happens when consumers lack information about the quality of the good. Here, we noted in particular that there could be an adverse selection problem if the lack of information is asymmetric. Specifically, when sellers know the quality of the good they are offering, but buyers do not, there is a real possibility that high-quality goods will not be profitable and will be withdrawn from the market, leaving only low-quality goods to be traded. Solving this problem requires that buyers somehow be assured pre-purchase of the product quality.

Here again, advertising could play a role. This is especially true for goods for which repeat purchases are important and whose quality buyers can ascertain *after* they try it—what economists refer to as experience goods. The argument is that because only high-quality goods will be purchased multiple times, high-quality goods have a discounted future revenue stream that can help defray the initial cost of expensive advertising. Hence, in this case, the mere fact of advertising provides useful information. It is a signal of quality regardless of whether the advertisement explicitly mentions any product specifications.

For credence goods, e.g., some elective surgery or perhaps an educational credential, the quality may not be easily known by a consumer even after purchasing and trying the good. For such goods, however, as well as for other products, advertising may still play an indirect role, even if not strictly informative role. Advertising revenues often support many of the digital platforms such as *TripAdvisor* that give consumers the opportunity to engage with others whose opinion they value, in part, precisely because they are consumers and not self-interested firms. At the same time, such sites not only serve consumers on one side but sell to advertisers on another as a means of financing that consumer service. Hence, these platforms are active in each of the two sides of an interconnected market. As such, they raise new issues about the role of advertising as one side of such two-sided platforms. We explore these issues in considerably more detail in Chapters 10–12.

## NOTES

1 However, in many cases it is difficult to capture enough of the value of information to cover its cost. This is because information has a non-rivalry in consumption feature in that once obtained by one consumer it can be shared at zero cost with many others. In other words, information has important public good aspects.

2 Adverse selection describes cases of imperfect information in which information is asymmetric before transactions are made, e.g., the seller knows the quality of a used car, but the buyer does not. Moral hazard describes cases in which the information becomes asymmetric after transactions are made, e.g., insured home-owners know whether they leave their doors unlocked (because if robbed they will be reimbursed), but the insurer does not.

3 The model presented in this section is based upon Salop and Stiglitz (1977).

4 Steves (2016, pp. 280–84).

5 Of course, there may be high-end restaurants and low-end eateries, and others in between, but so long as there are lots of restaurants within each type, i.e., so long as there are many perfect substitutes for each café or bistro of a given quality, our analysis still holds.

6 Note that the process of reaching $p = V$ does not need to go through this iterative process. Because $p = V$ is the unique equilibrium, each bistro can charge this price immediately knowing that others will, too. Note too that if $s \geq V - c$ does not hold, the equilibrium would be at $p = c + s$, so long as $s > 0$.

7 It should be clear that $P = V$ is the price a monopoly seller would charge. Recall that all $L$ consumers will pay as much as $V$ for one meal per day and will not buy any more meals that day no matter how much the price falls. So, reducing the price below $V$ gains no additional sales but raising it above $V$ would lose all sales. Hence, the profit-maximizing price is $P = V$. Diamond's (1971) path-breaking paper is the first to demonstrate this "knife-edge" result. Note that the long-run equilibrium is doubly inefficient here. Price exceeds marginal cost *and* average cost is not minimized.

8 The outcome also depends on how steeply sloped the left portion of the average cost curve is, i.e., how fast average cost rises as output declines below $q_C$.

9 Health insurance markets are often cited as a case where the adverse selection problem is most serious. For simplicity, imagine that there are equal numbers of two types of private individuals. One type has a 20% risk of needing $100,000 worth of medical expenses. The other type has only a 2% chance. The individuals know their type, but the insurance company does not. A policy that is actuarially fair would charge $11,000 to all individuals—reflecting the average 11% chance of a large medical need across the entire population. However, individuals in the healthier group will not pay this premium knowing that it costs more than the expenses it insures against. Knowing that only one group—those with the highest health risk—will insure, insurers will raise the premium to $20,000. This further insures that only this group will buy coverage. Solutions to this adverse selection problem typically involve mechanisms to make sure that all parties have insurance either via a subsidized mandate or public provision of insurance to everyone.

10 The First Amendment of the US Constitution protects free speech. While such speech does not include fraudulent product claims, it is not always easy to separate fact from fiction.

11 Somewhat surprisingly, Dale and Krueger (2014) have found that, with the exception of students from certain social groups such as Hispanics and Blacks, there are very small positive returns to graduating from a highly selective college. However, many other studies such as Hoxby (2009) and Hershbein (2013) do find a significant positive return.

12  See https://economistsview.typepad.com/economistsview/2006/04/markets_for_cre.html for some additional insights on shopping for credence goods (accessed March 23, 2021).

## 3.6 REFERENCES

Akerlof, G. 1970. "The Market for 'Lemons': Quality Uncertainty and the Market Mechanism." *Quarterly Journal of Economics* 84 (August), 488–500.

Dale, S., and A. Krueger. 2014. "Estimating the Effects of College Characteristics over the Career Using Administrative Earnings Data." *Journal of Human Resources* 49 (Spring), 325–58.

Diamond, P. 1971. "A Model of Price Adjustment." *Journal of Economic Theory* 3 (June), 156–68.

Hershbein, B. 2013. "Worker Signals Among New College Graduates: The Role of Selectivity and GPA." Upjohn Institute Working Paper, 13-190.

Hoxby, C. 2009. "The Changing Selectivity of American Colleges." *Journal of Economic Perspectives* 23 (Fall), 95–118.

Nelson, P. 1970. "Information and Consumer Behavior." *Journal of Political Economy* 78 (March/April), 311–29.

Nelson, P. 1974. "Advertising as Information." *Journal of Political Economy* 82 (July/August), 729–54.

Salop, S. C., and J. E. Stiglitz. 1977. "Bargains and Ripoffs: A Model of Monopolistically Competitive Price Dispersion." *Review of Economic Studies* 44, 493–510.

Steves, R. 2016. *Europe Through the Back Door*. Berkeley: Perseus Books.

# 4
# Non-Informative Advertising, Consumer Behavior, and Welfare

## 4.1 INTRODUCTION

Television became the dominant advertising medium in the latter half of the twentieth century. In the years following the Second World War, TV ads reached a rapidly growing television audience, introducing to potential consumers a wide array of new products from small ticket items such as ready-to-eat cereals, cleaning liquids, and instant coffee, to more expensive ones, such as clothes driers, dishwashers, and new color television sets. Initially, these TV ads had for the most part informational content, emphasizing unique attributes of the product, but over time the informative content of TV advertising declined. Television advertising became increasingly emotional or funny or entertaining, but contained less real information.[1]

A recent popular television series *Mad Men* followed the lives and fortunes of people in a Madison Avenue advertising agency world in this new era of television advertising. In the final episode, the main character, Don Draper, torn between the shallowness of the Madison Avenue world and the lifestyle and career that such a world had afforded him, sat Zen-like with fellow meditators on a California hillside green trying to reconcile these inner conflicts. Suddenly, a wry smile hinting some resolution and hope for the future spread across his face as he envisioned a new ad for Coke, an ad that in fact did debut in 1971.

This iconic "non-informative" ad features a large group of young people of differing ethnicities sitting on a hillside each holding a bottle of *Coca-Cola* and one by one, joining in a chorus of: *"I'd like to teach the world to sing in perfect harmony. I'd like to buy the world a Coke and keep it company."* It was widely watched in its day and was re-watched in the finale, triggering nostalgic remembrances for the millions of *Mad Men* viewers who recalled seeing that ad when it first aired.

After the *Mad Men* finale *Advertising Age* reported on the true story of how the Coke ad came to be.[2] In the early 1970s, the McCann-Erickson advertising agency had the Coca-Cola company as a client, and William Backer was the creative director handling the account. While flying to London, Backer's plane was diverted to an overnight stop in Ireland, which of course frustrated and annoyed many passengers. The following morning, Backer observed that the same passengers who had been so angry and distraught the night before were now laughing and bonding together, with many drinking a Coke. Backer later said that he suddenly saw that "Let's have a Coke" could mean more than just "Let's get a drink." It could instead be framed as a way of saying, "Let's keep each other company for a while." In his vision, Coke was not just a drink with refreshing attributes sold at a reasonable price, but rather it was a bond between people of different cultures. Drinking Coke was a way for the consumer to be part of this group—and to share in its values of respect for others and "peace throughout the land."

Backer's insight is potentially a powerful one. Advertising may work by changing consumers' views about how much they desire a product or by enhancing the enjoyment they get as they consume the product. Alternatively, it may allow them to feel that such consumption deepens their bond with others. If this is the way that advertising works, then the Chicago School perspective that advertising's main role in the marketplace is to provide information misses the mark.

In this chapter, we explore how advertising could affect consumer behavior even when such advertising contains no informative content regarding price, product attributes or quality. One such non-informative view of advertising is referred to as the persuasive view. Persuasive advertising alters consumers' tastes by persuading consumers that only Coke, and not a rival substitute, can satisfy their soft drink desires. The persuasive view implies that *Coca-Cola*'s advertising would make the demand for Coke less elastic. In other words, as the price of Coke rises, fewer consumers will want to switch to a lower-priced substitute.

An alternative non-informative view treats advertising instead as a complement to the good that is being advertised. This perspective is subtly different from the persuasive view. As a complementary good, advertising enhances the value of Coke to the consumer in a way similar to how butter enhances the value of toast, or perhaps how music can enhance a dining experience. Advertising does not change the consumer's tastes, but it does make consuming the product more enjoyable. If consumers think about Coke's hilltop singing ad while drinking their *Coca-Cola* beverage, they enjoy increased pleasure from drinking the beverage. We explore each of these two "non-informative" perspectives on advertising in the sections below.

Before beginning that discussion we should note that there are a number of models of advertising in which firms deliberately suppress the information content of their messaging. For example, Anderson and Renault (2006) present a model in which sellers' ads strategically avoid providing precise information on their stock so as to attract a larger set of shoppers with a broad variety of tastes. The optimal price to this eclectic group is lower than it would be to one with more specialized interests, and welfare is higher in this limited information world. An alternative approach is taken by Ellison and Ellison (2009) in which e-commerce firms obfuscate their true fees with transport costs and other charges that search engines may not pick up. This information suppression tends to lower social welfare.

However, the articles cited above are fundamentally rooted in the view that the mechanism by which advertising affects consumer behavior is by providing more or less information. In contrast, our focus in this chapter is on examining models in which advertising's effect works through a different, non-informative channel. We explore the strategic choice of information content in subsequent chapters.

# 4.2 PERSUASIVE ADVERTISING: CHANGING CONSUMER TASTES

The persuasive view of advertising reflects a long-standing approach evident in both the early popular work of Packard (1957) and the more formal analysis of economists, including Kaldor (1950) and Galbraith (1958). In this view, advertising is a way to persuade consumers to want products that they would not otherwise buy. More critically, advertising leads consumers to make mistakes and spend their money unwisely by paying too high a price for the wrong kinds of goods.

Fundamentally, the persuasive view is that advertising affects consumers' behavior by altering their preferences or tastes—leading them to prefer some goods that in the absence of such advertising they would not have valued so highly. From the viewpoint of social welfare, the persuasive view sees advertising as generally pernicious. Yet while this may be the case, some deeper analysis is necessary to confirm that suspicion. Suppose, for instance, that a persuasive medicinal drug ad enables a consumer to learn about a new medical condition; or that a persuasive ad for a food product reveals new ways to use the product. In both instances, the consumer's preferences for the advertised product change, yet in both it seems equally clear that this change is the result of beneficial consumer learning. In short, one has to do more than simply assert that advertising changes consumer tastes before concluding that it is therefore welfare-reducing.

More generally, it is important to recognize that in economics, we generally take as a starting point that consumers have *given* preferences, i.e., that "they know what they like." Accordingly, the consumer's problem is usually one of how to allocate scarce budget dollars over various goods and services in a way that yields the most preferred consumption package affordable. Suggesting that consumer tastes are endogenous, or that advertising changes a consumer's preferences, is somewhat at odds with this basic consumer choice paradigm.[3]

In particular, the evaluation of market outcomes from an efficiency viewpoint becomes considerably more difficult in a world of changing consumer tastes. A consumer whose tastes have changed because of advertising is analogous to two consumers—one with one set of tastes before advertising and one with a different set after advertising. An interpersonal comparison of utility between these two consumers is not truly possible any more than it is possible to compare the utility of a consumer who likes wine with that of a consumer who prefers ale. Any analysis of persuasive advertising must therefore confront this problem of interpersonal utility comparison if we want to say anything about economic efficiency and social welfare.[4]

## 4.2.1 A Simple Model of Persuasive Advertising

As noted, the view that advertising persuades consumers by altering their tastes has been a persistent theme among real-world practitioners, as well as social critics. A model that captures this basic argument can be traced back to Braithwaite (1928). We illustrate his basic analysis in Figures 4.1(a) and 4.1(b).

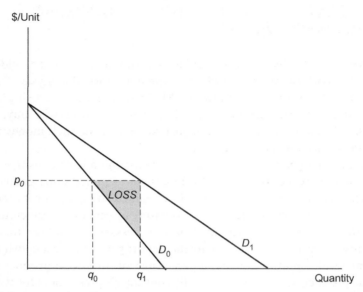

*Note:* Advertising persuades consumers to act erroneously as if their demand is $D_1$ rather than $D_0$. The shift to $D_1$ however does not alter the elasticity at any price nor does it change marginal cost. There is a welfare loss indicated by the shaded triangle equal to the amount by which the perceived value of the increased sales exceeds its true value indicated by the original demand curve.

**Figure 4.1(a)** Advertising distorts consumer spending and leads to a welfare loss

In both Figures 4.1(a) and 4.1(b), consumer preferences in the absence of advertising underlie the demand curves labeled $D_0$. In each figure, these pre-advertising demand curves are taken to represent consumers' true or innate preferences. In contrast, the demand curves labeled $D_1$ reflect consumer preferences *after* advertising. Braithwaite (1928) regards these demand curves, however, as essentially mistaken demands that reflect consumers' (perhaps temporary) misunderstanding of their needs and wants because of manipulative effects of persuasive advertising.

In the absence of advertising, a monopolist optimally sets the price $p_0$ and at that price consumers buy $q_0$ units. The monopolist engages in persuasive advertising of an amount $A$ for which the cost is $g(A)$, and in Figure 4.1(a), this shifts (rotates) the demand curve outward in a way that maintains the same elasticity of demand at each price. If in addition we also assume a constant marginal cost, the optimal price-cost markup does not change, and so the profit-maximizing price remains at $p_0$. However, at that price consumers now mistakenly increase their consumption to $q_1$. Given their true, innate preferences this amounts to a misallocation of scarce budget dollars. The loss from this is given by the shaded triangle.

Of course, the monopolist is not concerned about the loss to consumers. The monopolist is interested in maximizing its profit. With constant marginal cost $mc$ and a constant markup $p_0 - mc$, this will increase profit so long as the operating profit gain $(p_0 - mc)$

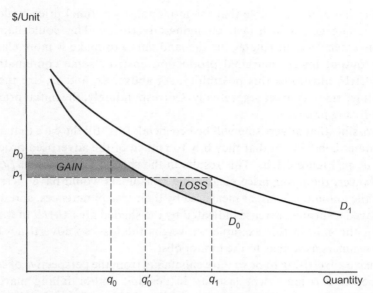

*Note:* Advertising persuades consumers to act erroneously as if their demand is $D_1$ rather than $D_0$. The shift to $D_1$ however increases the elasticity and leads to a lower price. The shaded trapezoid reflects a welfare gain due to the fall in price that would have led demand to increase from $q_0$ to $q_0'$ along the original, true demand curve. The shaded triangle reflects a welfare loss in that at the lower price consumers buy too much of the advertised good. It is possible that the gain exceeds the loss.

**Figure 4.1(b)** Advertising distorts consumer spending and leads to a welfare loss

$(q_1 - q_0)$ exceeds the cost of advertising $g(A)$. The monopolist will want to continue to increase the level of advertising until the marginal gain in operating profit just equals the marginal cost of advertising. From the viewpoint of economic efficiency, however, this outcome will result in too much advertising. The monopolist balances the marginal gain in operating profit against the marginal cost of advertising. However, the marginal social gain is less than that gain in operating profit precisely because the increase in demand does not reflect the true consumer valuation or the true consumer surplus from the increased consumption.

Because of the assumption of constant marginal cost and constant demand elasticity the profit-maximizing monopoly price does not change. It should be clear though that if that price rises, consumers will be doubly hurt. They would now pay a higher price (and therefore lose surplus) on the $q_0$ units that they would have bought even without advertising plus suffer the further distortion of buying too many units at too high a price. In short, Braithwaite's (1928) research implies that in this kind of world, firms with market power will do too much advertising and that this will hurt consumers if the post-advertising price is greater than or equal to the pre-advertising price.

On the other hand, it is possible that the monopolist's optimal price could fall after the monopolist engages in such taste-changing advertising. This could happen if the change in consumer demand rotates the demand curve to make it more elastic; if the expansion in output lowers marginal production cost; or some combination of the two. Figure 4.1(b) illustrates this possibility. As above, $D_0$ and $D_1$ are the pre- and post-advertising demand curves respectively. Correspondingly, the initial price is $p_0$ and the post-advertising price is $p_1$.

It is now possible that advertising will be beneficial. It is still the case that advertising distorts consumer behavior so that they buy too much of the advertised product in the amount $q_1 - q'_0$ in Figure 4.1(b). This results in the shaded area marked *LOSS* in the diagram. However, the lower price means that consumers would have increased their purchases by the amount $q'_0 - q_0$, as measured by their true preferences, and would have therefore enjoyed a surplus increase indicated by the shaded area *GAIN* in the diagram. As illustrated, the gain in this example outweighs the loss, so advertising brings net benefits to consumers as well as to the monopolist.

For persuasive advertising to be welfare enhancing from the perspective of consumers, there must be some rising price elasticity in demand and/or falling marginal cost. However, there is still no guarantee that the combined effect of these forces, even if they are present, will be large enough to produce a gain that is larger than the loss.

Braithwaite (1928) therefore carries the following message. Persuasive advertising that does not lead to a price decline is inefficient and harmful to consumers. Advertising that results in a price decline is necessary for advertising to be socially beneficial, but a price decline is not a sufficient condition. Figure 4.1(b) can be easily drawn such that the *LOSS* area exceeds the *GAIN* area.

## 4.2.2 Persuasive Advertising with Consumer Sovereignty

Braithwaite's (1928) model is somewhat remarkable in that it captures, in a straightforward way, much of the popular concern about persuasive advertising and its manipulation of consumer behavior. It does, however, conflict with the standard economic assumption that consumers know what they want—that they are sovereign. While this sovereignty assumption may seem strong, further consideration of the Braithwaite (1928) model helps clarify the problems one encounters in abandoning it.

Suppose that Braithwaite (1928) is correct and that consumers are "fooled" by the advertising into wanting to buy more of the advertised product. Even if this is true, it seems that for sensible consumers, the "fooling" would only be temporary. The advertising would then work to lure consumers into buying the good the first time. Yet once they wake up and realize that they have been "tricked" into buying too much, they would become less susceptible to advertising. In that case, the advertising effect is temporary and therefore less worrisome.

But, what if the change in consumer taste change is permanent? Consumer preferences after advertising have forever changed to favor more consumption of the advertised good. The trouble with that argument is that we can no longer claim that the lower demand curve ($D_0$ in Figures 4.1(a) and 4.1(b)) reflects consumers' tastes. If advertising has irrevocably changed their preferences then the post-advertising consumers are truly different from their pre-advertising selves. In turn, this implies that trying to compare the pre- and post-advertising welfare of those consumers is tantamount to the impossible comparison of the utilities of different consumers. Is there therefore any way we can say that there is too much advertising in such a world?

The above counterarguments to Braithwaite's (1928) analysis motivated what is, to date, probably the most ambitious attempt to tackle the issue of changing preferences—the well-known paper by Dixit and Norman (1978). In brief, they approach the evaluation of advertising in two ways. One is to take consumer preferences as those indicated by their pre-advertising demand curve and use the pre-advertising demand to evaluate overall social welfare before and after advertising. The second way follows the same method, but uses the demand curve reflecting consumer post-advertising tastes to evaluate the pre-advertising and post-advertising market outcomes.

Because there is no direct comparison of the pre-advertising market outcome with the post-advertising one, Dixit and Norman (1978) avoid the problem of interpersonal utility comparisons. That is, they recognize the difficulty of mixing the two sets of consumer tastes and demand curves in the same analysis. They also recognize that it is not clear *a priori* which set of tastes and associated demand curve best captures the welfare effects of advertising. Their view is that while we cannot be sure which set of consumer preferences is *true*, that should not matter if using either set points to the same conclusion. As we will see, this can in fact be the case, and can again lead to the conclusion that such persuasive advertising can be excessive—hurting consumers and causing overall economic inefficiency—if it results in any upward movement in the price.

We first consider the case of a monopolist in which the demand expansion leaves the price elasticity of demand, the optimal markup, and hence the optimal price unchanged. This is illustrated in Figure 4.2(a). Here too, we have again labeled $D_0$ as the demand implied by consumers' pre-advertising tastes, and $D_1$ as the demand implied by their post-advertising tastes. Marginal cost is constant and labeled $mc$. Finally, let the level of advertising be $A$ so that we may refer to a marginal change in advertising as $dA$.

We will assume an increase $dA$ in advertising lies behind the shift in the demand curve shown in Figure 4.2(a). If advertising costs are constant at $g$ per unit, then the cost of such a rise in advertising is $gdA$. The advertising increase $dA$ leads to a rise in output from $q_0$ to $q_1$. This amount may be regarded as the marginal impact of advertising, i.e.,

$$dq = q_1 - q_0 = \frac{\partial q}{\partial A} dA.$$

The questions that Dixit and Norman (1978) then ask are the following: (1) What incentive does the monopolist have to make this increase in advertising effort? (2) How does the monopolist's calculation of the gains and losses from a marginal increase in advertising compare with the social benefits and costs of such an increase?

The answer to the first question is clear from Figure 4.2(a). The rise in advertising enables the monopolist to sell $dq$ more units of output each at a price above cost or the amount ($p_0 - mc$). The net extra operating profit $d\pi$ gained is indicated by the rectangle

$ACEF = d\pi = (p_0 - mc)dq$. The net profit gain is this amount less the increased advertising cost or $(p_0 - c)dq - gdA = d\pi - gdA$. This net gain is the incentive that a monopolist has to increase advertising at the margin.

The next step is to work out the net marginal *social* benefit from an increase $dA$ in the level of advertising. This is a bit trickier because it depends a bit on whether we use the pre-advertising demand curve $D_0$ or the post-advertising demand curve $D_1$. Let us consider each in turn.

Using the pre-advertising tastes and demand, the net social benefit is given by the area of the trapezoid $ADEF$ less the advertising cost $gdA$. The amount $gdA$ is common to the measure of the net private monopoly benefit and to the net social benefit, and the social benefit is *smaller* than the private benefit by an amount equal to the area of triangle $ACD$.

If instead we use the post-advertising tastes and demand, the net social benefit is given by the trapezoid area $FBCE$ less the advertising expense $gdA$.[5] In this case, it appears that the social benefit is *larger* than the private benefit by an amount equal to the area of triangle $ABC$.

It may be tempting to say that these two triangle measures of the difference between the net private benefit and net social benefit of advertising cancel each other out and, therefore, that average net private benefit and net social benefit are the same. That turns out to be the right conclusion in this case, but the real reason for this is more fundamental, and slightly more technical.

The real reason that we can conclude that private and social benefits are equal in this case is that the measure of any difference—either triangle $ACD$ or triangle $ABC$—is what economists refer to as "second-order small." Remember, we are considering here the incentive at the margin to engage in a small amount of additional advertising $dA$. The increase in operating profit is:

$$\Delta\pi = (p_0 - mc)\frac{\partial q}{\partial A}dA \qquad (4.1)$$

If we denote the price elasticity of demand by $\varepsilon$ at the point $C$ then the area of either extra triangle can be written as:

$$ACD = ABC = \left[\frac{1}{2}\left(\frac{p_0}{q_1}\right)\frac{1}{\varepsilon}\right](dq)^2 = \left[\frac{1}{2}\left(\frac{p_0}{q_1}\right)\frac{1}{\varepsilon}\right]\left(\frac{\partial q}{\partial A}dA\right)^2 \qquad (4.2)$$

Because of the squared $dA$ term in (4.2), it goes to zero relatively quickly compared to (4.1) as $dA$ gets very small. This means that we can ignore these two triangles in our calculations. In turn, this implies that for this case in which advertising results in *no* increase in price, the private monopolist's gain from a small increase in advertising effort $dA$ is the same as the social welfare gain. Hence, in this case, we can rely on profit-maximizing decision-making to yield the socially efficient level of advertising effort. This result is reached regardless of whether one uses the pre-advertising tastes and demands or the post-advertising demands, and is immune to the problem of trying to make interpersonal utility comparisons.

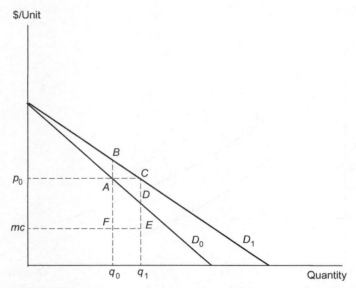

*Note:* Advertising shifts demand from $D_0$ to $D_1$ but leaves the elasticity of demand and equilibrium price unchanged at $p_0$. The firm gains profit of area **ACEF** less the cost of advertising. The net social gain using the initial demand curve is the trapezoid **ADEF** less the cost of advertising. The net social gain using the induced demand curve is the trapezoid **FBCE**. In each case, the triangle difference between the firm's gain and the social gain **ACD** or **ABC**, respectively, is second-order small. The level of advertising is asymptotically equal to the social optimum.

**Figure 4.2(a)** Welfare effects when advertising changes tastes but does not raise price

As Dixit and Norman (1978) stress, however, a different conclusion is reached if the increase in advertising raises the price as well as the output. We illustrate this case with Figure 4.2(b). The major difference between this case and the previous one is that with a rise in price, from $p_0$ to $p_1$, the monopolist's gain from a small increase in advertising $dA$ is now considerably larger. This is because in addition to the rectangle *ACEF* that we had in the previous diagram, the monopolist also gains the additional rectangle of profit $p_0 p_1 AG$ which is simply $q_0(p_1 - p_0) = q_0 dp$.

Under either set of consumer preferences, pre-advertising or post-advertising, the amount $q_0 dp$ reflects the transfer of consumer surplus to the monopolist on the first $q_0$ units that would have been bought under either set of tastes. It is *not* an increase in the total surplus or total social welfare however—just a transfer. It therefore provides an incentive to the monopolist to advertise, where from the viewpoint of society there is no real net gain.

Denote the increase in the total surplus or social welfare from a small increase $dA$ in advertising as $dW$. Denote the monopolist's profit gain from that same incremental advertising as $d\pi$. Then, again ignoring either the (roughly) triangular area $ABC$ or

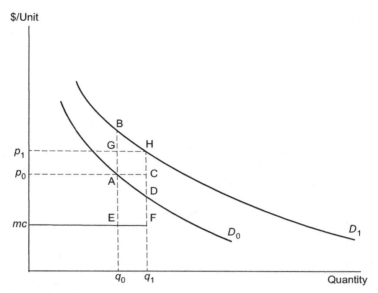

*Note:* Advertising shifts demand from $D_0$ to $D_1$ but decreases the elasticity of demand and raises the equilibrium price from $p_0$ to $p_1$. The firm gains profit of area **ACFE** plus $(p_1 - p_0)q_1$ less the cost of advertising. The net social gain using either the initial or induced demand curve is either the trapezoid **ADEF** or the trapezoid **EBHF**, respectively, again less the cost of advertising. The level of advertising likely exceeds the social optimum.

**Figure 4.2(b)** Welfare effects when advertising changes tastes but does not raise price

the (roughly) trapezoidal area **ADEF** as negligible for small $dA$, we have the following result:

$$dW = d\pi - q_0 dp \qquad (4.3)$$

Equation (4.3) implies when prices do not increase ($dp = 0$) then social welfare and private gains match identically, just as in the Figure 4.2(a) case discussed above. However, in any case that prices rise ($dp > 0$), a small increase in advertising $dA$ will generate a larger gain in private monopoly profit than it will in total welfare. The difference reflects the transfer of surplus from consumers to the monopolist that the higher price implies over the $q_0$ units bought without advertising. In turn, this implies that the monopolist will advertise excessively to the detriment of consumers. Put somewhat differently, if by starting from the profit-maximizing level of advertising we could reduce advertising by a small amount, this reduction would raise welfare.

Once again, these results hold whether one uses the pre-advertising demand curve or the post-advertising demand curve. Dixit and Norman (1978) argue that they also apply with even greater force to the cases of oligopoly and monopolistic competition. Intuitively, this is because in those cases the advertising could include a combative feature as well. Some of a firm's advertising is wasted as its effects are simply countered by the advertising of its rivals. Overall then, Dixit and Norman (1978) seem to make a strong case that persuasive advertising will be excessive.

### 4.2.3 Persuasion, Information, and Interpersonal Welfare Comparisons

Despite the results about wasteful advertising derived in Dixit and Norman (1978), it is perhaps fair to say that this perspective on advertising has not carried the day with economists. It is important to understand why. Basically, the Dixit and Norman (1978) analysis has not been persuasive because it omits a full consideration of the reasons behind any change in tastes or preferences, and because it also leaves open key questions about the interpretation of the behavior of a consumer whose tastes truly have been changed.

For example, one can argue that an ad providing consumers with information does change their tastes without manipulating them. Dixit and Norman (1980) have argued against this view, writing that providing a consumer with information simply gives them a tool to pursue their tastes more efficiently but leaves those tasted unaltered. Yet this seems not to be quite accurate in at least some cases. As suggested by our earlier examples of advertising for medicinal drugs or food products, advertising that changes tastes as the result of consumer learning likely has positive welfare effects. It does more than merely enable consumers to pursue their preferences more efficiently.

In light of the foregoing argument, economists have come to recognize that the line between persuasive and informative advertising is likely to be a fine one. Dixit and Norman's (1978) claim that for-profit firms will likely do too much persuasive advertising may in fact still hold when we apply a clear and strict definition of what persuasion means. But if advertising provides the consumer with information that expands their set of preferences, the social benefits of advertising providing this information could be substantial and more than the private gains to any one firm. This implies that advertising may be too little and not too much.[6] This point serves as an important counterbalance in any discussion of the welfare effects of advertising overall.

There is also a second somewhat more fundamental reason why the Dixit and Norman (1978) conclusions have not found wide acceptance among economists. This again concerns the nature of consumer tastes and what it means to change them. Consider Figure 4.2(b) once more. The area between demand curves $D_0$ and $D_1$ but above the post-advertising price $p_1$ is the consumer surplus enjoyed by consumers who now have post-advertising tastes *that they would not have enjoyed* with their pre-advertising preferences. This extra consumer surplus does not enter into the analysis in Dixit and Norman (1978), but an argument could be made that it should. After all, this is a gain that advertising creates. If that point is accepted, however, the social gains to persuasive advertising are much greater than what we derived above. Correspondingly, the case that persuasive advertising is excessive again becomes much weaker.

Of course, there is as well the argument against including this extra surplus in our calculations. To do so is really to compare the well-being or utility level of consumers with one set of tastes with the well-being or utility level of consumers with a different set of tastes. The fact that the consumers are the same people at different points in time—before advertising and after it—does not remove the problem. If their preferences are different, then they are in fact different consumers. But this is precisely the kind of interpersonal comparison of consumer utility that we want to avoid when trying to understand the impact of advertising on welfare or efficiency.[7]

One possible way forward, suggested by Stigler and Becker (1977), Fisher and McGowan (1979), and Becker and Murphy (1993) among others, is to put the level of advertising *directly* into consumers' utility functions. As the level of advertising changes, it now will alter consumers' choices over goods in their utility function, but this does not imply any change in their fundamental *preferences*. That is, the consumer's preference ordering, or utility function, will be unaltered. Their buying behavior though will change as the level of advertising consumed by the consumer changes. Because the utility function is the same both before and after advertising, comparisons of post-advertising utility with pre-advertising utility now become possible. This alternative approach lies at the heart of the complementary view of advertising to which we now turn.

## 4.3 ADVERTISING AS A COMPLEMENTARY GOOD

Recall that consumer utility maximization underlies the derivation of market demand. Each consumer chooses a set of goods $X_1, X_2, \ldots X_N$ that maximizes the utility function $U(X_1, X_2, \ldots X_N)$ given the prices of these goods $p_1, p_2, \ldots p_N$ and income $Y$. This optimization problem results in an optimal choice of commodity $X_i$ as a function of $p_i$, given the prices of the other goods and the consumer's endowment of income. Aggregating these demands across consumers then yields the market (Marshallian) demand curve for $X_i$ as a function of $p_i$, again, taking all other prices and consumers' incomes as given.

Stigler and Becker (1977) suggest a somewhat different approach to the consumer's utility maximization problem. In their view, the goods $X_i$ are not necessarily what enter the utility function directly. For example, a consumer likely does not value having a toothbrush, toothpaste, and floss in and of themselves. Instead, what the consumer really cares about is the dental hygiene that these products can be used to produce. Somewhat similarly, a consumer streaming music fundamentally cares about the quality of music-listening. The streaming device and speakers are just inputs to the production of that listening experience.

Effectively then, Stigler and Becker (1977) argue that the utility function ought really to be written as $U(Z_1, Z_2, \ldots Z_N)$ where the variable $Z_i$ measures the true concern of the consumer, e.g., dental hygiene, music enjoyment, and so on. These fundamental "goods" are in turn produced from the underlying market goods $X_1, X_2, \ldots X_N$ according to the consumer's internal "technology." It is here that there emerges a role for advertising.

Think again of the "*Coca-Cola* hilltop" commercial. Hearing this commercial, or even the consumer just knowing about it, may associate the values of peace and diversity with drinking Coke and enhance the consumer's enjoyment or pleasure taken in each sip. In fact, some neuroscience experiments lend support to this view. McClure et al. (2004) monitored the brain scans of 67 volunteer subjects while they were tasting a drink which could be either Coke or Pepsi. Before the scan the researchers determined each subject's preference for Coke versus Pepsi by asking them directly and by doing blind taste tests. The subjects then sipped each of the beverages while the researchers scanned their brains using functional magnetic resonance imaging (fMRI), which measures the blood flow in regions of the brain and differentiates the brain activity levels. Before taking a sip, the subjects saw either anonymous cues of flashes of light or they saw pictures of a Coke or Pepsi can.

The idea was to see which specific regions of the brain were activated when the subjects had only taste information when they took a sip versus what happened when they also had brand identification. The researchers found no influence in the MRI of brand knowledge for Pepsi. However, the identity of the Coke label did have an effect, activating areas in the dorsolateral prefrontal cortex and the hippocampus of the brain. These areas are associated with emotion and affect and can therefore influence the subject's enjoyment or preference.

The results of this study suggest that when consumers drank Coke, they received greater pleasure (utility) when informed they were drinking Coke than they did when they were unaware of the brand of cola they were consuming. More generally, the results of the study suggested that two separate brain activations—one corresponding to taste and the other to cultural influence—interact to determine the subjects' preferences.[8] These findings would not be at all surprising to people working in the advertising industry. They have long believed that cultural messages affect consumers' enjoyment of brands and satisfy consumers' tastes or preferences. Indeed, advertisers held those beliefs for a century before there was any neuroscientific evidence to back them up.

More formally, if $Z_1$ is drinking enjoyment; $X_1$ is the *Coke* beverage; and $A_i$ is *Coca-Cola* advertising, the complementary approach taken by Stigler and Becker (1977) suggests that we may write:

$$Z_1 = f(A_1)X_1 \tag{4.4}$$

Here $f(A_1)$ is a continuous function with $f'(A_1) > 0$ and $f''(A_1) < 0$ defined over all non-negative values of $A_1$ and $f(0) \geq 0$. In other words, more *Coca-Cola* advertising increases the pleasure from drinking Coke, but does so at a diminishing rate. If, for simplicity, we assume that only *Coca-Cola* advertises, we then have the following representation of a consumer's utility function:

$$U[Z_1, Z_2, \ldots Z_N] = U[f(A_1)X_1, Z_2, \ldots Z_N] \tag{4.5}$$

A subtly different approach to modeling advertising's complementarity in the consumer's utility function is taken in the later work of Becker and Murphy (1993). In their model, the fundamentals in the utility function are the market goods $X_i$ as in the conventional treatment. However, advertising also enters into the consumer's utility function: $U = U(X_1, X_2, \ldots X_N, A_1)$ for the case in which $X_1$ is the good being advertised.

A simple example with just two goods $X_1$ and $X_2$, where again $X_1$ is the advertised good, is:

$$U(X_1, X_2, A_1) = X_1^\alpha X_2^\beta + min\ (\alpha A_1, X_1) \tag{4.6}$$

Here, $X_1$ and $X_2$ are substitute goods in consumption, but the goods $A_1$ and $X_1$ are complements as indicated by the second term.[9] As the volume of advertising $A_1$ increases, so does the marginal utility of and the willingness to pay for good $X_1$. Likewise, the marginal utility of advertising $A_1$ rises as more of the good $X_1$ is consumed. The central implication of either the Stigler and Becker (1977) or Becker and Murphy (1993) model is that an increase in advertising shifts or rotates the market demand curve outward.

Again though, the fact that advertising enters directly into the utility function implies that any such shift in demand does *not* reflect a change in consumer tastes. We would expect the demand for a product $X_1$, say, automobiles, to change if there was a change in the supply of a complementary product $X_2$, say, gasoline. That is what is happening now except that the "complementary good" is advertising for $X_1$. Because the underlying preferences have not changed, the pre-advertising and post-advertising demand curves can now be used to make direct comparisons of welfare effects in the pre-advertising and post-advertising market outcomes. Each demand curve reflects the same utility function or consumer preferences—the difference is the amount of advertising, which in turn affects demand.[10]

Dixit and Norman (1978) concluded that a monopolist will advertise excessively if the advertising leads to a price increase. Does this still hold when the shift in demand is no longer associated with a different underlying utility function? We investigate this issue in Figure 4.3.

In Figure 4.3, the pre-advertising market demand $D_0$ is described by the linear inverse demand curve: $P = V_0 - \mu Q$, where both the intercept $V_0$ and the slope term $\mu$ are positive. Without loss of generality, we normalize the measure of units so that the slope parameter $\mu = 1$. Hence, the equation for $D_0$ becomes: $P = V_0 - Q$. For simplicity, we also assume a constant marginal cost of $c = 0$. A profit-maximizing monopolist will produce $Q_0^* = \dfrac{V_0}{2}$ and charge $P_0^* = \dfrac{V_0}{2}$. Hence, the pre-advertising profit is: $\pi_0 = \dfrac{V_0^2}{4}$.

Suppose that the post-advertising demand $D_1$ is given by the linear equation: $P = V_1 - \left(\dfrac{V_1}{V_0}\right)Q$, where $V_1 > V_0$. For this example, we have specifically chosen the slope of the new demand curve to be $\left(\dfrac{V_1}{V_0}\right)$ so that, after advertising, the profit-maximizing output is still $\dfrac{V_0}{2}$. However, the profit-maximizing price is now: $P_1^* = \dfrac{V_1}{2}$. In other

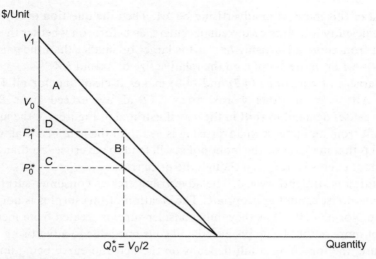

*Note:* Advertising shifts the demand curve out as shown. The monopolist gains area *B+C* as extra profit less the advertising cost. The net welfare gain is area *A+B* less the advertising cost. The latter is greater than the former, implying that the monopolist's advertising level will be *too low* despite the fact that it raises the equilibrium price.

**Figure 4.3** Welfare and monopoly advertising level when advertising is a complement

words, advertising has rotated the demand curve outward in such a way that the firm continues to produce its pre-advertising output level, but now sells this production at a higher price. The firm now earns profit of $\pi_1 = \dfrac{V_1 V_0}{4}$. Dixit and Norman (1978) state that when persuasive advertising raises prices, as advertising clearly does here, the profit gain to the monopolist exceeds the social welfare gain overall. Therefore, they argue that such advertising will be inefficiently excessive. As we will see, however, that is not the case when advertising is a complementary good.

From above, the increase in profit before any advertising cost is:

$$\Delta\pi = \pi_1 - \pi_0 = \frac{V_1 V_0}{4} - \frac{V_0^2}{4} = \frac{V_0(V_1 - V_0)}{4} \tag{4.7}$$

This is equivalent to the sum of areas *B* and *C* in Figure 4.3.

The increase in total welfare, $\Delta W$ again before taking account of any advertising cost is the sum of areas $B + C$ in the figure. This, unlike Dixit and Norman (1978), is equivalent to the entire area beneath demand curve $D_1$, but above demand curve $D_0$ up to the value of $Q_0^* = \dfrac{V_0}{2}$. Hence, we may write:

$$\Delta W = \int_0^{v_0/2} \left[ V_1 - \frac{V_1}{V_0} Q \right] dQ - \int_0^{v_0/2} [V_0 - Q] \, dQ$$

$$= \left( \frac{V_1 V_0}{2} - \frac{V_1 V_0}{8} \right) - \left( \frac{V_0^2}{2} - \frac{V_0^2}{8} \right) = \frac{3V_0(V_1 - V_0)}{8} \tag{4.8}$$

Let the cost of this increase in advertising be $\Delta A$. Then the question of whether advertising is inefficiently too large or too small centers, as before, on whether the gain to the monopolist from more advertising $\Delta\pi - \Delta A$ is larger or smaller than the gain to society overall $\Delta W - \Delta A$ or, more simply, on the relative size of $\Delta\pi$ and $\Delta W$.

A comparison of equations (4.7) and (4.8) makes it clear that for all $V_1 > V_0$, we must have $\Delta W > \Delta\pi$. In other words, areas $A+B$ always exceed areas $B+C$. When advertising causes demand to shift in the way illustrated in Figure 4.3, the monopolist's gain in profit from an increase in advertising is *less* than the gain in social welfare. The implication is that in this case, the monopolist will tend to advertise *less* than the socially optimal amount. This is true even though the price rises.

The intuition is straightforward. The advertising creates consumer surplus (area A) that the monopolist cannot appropriate. The creation of this surplus is not considered in Dixit and Norman (1978) as they only consider surplus created from increased consumption or more output being produced and consumed due to advertising.

To be sure, the foregoing result depends on the demand curve being linear and on advertising shifting demand in the way described.[11] It is, however, a useful case to consider because there is no expansion in output and *only* a rise in price. In that sense, it is one in which we might expect the Dixit and Norman (1978) result that a firm with monopoly power will inefficiently advertise *too much* to continue to hold. The fact that the opposite conclusion obtains—that the monopolist likely advertises inefficiently *too little*—makes it clear that once we treat advertising as a complement to the advertised product, the Dixit and Norman (1978) assertion no longer holds.

Of course, advertising, even when complementary, may be excessive for other reasons. Firms with market power may spend excessively on advertising either due to their imperfect competition with existing rivals, or to make it difficult for new rivals to enter their market and compete. Indeed, early but still influential work by Bain (1956) identified incumbent firm advertising to be the most important barrier to entry in a large range of US manufacturing industries. We explore this role of advertising further in Chapter 7.

However, complementary advertising strategies do not depend on firms having market power to be profitably adopted. Even perfectly competitive firms may advertise in this case. If that happens, then the firm's demand for the advertised product could be perfectly elastic. However, perfectly competitive firms, such as those found in the retail sector, may find it optimal to provide services to customers that enhance their consumption experience of the good.

## 4.4 PERSUASIVE VERSUS COMPLEMENTARY ADVERTISING AND ADVERTISING PRACTICE

Real-world practitioners in the advertising business depend on the success of their campaigns for their livelihood. They have an even stronger incentive than economists to determine how advertising works. It is reassuring that our taxonomy of how advertising works—through information, persuasion, or complementarity—matches reasonably well with the logic that real-world practitioners adopt in designing actual promotional campaigns.

Advertising campaigns, especially for new product releases, often do provide consumers with valuable learning experiences. We see this in ads for new drug treatments for, say, insomnia or arthritis. In contrast, some campaigns, particularly those for luxury goods, seem designed to persuade consumers that they do have a desire for a new piece of jewelry or a cruise vacation, perhaps a desire that they had not previously recognized. At the same time, a great deal of advertising in recent decades seems to fit the complementary view.

Consider, for example, AirBnB's Open Homes initiatives. This allows users to donate free housing to refugees or victim of natural disasters. State Farm's Neighborhood of Good similarly connects people with volunteering opportunities. These digital experiences clearly promote the AirBnB and State Farm brands. Yet they also facilitate real-world interactions that consumers value, enhancing their experience with these firms when they purchase holiday rentals or insurance. Somewhat similarly, consumers may feel better about using Dove products after watching a Dove Beauty Sketch commercial.

For practitioners of advertising, the view that advertising can affect demand via its complementarity with the advertised product rather than by persuading consumers to change their preferences suggests an important shift in the creative starting point of a promotional campaign. Rather than beginning with the question of how advertising can *affect* consumer preferences, the question now is how advertising can *respond* to consumer preferences.

Understanding this change in focus could be particularly important in the digital age. Digital technology allows advertising to be more easily tailored and targeted to specific individuals. In addition, digital advertising that is appreciated or enjoyed by a digital viewer can be quickly shared with that viewer's social network. This is the logic underlying the now-popular practitioner's view that advertising should "focus on making an impression not buying one."[12] The Dove Beauty Sketches for example were clearly designed to give consumers not only a more positive experience when using *Dove* shampoo or skin-care products, but also a reason to talk about the advertisements and advocate for their implicit messages with others after the ad has been viewed.

## 4.5 SUMMARY

We have focused in this chapter and the previous one on how advertising affects consumer behavior and market demand. In Chapter 3, we considered how advertising can affect behavior by providing consumers with information about prices and products explicitly or implicitly as a signal of things the consumer cannot observe pre-purchase. In this chapter, we discussed the persuasive dimension of advertising and considered how persuasion could change a consumer's preferences for a good and what this means for understanding the efficiency of advertising. An alternative way advertising could work is as a complement to the good being advertised. In this view, an ad enhances the consumer's pleasure from consuming the good.

Which of these two, non-information mechanisms, if either, is the dominant one is important for any complete evaluation of the efficiency or welfare effects of advertising. Even in the simple case of monopoly there is good reason to believe that persuasive advertising is likely to be excessive from the viewpoint of social inefficiency. There is much less reason to believe this is what happens if instead advertising is viewed as a complement to the advertised product.

There are some clear difficulties with the persuasive approach where advertising is a way to change consumer tastes. When this is the way that advertising works, it becomes difficult to compare pre- and post-advertising outcomes for the same reason that it is difficult to compare someone who likes warm weather holidays on a beach with someone who likes her holidays in a city going to museums. If advertising changes tastes, then comparing consumers pre- and post-advertising is equivalently comparing two different people or groups of people.

Moreover, if the view that persuasive advertising works by manipulating or tricking consumers into making a mistaken purchase is correct, a number of difficult questions quickly follow. Do the consumers who were manipulated into mistakenly choosing Brand X ever learn that Brand X is not their best option? If they do, then the manipulation has just a short-run distortionary impact at worst. If they do not learn though, then it seems likely that their preferences really have changed in a fundamental way such that the later purchases of Brand X cannot be classified as mistakes. Moreover, if consumers understand that advertising is trying to manipulate them to make unwarranted purchases, should they not be able to take preventive action to thwart that effort? Alternatively, if consumers cannot take any such preventive action, is there not a clear market opportunity for some firm to help consumers learn and avoid market mistakes?

Advertising that affects consumer demand because it is a complement to the advertised product is different from persuasive advertising. Complements are goods that enter directly into the utility function. Changes in advertising therefore imply changes in the level of the various goods in the utility functions and not changes in the function itself. So, comparison of pre- and post-advertising market outcomes is now possible. Such a complementary view of advertising is perhaps a better fit for understanding recent trends in advertising that respond to consumer preferences with a view to building brand identity and value.

Whether the ad is designed to persuade, to inform, or to complement likely depends on context—the kind of good: new or old; experience or search: the kind of consumer, young or old, urban or rural—and also the nature of competition in the marketplace. In turn, advertising will likely be part of any firm's competitive strategy, and could influence a market's structure, say, by acting as an entry barrier that blocks new firms. We explore the links between advertising and competitive strategy and outcomes in subsequent chapters.

1 Teixera (2014) analyzes a random sample of 60 TV ads from the 1950s to the 2000s and finds that the percentage of time in the ad that was dedicated to pure entertainment was about 13 percent in the 1950s–1970s. However, by 2000 the percentage had increased to 38 percent. The Chicago School view that this "non-informative" content of advertising could be a way to signal product quality stretches our credulity, particularly when it comes to ads for products that are pretty well-known by consumers, such as Coca-Cola, Tide, Cheerios or Listerine.

2 You can view the "hilltop" Coke ad at https://www.youtube.com/watch?v=1VM2eLhvsSM.

3 In the informative case, one may argue that consumer preferences are given at a more primal level and that advertising simply helps consumers satisfy those preferences more efficiently, e.g., at lower cost.

4 The ancient Roman expression, "de gustibus non est disputandum," roughly, "there's no arguing about taste," captures this idea.

5 Dixit and Norman (1978) only consider surplus created on the additional units of output $q_0$ to $q_1$ that are consumed.

6 See Shapiro (1980) for a short but effective statement of this argument.

7 Elegant as it is, the Dixit and Norman (1978) model does not truly address this fundamental issue as Fisher and McGowan (1979) noted in an early comment.

8 McClure et al. (2004).

9 In equation (4.6) the goods $A_1$ and $X_1$ are strict complements.

10 In the models discussed in this chapter, the firm selects the amount of advertising that each consumer receives and "sells" or rations this amount at a zero price, i.e., the cost of advertising is covered by revenue from sales of the advertised product. In principle, a general utility function representation of the Becker and Murphy (1993) model permits advertising to be a "good" (or a "bad") for which there is a market. Note too that just as perfectly competitive firms may be induced to supply complementary service with their products, so too might they be induced to supply complementary advertising. See Nichols (1985).

11 Advertising that leads to the demand rotation in Figure 4.3 could be characterized as "building value" because it raises the willingness to pay for those consumers who were already buying the product. In contrast, advertising that leads to the rotation shown in Figures 4.1(a) and 4.2(a) could be described as "extending the reach" of a brand as it now has the greatest impact on the willingness to pay of consumers who were not previously buying the good.

12 Aziz (2018).

# 4.6 REFERENCES

Anderson, S., and R. Renault. 2006. "Advertising Content." *American Economic Review* 96 (March), 93–113.

Aziz, Afdhel. 2018. "Building a Better Brand." *Ad Age* (February 5), 12–18.

Bain, J. 1956. *Barriers to New Competition*. Cambridge, MA: Harvard University Press.

Becker, G., and K. Murphy. 1993. "A Simple Theory of Advertising as a Good or Bad." *The Quarterly Journal of Economics* 108 (November), 941–64.

Braithwaite, D. 1928. "The Economic Effects of Advertisement." *Economic Journal* 38 (March), 16–37.

Dixit, A., and V. Norman. 1978. "Advertising and Welfare." *The Bell Journal of Economics* 9 (Spring), 1–17.

Dixit, A., and V. Norman. 1978. "Advertising and Welfare: Reply." *The Bell Journal of Economics* 10 (Autumn), 728–29.

Dixit, A., and V. Norman. 1980. "Advertising and Welfare: Another Reply." *The Bell Journal of Economics* 11 (Autumn), 753–54.

Ellison, G., and S. F. Ellison. 2009. "Search, Obfuscation, and Price Elasticities on the Internet." *Econometrica* 77 (March), 427–52.

Fisher, F. M., and J. J. McGowan. 1979. "Advertising and Welfare: Comment." *The Bell Journal of Economics* 10 (Autumn), 726–27.

Galbraith, J. K. 1958. *The Affluent Society*, Boston, MA: Houghton-Mifflin Company.

Kaldor, N. V. 1950. "The Economic Aspects of Advertising." *The Review of Economic Studies* 18 (January), 1–27.

McClure, J. L., D. Tomlin, K. S. Cypert, L. Montague, and P. Montague. 2004. "Neural Correlates of Behavioral Preference for Culturally Familiar Drinks." *Neuron* 44 (October 14), 379–87.

Nichols, L. 1985. "Advertising and Economic Welfare." *American Economic Review*, 75 (March), 213–18.

Packard, V. 1957. *The Hidden Persuaders*. New York: D. McKay Company.

Shapiro, C. 1980. "Advertising and Welfare: Comment." *The Bell Journal of Economics* 11 (Autumn), 749–52.

Stigler, G., and G. Becker. 1977. "De Gustibus Non Est Disputandum." *American Economic Review*, 67 (March), 76–90.

Teixeira, T. 2014. "The Rising Cost of Consumer Attention: Why You Should Care, and What You Can Do About It." Harvard Business School Working Paper.

# 5
# Advertising and Competition

## 5.1 INTRODUCTION

Many of the goods that we buy on a daily, or weekly, or monthly basis are convenience goods. These goods are relatively inexpensive and consumed frequently. Stores are well stocked with such goods. Toothpaste, detergent, yogurt, cereal, frozen pizza, cookies, and bottled beverages are just a small sample of the convenience goods that end up in millions of consumers' shopping baskets each day. Indeed, there are usually many different brands of convenience goods to choose from. How do consumers choose which brand to buy? How do they know which brand matches their preferences or which brand gives a consumer the best value? Expending a lot of effort searching for information about which brand to buy would be very costly if consumers had to do all the searching themselves. Instead, consumers may find advertising to be a helpful guide to their buying decisions.

Many convenience goods, such as *Tide*, *Crest*, *Cheerios*, and *Yoplait*, are in fact known by their advertised brand names. Their advertisements are often memorable for their creativity and catchiness. Think of *Tide*'s 2018 Super Bowl ad.[1] Running a branded advertising campaign on national television is costly. TV commercials can cost anywhere from $50,000 to $750,000 to write, shoot, and produce.[2] Moreover, production costs are not the only expense. There is also the cost of airtime. *AdWeek*, a marketing and media publication, reports that in 2018 the television network CBS charged rates for a 30-second commercial spot ranging from $29,000 to $110,000 on average, while FOX charged between $61,000 and $688,000. The rates vary by the programming offered, with live sports shows typically getting the highest advertising rates.[3]

No matter how often an ad is aired there will always be some consumers whom the ad did not reach. The increasing cost of reaching consumers is a clear constraint on a firm's advertising effort. But how is this effort affected when, as in the case of convenience goods, there are multiple brands and competition for consumers? More generally, how does the incentive to advertise and inform consumers change when there is competition in the market? The more consumers that know about the availability of rival products, the greater is the potential for consumers to compare prices and switch from one brand to another.

In this chapter we explore how competition affects firms' incentives to advertise to inform consumers about their brands. To model competition among different brands, we adopt a spatial approach to product differentiation that is based on Hotelling (1929). This approach is similar in spirit, but formally different from Chamberlin's model of monopolistic competition, which we introduced in Chapter 1. Both approaches have in common the insight that consumers do prefer variety. Consumers like different kinds of cereals, different kinds of ice creams and beverages. Competitive firms in these markets respond by differentiating their products or brands.

The key difference between these two variants of monopolistic competition is that the spatial model uses a kind of geographic analogy to model product differentiation. Different brands are located on a "product differentiated" map, so that more similar brands are "closer" together, and dissimilar ones "far apart." Consumers will prefer those brands that match their preferences more "closely." Hence, competition in a spatial model has a more localized effect.

Before beginning, it is helpful to note that for many goods it is the manufacturer who arranges the national or global market advertising regarding what is special about its product for which it has developed a brand name. For example, Procter & Gamble promotes the *Tide* detergent brand on national media platforms. Typically, in those kinds of ads there is no mention of price. This is largely because the manufacturer sells their brand of the convenience good at a wholesale price to a retailer, e.g., supermarket, who sets the retail price of the brand to consumers. The retailer may then advertise the price of its brands in local media outlets, often with assistance from the manufacturer to ensure adequate promotion of the brand at the retail level in a manner consistent with the national brand image. For simplicity, we treat the manufacturer and retailer as the same "firm" in this chapter and consider advertising that is done by the "firm" to include information on price as well as on the brand's attributes.

## 5.2 A SPATIAL MODEL OF PRODUCT DIFFERENTIATION

In this section, we explore how a firm's advertising is affected by the cost of advertising and by competition among different brands in a spatial model of competition.[4] Take the market for ice cream where some consumers like vanilla ice cream, some like chocolate, some prefer strawberry, and some like full fat ice cream, while others prefer low fat. For the moment, assume that each firm markets its own flavor or fat content brand of ice cream. As a result, each firm's ice cream product will be a "close" or "distant" match to what some consumers most prefer. Chocolate chip ice cream is likely viewed as closer to vanilla or to chocolate ice cream than it is to strawberry. Ninety percent full fat ice cream is closer to the 100 percent full fat brand than it is to a low-fat brand and so on. Those who most prefer vanilla will likely choose chocolate chip ice cream over the strawberry brand if both are offered at the same price. Those who really want full fat ice cream will choose the 90 percent full fat brand over the

---

0           *X*                                            1

*Note:* Consumers are distributed uniformly along the linear market with one firm located at each end. In addition to paying the product price, a consumer located at $X$ incurs a transport or disutility cost of $tX$ if she buys from the firm located at 0 and a transport or disutility cost of $t(1 - X)$ if she buys from the firm located at 1.

**Figure 5.1 The linear market**

low-fat rival if those are the only two choices and, again, assuming they are priced the same.[5]

More precisely, we model consumer preferences for this kind of product differentiation by imagining that consumers can be located at different points along a line of unit length, where the geographic location refers to the consumer's taste or preference for a variety of good. Specifically, where a consumer is located on the line, some point $x$ between 0 and 1, describes the consumer's *most* preferred variety of the good. We then suppose that each consumer has the *same* maximum willingness to pay $V$ for the consumer's most preferred variety. Each consumer is also assumed to buy at most one unit of a variety of the good per period.

There are two firms, firm 1 and firm 2, in the market, each producing a variety of the good at end points on the unit line. Good 1 is located at point 0, and good 2 is located at point 1. Figure 5.1 illustrates this setting. For a consumer to buy either one of these goods the consumer incurs a cost that measures the disutility incurred by the consumer when the consumer is not able to consume the most preferred product. This disutility cost will depend on how far either good 1 or good 2 is from the consumer's most preferred good.

Specifically, we assume that consumers incur a "travel" or disutility cost $\tau$ per unit of distance so that a consumer located at point $x$ on the line incurs a disutility cost of $\tau x$ when consuming good 1 and a disutility cost of $\tau(1 - x)$ when consuming good 2. In other words, a consumer will not generally regard the two goods as perfect substitutes.

As in our ice cream examples above, even when the firms charge the same price so that $p_1 = p_2$, consumers who are located closer to firm 1 will prefer its brand and those closer to firm 2 will prefer the variety of good that it offers. Moreover, if firm 1 were to raise its price a bit the firm would not lose all its customers as it would have when all consumers view the two brands as perfect substitutes (i.e., when $\tau = 0$). Apart from their location, the two firms are identical with each incurring a fixed cost $F$ and a constant marginal cost of $c$.[6]

Each consumer $x$ buys at most one unit of the product either from firm 1 or firm 2. For any consumer $x$, the surplus obtained from a purchase is:

$$U_x = V - \tau x - p_1 \geq 0 \qquad \text{if the consumer } x \text{ buys brand 1, and}$$
$$U_x = V - \tau(1 - x) - p_2 \geq 0 \qquad \text{if the consumer } x \text{ buys brand 2} \qquad (5.1)$$
$$U_x = 0 \qquad \text{if the consumer } x \text{ does not buy}$$

Suppose that the value $V$ common to all consumers is sufficiently high that for any plausible set of prices $p_1$ and $p_2$ each consumer will buy from one of the two firms. In that case, we can identify a marginal consumer whose location $x^M$ is such that the consumer is indifferent between purchasing either of the two products. That is:

$$V - p_1 - \tau x^M = V - p_2 - \tau(1 - x^M) \tag{5.2}$$

Solving for $x^M$ in equation (5.2) we find that the location of this consumer depends on the prices set by the two firms. Specifically:

$$x^M(p_1, p_2) = \frac{1}{2} + \frac{p_2 - p_1}{2\tau} \tag{5.3}$$

All consumers located to the left of $x^M(p_1, p_2)$, i.e., all consumers for whom $x$ satisfies $0 \le x < x^M(p_1, p_2)$, will buy from firm 1. Likewise, all consumers with location preference $x$ satisfying $x^M(p_1, p_2) < x \le 1$ will buy from firm 2. At $x^M(p_1, p_2)$ the consumer is indifferent and so they will randomly choose between either good.

Let the density of consumers who live along the line be given at $H$. We can then write the demand for each firm as a function of its price and its rival's price as follows:[7]

$$q_1(p_1, p_2) = H x^M(p_1, p_2) = H\left(\frac{1}{2} + \frac{p_2 - p_1}{2\tau}\right)$$
$$q_2(p_1, p_2) = H[1 - x^M(p_1, p_2)] = H\left(\frac{1}{2} + \frac{p_1 - p_2}{2\tau}\right) \tag{5.4}$$

It follows that profit for each firm can be written as a function of the prices set by each firm:

$$\pi_1(p_1, p_2) = (p_1 - c)H\left(\frac{1}{2} + \frac{p_2 - p_1}{2\tau}\right) - F$$
$$\pi_2(p_1, p_2) = (p_2 - c)H\left(\frac{1}{2} + \frac{p_1 - p_2}{2\tau}\right) - F \tag{5.5}$$

Firm 1 and firm 2 both understand that their profits depend on what price they set and what price their rival sets. Firm 1 wants to choose a price $p_1$ that maximizes its profit given its best guess of the price firm 2 is going to set. Similarly, firm 2 wants to choose a price, $p_2$, that maximizes its profit given its best guess of the price firm 1 is going to set.

Let's examine how firm 1 chooses its profit-maximizing price $p_1^*$. The firm wants to find $p_1^*$ that solves the first-order necessary condition that $\dfrac{\partial \pi_1(p_1^*, p_2)}{\partial p_1} = 0$; that is, $p_1^*$ solves $\dfrac{(p_2 - p_1^* + t)}{2t} - \dfrac{1}{2t}(p_1^* - c) = 0$. Rearranging this implies that:

$$p_1^* = \frac{c + \tau + p_2}{2} \tag{5.6}$$

To set its optimal price $p_1^*$, firm 1 must make a guess of what price firm 2 will set. Firm 1 knows that firm 2 will want to choose a price $p_2^*$ that maximizes its profit, and so it reasons that firm 2 will solve $\frac{\partial \pi_2(, p_1, p_2^*)}{\partial p_2} = 0$, which implies $p_2^* = \frac{p_1 + c + \tau}{2}$. Knowing that this is how firm 2 will respond to any price it sets, firm 1 sets its price by substituting this pricing rule for firm 2 into equation (5.6). That is, firm 1 solves $p_1^* = \dfrac{\frac{p_1^* + c + \tau}{2} + c + \tau}{2}$.

Solving then for $p_1^*$ yields: $p_1^* = c + \tau$.

Because the two firms have identical costs and their demand functions are symmetric or mirror opposites, they will behave identically. In other words, firm 2 solves the same problem firm 1 solves, implying that $p_2^* = c + \tau$. In other words, the symmetry of the firms implies that in any equilibrium outcome, $p_1^* = p_2^*$. Hence, equation (5.6) implies that the equilibrium prices are:

$$p_1^* = p_2^* = c + \tau \tag{5.7}$$

In turn, this implies that the marginal consumer is located at the midpoint or that $x^M = \frac{1}{2}$, so that the two firms share the market equally, each serving $\frac{H}{2}$ customers. Profit for each firm is therefore:

$$\pi_1 = \frac{\tau H}{2} - F = \pi_2 \tag{5.8}$$

Total consumer surplus is the difference between each consumer's maximum reservation price $V$ and the equilibrium price $c+\tau$, times the mass of consumers $H$, less the sum of consumer transport or disutility costs. Hence, total consumer surplus in the market is:

$$CS = H(V - c - \tau) - 2H \int_0^{1/2} \tau x \, dx = H\left[V - (c + \tau) - \frac{\tau}{4}\right] \tag{5.9}$$

Total producer surplus is $PS = \tau H - 2F$. Hence, overall welfare or the total surplus $TS$ is:

$$TS = CS + PS = H\left(V - c - \frac{\tau}{4}\right) - 2F \tag{5.10}$$

This spatial duopoly will serve as our baseline model. It is worth noting some of its key features. Consumers' taste for variety, as reflected in the disutility cost parameter $\tau$, permits the firms to charge prices above marginal cost even though price competition is very real in the market. Indeed, the extent of the markup over cost is directly related to the parameter $\tau$, which measures the strength of attachment to the consumer's most preferred variety. It may also be thought of as a measure of brand loyalty—consumers are willing to pay more for the "nearest" brand as $\tau$ rises.

Finally, we note it is relatively straightforward to extend the duopoly model to include more firms. However, to keep the market conditions symmetric so that each firm has a competitor on either side of its location we "bend" the line around into a circle. In that case, as we show in the appendix to this chapter, one can solve for the equilibrium number of firms in a manner consistent with Chamberlin's (1933) zero-profit condition for monopolistic competition.[8] We show there that the long-run market equilibrium will inefficiently have too many firms, which is consistent with Chamberlin's (1933) conjecture about monopolistic competition.

# 5.3 INFORMATIVE ADVERTISING, COMPETITION, AND WELFARE

When the marketplace offers more than one variety, consumers will match their preferences to the option that best suits them. This matching depends, of course, on consumers knowing the range of varieties that are available for purchase. In our baseline model, we implicitly assumed that consumers living along the line knew of the availability and the prices of the two varieties. If, however, consumers are not perfectly informed, then the two firms would have the incentive to "get the word out" to potential consumers. Advertising, particularly in convenience goods markets, is a great way to do this. We will assume here that consumers are uninformed about a firm's product unless they receive and pay attention to an advertising message sent by the firm. Both firms must now think about advertising strategies as well as pricing decisions when competing in this market.

The "attention" qualifier is important. When a firm airs a commercial, it is quite likely that some consumers either will not receive it or, if they do, will not pay attention to it. In other words, it is likely that there will always be some uninformed consumers in the market. These are consumers who are just not aware of a firm's brand of the product. More formally, let there be a proportion $\theta_1$ of the $H$ consumers who have been informed of firm 1's product. Likewise, let there be a proportion $\theta_2$ of the $H$ consumers who are informed of firm 2's product. For $i = 1, 2$, each firm $i$ chooses both the price $p_i$ and the $\theta_i$ the proportion of consumers to inform.

It is reasonable to assume that it becomes increasingly costly for a firm to inform a greater proportion of consumers. Specifically, we assume that the relationship between a firm's total advertising cost, or expenditure, and the proportion of consumers informed is given by $A_i(\theta_i) = \alpha \frac{\theta_i^2}{2} H, i = 1, 2$. In this case, the marginal cost of increasing the proportion of informed consumers about the firm's brand is: $\frac{dA_i}{d\theta_i} = \alpha \theta_i H$. The coefficient or parameter $\alpha$ is a key measure of how quickly advertising costs increase. When consumers in a market are distracted and nonattentive to advertising, then $\alpha$ could be relatively high compared to when consumers listen or seek out informative advertising. Compare, for example, how attentive consumers are to the advertising about cheap flights compared with how attentive they are to ones for cleaning detergents.

For any values of $\theta_1$ and $\theta_2$ that the firms choose, the market will be characterized by four distinct groups of consumers. There will be a proportion $\theta_1\theta_2$ that knows about both firm 1's and firm 2's brands of products. There will also be both a proportion $\theta_1(1 - \theta_2)$ of consumers that will know only of firm 1's brand, and an equally large proportion $\theta_2(1 - \theta_1)$ that will know only of firm 2's brand. Finally, there will be a proportion of consumers in the market who are completely uninformed, $(1 - \theta_1)(1 - \theta_2)$; they will not know about either firm's product.

The different groups of consumers informed by firms' advertising are also distributed uniformly along a line of unit length. That is, there is no targeting of advertising to specific consumers. For example, if $\theta_1 = \theta_2 = \frac{1}{2}$, then there are $\frac{H}{4}$ consumers who know only about firm 1's product and these consumers will be distributed uniformly along the line from 0 to 1. Likewise, there will be $\frac{H}{4}$ consumers who know only about firm 2's products and they are also uniformly distributed along the line; a group of $\frac{H}{4}$ consumers, uniformly distributed, will know about both products, and finally a group $\frac{H}{4}$ of consumers, again uniformly distributed, who remain uninformed about either product. When $\theta_1 = \theta_2 = 1$, all $H$ consumers in the market are fully aware of the availability of both products as in our baseline model.

Firm 1's potential consumers include the fraction of customers $\theta_1(1 - \theta_2)H$ who have received only the advertising of firm 1 and the fraction who have heard the commercials of both firms, $\theta_1\theta_2H$. Symmetrically, firm 2's potential market includes the $\theta_2(1 - \theta_1)H$ consumers who have heard only its advertising message and the $\theta_1\theta_2H$ consumers that have heard or received both messages. Each consumer has the same maximum reservation price $V$ and we will assume that prices are such that a fully informed consumer will buy either brand. Because firms cannot tell what information about brands a consumer has when the consumer buys its product, each firm must charge the same price to all consumers that buy its product.

The subgroup $\theta_1(1 - \theta_2)H$ of consumers who know only about brand 1 are firm 1's captive market. Firm 1 is competing with firm 2 only for the $\theta_1\theta_2H$ or perfectly informed consumers. Any price at which a consumer in the perfectly informed group would buy firm 1's brand is such that all consumers in the captive group $\theta_1(1 - \theta_2)H$ will also buy the brand. Similarly, for firm 2, any price at which a consumer in the perfectly informed group would buy firm 2's brand is such that all consumers in its captive group $\theta_2(1 - \theta_1)H$ will also buy the brand.

It is competition for those $\theta_1\theta_2H$ informed consumers that determines the prices set by the two firms. That is, in the subgroup of $\theta_1\theta_2H$ informed consumers, uniformly distributed along the line, there is, for prices $p_1$ and $p_2$, again a marginal consumer $x^M$ for whom $V - p_1 - \tau x^M = V - p_2 - \tau(1 - x^M)$ as in equation (5.2). Therefore, the marginal consumer again satisfies: $x^M(p_1, p_2) = \frac{(p_2 - p_1 + \tau)}{2\tau}$.

We can now write the demand function facing firm 1, which will depend upon the advertising strategies $(\theta_1, \theta_2)$ and prices $(p_1, p_2)$ of both firms. There will be two components to firm 1's customers, its captive market and its share of the informed market, i.e., those informed consumers whose location lies in the interval $[0, x^M(p_1, p_2)]$.

$$q_1(\theta_1, \theta_2, p_1, p_2) = \left[\theta_1(1 - \theta_2) + \theta_1\theta_2\left(\frac{(p_2 - p_1 + \tau)}{2\tau}\right)\right]H \qquad (5.11)$$

Symmetrically, firm 2's demand is:

$$q_2(\theta_1, \theta_2, p_1, p_2) = \left[\theta_2(1-\theta_1) + \theta_1\theta_2\left(\frac{(p_1 - p_2 + \tau)}{2\tau}\right)\right]H \qquad (5.12)$$

Accordingly, the profits earned by firm 1, $\Pi_1$, and those earned by firm 2, $\Pi_2$, are:

$$\pi_1(\theta_1, \theta_2, p_1, p_2) = (p_1 - c)\left[\theta_1(1-\theta_2) + \theta_1\theta_2\left(\frac{(p_2 - p_1 + \tau)}{2\tau}\right)\right]H - \frac{\alpha\theta_1^2 H}{2} - F \quad (5.13)$$

and

$$\pi_2(\theta_1, \theta_2, p_1, p_2) = (p_2 - c)\left[\theta_2(1-\theta_1) + \theta_1\theta_2\left(\frac{(p_1 - p_2 + \tau)}{2\tau}\right)\right]H - \frac{\alpha\theta_2^2 H}{2} - F \quad (5.14)$$

Each firm must choose the price to set $p_i$ and the amount of advertising effort $\theta_i$. Consider these decisions from the viewpoint of firm 1. It has the following two, first-order necessary profit-maximizing conditions:

$$\frac{\partial \pi_1(p_1^*, p_2, \theta_1, \theta_2)}{\partial p_1} = \theta_1(1-\theta_2) + \theta_1\theta_2\left(\frac{(p_2 - p_1^* + \tau)}{2\tau}\right) - (p_1^* - c)\frac{\theta_1\theta_2}{2\tau} = 0 \qquad (5.15)$$

$$\frac{\partial \pi_1(p_1, p_2, \theta_1^*, \theta_2)}{\partial \theta_1} = (p_1 - c)\left[(1-\theta_2) + \theta_2\left(\frac{(p_1 - p_2 + \tau)}{2\tau}\right)\right] - \alpha\theta_1^* = 0 \qquad (5.16)$$

Solving (5.15) and (5.16) for the optimal values of $p_1^*$ and $\theta_1^*$ we obtain:

$$p_1^* = \frac{(1-\theta_2)}{\theta_2}\tau + \frac{p_2 + c + \tau}{2} \qquad (5.17)$$

$$\theta_1^* = \frac{(p_1^* - c)}{\alpha}\left[1 - \theta_2 + \theta_2\left(\frac{p_2 - p_1^* + \tau}{2\tau}\right)\right] \qquad (5.18)$$

At this point, we see that the two firms are like identical twins and will in equilibrium set the same price, $p_1^* = p_2^* = p^*$, and adopt the same advertising strategy $\theta_1^* = \theta_2^* = \theta^*$. With this insight, we can solve equation (5.17) to find that:

$$p_1^* = p_2^* = p^* = c + \frac{(2-\theta^*)}{\theta^*}\tau \qquad (5.19)$$

The result in (5.19) may then be substituted into (5.18) to yield:

$$\theta_1^* = \theta_2^* = \theta^* = \frac{(2-\theta^*)\tau}{\alpha\theta^*}\frac{(2-\theta^*)^2}{2} \rightarrow \frac{2\alpha\theta^{*2}}{\tau} = (2-\theta^*)^2 \qquad (5.20)$$

Solving for $\theta^*$ then yields:

$$\theta^* = \frac{2}{1 + \sqrt{2\alpha/\tau}} \qquad (5.21)$$

The substitution of (5.21) back into (5.19) then implies:

$$p^* = c + \sqrt{2\alpha\tau}$$

(5.22)

Together, equations (5.21) and (5.22) describe the equilibrium price and advertising strategies for a spatial duopoly model of informative advertising. These outcomes generate several insights. Before turning to these, however, we must check one condition. Because we assumed that some consumers in the market remain uninformed, it is important to check that in equilibrium $\theta^* < 1$. If this condition does not hold and all consumers are perfectly informed, then the equilibrium is the one corresponding to the full-information case that was our baseline model.

For $\theta^* < 1$ to hold, equation (5.21) makes clear that the advertising cost parameter must be such that $\alpha > \tau/2$. The parameter $\alpha$ measures how steep the marginal cost is of increasing the fraction of informed consumers. To ensure that some consumers remain uninformed, we must assume that $\alpha$ is sufficiently large relative to consumers' preference for variety, as measured by the parameter $\tau$.

The first insight follows directly from the necessary condition that $\alpha > \tau/2$. As (5.22) makes clear, the equilibrium prices set when at least some consumers are not fully informed about brands are greater than $c + \tau$, the prices that firms set in the baseline model when consumers *are* perfectly informed. In part, the higher price is necessary to fund the cost of advertising that firms must incur to inform consumers about the market. Otherwise consumers do not participate in this market. However, the higher price set by each firm also partly reflects the fact that each firm has a captive market. That is, those customers who know only about the firm's brand and not about the rival brand. The captive market dampens the incentive to compete in price for fully informed consumers.

Another insight is that an increase in the degree of specialization or preference for variety in consumer tastes—an increase in $\tau$—causes both price and advertising to increase. Prices are higher and advertising expenses are larger when differences in product brands matter more to consumers. It is important to understand though that advertising does not play a causal role in these results. Advertising is not the reason why consumers have specialized tastes. Instead, it is the fact that consumers have specialized tastes to begin with that both encourages firms to advertise their product differences extensively and to enjoy some market power by selling at price above unit cost.

We return to this point in subsequent chapters where we examine the empirical evidence on the impact of advertising on brand competition. At this point, it is helpful to recognize that this result means that we should expect real-world data to show a positive relation between higher prices and higher advertising expenses, as well as between higher advertising and stronger consumer preferences for brands of products—less consumer switching across brands.

The final insight comes from exploring the relationship between firm profitability and the cost of advertising. Let's return to the equation for a firm's profit and substitute the optimal price $p^* = c + \sqrt{2\alpha\tau}$ and advertising strategy $\theta^* = \dfrac{2}{1 + \sqrt{\dfrac{2\alpha}{\tau}}}$ into the profit

equations (5.13) and (5.14), which yields the following expression for the profit of each firm:

$$\pi_1 = \pi_2 = \frac{2\alpha}{(1 + \sqrt{2\alpha/\tau})} H - F \qquad (5.23)$$

Inspection of equation (5.23) reveals that each firm's profit is increasing in the parameter $\alpha$, which is a measure of the marginal cost of advertising.

How is it that making it more expensive for firms to inform consumers about their brands results in increased firm profitability? The answer is that informative advertising is generally pro-competitive.[9] As $\alpha$ falls, firms do more advertising. This has two effects. One is to raise the number of consumers that know of at least one product. The other is to increase the number of consumers who know of both goods. With *both* firms increasing their advertising efforts, this latter group of fully informed consumers will grow proportionately larger. Hence, following a fall in $\alpha$, each firm will serve a customer base that now has proportionately more fully informed consumers who can compare prices across firms. Price competition intensifies, and both price-cost margins and profits fall. On the other hand, exactly the opposite happens when $\alpha$ rises and advertising becomes more costly.

From a welfare perspective, clearly this kind of informative advertising is desirable relative to no advertising because, by assumption, consumers are not informed without advertising. But whether the level of advertising that is chosen by the two firms is socially optimal is less clear. When firm 1 increases its advertising effort, consumers enjoy two positive effects. First, more consumers will now be at least partially informed, and the market will expand. Second, more consumers will be fully informed, and this will permit more consumers to buy from the firm whose product offers better value to them. Both effects raise the total consumer surplus. However, firm 1 is interested only in what happens to profit and not to consumer surplus, so neither effect will be fully incorporated into firm 1's advertising decision. This suggests that total advertising will be too low from a social welfare perspective.

However, there is another effect. This is that additional advertising by a firm intensifies price competition and, therefore, lowers both firms' profits. Yet again, each firm cares only about its own profits, so they ignore the negative impact on its rival. Hence, this third effect suggests that a firm, ignoring this negative externality, will advertise too much relative to the social optimum.

For the duopoly case, it is possible to show that the effects on consumer surplus dominate, and in equilibrium, firms advertise too little relative to the social optimum. However, as we consider a market with more firms, the advertising by any one firm has an increasingly small effect on the number of informed consumers. As a result, some of the positive effects on consumer surplus are less important and the welfare conclusion becomes less clear.[10]

# 5.4 PERSUASIVE ADVERTISING, COMPETITION, AND WELFARE

As discussed extensively in Chapter 4, there is a long and popular tradition—also backed by real-world experiences—that advertising does more than simply inform but acts as well to affect consumers' preferences. We now consider such persuasive advertising in the context of a duopoly along the Hotelling line.[11] Recall that in the baseline model, the consumer surplus that consumer $x$ obtains from buying firm 1's product is given by: $V - p_1 - \tau x$, while the utility from buying firm 2's good is: $V - p_2 - \tau(1-x)$. The parameter $\tau$ indicates the intensity of consumers' preferences, or how much they dislike buying a product variety different from their most preferred type. Alternatively, $\tau$ may be viewed as indicating how different consumers perceive different products to have different values, where an increase in $\tau$ means that consumers regard even products that are "close" to each other to be significantly different from each other.

Specifically, we will assume that $\tau$ measures consumers' perception of differences and it is a function of the advertising efforts, $\theta_1$ and $\theta_2$, of both firms. That is:

$$\tau(\theta_1, \theta_2) = \tau_0 + \theta_1 + \theta_2 \tag{5.24}$$

In other words, the effect of firms' advertising in this model is to make the differences between their products more important in the eyes of consumers. If such persuasive advertising were absent or if it had no effect, the taste parameter $\tau$ would be constant at $\tau_0$ in equation (5.24) and the model would simply revert to that of our baseline case. As in the informative advertising model, we will assume that the cost of a firm's advertising effort $A(\theta_i)$ is: $A(\theta_i) = \alpha \dfrac{\theta_i^2}{2} H$.

We will make a subtle change to the informative advertising model. In a world where advertising provides information about the availability and price of a product, the pricing and advertising decisions can be treated as simultaneous choices. However, when advertising is used to affect consumer views regarding the substitutability among brands, we must recognize that it takes time to create and design an advertising campaign. It makes more sense in this context to let firms first decide upon their advertising effort or $A(\theta_i)$, and then set price $p_i$ to maximize profits given that advertising strategy and the new consumer preferences for products that it will create.

In this two-step or stage decision-making process, we proceed by working backwards. We first solve for the equilibrium prices, $p_1^*, p_2^*$, in the second stage, given the first-stage advertising choices that each firm has made, i.e., $\theta_1$ and $\theta_2$. This allows us to find the equilibrium profit for either firm as a function of the advertising choices $\theta_1$ and $\theta_2$. We then find the advertising choices that will maximize each firm's profit function conditional on the firm subsequently setting the profit-maximizing price in stage two.

We wish to focus on advertising as a persuasive influence, not an informative one. In other words, we now assume that consumers know the location and price of both products as in the baseline case. Again though, we now permit advertising to alter the consumer taste parameter $\tau$ as shown in equation (5.24). This suggests that we can use our baseline model to solve for the stage two profit-maximizing prices by simply substituting the value in (5.24) in for $\tau$:

$$p_1^* = p_2^* = p^* = c + \tau = \tau_0 + \theta_1 + \theta_2 \tag{5.25}$$

Equation (5.25) tells us the profit-maximizing prices for any given levels of persuasive advertising effort, $\theta_1$ and $\theta_2$. Using these stage two prices, each firm can work out in stage one what would be the profit-maximizing persuasive advertising campaign or effort to engage in. For example, firm 1 can see that in stage 1, by substituting equation (5.25) into the equation for profit that its profit, from any advertising choices $\theta_1$, $\theta_2$ will be:

$$\pi_1(\theta_1, \theta_2) = (\tau_0 + \theta_1 + \theta_2)\frac{H}{2} - \frac{\alpha \theta_1^2}{2} H - F \tag{5.26}$$

Similarly, for firm 2:

$$\pi_2(\theta_1, \theta_2) = (\tau_0 + \theta_1 + \theta_2)\frac{H}{2} - \frac{\alpha \theta_2^2}{2} H - F \tag{5.27}$$

Given its rival's advertising choice $\theta_j$, each firm $i$ chooses its own advertising level $\theta_i^*$ to maximize its profit. When we solve for the equilibrium advertising choices, we find:

$$\theta_1^* = \theta_2^* = \theta^* = \frac{1}{2\alpha} \tag{5.28}$$

Equation (5.28) says that advertising efforts to change the value of consumers' perceived brand differences fall as the parameter affecting the cost of advertising $\alpha$ increases. Given the advertising efforts and prices of the two firms, we then find that the profit of each firm is:

$$\pi_1 = \pi_2 = \left(\tau_0 + \frac{1}{\alpha}\right)\frac{H}{2} - \frac{H}{8\alpha} - F = \tau_0 \frac{H}{2} + \frac{3H}{8\alpha} - F \tag{5.29}$$

Unlike in the informative case, a rise in the advertising cost parameter $\alpha$ now reduces profits. However, relative to the baseline model, persuasive advertising and the higher resulting prices do lead to higher profit for each firm.

This approach to how persuasive advertising works on consumers has an unambiguous impact on welfare. Clearly, persuasive advertising raises the disutility parameter $\tau$ and hence, equilibrium prices. Moreover, persuasive advertising, unlike informative advertising, does not expand the market by informing more consumers. It simply intensifies their brand loyalty. The higher prices that firms can then set therefore simply transfer surplus from consumers to producers. They do not create value for consumers. Moreover, persuasive advertising is costly—it increases disutility costs to consumers and is an expensive activity for firms. Each firm chooses its advertising level $\alpha$ based on its profitability—its revenue gain relative to that advertising expense at the margin. Yet because the rise in profit does not reflect an increase in the total surplus but merely a transfer from consumers to the firm, that calculation necessarily overstates the social value of persuasive advertising. The model yields an unambiguous result that persuasive advertising is excessive.

## 5.5 COMPLEMENTARY ADVERTISING, COMPETITION, AND WELFARE

Let's now consider how advertising as a complementary good works in our model of spatial competition. The idea that advertising can be a complement to the brand being advertised means that the consumer's enjoyment of the brand increases as the consumer receives advertising for that brand. Hence, we now assume that the firm's advertising effort is valued by the consumer when the consumer buys the firm's brand of product. If the consumer does not buy the brand, then the consumer does not get any value from the firm's advertising. That is, advertising consumed jointly with the branded product has value but without such consumption, the advertising itself brings no additional pleasure. In all cases, however, advertising does not change consumer preferences regarding what they like or dislike as it did in the persuasive advertising model above.

Suppose that $\theta_i$ is the advertising effort of firm $i$, where $i = 1, 2$. We capture the complementary effect of advertising by assuming that consumer $x$, whose most preferred product is at location $x$, enjoys a surplus $V + \theta_1 - p_1 - \tau x$ if the consumer buys from firm 1, or a surplus $V + \theta_2 - p_2 - \tau(1 - x)$ if the consumer buys from firm 2.[12] If the consumer does not buy a good, the consumer gets zero surplus. The marginal consumer denoted by $x^M$ satisfies:

$$x^M(p_1, p_2; \theta_1, \theta_2) = \frac{1}{2} + \frac{(p_2 - p_1)}{2\tau} + \frac{(\theta_1 - \theta_2)}{2\tau} \tag{5.30}$$

When advertising is designed as a complement to affect the consumer's enjoyment of a brand, it is again likely to take time to create and design an effective advertising campaign. Similar to the persuasive advertising case, it makes sense in this context to let a firm $i$, $i = 1, 2$, decide upon its advertising effort $\theta_i$ given the cost $A(\theta_i)$ in the first stage, and then set price $p_i$ in the second stage to maximize profits given the new consumer valuations for the firms' brands. We apply backward induction to determine the second-stage prices and profit implied by the advertising efforts chosen in the first stage. We then choose, in the first stage, the advertising efforts consistent with firm profit maximization.

Given advertising efforts $\theta_1$, $\theta_2$ chosen in the first stage, the profit that each firm could earn in the second stage is:

$$\pi_1(p_1, p_2; \theta_1, \theta_2) = (p_1 - c)\left[\frac{1}{2} + \frac{(p_2 - p_1)}{2\tau} + \frac{(\theta_1 - \theta_2)}{2\tau}\right]H - \frac{\alpha\theta_1^2}{2}H - F$$

and

$$\pi_2(p_1, p_2; \theta_1, \theta_2) = (p_2 - c)\left[\frac{1}{2} + \frac{(p_1 - p_2)}{2\tau} + \frac{(\theta_2 - \theta_1)}{2\tau}\right]H - \frac{\alpha\theta_2^2}{2}H - F \tag{5.31}$$

The first-order necessary condition for profit maximization for firm, $\dfrac{\partial \pi_1(p_1^*, p_2; \theta_1, \theta_2)}{\partial p_1} = 0$ can be written as:

$$\left[ \frac{1}{2} + \frac{(p_2 - p_1^*)}{2\tau} + \frac{(\theta_1 - \theta_2)}{2\tau} \right] - \frac{(p_1 - c)}{2\tau} = 0 \tag{5.32}$$

Solving for $p_1^*$, we find:

$$p_1^* = \frac{(c + \tau)}{2} + \frac{(\theta_1 - \theta_2)}{2} + \frac{p_2}{2} \tag{5.33}$$

By the symmetry of the two firms, we then have that:

$$p_2^* = \frac{(c + \tau)}{2} + \frac{(\theta_2 - \theta_1)}{2} + \frac{p_1}{2} \tag{5.34}$$

Solving for prices $p_1^*$, $p_2^*$, we find:

$$p_1^* = c + \tau + \frac{(\theta_1 - \theta_2)}{3} \text{ and } p_2^* = c + \tau + \frac{(\theta_2 - \theta_1)}{3} \tag{5.35}$$

We substitute the outcome of stage two price competition into stage one profits for each firm. That is, firm 1's profit in stage 1 is:

$$\pi_1(\theta_1, \theta_2) = \left( \tau + \frac{\theta_1 - \theta_2}{3} \right) \left[ \frac{1}{2} + \frac{(\theta_1 - \theta_2)}{6\tau} \right] H - \frac{\alpha \theta_1^2}{2} H - F \tag{5.36}$$

Firm 1 maximizes $\Pi_1(\theta_1, \theta_2)$ with respect to $\theta_1$. Solving for the first-order condition for profit maximization $\dfrac{\partial \pi(\theta_1^*, \theta_2)}{n \partial \theta_1} = 0$ and again relying upon the symmetry of the two firms, we obtain:

$$\theta_1^* = \theta_2^* = \theta^* = \frac{1}{3\alpha} \tag{5.37}$$

These profit-maximizing advertising strategies imply that in stage two the equilibrium prices set by the two firms [equations (5.35)] are: $p_1^* = p_2^* = p^* = c + \tau$, exactly the same as in the baseline case!

From the viewpoint of firms then, complementary advertising is combative in the sense that it incurs costs but brings in no additional revenue. However, a firm cannot risk not engaging in such advertising as then it is vulnerable to its rival's advertising swaying consumers to the rival brand. But when both firms advertise, neither firm gains consumers. Both firms would prefer to limit these costly advertising efforts if they could credibly do so.

From a welfare standpoint, the complementary advertising outcome increases welfare compared to the no-advertising baseline case. Each of the $H$ consumers now gets the good *plus* advertising that they value at $\theta^* = \dfrac{1}{3\alpha}$ for a total gain of $\dfrac{H}{3\alpha}$ in consumer surplus.

This comes at the expense of both firms' profits, or a total cost of $\alpha\theta^{*2} = \dfrac{H}{9\alpha}$. So, in equilibrium, there is a net gain of surplus equal to $\dfrac{2H}{9\alpha}$ relative to the baseline case.

It is also straightforward to show that the equilibrium advertising level in this case is too small relative to the optimum level. At any value of $\theta$ common to both firms, the net welfare change is:

$$dW = Hd\theta - 2\alpha\theta Hd\theta = H\left(1 - \frac{2}{3}\right)d\theta = H\frac{d\theta}{3} > 0 \qquad (5.38)$$

In other words, at the market level equilibrium $\theta^* = \dfrac{1}{3\alpha}$, a further small increase in advertising would be welfare-improving. Each firm would see only the higher cost of more advertising, but consumers value that extra advertising and their gain would more than offset those expenses.

## 5.6 SUMMARY

In this chapter, we have explored how advertising affects competition when products are differentiated. To model competition among firms, we have adopted a simple duopoly spatial model of product differentiation. Nevertheless, the results derived are suggestive of the likely impact of advertising on both consumer and producer surplus in each case.

When advertising serves generally to inform consumers, its impact is generally pro-competitive. Fully informed consumers who understand the prices and range of products available to them are more responsive to price differentials, i.e., demand becomes more elastic. Price competition intensifies, and margins and firm profitability fall as consumer surplus rises. Welfare, as measured by the sum of consumer and producer surplus, also rises relative to a no-advertising case. When there are only two firms, the level of informative advertising efforts chosen by the two firms is less than that which would maximize welfare. However, as we increase the number of firms competing in the market, the outcome approaches the efficient level of advertising.

In contrast to informative advertising, persuasive advertising is generally not pro-competitive. It tends to tie consumers more closely to brands—lowering their price sensitivity (reducing demand elasticity) and thereby permitting higher prices and profits. Those higher profits reflect a transfer of surplus from consumers to producers, but not an increase in the total surplus. As firms' persuasive advertising efforts work to transfer surplus from consumers, because such efforts are costly, there will be excessive persuasive advertising from a social welfare perspective.[13]

When advertising serves as a complement to the advertised good, the impact on welfare is different. Firms' advertising efforts to provide this complement do yield additional value to consumers even if they do not increase firm profits or lower product prices. Relative to the no-advertising baseline, firms' advertising efforts raise welfare. However, the advertising efforts chosen by firms will fall short of the level that would maximize total welfare in the market. In this sense, we can say that complementary advertising may be undersupplied.

Two other points also deserve to be noted. First, in both the informative and complementary cases, advertising has a strongly combative feature. That is, the advertising efforts of each firm can work to cannibalize each other's profit with no gain in profit overall. To the extent that this is the case, the cost of such advertising efforts reflects a social waste of resources unless there are important consumer benefits. Such benefits potentially exist in the informative and complementary cases but, if the reality includes an element of persuasive advertising the overall welfare impact could still be negative.

Second, advertising is a strategy chosen by firms. Accordingly, some care must be taken when trying to identify a causal relationship between advertising and profitability. Firms have an incentive to advertise those products that earn a high markup. This does not mean that advertising causes the high markup. It could be the strength of consumers' preferences for specific brands that generates the high profits as well as encourages advertising efforts to exploit those preferences. We will return to these points about the relationship between profitability and advertising in subsequent chapters when we review empirical findings on this topic.

## NOTES

1 See https://www.youtube.com/watch?v=IIW3l-ENHdA.

2 See https://yourbusiness.azcentral.com/average-cost-national-advertising-campaigns-26091.html (accessed 12 August, 2020).

3 See https://adage.com/article/media/tv-pricing-chart/315120 (accessed 2 October, 2020). Fox had more live sports.

4 The model that we present is a simplified version of Grossman and Shapiro (1984), which in turn is an extension of Butters' (1977) model of informative advertising. Advertising conveys information on product existence and price in the context of monopolistic competition.

5 The assumption of one flavor or one fat content of ice cream per firm is made for illustration. We may just as easily consider the frozen dessert market in which say one firm offers ice cream (in many flavors, one offers frozen yogurt (again in many flavors) and so on. Our assumption is simply that there is a product space in which distance can be meaningfully measured.

6 If there was not a sunk cost $F$, then as long as $c < V$ it would be technically possible to produce and market every consumer's preferred variety.

7 In deriving the demand for brand 2 note that $1 - x^M (p_1, p_2) = 1 - \frac{(p_2 - p_1 + \tau)}{2\tau} = \frac{(p_1 - p_2 + \tau)}{2\tau}$.

8 This exposition is based on Salop (1979).

9 Stigler (1961) appears to be the first to articulate this point. Benham (1972) provides some early empirical support as well.

10 Grossman and Shapiro (1984) find that once that number reaches four or five, one firm's advertising mainly serves to take profit from rivals rather than create additional surplus. Given the positive marginal costs of advertising this implies that the equilibrium advertising level will be too high.

11 The analysis in this section and the following one draws heavily from Von der Fehr and Stevik (1998).

12  We use this additive approach here for simplicity. We could alternatively consider a multiplicative approach in which consumer $x$ gets utility $(1 + \theta_1)V - p_1 - \tau x$ if buying from firm 1 and $(1 + \theta_2)V - p_2 - \tau(1 - x)$ if buying from firm 2. This does not materially change the results, however.

13  Our analysis is set in a framework of symmetric firms facing a symmetric distribution of consumers. The results may differ in an asymmetric setting. Suppose for example that the duopoly is comprised of a dominant firm whose product is preferred by most consumers and a smaller firm whose product is less well liked. If advertising works by shifting the distribution in favor of the advertised product, it may then be the small firm that advertises heavily. In turn, this may lead the dominant firm to cut its price thereby intensifying price competition. See Bloch and Manceau (1999).

# 5.7 REFERENCES

Benham, L. 1972. "The Effect of Advertising on the Price of Eyeglasses." *Journal of Law & Economics* 15 (October), 337–52.

Bloch, F., and D. Manceau. 1999. "Persuasive Advertising in Hotelling's Model of Product Differentiation." *International Journal of Industrial Organization* 17 (May), 557–74.

Butters, G. R. 1977. "Equilibrium Distributions of Sales and Advertising Prices." *The Review of Economic Studies* 44 (October), 465–91.

Chamberlin, E. H. 1933. *The Theory of Monopolistic Competition.* Cambridge, MA: Harvard University Press.

Grossman, G., and C. Shapiro. 1984. "Informative Advertising with Differentiated Products." *The Review of Economic Studies* 51 (January), 63–81.

Hotelling, H. 1929. "Stability in Competition." *Economic Journal* 39 (March), 41–57.

Salop, S. 1979. "Monopolistic Competition with Outside Goods." *The Bell Journal of Economics* 10 (Spring), 141–56.

Stigler, G. 1961. "The Economics of Information." *Journal of Political Economy* 69 (June), 213–25.

Von der Fehr, N.-H., and K. Stevik. 1998. "Persuasive Advertising and Product Differentiation." *Southern Economic Journal* 65 (July), 113–26.

# 5.8 APPENDIX—MONOPOLISTIC COMPETITION IN A SPATIAL SETTING

We provide here a brief description of the monopolistic competition model due to Salop (1979). There are $n$ firms symmetrically located around a circle normalized to have a circumference of 1. Hence, the distance between any two firms is $1/n$. Each firm has a constant marginal cost of $c$ and a fixed cost of $F$. The $n$ firms serve a mass of $H$ consumers uniformly distributed around the circle. Each consumer is denoted by the location $x$ on the circle of their most preferred product version, with $x$ running from 0 to 1. Consumer $x_h$ therefore lies in the interval between two firms, $j$ and $j+1$, with $h = j$ indicating that the consumer's most preferred product location is identical to the location of firm $j$'s product. Consumer $x_h$ has a reservation price $V$ and buys at most one product per unit of time. We will assume that $V$ is sufficiently high that $x_h$ buys from either $j$ or $j+1$. In choosing between these two products, consumer $x_h$ selects that product from which they get the highest surplus. That is, consumer $x_h$:

Buy one unit from firm $j$ if: $\quad V - \tau|x_h - j| - p_j > V - \tau|x_h - (j+1)| - p_{j+1}$,

Buy one unit from firm $j+1$ if: $\quad V - \tau|x_h - (j+1)| - p_{j+1} > V - \tau|x_h - j| - p_j$, $\quad$ (A5.1)

Indifferent between $j$ and $j+1$ if: $V - \tau|x_h - j| - p_j = V - \tau|x_h - (j+1)| - p_{j+1}$

where $|x_h - j|$ is the absolute value of the distance between consumer $x_h$ and firm $j$.

We will assume that firm $j+1$ is to the right of firm $j$. The point of indifference marks the location of the marginal consumer $x^M_{Right}$ on this side of $j$'s market. Given that the distance between $j$ and $j+1$ is $1/n$, we can solve for $x^M_{Right}$.

$$x^M_{Right} = \frac{2j+1}{2n} + \frac{p_{j+1} - p_j}{2\tau} \qquad (A5.2)$$

For example, let there be $n = 4$ firms and $j = 3$ so that $j+1 = 4$. If both firm 3 and firm 4 charge the same price, then the marginal consumer $x^M$ would lie at location 7/8—exactly half way between firms 3 and 4 completely analogous to the simple Hotelling model.

Of course, firm $j$ also competes with firm $j-1$ to its left. By analogous reasoning, we then have that the marginal consumer $x^M_{Left}$ on this side of firm $j$ satisfies:

$$x^M_{Left} = \frac{2j-1}{2n} + \frac{p_j - p_{j-1}}{2\tau} \qquad (A5.3)$$

Continuing with our earlier example, if $j = 3$, then $j - 1 = 2$. So, with firms 2 and 3 charging the same price, the marginal consumer on firm $j$'s left-hand side would be located at 5/8 or exactly halfway between firms 2 and 3.

The total demand facing firm $j$ is the mass of consumers from $x^M_{Left}$ to $x^M_{Right}$. So, firm $j$'s demand is given by:

$$q_j(p_{j+1}, p_j, p_{j-1}) = H(x^M_{Right} - x^M_{Left})$$

$$= H\left[\left(\frac{2j+1}{2n} + \frac{p_{j+1} - p_j}{2\tau}\right) - \left(\frac{2j-1}{2n} + \frac{p_j - p_{j-1}}{2\tau}\right)\right] \qquad (A5.4)$$

$$= H\left(\frac{1}{n} + \frac{p_{j+1} + p_{j-1}}{2\tau} - \frac{2p_j}{2\tau}\right)$$

Therefore, firm $j$'s profits are:

$$\pi_j(p_{j+1}, p_j, p_{j-1}) = (p_j - c)\left(\frac{1}{n} + \frac{p_{j+1} + p_{j-1}}{2\tau} - \frac{2p_j}{2\tau}\right) - F \qquad (A5.5)$$

The first-order profit-maximizing condition is:

$$\left(\frac{1}{n} + \frac{p_{j+1} + p_{j-1}}{2\tau} - \frac{2p_j}{2\tau}\right) - \frac{2(p_j - c)}{2\tau} = 0 \qquad (A5.6)$$

In turn, the assumption of symmetry such that $p_{j-1} = p_j = p_{j+1} = p$ then implies:

$$p = c + \frac{\tau}{n} \qquad (A5.7)$$

As intuition suggests, more firms lead to more competition and to a lower markup over price. Note that the symmetry assumption also implies that each firm serves $H/n$ consumers. Hence, each firm has profit of $II = H\left(\frac{\tau}{n}\right)\left(\frac{1}{n}\right) - F = \frac{H\tau}{n^2} - F$. Following Chamberlin (1933), we assume that entry occurs in the long run until all firms just break even so that long-run firm profit $\varPi = 0$. This allows us to solve for the equilibrium number of firms $n$ as:

$$n = \sqrt{\frac{H\tau}{F}} \qquad (A5.8)$$

The equilibrium number of firms increases with both market size $H$ and the strength of consumer preferences for specific varieties $\tau$, but decreases as the fixed cost $F$ incurred by each firm rises. Again, these results are intuitively plausible.

However, the competitive equilibrium number of firms is not optimal. To see this, we start by recognizing that given that the entire mass of $H$ consumers is served, the total value created is $HV$, and the total variable production cost $Hc$ will be incurred regardless of the number of firms $n$. The question of the optimal number $n^*$ of firms then does not center on either of these two factors. What is relevant from the viewpoint of maximizing welfare then is the sum of the remaining two factors—namely the total transport or disutility costs consumer incur by consuming varieties far from their preferred one and the total fixed cost $F$ summed across all firms.

For any value of $n$, each firm in a symmetric equilibrium serves $H/n$ consumers extending $1/2n$ to the firm's right and $1/2n$ to the firm's left. The total disutility costs $TC_i$ associated with any one firm is then:

$$TC_i = 2H \int_0^{1/2n} \tau x dx = \frac{\tau H}{4n^2} \qquad (A5.9)$$

Summing this up over all $n$ firms then gives a total transport cost for any value of $n$ equal to $\frac{H\tau}{4n}$. The total fixed cost for any value of $n$ is $nF$. The optimal number $n^*$ minimizes the sum of these two costs $\frac{H\tau}{4n} + nF$. Straightforward calculus then yields:

$$n^* = \frac{1}{2}\sqrt{\frac{H\tau}{F}} \qquad (A5.10)$$

Thus, the efficient or socially optimal number of firms is only half as many as the number of firms that survive in a monopolistically competitive equilibrium in the long run. Just as Chamberlin's (1933) less formal argument implied, the incentive to carve out a market niche in which a firm has some market power leads to excessive product differentiation and too many varieties or niche firms. It is this circular framework of product differentiation in which Grossman and Shapiro (1984) set their model of informative advertising.

# 6
# Advertising and Consumer Behavior: Empirical Evidence

## 6.1 INTRODUCTION

We have seen some empirical evidence on the role and impact of advertising. In the current chapter, we focus on evidence regarding the primary function of advertising efforts—whether it serves to inform; to persuade; or as a complement to the advertised product. In Chapter 7, we examine evidence on how advertising affects competition and market outcomes. Our primary goal is to provide some sense of where the balance of the evidence lies on these issues. However, we focus on specific studies to convey both the general nature of empirical economic research and the myriad difficulties that attend any effort to identify causal relationships using social and economic data.

## 6.2 A BRIEF REVIEW OF EMPIRICAL METHODS

An economic model of consumer and firm behavior yields predictions about what we expect to happen in the marketplace. The validity of such a model depends on how well it is supported by empirical evidence. While economic models and the derivation of the results that they yield often provide valuable insights, it is how well the predictions of those models fare when tested against actual data that establishes their validity.

For example, suppose we have an economic model predicting that a consumer's weekly expenditure on fast food depends on the individual's level of education, weekly income, gender and the number of outlets within 5 miles of the consumer's home. A measure of the extent to which each of these variables is important is an open question. If our model predicts a negative relationship between income and fast food expenditures, we would like to know the strength of this relationship, i.e., precisely how much more do lower income earners spend on fast food than high income earners, all else equal.

Answering this question requires the use of statistical techniques. If we have the data on fast food expenditures, education, income, gender and the number of outlets, we can begin to think about how to test the economic model. The tool most used in the economist's tool kit is a linear regression model. It specifies the expected value of the key variable of interest, $y_i$, in this case fast food expenditure, conditional on a linear combination of $k$ independent variables, the $x_k$'s, or education, gender, number of food outlets and so on.[1]

In our example, the data sample might consist of observations from a survey of $n$ individuals over the age of 21 years, reporting for each individual $i$ the amount spent on fast food ($FFExpend_i$) in a specific week, as well as the individual's total years of schooling ($YrsSchool_i$), weekly income ($Income_i$), and a binary variable ($Gender_i$) equal to 1 if individual $i$ is female and 0 otherwise. In this framework, $FFExpend$ would be the $y$ variable and the remaining variables ($YrsSchool$, $Income$, and $Gender$) are the $x$'s.

Of course, it is unlikely that these three variables will perfectly account for the fast food spending of every individual in the sample. Therefore, to pick up the effects of any other factors that we do not observe, we add an error term $\varepsilon$ to complete the model's specification. The regression model for this case would then be that, for any individual $i$ in our sample, spending on fast food is:

$$FFExpend_i = \beta_0 + \beta_1 YrsSchool_i + \beta_2 Income_i + \beta_3 Gender_i + \varepsilon_i \qquad (6.1)$$

We can allow for some nonlinear effects in the relationship by replacing a variable such as $YrsSchool$ with its squared value or with its logarithmic value or with some other nonlinear transformation. The linearity of the regression model refers to additive linearity in the coefficients or $\beta_k$, and not to the $x$ variables.

Given the sample of $n$ observations, regression techniques such as ordinary least squares (OLS) may be applied to estimate the $\beta_k$ coefficients. It is important to point out at the outset that a sample is truly just a sample. That is, the data does not include the entire universe of all observations on, say, education and fast food expenditures, but only a random sample or subset of the greater population. Many other samples are possible to draw from the population, and each will give rise to a somewhat different set of $\beta_k$ estimates. The $\beta_k$ estimates are, therefore, themselves random variables, each with a distribution mean and variance.

Fortunately, the OLS technique provides estimates of not only the true $\beta_k$, but also of the variance of the associated sampling distributions. In other words, each $\beta_k$ estimate may be taken as an estimate of the true population-wide $\beta_k$, and the precision of that estimate may be measured by the associated sample variance for that coefficient. In turn, this permits hypothesis testing and statistical inference.

Consider again the model that we wish to estimate in equation (6.1). The $x$ variable, Gender, is a binary dummy variable equal to 1 if the individual $i$ is female and 0 otherwise. Evidence that women tend to consume less fast food than men would be found if our estimate of $\beta_3$, denoted by $\hat{\beta}_3$, is negative, i.e., if $\hat{\beta}_3 < 0$. Yet while finding that $\hat{\beta}_3 < 0$ might be suggestive, it would not in itself be necessarily compelling. The reason is again that $\hat{\beta}_3$ is a random variable, and it is therefore entirely possible that one could obtain a negative value for $\hat{\beta}_3$ in one sample even though the true value of $\beta_3$ is zero or positive.

However, just as $\hat{\beta}_3$ is an estimate of its true value, the estimate of the variance of $\hat{\beta}_3$, denoted as $var(\hat{\beta}_3)$, is similarly a good statistical guess of the variance in the $\hat{\beta}_3$ estimates one would observe across many different samples, each having the size $n$. If that variance is small, we can be reasonably sure that our $\hat{\beta}_3$ estimate would not change too much even if we measured it over many data samples. If it is large, however, we cannot be very confident that our finding is robust.

Whether a coefficient's sampling variance is large or small is a relative question. The conventional measure is the ratio of $\hat{\beta}_k$ to the square root of $var(\hat{\beta}_k)$, or in our example, the measure is the $t$-statistic: $t = \hat{\beta}_3/std\ dev(\hat{\beta}_3)$.[2] Under standard assumptions regarding the random error term $\varepsilon_i$, this $t$-statistic follows what is called the Student's $t$ distribution with $n - k - 1$ degrees of freedom. As a rough guide, we can say that with sample sizes of $n \geq 35$, a $t$-value that is either greater than +2 or less than –2 tells us that the probability of observing the $\hat{\beta}_3$ value that we found, when the true value of $\beta_3$ is zero, is 5 percent or less.

Suppose that the dependent $y$ variable in equation (6.1) is measured in dollars, and the regression analysis yields $\hat{\beta}_3 = -6.20$ and $std\ dev(\hat{\beta}_3) = 3.05$, so that we compute the $t$-statistic $t = -2.04$. With a sample size of $n = 40$, this $t$-statistic is sufficiently large that we can infer that women spend less than men on fast food and that this finding is statistically significant at the 5 percent level. In other words, given the sample data, there is only a 5 percent chance that there is no gender difference in fast food spending. Had our estimates instead been $\hat{\beta}_3 = -4.76$ and $std\ dev(\hat{\beta}_3) = 2.80$, we would have $t = -1.70$, which would lower the significance level of our findings to 10 percent. We still might feel confident that the effect of gender is not zero, but we would not be quite as confident as in the earlier case. Note too, that in each case, the coefficient itself, whether –6.20 or –4.76, is the best guess of how much smaller the amount of weekly spending on fast food done by women is than men, given their education and income. Of course, we could conduct similar tests on the other coefficient estimates as well.

Beyond testing the value of various coefficient estimates, we can also ask a slightly different question. This is whether our linear model does a good job of capturing the variation in fast food spending across the individuals in our sample. One way to do this is to use the estimated $\hat{\beta}_k$ values to form a prediction for the fast food expenditures of everyone in the sample. That is, we can form the predicted value $\hat{y}_i$ for each observation such that:

$$\hat{y}_i = \hat{\beta}_0 + \hat{\beta}_1(YrsSchool)_i + \hat{\beta}_2(Income)_i + \hat{\beta}_3(Gender)_i \qquad (6.2)$$

Associated with this prediction for each observation, there will be a residual or forecast error $u_i$ measuring the difference between the actual value $y_i$ and the predicted value $\hat{y}_i$. That is:

$$u_i = y_i - \hat{y}_i \qquad (6.3)$$

The residuals $u_i$ measure the extent to which the fitted model fails to predict or explain the actual $y_i$ values. Of course, these will be different for each observation. That is, the actual $y_i$ value and the model's predicted value $\hat{y}_i$ will vary across observations, as will the prediction error $u_i$. However, an important feature of the OLS estimation procedure is that the mean $\bar{y}$ of the actual $y_i$ is also the mean of the predicted $\hat{y}_i$ values. Hence, the ratio of the variation of the $\hat{y}_i$ to the variation in the $y_i$ about that mean value is an intuitive measure of the proportion of the variation in the observed $y_i$ values that the fitted model can explain. This ratio is known as the $R^2$ value and it is commonly used as a "goodness of fit" measure. It is a measure of how well the estimated relationship fits or explains the data.[3] More formally, we can write:

$$R^2 = \frac{\Sigma(\hat{y}_i - \bar{y})^2}{\Sigma(y_i - \bar{y})^2} \tag{6.4}$$

The $R^2$ value is bounded between 0 and 1. Higher $R^2$ values are interpreted as indicating a better "fit" of the data. The intuition is that as $R^2$ rises, the variation in the $\hat{y}_i$ values predicted by the model better matches or "explains" better the variation in the $y_i$ values observed in the sample data.

Even though the $R^2$ is commonly reported in empirical studies its use as a goodness of fit measure is somewhat limited for at least two reasons. First, if there is a lot of natural random variation in the actual data, then even a correctly specified model with accurate $\hat{\beta}_k$ estimates will have a relatively low $R^2$. Second, we are often interested in investigating different ways to characterize a relationship. For instance, we might want to consider replacing fast food expenditures with the (natural) log of fast food expenditures. Unfortunately, we cannot compare the estimation results of this alternative specification by comparing the $R^2$ value to what we found in our earlier specification. The $R^2$ measure is not robust to such transformations of the dependent variable.

As a test of the model's validity we are interested in a statistically rooted measure of the model's overall performance. In this regard, a useful reported value is the regression's $F$-statistic. This measure is very much like the $t$-statistic for an individual coefficient estimate, but the difference here is that it jointly tests whether *all* the $\hat{\beta}_k$ estimates are significantly different from zero.

We earlier defined the residuals from an estimated model as $u_i = y_i - \hat{y}_i = y_i - \hat{\beta}_0 - \hat{\beta}_1 x_{1i} - \hat{\beta}_2 x_{2i} - ... - \hat{\beta}_k x_{ki}$. Consider the residuals $e_i$ from a very simple alternative model, namely, $e_i = y_i - \hat{\beta}_0$. In other words, this alternative simple model imposes $k$ restrictions on the regression estimation in that it implicitly sets the coefficients on the $k$ independent variables equal to 0. Effectively, this restricted version says that one can predict $y_i$ (fast food expenditures in our example) simply as the average value of $y_i$, while the original unrestricted model uses other data (e.g., income, education, and gender) to improve on that simple prediction. It follows that the variation in $e_i$ residuals will be larger than the variation in the $u_i$ residuals as the latter are from a model using more information to make its predictions. When is this difference large enough to suggest that the restricted alternative is *too* simple? In other words, when does the original unrestricted model reduce the prediction errors sufficiently to be deemed statistically significant?

The regression $F$-statistic provides an answer to these questions. Its value is:

$$F = \frac{(\Sigma e_i^2 - \Sigma u_i^2)/k}{\Sigma e_i^2/(n-k-1)} \tag{6.5}$$

This statistic has the $F$ distribution with $k$ and $n - k - 1$ degrees of freedom in the numerator and denominator, respectively.

Like the $R^2$ value, the regression $F$-statistic is also commonly reported. It is really a way of testing whether the estimated model is capturing anything useful in predicting or "explaining" the dependent variable $y_i$. Turning again to our fast food example, suppose again that we have $n = 40$ observations and that the $F$-statistic is 2.55. Given that we have three regressors or different $x$ variables the numerator has $k = 3$ degrees of freedom and the denominator has $n - k - 1 = 36$ degrees of freedom. Referring to a standard $F$ table, we find that the level of significance, or the $p$-value, is not quite 5 percent, but rather is well below 10 percent. Roughly speaking, there is less than a 10 percent chance that *YrsSchool*, *Income*, and *Gender* are not important for explaining fast food expenditures. In other words, our model "fits" the data reasonably well in that it captures some of the main reasons that fast food expenditures differ among individuals.

Regression analysis is a powerful tool for testing the predictions of economic models and identifying important economic relationships. However, like every tool, regression analysis has its limitations. The statistical inferences discussed above are only valid if some key assumptions regarding the data are satisfied. Chief among these assumptions is that the error terms $\varepsilon_i$ are independent of the $x_{ki}$ variable, formally, $E(\varepsilon_i | x_{1i}, x_{2i}, \ldots x_{ki}) = 0.$[4]

There are several reasons why the assumption of independence may not hold. One reason is that an $x_i$ variable may itself be endogenous along with the $y_i$ variable. Consider again our fast food expenditure example. Suppose that eating fast food and therefore spending money on fast food is bad for a person's health and that bad health tends to reduce income. Then in addition to the hypothesized effect of *Income* on *FFExpend*, there is also an influence of *FFExpend* on *Income*. As a result, a random shock that makes $\varepsilon_i$ larger, will also make *FFExpend* larger. In turn, as *FFExpend* rises, there is a direct relation between $\varepsilon_i$ and $Income_i$. The associated $\beta_2$ coefficient will be biased as a measure of how changes in *Income* affect *FFExpend* alone because it not only reflects that effect, but also reflects the reverse influence of *FFExpend* on *Income*, and we will not be able to sort out these two separate effects.

Another reason that the assumption of independence between the $x_{ki}$ and the $\varepsilon_i$ may not hold is that the estimated regression may be mis-specified. For example, we may be leaving out an important causal factor. Suppose that individuals with dependent children tend to spend notably more on fast food than individuals without children. Because the model includes no indicator of dependent children, this effect will be one of the unobserved factors captured by the error term $\varepsilon_i$. Suppose as well, however, that family size or the number of dependent children is smaller for individuals with more education. Then movements in the error term $\varepsilon_i$ will be correlated with movements in the *YrsSchool* variable. The estimated $\beta_k$ coefficient for *YrsSchool* is biased as it will in this case reflect both the effect of the individual's education and the number of dependents.

In short, there are several reasons that the regression $\hat{\beta}_k$ may be biased estimates of the true $\beta_k$ values.[5] Of course, economists are aware of these problems and have developed useful "fixes." However, as we will discuss later, such "fixes" are often not easy to implement. In any case, it will be helpful to keep the potential for biased results in mind as we review empirical work in this chapter and the next.

## 6.3 EVIDENCE THAT ADVERTISING IS INFORMATIVE

We consider in this section two studies that provide evidence of the hypothesis that advertising serves to inform customers rather than to persuade them or to provide them with a complementary good. The first of these studies is the Hosken and Wendling (2013) study of prescription drug advertising that is made directly to consumers—a practice that has been legal in the US only since 1997.

Hosken and Wendling (2013) use data from the Medical Expenditure Panel Survey (MEPS) over the years 1997 through 2004 to explore a simple question. Does Direct to Consumer (DTC) advertising lead individuals with previously undiagnosed conditions to have a checkup? The underlying intuition is straightforward. Many consumers do not know their medical condition, but they may observe symptoms. Yet even after observing symptoms, many consumers may not get a checkup because going to a doctor takes time and effort, which will not be worthwhile if the symptoms do not mean much, or if even when the symptoms may indicate a serious condition there is no effective treatment for it. DTC advertising may reduce a consumer's reluctance to seek a medical opinion on both counts. Such advertising may alert consumers that their symptoms do suggest a serious condition. It may also inform consumers that there is an effective treatment for any illness that they fear they may have.

An appealing aspect of the Hosken and Wendling (2013) study is that it does not pursue the issue of how DTC advertising for one arthritis drug switches demand from a rival drug. That would involve explicit consideration of the persuasive feature of advertising. While this would be difficult to measure in any case, such an investigation faces hurdles in the prescription drug case because the choice of a prescription drug is typically made by a patient's doctor and not the patient. By focusing simply on the decision to seek medical attention, Hosken and Wendling (2013) concentrate their analysis on whether advertising imparts useful information to consumers.

### 6.3.1 A Linear Probability Model Approach

Hosken and Wendling (2013) use the MEPS data to select those individuals who have no previously diagnosed medical condition and who, therefore, are not taking (presumably) regular prescriptions or receiving other medical treatment. They divide the sample into six-month periods and record whether the previously undiagnosed individual went in for a checkup or not in that six-month period. They then use regression analysis to examine whether this decision was affected by the total amount of DTC advertising done during that same six-month period, where total advertising is measured using data from the market research group, TNS Media Intelligence.

Because the MEPS data provides substantial information including age, biological sex, race, geographic region, education, and health insurance status, Hosken and Wendling (2013) can include as $x$ variables these many other individual characteristics as well. This allows them to measure the effect of DTC advertising controlling for these other possible influences on the checkup decision.

In brief, the regression estimated by Hosken and Wendling (2013) is:

$$Checkup_{it} = \beta_0 + \beta_1 DTC_t + \sum \delta_k x_{ik} + \sum \lambda_j z_{ijt} + \sum \theta_t YR_t + \varepsilon_{it} \qquad (6.6)$$

The variable $Checkup_{it}$ is a 1,0-variable indicating whether the previously undiagnosed individual $i$ went in for a checkup in period $t$. $DTC_t$ is the (natural) log of total direct-to-consumer advertising expenditures made in that same period $t$.[6] Using the natural log means that the coefficient $\beta_1$ measures the impact on the checkup decision of a percentage point increase in DTC advertising expenditures. The $x_{ik}$ are a set of $k$ individual characteristics such as race or sex that do not change over time while the $z_{ijt}$ are the set of those $j$ individual characteristics, e.g., income and health insurance status, that do change over time, and the $YR_t$ variables are 1,0 dummies for each period meant to capture any direct effects of time itself.

The coefficient of key interest is $\beta_1$, the estimated effect of DTC advertising. What does this coefficient measure? Recall that the dependent variable $Checkup_{it}$ is either 1 (if the individual went in for a checkup in that period) or 0 (if they did not). It is useful to think of this variable as a coin flip (either Heads or Tails) with the probabilities of either going for a checkup or not determined by the right-hand-side variables. Because the regression explains this probability as a linear combination of those explanatory variables, it is generally referred to as the linear probability model. Within this framework, the estimated $DTC_t$ is interpreted as the effect that a given percentage point rise in DTC advertising has on the probability that a previously undiagnosed individual gets a checkup in that six-month interval.

Hosken and Wendling (2013) estimate that $\beta_1 = 0.069$ with an estimated standard error of 0.029. This means that a 10 percent increase in DTC spending would increase the probability of a previously undiagnosed individual going to the doctor for a checkup by 6.9 percent. Moreover, as the standard error of this estimate is 0.029, the $t$-statistic is $t = 2.38 = (0.069/0.029)$, which is significant at the 2 percent level. That is, the advent of DTC advertising appears to have raised the probability of individuals getting a medical checkup.

The typical checkup exam is explicitly meant to diagnose conditions early, before a patient is aware that they have a serious condition. As a result, checkup visits are the primary source of the timely diagnosis of serious disease. As early detection is typically critical for successful treatment, inducing individuals to get regular checkups is crucial to better health outcomes. The Hosken and Wendling (2013) finding implies that DTC advertising of prescription drugs provides useful information in that it leads to a significant increase in individuals getting checkups.

## 6.3.2 Latent Variables and Logit Estimation

One potential problem with this part of the Hosken and Wendling (2013) study is that the dependent $y_i$ variable is recorded as either 1, indicating the individual went in for a checkup, or 0, the individual did not. But for any combination of the estimated coefficients and right-hand-side variables, the predicted $\hat{y}_i$ variable is unlikely to be either 1 or 0. The fact that we want to interpret the $\hat{y}_i$ values as probabilities (i.e., not either 1 or 0) is not necessarily a problem. This interpretation does become problematic however if, for some observations, the predicted $\hat{y}_i$ values are either less than 0 or greater than 1. Such outcomes cannot obviously be interpreted as probabilities.[7]

If we had an explicit measure of the probability of an individual going in for a checkup, then we could use that directly as our left-hand-side variable. However, we do not "see" those probabilities directly. All we can code is the 1 or 0 measure of whether the individual had a checkup or not. The probabilities that we estimate are therefore latent measures that we need to infer from the data in a way that avoids the problems of the linear probability model above.

Consider a $y_i$ variable that is either 1 or 0, such as getting a checkup or not, or voting Democrat or not. Individuals who go to the doctor or vote will differ in their observed levels of income, education, and other $x_i$ variables, and these differences may explain some of the variation in the unobserved likelihood or probability, which we denote as $y_i^*$, that the variable $y_i$ is either 1 or 0. There will also be additional unobserved factors $u_i$ that are important in determining this variable. We assume that these unobserved factors are random and are symmetrically distributed around a zero mean. For any individual $i$, the unobserved latent variable or probability $y_i^*$ will be the result of the linear combination of $k$ different $x_i$ variables, i.e., $\sum \beta_k x_{ki}$, and the random $u_i$.

We assume that the observed actual variable $y_i$ ($= 1,0$) is generated as follows:

$$\text{If } y_i^* = \sum \beta_k x_{ki} + u_i < 0, \text{ then } y_i = 0$$
$$\text{If } y_i^* = \sum \beta_k x_{ki} + u_i \geq 0, \text{ then } y_i = 1 \tag{6.7}$$

Equation (6.7) says that one will observe the outcome $y_i = 1$, so long as the random factor $u_i$ is not "too negative," specifically, so long as $u_i \geq -\sum \beta_k x_{ki}$. Algebraically, this is the same as the condition that $u_i \leq \sum \beta_k x_{ki}$. Because the $u_i$ are assumed to be random, they are drawn from a probability distribution. This means that the probability that we observe $y_i^* = 1$, is just the probability that $u_i$ is less than or equal to $\sum \beta_k x_{ki}$, or $\Pr(u_i \leq \sum \beta_k x_{ki})$. In turn, this is simply the cumulative distribution of $u_i$ at $\sum \beta_k x_{ki}$.

If we assume a distribution for the random variable $u_i$, then the question becomes what set of $\beta_k$ coefficients best fits the data in terms of generating predicted $\hat{y}_i$ values that match the actual 1 or 0 values of $y_i$. One common assumption is that the $u_i$ distribution is logistic.[8] The logistic distribution is very similar to the normal distribution except that it has fatter tails. In our case, the assumption of a logistic distribution for $u_i$ means:

$$\text{Probability } (y_i = 1) = \frac{e^{\sum \beta_k x_{ki}}}{1 + e^{\sum \beta_k x_{ki}}}$$

$$\text{Probability } (y_i = 0) = 1 - \frac{e^{\sum \beta_k x_{ki}}}{1 + e^{\sum \beta_k x_{ki}}} = \frac{1}{1 + e^{\sum \beta_k x_{ki}}} \qquad (6.8)$$

A *logit* regression directly estimates the $\beta_k$ for this case.[9] Given these $\hat{\beta}_k$ estimates, the linear combination $\sum \hat{\beta}_k x_{ki}$ will generate predicted $\hat{y}_i$ values, either 1 or 0, for each observation. As noted, the $\hat{\beta}_k$ estimates will be chosen to best fit the observed data.[10]

It is useful to be clear about what the linear combination $\sum \hat{\beta}_k x_{ki}$ estimated by the logit procedure explicitly measures. One way to understand it is to think about the *odds ratio* common to sports betting. Consider the binary outcome that your favorite sports team either wins its next game ($y_i = 1$) or loses it ($y_i = 0$). If there is a two-thirds chance of winning and observing $y_i = 1$ and a one-third chance of losing and observing $y_i = 0$, then, the odds ratio for your team winning is $\frac{2/3}{1/3}$ or 2 to 1. Alternatively, if your team's chance of winning is just 50 percent, the odds ratio is $\frac{1/2}{1/2}$ or 1 to 1 (even odds). In general, the odds ratio for a binary 1,0 event is:

$$\textit{Odds Ratio} = \frac{Prob(y_i=1)}{Prob(y_i=0)} = \frac{Prob(y_i=1)}{1 - Prob(y_i=1)} \qquad (6.9)$$

The odds ratio for the logit case is the ratio of the two expressions in (6.8). Consequently, the definition of the odds ratio implies that the (natural) log of the odds ratio is then:

$$\ln \left( \frac{e^{\sum \beta_k x_{ki}}}{1 + e^{\sum \beta_k x_{ki}}} \middle/ \frac{1}{1 + e^{\sum \beta_k x_{ki}}} \right) = \ln(e^{\sum \beta_k x_{ki}}) = \sum \beta_k x_{ki} \qquad (6.10)$$

In other words, given the assumption that the random term has a logistic distribution, the logit coefficient estimates $\hat{\beta}_k$ simply map the log of the odds ratio for any set of $x_{ki}$ values. This is important because the log of the odds ratio ranges from $-\infty$ to $+\infty$. Hence, we no longer have the problem that the linear combination $\sum \hat{\beta}_k x_{ki}$ may predict values outside the permissible range as we had with the linear probability model and a permissible range of $[0,1]$.

The log of the odds ratio transformation also means that the logit coefficient estimates $\hat{\beta}_k$ no longer directly measure the change in the probability of an event, e.g., getting a checkup. Instead, we must use the chain rule in calculus to derive that the change in the probability that $y_i = 1$ for a small change in a given variable $x_i$ is:

$$\frac{\partial \text{ Probability } (\hat{y}_i = 1)}{\partial x_i} = \partial \frac{\partial \text{ Probability } (\hat{y}_i = 1)}{\partial (\sum \hat{\beta}_k x_{ki})} \frac{\partial (\sum \hat{\beta}_k x_{ki})}{\partial x_{ki}} = \frac{e^{\sum \hat{\beta}_k x_{ki}}}{(1 + e^{\sum \hat{\beta}_k x_{ki}})^2} \beta_k \qquad (6.11)$$

Returning to the Hosken and Wendling (2013) study, they also perform a logit estimation of impact of DTC advertising on the probability that a previously undiagnosed individual visits a doctor for a checkup. Using (6.11) to determine this effect, they again find that a 10 percent rise in DTC advertising significantly raises this checkup probability by close to 7 percent. As this is roughly the same estimate as the linear probability model gave, the result seems to be robust. In all estimations, the Hosken and Wendling (2013) study supports the view that DTC advertising informs consumers about potential health issues and leads them to seek a checkup.

Our second study of informative advertising is based on Ackerberg (2001), which studies the introduction of a new yogurt product by Yoplait, the second largest yogurt company in the US. In April of 1987, the company introduced Yoplait 150 as its first entry into the low-calorie and low-fat yogurt product line.

This introductory period falls within the time frame of data collected by the A. C. Nielsen Co. for just under 2,000 households split roughly evenly between Sioux Falls, South Dakota and Springfield, Missouri. That data included scanner readings used to monitor the shopping trips and purchases of these households. It also included recordings from TV meters installed by the Nielsen Company in the consumers' homes. These meters allowed Nielson to monitor the households' television viewing. Unlike Hosken and Wendling (2013), the study in Ackerberg (2001) has a direct measure of everyone's exposure to Yoplait 150 advertising over the 12 months starting three months after the Yoplait 150 introduction. The data are a panel of observations covering consumers in two cities at weekly intervals over a one-year period.

Ackerberg (2001) considers two broad effects that Yoplait advertising could have. The first of these is an information effect. The advertising could either inform consumers of the good's existence (Grossman and Shapiro, 1984) or it could signal quality or other information about the product's attributes (Nelson, 1970). The advertising could also work to persuade consumers, or it could complement the consumption of the yogurt.

Ackerberg (2001) argues that if advertising plays an informative role then it should have little effect on experienced consumers who have been informed. Once a consumer has bought the product, they presumably know it, so informative advertising should have little effect on the buying behavior of these experienced consumers. Of course, firms do market different versions of their product, e.g., Yoplait 150 is available in different flavors. So, it may take consumers several tries to become fully informed and, in that case, informative advertising may continue to play a role as that learning process continues. However, it is a role that should diminish as the consumer becomes more experienced with the product.

Ackerberg (2001) presents several regressions using a variant of the logit procedure known as multinomial logit (MNL). This estimation technique allows for the dependent variable to have more than two discrete outcomes, which in this case are: buy Yoplait 150, buy a rival brand, or buy no yogurt.[11] The independent explanatory variables $x_{it}$ include: (1) ADS, the amount (measured in time) of Yoplait 150 advertising the household has seen up to the time of purchase divided by the total time spent watching television; (2) OWN PRICE, the price of Yoplait 150 in the relevant market at the time of purchase; (3) RIVAL PRICE, the average price of rival yogurt brands; (4) NUM PREV, the number of times (perhaps zero) the household had purchased Yoplait 150

**Table 6.1** Logit estimated effect of advertising in the low-fat yogurt market (dependent variable: purchase (or not) of Yoplait 150 by household I at time t)

| Independent variable | Coefficient | Std. error | Coefficient | Std. error |
|---|---|---|---|---|
| ADS*INEXPERIENCED | 2.041 | (0.723)* | – | – |
| ADS*EXPERIENCED | 0.904 | (0.635) | – | – |
| ADS | – | – | 1.716 | (0.764)* |
| ADS*(NUM PREV) | – | – | –0.148 | (0.063)* |
| COUPON | 2.730 | (0.744) | 2.736 | (0.742)* |
| OWN PRICE | –4.900 | (0.332)* | –4.896 | (0.335)* |
| RIVAL PRICE | 0.761 | (0.192)* | 0.761 | (0.217)* |

*Note:* *Indicates significant at the 5% level or higher.

prior to the time of purchase. There is as well a dummy variable EXPERIENCED or INEXPERIENCED, which are 1,0 variables indicating whether the household had any previous purchases of Yoplait 150, and several other variables to control for such factors as household income and region.

Some of Ackerberg's (2001) main results are summarized in Table 6.1.

The first two columns describe the key results from a logit model that explicitly tests whether advertising has a differential effect on consumers that have previously bought the product (ADS*EXPERIENCED) versus those who have no experience with it (ADS*INEXPERIENCED). This hypothesis is largely verified. The coefficient on advertising is positive and highly significant, but only for those who have not yet tried the new product.[12]

In the first regression (columns 1 and 2), the assumption is that a household becomes fully informed after just one purchase of Yoplait 150. This would likely be the case if the important information provided by advertising was simply knowledge of the good's existence and availability. Once a household has bought the product, it presumably knows this information. However, learning brand characteristics such as taste, calories, and so on may take a little longer and may be facilitated by further advertisements.

The second regression (columns 3 and 4) in Table 6.1 tries to dig deeper into the informative role played by advertising. It includes ADS alone as an independent explanatory variable to measure the effect of advertising on consumers with no previous purchases, but also includes an interaction term ADS*NUMPREV that permits the impact of advertising to change with the number of Yoplait 150 purchases made in prior weeks.

Again, the evidence confirms that advertising primarily affects the buying choice of relatively inexperienced consumers. The coefficient on ADS alone is positive and significant, indicating that advertising has an important effect on consumers with no previous Yoplait 150 purchases. However, the coefficient on ADS*NUMPREV is negative and significant, indicating that the initial impact declines rapidly as consumers become more experienced with the Yoplait product.

Across all regression specifications considered, Ackerberg's (2001) estimates imply that advertising raises the probability of an initial Yoplait 150 purchase (but not later ones) by roughly 15 percent. It is useful to note that the other coefficient estimates reported in Table 6.1 appear quite sensible. A higher price for Yoplait 150 itself significantly depresses sales with an implied price elasticity of roughly 2.8. Conversely, higher prices for rival yogurt products as well as having store coupons both significantly increase Yoplait 150 sales.

Ackerberg's (2001) empirical study thus offers robust evidence that advertising provides consumers with information. The advertising appears primarily to make consumers aware of the product's features and availability. Once a consumer tries and learns about the product and its attributes, advertising has a diminished effect on the consumer's buying behavior.

Ackerberg (2001) and Hosken and Wendling (2013) are two of many empirical studies that offer clear support for the claim that advertising plays an informative role. Like Ackerberg (2001), the study by Terui et al. (2011) investigates consumer choices of laundry detergents and instant coffee brands. They begin with a model of consumer behavior in which advertising serves to influence consumer choices by affecting the brands that a consumer considers, but the advertising has no effect once a threshold level that made the consumers aware of the brand has been reached. They contrast this model with one in which advertising has a continued direct effect beyond a threshold. Using various goodness of fit measures to compare the two approaches, they find that the first type of model fits consumer choices far better.

The empirical study in Anand and Shachar (2011) looks at the impact of the TV networks' advertising for their television programs. Anand and Shachar (2011) generate a measure of matching that links consumer characteristics, e.g., age and gender, to the type of show enjoyed by viewers with those characteristics. Better matches are indicated by a higher numerical match score. Anand and Shachar (2011) use Nielsen data that recorded the shows and ads viewed by 1,675 individuals over one November week in 1995. These data record what was watched on each household TV but also record the individuals who were watching. Anand and Shachar (2011) are thus able to detect any influence of ads seen on Monday or Tuesday with shows watched on Wednesday through Friday.

Anand and Shachar (2011) find that those consumers exposed to more ads earlier in the week for shows aired later in the week, made better matches in their later-week watching. That is, those exposed to more ads later watched shows that yielded higher match scores in terms of the measured affinity between the watcher's demographic characteristics and the show's features. Their results therefore indicate that the informative role for advertising works in two ways. By informing viewers who, for example, prefer crime shows to sitcoms, the viewers learn not only what shows they want to watch, crime shows, but they also learn what shows, sitcoms, they do not want to watch.[13]

# 6.4 EVIDENCE THAT ADVERTISING IS PERSUASIVE

Distinguishing between informative, persuasive, and complementary advertising is, in practice, a difficult exercise. Providing information about a product can be part of a persuasive advertising or "branding" strategy to make consumers want that brand of good. Casual observation of media advertising suggests that firms do place a considerable weight on the *presentation* of their messages, i.e., on the design features of how an ad is staged. This in turn suggests that such presentation features—which convey nothing about a product's price, quality, or availability—have a direct impact on consumer behavior or demand. In this light, one can argue that marketing messages are designed in such a way to make consumer preferences less sensitive to price differences. We consider here two studies that try to uncover such "persuasive" effects for advertising.

Our first study investigating the purely persuasive effects of advertising comes from a field experiment conducted by Bertrand et al. (2010). In this experiment, the researchers worked with a lender in South Africa and analyzed how persuasive strategies may affect the demand for consumer credit. The loan market in question was one for relatively short-term (typically about four months), and relatively small ($150) cash loans. The borrowers in this market usually cannot borrow from commercial banks either because they do not have either a sufficiently long credit history or enough collateral (or both). The lending company was well known and had made previous loans (that had been repaid) to each of the 53,194 consumers in the study.

The design of the experiment was relatively straightforward. In brief, the lender randomized how the messages advertising a new credit opportunity were sent to the 53,194 potential customers (borrowers). The messages were fliers and they differed in terms of both the interest rate offered on the loan and various features of the presentation. The basic template of each flier announced to the consumer that they were eligible for a new cash loan at a given interest rate on a limited time basis. Each flier also included randomized variations on several features of the basic template.

To begin with, different consumers were offered different interest rates, and virtually all offered rates were below the lender's standard rates. Some consumers received fliers indicating that they were eligible for one of four possible loans that differed in the amount borrowed and maturity date, with the monthly payment shown for each. Other consumers were offered only one such loan. Some fliers compared the offered interest rate to those offered by rival lenders and some did not.

There was also significant variation in the non-informative aspects of the flier. Eighty percent of the sample received a flier with a photo of someone typically identified as a customer consultant or area manager. However, not all photos were the same. In some cases, the photo showed a smiling young man; in others, a smiling young woman. The ethnicity of the person in the photo also varied.

Another randomized feature was that some fliers also included suggestions of how the loan might be used, e.g., to buy an appliance or to repair a home, while some recipients were sent fliers that offered no suggestions. For some, applying for a loan automatically entered them in a lottery with a small chance of winning a new cell phone. Others were not given this offer. Another variation came by way of letting randomly selected consumers know that the lender could speak their language and suggesting to the consumer that the offer was a special offer just for them.

The use of such a randomized control trial (RCT) permits economists to test hypotheses in a way that overcomes many of the data problems confounding linear regression estimations. As noted earlier, such regressions are often based on data that may reflect some unobserved factors, and these factors then confound the interpretation of the regression estimation. For example, estimating how demand responds to changes in price is typically based on observations of consumer purchases in response to, say, an increase in price. While the underlying theory is sound, a simple estimation of the change in the quantity purchased in response to, say, a price increase ignores the fact that such a price rise also induces firms to supply more quantity of the product. A demand shock that pushes the demand curve outward will lead to a new market outcome with both a higher volume of output and a higher price. But a researcher looking at the data as reflecting only consumer demand may erroneously conclude that the demand curve slopes upward!

With the RCT approach of the Bertrand et al. (2010) study, however, such endogenous supply shocks and other potential factors are largely controlled. The price and other variables that consumers see are not the result of an actual market process, but the exogenous randomized choice of how the experiment was designed. Thus, applying regression analysis to the data generated by an RCT should, in principle, avoid the endogeneity issues that arise when regression techniques are applied to observational data taken directly from non-controlled, real-world observations. Indeed, the RCT approach can be thought of as duplicating the kind of experimental testing done in a natural science laboratory. RCTs thus provide a way to vary which subjects receive certain treatments and which do not, thereby providing a straightforward way to measure the effects of those treatments.

Historically, the use of such randomized control trials has been limited in economics for a variety of practical reasons, including cost. However, in recent years they have become an increasingly important tool as computational and communication technologies have made this approach more cost-effective.

Using their RCT-generated data, Bertrand et al. (2010) estimate several regressions based on both the full sample of potential borrowers in the trial as well as on the sample of only those potential loan applicants who are male. Two alternative variables are used. One is simply whether the potential borrower applied for a loan before the offer deadline. The other is whether the potential borrower both applied for and received a loan before that deadline. We report here only the key results of their findings on the decision to apply for a loan when it is the full sample.

Before discussing the Bertrand et al. (2010) results, it is useful to observe that here again we have a binary (1,0) choice—either to apply or not to apply for a loan—as the dependent variable. Bertrand et al. (2010) could therefore use the logit estimation procedure discussed earlier. Instead though, they use an alternative estimation procedure known as probit. This is nearly the same as the logit technique except that it assumes

**Table 6.2** Probit estimated effect of price and persuasive advertising on loan applications (dependent variable: application (or not) for loan by specified offer deadline)

| Independent variable | Coefficient | Std. error |
|---|---|---|
| INTEREST RATE (%) | −0.0025*** | (0.0007) |
| NO PHOTO | 0.0013 | (0.004) |
| FEMALE PHOTO | 0.0057** | (0.0026) |
| ONLY 1 EXAMPLE LOAN | 0.0068** | (0.0028) |
| CELL PHONE RAFFLE | −0.0023 | (0.0026) |
| NO SUGGESTED LOAN USE | 0.0059** | (0.0029) |
| COMPETITOR'S RATES | −0.0002 | (0.0031) |
| SAME LANGUAGE | −0.0043 | (0.0031) |

*Note:* **Indicates significant at the 5% level; ***indicates significant at the 1% level.

that the underlying random shock or error term has a normal rather than a logistic distribution. Their key results are shown in Table 6.2.

The results reported in Table 6.2 are interesting. As expected, the price or the interest rate offered matters. Consumers receiving offers with higher interest rates are significantly less likely to apply for a loan, with the estimates suggesting a demand price elasticity of 0.28. Mentioning the comparable rates offered by rival lenders in the flier, however, does not appear to have any significant impact. Nor does the possibility of winning a free cell phone have much effect on consumer behavior.

However, the psychological cues concerning choice that were embedded in the flier appear to be important. Consumers are more likely to apply for a loan when only one example of the principle and monthly payments is shown as opposed to four. Bertrand et al. (2010) interpret this as indicating an aversion to having "too much" choice.

Somewhat similarly, suggesting possible uses for the loan such as purchasing an appliance or making house repairs negatively impacts the likelihood of applying. Suggesting possible purchases afforded by the loan could lead consumers to think about how they might use the loan. This induces a kind of deliberative thinking process, and thereby enables consumers not to give in to impulse, but instead to recall their innate bias against further borrowing. This interpretation is supported by the fact that less than 8.5 percent of this sample applied for a loan.

More important in view of our interest in the role of persuasive advertising is the finding that the inclusion of a photo of an attractive young woman in the flier significantly raises the probability of applying for credit. Furthermore, this effect is quite sizable. Including a photo of a woman raises the likelihood of a loan application by as much as would a decrease of 25 percent in the interest rates (e.g., a fall from 8 percent to 6 percent).

It is difficult to see this result as indicating anything other than a purely persuasive effect of marketing. Moreover, further investigation of this effect reveals that it is male applicants that are responsive to fliers that include a photo of a woman. This appears to strengthen the persuasive interpretation. If the inclusion of a photo contained useful information, it would presumably influence female loan application rates, but it does not.[14]

In the absence of any evidence that including the photo of an attractive young woman in the mailed advertisement has any informative effect, Bertrand et al. (2010) interpret the large positive demand effect of including a female photo as strong evidence that advertising can have persuasive impact, inducing consumers to act somewhat impulsively and perhaps against their better judgment. It is difficult to argue with this interpretation.[15]

A second and more recent study finding evidence of purely persuasive advertising is the investigation by Hastings et al. (2017) into the privatization of the Mexican social security program. Like many countries, Mexico decided to move its social security program from a pay-as-you-go system to a fully funded system in which worker contributions would be invested in yield-earning securities rather than being used to finance the current consumption of the elderly population.

The change in how worker contributions were used came into effect in 1997. Starting in that year, all new contributions to a worker's retirement fund had to go into an investment portfolio managed by a private financial firm. There were 17 firms (called Afores) approved to manage workers' new retirement accounts. Workers were free to choose any one of these firms as an investment vehicle for the 6.5 percent of their salary that they contributed to their fund each period.

Tight regulations restricted the Afores' investment portfolios, but each firm was free to establish its own pricing scheme. The format of those schemes was standard. Each Afore generally charged a load fee of $\alpha_L$ on new contributions. For example, if a worker deposited 1,000 pesos the worker's account would be credited with that amount less the load fee. Somewhat surprisingly, the Afores set the load fee as a percentage of the worker's salary. If the load fee was 1 percent or 0.01 then a worker with a monthly salary of 15,384 pesos would deposit 6.5 percent of this amount or 1,000 pesos each month. In this case, the load fee would be $0.01 \times 15,384 = 153.85$ pesos and the individual's account would be credited with only $1000 - 153.85 = 846.15$ pesos implying an effective load fee of 15.4 percent.

In addition to the load fees, the Afores also charged management or balance fees as a percentage of the size of the worker's retirement account. If the Afore chosen by the worker set a balance fee of 2 percent and the worker had a balance of 100,000 pesos, the worker would be charged 2,000 pesos a year. In short, the effective "price" that a worker needed to consider when making the choice of an Afore depended on the worker's current and expected future income, their time horizon, endowment balance, and a host of other demographic factors.

Hastings et al. (2017) used data for over 500,000 workers to construct a measure of the true cost $C_{i,j}$ each worker $i$ would face in investing with each Afore $A_j$. They then organized these data into 3,699 separate cells based on individual demographic characteristics and the relevant municipality. Within each of these cells, denoted by $C$, the following random utility relationship for a worker $i$ investing in Afore $j$ is assumed to hold:

$$U_{i,j} = \lambda_{i,C} P_{i,C} + \delta_{j,C} + \varepsilon_{i,j} = (\lambda_C + \gamma_C W_i)P_{i,j} + \delta_{j,C} + \varepsilon_{i,j} \qquad (6.12)$$

where $P_{i,C}$ is a measure of the effective price that worker $i$ faces if the worker invests with Afore $j$, which depends on the worker's characteristics and the Afore's fee structure. The intercept term $\delta_{j,C}$ is a measure of the brand strength Afore $j$ has in cell $C$. The coefficient $\lambda_{i,C}$ is a measure of the price sensitivity of worker $i$ in cell $C$ and it can be broken down into two parts. One is the basic price sensitivity $\lambda_C$ common to all workers in cell $C$. The other reflects the wage $W_i$ of the worker as price sensitivity may change with an individual's income. The $\varepsilon_{i,j}$ are random terms.

As in the Ackerberg (2001) study discussed earlier, we again have a discrete dependent variable with more than two possible outcomes. So, Hastings et al. (2017) also use the generalization of the logit procedure known as multinomial logit (MNL) to estimate the equation in (6.12) across all the cells. This procedure yields 3,699 values of the basic price sensitivity measure $\lambda_C$ (one for each cell) and 62,883 values for the Afore brand strength measure $\delta_{j,C}$ (one for each cell-Afore observation, noting that there are 17 Afores).

Hastings et al. (2017) also have data on the number of sales personnel Afore $j$ had in municipality $m$. Using these data, they construct a measure of total sales force efforts by all Afores in each cell $A_C$; and a measure of the sales effort of each Afore $j$ in each cell, $a_{j,C}$. This allows the estimation of two additional regressions. The first tests whether the basic price sensitivity of workers in a cell $C$ is related to their exposure to overall sales efforts of the Afores $A_C$ in that cell. The second tests whether the individual brand strength $\delta_{j,C}$ of the Afore $j$ in cell $C$ is affected by Afore $j$'s sales effort in that cell $a_{j,C}$. Their basic results are shown in Table 6.3.

The results are striking. Overall, workers are obviously less likely to choose an Afore with higher prices. The average price coefficient (not shown) is –0.388. However, the first row in Table 6.3 indicates that such price sensitivity decreases significantly (the coefficient becomes more positive) the more the workers are exposed to sales efforts by Afores. Similarly, each Afore's brand strength significantly increases with worker exposure to that Afore's sales efforts.

These effects are also large. A one-standard deviation change in Afore-combined sales efforts in a cell decreases price sensitivity by 30 percent. A similar one-standard

**Table 6.3** Effect of sales intensity on price sensitivity and Afore brand strength

| Dependent variable | Estimated effect of sales activity | Std. error |
| --- | --- | --- |
| PRICE SENSITIVITY | 0.046*** | (0.012) |
| BRAND STRENGTH | 4.499*** | (0.031) |

*Note:* ***Indicates significant at the 1% level.

deviation in an Afore's individual sales efforts increases its brand strength by 51 percent. In short, sales activity by Afores both decreases price sensitivity and increases intrinsic brand strength, i.e., it both rotates and shifts out an Afore's demand curve. Hastings et al. (2017) also provide evidence that these effects are stronger for younger male workers, and lower-wage workers. They further show that the brand strength effects are not due to an Afore being affiliated with a bank and having lots of branches in a municipality.

The Hastings et al. (2017) paper supports the view that the sales activity in the privatized Mexican pension market had strong persuasive effects in so far as it tied consumers much more closely to firms. As a result, consumers were less likely to switch to rivals even though the basic product offered by each firm is similar and even though rival prices may be much lower. Hastings et al. (2017) also provide evidence that the Afore with the largest market shares typically had not only the largest sales forces, but also the highest prices.

These findings are not unique. Agarwal and Ambrose (2008) find that mortgage applicants who initiated their applications as the result of a direct mail promotion selected more expensive mortgages, all else equal, than those who applied for mortgages "de novo." Somewhat similarly, Gurun et al. (2016) show that those institutions who initiate mortgages and who advertised more also charged higher mortgage rates. They also targeted their advertising to less educated borrowers, all of whom ended up paying significantly higher interest rates than other buyers with similar characteristics. In other words, these additional studies suggest that advertising by lenders was directed to steer or persuade relatively uninformed consumers to more expensive mortgages—and not to inform them about their best options.

## 6.5 EVIDENCE OF ADVERTISING AS A COMPLEMENTARY GOOD

Let us now consider empirical evidence that supports the view that advertising is a complement to the advertised good, as suggested by Becker and Murphy (1993). Complementarity in economics has a precise definition. It holds for two goods $x_1$ and $x_2$ if a fall in the price of, say, $x_1$ increases the quantity demanded of *both* $x_1$ and $x_2$, rather than leading to substitution into $x_1$ from $x_2$. In the context of advertising the price of which to the consumer is zero, this implies that as more advertising is "consumed," more of the good ought to be purchased.

This is a somewhat conventional outcome reflecting the way that advertising can raise consumer demand, an effect common to informative and persuasive advertising. However, the difference with complementarity is that it also implies that as consumers buy more of the good, they ought also to "consume" more advertising—something not predicted by either the informative or persuasive models.

Testing the advertising-as-complement hypothesis is difficult. The reason is that data regarding its unique prediction that consumers will *choose* to consume more advertising of the goods they consume is not readily available. For the most part, what we have is data on, say, the number of ads to which the consumer was exposed, and this is often not an active choice on the part of consumers.

Some evidence comes from psychological studies. In an early paper, Mills (1965) allowed a sample of college women to rank a set of products within different categories and then to choose one from each classification. After rating the interests of the women in reading advertisements for each product, Mills (1965) found a strong positive correlation between their ranking and choice of products, on the one hand, and their interest in a product's advertisements on the other. Somewhat similarly, Korgaonkar and Moschis (1982) find that consumer involvement in purchasing a product is positively related to subsequent search for news about the product in the media.

More direct evidence on the complementary advertising hypothesis is provided in a recent paper by Tuchman et al. (2018). These authors test *both* parts of the above prediction using a large and rather unique data set on consumer spending and advertising exposure. In brief, their data covers 6,437 households over an 18-month period. During this time, household members made a combined total of over 117,000 purchases and were exposed to over 1.4 million ads.

What makes the study unique is that the researchers were able to use a measure of how much of each ad was skipped. A monitor was attached to each TV in each household, recording not only the time, day, and show watched, but also measuring any time the TV was switched off, the channel changed, or an attached gaming console was activated so that ad avoidance could be calculated. This, in turn, permits a measure of how much of each ad was actually "consumed."

In addition, household spending receipts were monitored so that purchases of products by the eleven advertised brands could be observed. Together, these data allow direct testing for any effect consumption of the product had on consumption of the advertising for that product. The key results of the Tuchman et al. (2018) study are shown in Table 6.4.[16]

The first three columns show the results of a regression in which the dependent variable is the amount of brand $j$'s product consumed by household $i$, in period $t$. As this is essentially an equation describing household demand, this regression includes two key variables (along with some other variables not reported here). These are: $A_{i,j,t}$ or the amount of $j$-product advertising consumed by the $ith$ household in the prior two weeks, and the product price.

**Table 6.4** Advertising as a complement

| Effect of advertising consumption on product consumption | | | Effect of product consumption on advertising consumption | | |
|---|---|---|---|---|---|
| Variable | Coefficient | Std. error | Variable | Coefficient | Std. error |
| $A_{i,j,t,14}$ | 0.1251*** | (0.021) | $Q_{i,j,t,14}$ | 0.039** | (0.019) |
| Price | −11.993*** | (2.74) | — | — | — |

*Note:* ***Indicates significant at the 1% level; **indicates significant at the 5% level.

The results reported are entirely plausible. Advertising for brand $j$ tends to raise the consumption of brand $j$, while setting the price of brand $j$ higher reduces consumption. Both coefficients have the expected sign—positive for advertising and negative for prices—and both are significant at the 1 percent level.

The next three columns show the results of a regression in which the dependent variable is the percentage of the $r$th ad of the $j$th brand watched by household $i$ in period $t$. This equation represents the explicit test of the complementarity hypothesis in that the key independent variable is the amount of brand $j$'s good consumed by household $i$ over the 14 days prior to the current period $t$. Note that the estimated coefficient for this variable is both positive and again highly significant. In other words, more consumption of a firm's product leads consumers subsequently to "consume" or watch more of that firm's advertising on television. This prediction is unique to the complementary view of the role of advertising—consumers enjoy watching advertising for the products they choose to consume.

## 6.6 SUMMARY

The empirical testing of economic models requires data as well as the statistical analysis of those data. Economists typically use regression estimation procedures to test economic hypotheses and to tease out causal relationships implied by the theory. However, great care must be taken to ensure that the estimation procedure correctly specifies the relationship and controls for variables that might otherwise cause a correlation to be mistaken as a causal effect.

When the dependent variable to be explained by the data is a discrete or binary variable, e.g., "purchase" or "no purchase," or "buy brand 1" versus "buy brand 2" versus "buy brand 3," the use of regression techniques such as logit or multinomial logit are the appropriate choices and they yield more reliable information regarding the standard errors of any parameter estimates.

In this chapter, we have reviewed how to use these regression techniques to test whether the effect of advertising on consumer demand works through informative, persuasive, or complementary channels. Designing empirical tests that clearly distinguish one of these mechanisms from another is particularly difficult. Nevertheless, in recent decades economic literature has provided empirical evidence that overcomes many of the challenges.

There is strong evidence that providing information is an important function of a great deal of advertising. This evidence implies that in many cases, advertising works to make consumers aware of a product (e.g., a new low-fat yogurt) or a service (e.g., a medical exam to investigate the source of uncomfortable symptoms). Once the information has been received, however, the effect of advertising appears to fall considerably.

At the same time, there is credible evidence that advertising can also work to persuade consumers, and often does so in a way that seems to disadvantage the consumer. Persuasive techniques such as attractive visual cues (attractive women on ads) that carry little information appear to have statistically significant effects on consumers' decisions and these effects have economic consequences. Far from directing consumers to the most cost-effective product, persuasive advertising efforts can induce consumers to buy expensive products of no better quality or match than lower-price alternatives.

The fact that many of the empirical studies reporting these effects are set in markets for financial products, such as loans or mortgages or pension funds, suggests that persuasive advertising may be most prevalent in markets where many consumers may not know how to use financial information effectively in their decision-making. Moreover, there is no expert intervening to guide their product choice as there is in the case of a doctor prescribing their medications.[17]

It is a challenge to find data that allows us to test the complementary view of advertising. However, it is likely that this data challenge will become more surmountable as we move into a digital age where both purchases and the amount of time a viewer spends viewing or consuming online advertising becomes more measurable. The one study explicitly testing whether television advertising plays a complementary role does find strong evidence of such a complementary effect.

Whether advertising is informative, persuasive, or complementary has different implications for how advertising affects consumer welfare and market efficiency. In this chapter, we have focused mostly on empirical studies that investigate the effect of advertising on consumer behavior. In the next chapter, we look at empirical studies investigating the effect of advertising on market competition. The effect of advertising on competition will of course depend on the channel through which advertising affects consumer demand, so we can also expect to learn more about the mechanism of advertising's impact in the next chapter.

## NOTES

1  Formally we write, $E\{y_i|x_{i1}, x_{i2}, \ldots x_{ik}\} = \beta_0 + \beta_1 x_{i1} + \beta_2 x_{i2} + \ldots \beta_k x_{ik}$.

2  The standard deviation (std dev) is equal to the square root of the variance.

3  Equivalently, $R^2 = 1 - \dfrac{\sum u_i^2}{\sum(y_i - \overline{y})^2}$. Note, the OLS estimating procedure generates $\hat{\beta}_k$ estimates that set the mean of the residual term to 0.

4  Recall that the unconditional expectation of the error term is $E(\varepsilon_i) = 0$.

5  We have focused on the assumption $E(\varepsilon_i|x_{1i}, x_{2i}, \ldots x_{ki}) = 0$, which is crucial for the $\hat{\beta}_k$ coefficient estimates to be unbiased. Additional assumptions about the error term are needed to ensure that the coefficient variances are also estimated correctly as these are needed for any hypothesis testing. The standard assumption in this respect that the $\varepsilon_i$ are independent draws each from a distribution with a constant variance, typically a normal distribution. Violation of this assumption will not usually lead to biased $\hat{\beta}_k$ estimates, but it will invalidate standard significance tests.

6  Hosken and Wendling (2013) tailor $DTC_t$ to spending that is relevant to the individual. Thus, if the $i$th individual in year $t$ is female, $DTC_t$ will not include advertising expenditures on erectile dysfunction drugs. Similarly, if that individual is either male or a 55-year-old female, it will not include advertising expenditures on birth control drugs.

7  In addition, the errors will not be distributed normally.

8   If $u$ is a random variable with a logistic distribution, its cumulative distribution is: $F(u) = \dfrac{e^u}{1 + e^u}$.

9   If the $u_i$ are assumed to be distributed normally, the *probit* estimation procedure is used.

10  By "best fits" we mean the $\hat{\beta}_k$ estimates are chosen to maximize the likelihood function or the likelihood of observing the sample data given the distribution of the random error terms $u_i$.

11  Similarly, to the binomial logit regression discussed above, the MNL procedure again estimates the log of the odds ratio for any choice *relative* to some baseline "not" or reference choice, e.g., the log odds ratio for choosing Yoplait 150 *relative* to not buying yogurt at all; and the log odds ratio for choosing a rival brand *relative* to not buying yogurt at all. If these are the only three choices, the probabilities for all three choices are known once we know the odds ratio and probabilities for any two choices.

12  Tests on the equality of two coefficients, ADS*INEXPERIENCED and ADS*EXPERIENCED yield a *t*-statistic in the range of 1.5 to 1.6, which are significant at roughly the 10 percent level.

13  Erdum et al. (2008) use a Bayesian approach in which advertising interacts with consumer brand experience to provide the basis for consumer updates to their expected utility from choosing that brand over others. They find that imprecise or mis-informative advertising of a product's attributes that clashes with consumers' experiences from using the product creates consumer uncertainty that depresses sales—incentivizing firms to provide accurate information in their advertising. We return to this study in Chapter 9, where we examine the role of advertising as a signal.

14  Including the photo of an attractive young man had no effect on the loan application rates of either male or female consumers.

15  It is possible that the female photo allows the ad to play a complementary role. However, since the loan is not a good itself but rather the means to purchase (typically) a necessity, it is difficult to see any relevant complementarity.

16  Tuchman et al. (2018) use an instrumental variables (IV) technique to control for the endogeneity of recent quantity consumption. Hastings et al. (2017) use an IV approach to control for the endogeneity of firms' advertising efforts. We describe IV methods more fully in Chapter 7.

17  We have not considered here the possibility that even persuasive advertising may be informative as a signal of the underlying quality of experience goods as suggested by Nelson (1970, 1974). We will consider this topic in Chapter 9.

## 6.7 REFERENCES

Ackerberg, D. 2001. "Empirically Distinguishing Informative and Prestige Effects of Advertising." *RAND Journal of Economics* 32 (Summer), 316–33.

Agarwal, S., and B. W. Ambrose. 2008. "Does It Pay to Read Junk Mail? Evidence on the Effect of Advertising on Home Equity and Credit Choices." Federal Reserve Bank of Chicago, Working Paper, WP 2008–09.

Anand, B., and R. Shachar. 2011. "Advertising the Matchmaker." *RAND Journal of Economics* 42 (Summer), 205–45.

Becker, G., and K. Murphy. 1993. "A Simple Theory of Advertising as a Good or Bad." *Quarterly Journal of Economics* 108 (November), 941–64.

Bertrand, M., D. Karlan, S. Mullainathan, E. Shafir, and J. Zinman. 2010. "What's Advertising Worth? Evidence from a Consumer Credit Marketing Field Experiment." *Quarterly Journal of Economics* 125 (February), 263–306.

Erdum, T., M. P. Keane, and B. Sun. 2008. "A Dynamic Model of Brand Choice When Price and Advertising Signal Brand Quality." *Marketing Science* 27 (November–December), 1111–25.

Grossman, G., and C. Shapiro. 1984. "Informative Advertising with Differentiated Products." *Review of Economic Studies* 51 (January), 63–81.

Gurun, U., G. Matvos, and A. Seru. 2016. "Advertising Expensive Mortgages." *Journal of Finance* 71 (October), 2371–2416.

Hastings, J., A. Hortaçsu, and C. Syverson. 2017. "Sales Force and Competition in Financial Product Markets: The Case of Mexico's Social Security Privatization." *Econometrica* 85 (November), 1723–61.

Hosken, D., and B. Wendling. 2013. "Informing the Uninformed: How Drug Advertising Affects Check-Up Visits." *International Journal of Industrial Organization* 31 (March), 181–94.

Korgaonkar, P., and G. Moschis. 1982. "An Experimental Study of Cognitive Dissonance, Product Involvement, Expectations, Performance and Consumer Judgment of Product Performance." *Journal of Advertising* 11 (September), 32–44.

Mills, J. 1965. "Avoidance of Dissonant Information." *Journal of Personality and Social Psychology* 2 (April), 589–93.

Nelson, P. 1970. "Information and Consumer Behavior." *Journal of Political Economy* 78 (March/April), 311–29.

Nelson, P. 1974. "Advertising as Information." *Journal of Political Economy* 82 (July/August), 729–54.

Terui, N., M. Ban, and G. M. Allenby. 2011. "The Effect of Media Advertising on Brand Consideration and Choice." *Marketing Science* 30 (January–February), 74–91.

Tuchman, A., H. Nair, and P. M. Gardete. 2018. "Complementarities in Consumption and the Consumer Demand for Advertising." *Quantitative Marketing and Economics* 16, 111–74.

# 7
# Empirical Evidence on Advertising and Market Outcomes

## 7.1 INTRODUCTION

In this chapter, we explore the empirical evidence of the impact of advertising on market performance. Does advertising make markets work better or not? To answer this question, we review the empirical findings on how advertising affects such outcomes as market structure (i.e., the number and size of firms), the firms' profitability and market prices. Our primary goal is to provide some sense of where the balance of the evidence lies on these issues. We have tried to choose specific empirical studies that illustrate both the general nature of empirical research on advertising as well as the myriad difficulties of identifying causal relationships using social and economic data.

Before we review the empirical literature on this topic, we first look at how advertising fits into the profit-maximizing goal of the firm and work out what level of advertising expenditure maximizes the firm's profit. This is an important question for the firm. Advertising is an expensive activity—for example, Loctite, a company that manufactures glue, decided in 2015 to spend its entire annual $4.5 million advertising budget on a Super Bowl ad. It was the first time Loctite advertised during the Super Bowl. This was a bold move. Their eye-catching ad featured a diverse group of people hip-hop dancing to a Jamaican reggae beat. Everyone dancing on the stage was wearing a fanny pack with the Loctite logo and they pulled from the packs Loctite glue to fix things like eyeglass frames, a unicorn brooch, and even a marriage. No doubt the estimated 184 million people that were expected to watch the Super Bowl that year affected their decision, but what kind of conjectures on demand for their product made this high-stake bet seem worth taking? This is what we investigate first.

## 7.2 PROFIT MAXIMIZATION AND THE DORFMAN-STEINER CONDITION

Running an advertising campaign is costly. Not only does the firm need to pay for the cost of ad space on various media platforms, but it must also expend considerable resources in the creation and production of the advertising messaging. Advertisements on national television are among the most expensive campaigns. Commercials can cost anywhere from $50,000 to $750,000 to write, shoot and produce.[1] On top of production costs, there are the rates for airtime, which vary by networks and times, ranging from $35,000 to $2 million for a 30-second spot.

A firm will expend such considerable resources on advertising only if it conjectures that it is profitable to do so. It is profitable to do only if advertising increases consumer demand. This means of course that the firms we consider must not be perfect competitors able to sell as much as they want at the going price. Instead, the type of firm we examine will typically face a downward-sloping demand curve, in which selling more requires lowering the price unless the demand curve shifts out. That is the goal of advertising—to sell more by pushing out the demand curve and not having to lower price.

Advertising is then a strategy the firm employs to shift out its demand curve. This means that consumer demand depends not only upon the price the firm sets for its product, but also upon the amount of advertising that the firm does for that product. For a monopoly firm,[2] we can describe these relationships by a demand function $Q^D(P,A)$ where $P$ is the product price and $A$ is the amount of advertising messages sent, measured as seconds of television or radio time, or page space in newspapers or magazines, or digital banner ads, or on search engine auctions. For a given level of advertising, the firm's demand is decreasing in price, and for a given price, the amount demanded is increasing in advertising.

To describe how responsive consumer demand is to either a change in price or a change in advertising, it is helpful to use the concept of elasticity. Recall that an elasticity measure is a ratio of the percentage change in one variable in response to a percentage change in another variable. The price elasticity of demand is the percentage change in the quantity demanded to a percentage change in price, holding constant the firm's advertising strategy, or the amount $A$. The price elasticity of demand can be written as

$$E_P = \frac{\frac{\partial Q}{Q}}{\frac{\partial P}{P}} = \frac{\partial Q}{\partial P}\frac{P}{Q}, \text{ where } \frac{\partial Q}{\partial P} \text{ measures the slope of the demand curve at the chosen}$$

price $P$ and given level of advertising $A$. The slope of the demand curve is negative. Hence, this elasticity measure will also be negative.[3]

We can similarly define the advertising elasticity of demand as the percentage change in the quantity demanded to a percentage change in advertising, holding constant the firm's price, $P$. The advertising elasticity of demand can be written as $E_A = \dfrac{\frac{\partial Q}{Q}}{\frac{\partial A}{A}} = \dfrac{\partial Q}{\partial A}\dfrac{A}{Q}$,

where $\dfrac{\partial Q}{\partial A}$ measures the shift in the demand curve for a small change in advertising at the

chosen price $P$. The elasticity of demand with respect to advertising is a positive number.

We have discussed the ways advertising could affect consumer demand. If advertising is informative and provides details to the consumer about the product—where it is available and how much it costs—then advertising effectively increases the number of consumers who will be deciding how much of the good to buy. If advertising is either persuasive or complementary, it can change the intensity of the consumer's preference for the good. As a result of persuasive advertising, each consumer is willing to give up more to have the good. An advertising campaign is likely to combine the informative, persuasive, and complementary roles, and the advertising elasticity of demand measures just how responsive consumer demand in total is to advertising.

From the cost side, let's suppose that every unit of advertising space or advertising message costs the firm $T$ dollars.[4] In addition, suppose that to produce a unit of output costs $c$ dollars. There could be sunk costs to build production facilities as well as sunk costs for advertising, but these costs do not vary with either the amount of advertising space or the level of production.

The decisions facing the firm are to choose a level of advertising $A$, and a level of production $Q$ (or price $P$), that will together maximize profit. Let us first work out the profit-maximizing quantity of output $Q$ to produce for a given number of advertising messages, $A$. To do this, we write the firm's inverse demand function as $P(Q,A)$. The inverse demand $P(Q,A)$ tells us the price consumers are willing to pay for an additional unit of the good at quantity $Q$, when advertising $A$ is constant, and the price consumers are willing to pay per unit when advertising $A$ is increased for a given quantity $Q$ of the product. We can write the firm's profit function as follows:

$$\pi(Q, A) = P(Q, A)Q - cQ - TA = [P(Q, A) - c]Q - TA \qquad (7.1)$$

Holding the amount of advertising $A$ constant, we find the profit-maximizing quantity $Q^*$ by solving for:

$$\frac{\partial \pi(Q^*, A)}{\partial Q} = \frac{\partial P(Q^*, A)}{\partial Q} Q^* + P(Q^*, A) - c = 0 \qquad (7.2)$$

This expression for the profit-maximizing amount of output $Q^*$ in (7.2) can be rewritten as:

$$\frac{P(Q^*, A) - c}{P} = -\frac{\partial P(Q^*, A)}{\partial Q} \frac{Q^*}{P} \qquad (7.3)$$

Observe that the right-hand side of (7.3) is the inverse of the price elasticity of demand so we can rewrite the profit-maximizing condition for $Q^*$ as:

$$\frac{P(Q^*, A) - c}{P} = -\frac{1}{E_P} = \frac{1}{|E_P|} \qquad (7.4)$$

The firm chooses an output level where the price-cost margin, as a percentage of price, is equal to the inverse of the elasticity of demand at that price. The more inelastic is the demand curve the higher is the price-cost margin, or alternatively the more elastic is the firm's demand curve the lower is the price-cost margin.

Now let's find the profit-maximizing quantity of advertising $A^*$ to create and disseminate for a given quantity of output $Q$. Holding the amount of output $Q$ constant, we find the profit-maximizing quantity $A^*$ by solving for:

$$\frac{\partial \pi(Q, A^*)}{\partial A} = \frac{\partial P(Q, A^*)}{\partial A} Q^* - T = 0 \tag{7.5}$$

This expression for the profit-maximizing amount of output $A^*$ in (7.5) can be written as (note that we have multiplied both sides of the equation above by $A^*$):

$$A^* T = \frac{\partial P(Q^*, A)}{\partial A} Q^* A^* \tag{7.6}$$

Dividing both sides of (7.6) by sales $P^* Q^*$ at the optimal quantity $Q^*$ and optimal advertising $A^*$, it follows that:

$$\frac{A^* T}{P^* Q^*} = \frac{\partial P(Q^*, A^*)}{\partial A} \frac{Q^* A^*}{P^* Q^*} \tag{7.7}$$

We can further manipulate the right-hand side of (7.7) by multiplying it by $\frac{\partial Q}{\partial Q}$ (which is just equal to 1) and rearranging it so that we have:

$$\frac{A^* T}{P^* Q^*} = \frac{\partial P(Q^*, A^*)}{\partial Q} \frac{Q^*}{P^*} \frac{\partial Q A^*}{\partial A Q^*} \tag{7.8}$$

Observe that the right-hand side of (7.8) is the inverse of the price elasticity of demand multiplied by the advertising elasticity of demand evaluated at the optimal advertising and quantity strategies. Therefore, we can summarize the profit-maximizing strategy of the firm more simply: choose a quantity of output and advertising such that the ratio of advertising expenditure to sales is equal to the ratio of the advertising elasticity of demand to the price elasticity of demand. That is:

$$\frac{A^* T}{P^* Q^*} = \frac{E_A}{|E_P|} \tag{7.9}$$

Equation (7.9) is a key result, known as the Dorfman-Steiner condition after the pioneering paper on advertising written by Dorfman and Steiner in 1954. The firm will advertise until the ratio of dollar advertising to dollar sales equals the ratio of the advertising elasticity of demand to the price elasticity of demand.

The Dorfman-Steiner condition is a useful reference point for understanding the advertising behavior of a firm. The more price *inelastic* is demand, the larger is $(P-c)/P$, the *more* the firm should spend on advertising. It can then sell more without lowering price too much. On the other hand, the *more advertising elastic* is demand, or the greater is $E_A$, the *more* the firm should spend on advertising. When $E_A > 1$ the firm can spend a little more on advertising and sell proportionately more output. The ratio of the two elasticities measures different aspects of consumer response, indicating to the firm what proportion of sales revenue it should spend on advertising.

The Dorfman-Steiner condition identifies a positive relationship between the firm's profit, as measured by its price-cost margin, and its advertising expenditure. Observation of such a positive relationship in real-world data has often been erroneously interpreted to mean that advertising is used by the firm to achieve market power by making other products seem less substitutable. Advertising is argued to make the firm's customers less likely to switch brands in response to a competitor lowering its price. This is not, however, what the Dorfman-Steiner condition says. Rather, the condition says that advertising will be greater for a product whose price elasticity of demand is low. It does not say that advertising *causes* the price elasticity of demand to be low.

To put it somewhat differently, the Dorfman-Steiner condition says that advertising will be more intense the more market power or the higher is the price-cost margin in the industry, all else equal. Rather than the heavy advertising causing the market power, it is in fact the market power, or the low-price elasticity of demand, that gives the firm a strong incentive to advertise. Alternatively, think about the perfectly competitive firm that faces a perfectly elastic demand curve and sells at price equal to unit cost. The perfectly competitive firm has no market power and a zero price-cost margin. It also has no need to advertise—the firm can sell as much as it wants at the current price.

An important insight of the Dorfman-Steiner condition is what it says about how the firm's advertising-to-sales ratio changes in response to changes in the cost of advertising. The condition makes clear that even if the cost of advertising, in this case $T$, increases, the firm's advertising-to-sales ratio will not change unless the ratio of the advertising elasticity of demand relative to the price elasticity of demand changes. If these elasticities are not affected, the ratio of advertising expenditure to sales across industries will not be materially affected by changes in the cost of advertising.

It bears repeating that a key implication of equation (7.9) is that advertising expenditures will increase as a firm's price-cost margin and profitability grow. As noted, this means that we should expect a positive relationship between advertising intensity and profitability. That is, the Dorfman-Steiner condition makes clear that we should expect to find a positive relationship between a firm's advertising expenditure and the price elasticity of its demand. That prediction reflects a causality running from the price elasticity to the advertising expense—not the other way around. It may still be the case that there is some causal relation by which advertising does reduce the price elasticity of demand. However, that effect can only be found in actual data *after* taking account of the causal relation identified by Dorfman-Steiner.

## 7.3 EMPIRICAL CHALLENGES: REGRESSION BIAS, SIMULTANEITY, AND INSTRUMENTAL VARIABLES

Our discussion of the Dorfman-Steiner condition and the problem of finding a causal relation running from advertising to market power is really an illustration of a more general point. This is that all empirical work based on observed data must address the problem of "endogeneity." In our case, for example, the advertising expenditures that a firm makes are taken *in response* to the market environment that the firm inhabits. So, the observed market outcomes, such as market structure, profitability, and advertising intensity, are all endogenously determined, i.e., they are all jointly determined by under-lying optimizing behaviors of firms and consumers. We cannot use one endogenous variable, say, advertising to "explain" fundamental movements in another endogenous variable, say, profitability. Both are determined jointly by other factors such as con-sumer tastes and firm production costs.

To understand this point it is helpful to see what endogeneity means in terms of regression analysis, in part because doing so makes it easier to see a possible "fix" for the problem. Suppose, for example, we have data on a set of variables $Y$, $X_1$, $X_2$, and $X_3$, and a hypothesis that implies $Y$ is determined as a linear function of the $X$'s. Allowing for random variation in other unobserved influences on $Y$, we can try to estimate with our data the regression:

$$Y_i = \beta_0 + \beta_1 X_{1i} + \beta_2 X_{2i} + \beta_3 X_{3i} + u_i \tag{7.10}$$

where $i$ denotes the $i$th observation and $u_i$ is a normally distributed random variable with mean zero reflecting unobserved random factors. Such a linear relationship can be estimated by Ordinary Least Squares (OLS), and the OLS coefficients $\hat{\beta}_0, \hat{\beta}_1, \hat{\beta}_2$, and $\hat{\beta}_3$ will be unbiased estimates of the true coefficients $\beta_0, \beta_1, \beta_2,$ and $\beta_3$ so long as the X variables are uncorrelated with the random error term $u_i$.

However, that unbiased quality will not obtain if say $X_1$ is itself an endogenous variable, where the variable $Y$ along with $X_2$ and/or $X_3$ determine $X_1$. That is if:

$$X_{1i} = \theta_0 + \theta_1 Y_i + \theta_2 X_{2i} + \theta_3 X_{3i} + v_i \tag{7.11}$$

where $v_i$ is again, a mean-zero normal random variable.

Equation (7.11) says that each $X_{1i}$ observation is a linear combination of the other $X_i$ variables, the random term $v_i$, and the $Y_i$. Since $Y_i$ is affected by the random term $u_i$, this means that this random term also affects the $X_{1i}$ observations. Therefore, $X_{1i}$ and $u_i$ are *not* independent, which is a key assumption for unbiased estimates in OLS.

If the coefficient $\theta_1$ in (7.11) is positive, then a positive random shock ($u_i > 0$) will make both $Y_i$ and $X_{1i}$ rise. Unless this endogeneity is recognized, the researcher may conclude that $X_1$ has a strong positive effect on $Y$, i.e., that $\beta_1$ in (7.10) is strongly positive. Yet that conclusion would be wrong because the estimate of $\beta_1$ will not be capturing just the effect of $X_1$ on $Y$. It will also reflect the reverse causality from $Y$ to $X_1$. Thus, because the coefficient estimate $\hat{\beta}_1$ reflects this additional factor, it will be a biased estimate of the true impact that $X_1$ by itself has on $Y_i$.

The parallel between this example and the relationship between profitability and advertising should be clear. Advertising is an endogenous variable that the Dorfman-Steiner result implies is influenced by profitability as much as it influences profitability. Hence, separating out the causal effect flowing from advertising to profitability (or to another variable such as market structure) will require a statistical method that can disentangle these two forces.

The broader lesson is that OLS regressions provide valid coefficient estimates only if each of the $X_k$ variables on the right-hand side is uncorrelated with the random disturbance term. Otherwise, the coefficients estimated for the $X_k$ variables will be biased because they will inevitably reflect some of the effects of those random disturbances rather than just the impact of the $X_k$ variables alone.

When economic theory suggests that a regression right-hand-side variable is endogenous, the potential for correlation between that variable and the random disturbance term becomes very real. Is there a fix for the endogeneity problem? Can we, in the case above, get an unbiased estimate of the effect of $X_1$ (and the other variables) on $Y$?

The answer is a qualified yes. What is required is that we find an alternative variable $Z$ that satisfies two key requirements. First, it must be useful for predicting $X_1$; that is, $Z$ must be significantly correlated with $X_1$. Second, $Z$ should not be important in explaining $Y$ apart from its ability to explain $X_1$. In particular, $Z$ cannot be a variable like $X_2$ or $X_3$ that belongs in the equation determining $Y$ in the first place. More formally, we need the correlation of $Z$ and $X_1$ to be non-zero, while the correlation of $Z$ and $u$ should explicitly be zero.

The variable $Z$ is called an instrument and the fix for the problem of endogeneity in this case is called the instrumental variables (IV) technique or, as we describe here, a two-stage least squares (2SLS) estimation. The first stage is to run a regression of $X_1$ on the variables $Z$, $X_2$, and $X_3$ as follows:

$$X_{1i} = \lambda_0 + \lambda_1 Z_i + \lambda_2 X_{2i} + \lambda_3 X_{3i} + e_i \tag{7.12}$$

OLS estimation of equation (7.12) will yield coefficient estimates $\hat{\lambda}_0, \hat{\lambda}_1, \hat{\lambda}_2$, and $\hat{\lambda}_3$. Using these, we may then construct for each observation a synthetic value $\hat{X}_{1i}$ given by:

$$\hat{X}_{1i} = \lambda_0 + \lambda_1 Z_i + \lambda_2 X_2 + \lambda_3 X_3 \tag{7.13}$$

Because $\hat{X}_{1i}$ is a linear combination of variables that are uncorrelated with the $u_i$ of equation (7.10), it too must be uncorrelated with $u_i$. That is, $\hat{X}_{1i}$ is *not* endogenous. As a result, we may then estimate equation (7.10) with OLS, but with the fitted values $\hat{X}_{1i}$ replacing $X_1$. That is, the second stage is now to estimate the regression:

$$Y_i = \beta_0 + \beta_1 \hat{X}_{1i} + \beta_2 X_{2i} + \beta_3 X_{3i} + u_i \tag{7.14}$$

in which $\hat{X}_{1i}$ replaces the original $X_{1i}$ variable as a sort of proxy. Estimation of this regression will yield consistent estimates of the coefficient of interest $\beta_1$. Consistency means that any bias will diminish toward zero as the sample size grows large.

There are many reasons that a right-hand-side regressor such as $X_1$ or $X_2$ may be correlated with the shock term $u$ Reverse causality is just one form that the problem of endogenous right-hand-side regressors can take. Whatever the source of the endogeneity problem, an instrumental variable or 2SLS approach can generally be used to resolve it. However, doing so requires finding a good "instrument." This is not always so easy. A good instrumental variable must satisfy the double requirement that it is significantly correlated with the endogenous $X$ variable in question, but uncorrelated with the regression's random error.

# 7.4 ADVERTISING, PROFITABILITY, AND CONCENTRATION: A LOOK AT THE DATA

Recent data on the annual advertising expenditures of over 4,300 US companies across more than 300 industries has for many decades been collected by both Schonfeld and Associates and *Advertising Age*.[5] These data show that in 2017, for example, the firms doing the most advertising were familiar corporate giants with Comcast heading the list ($5.7 billion) and Procter & Gamble second ($4.4 billion). Other firms in the top ten included AT&T, Verizon, GM, Ford, and Alphabet.

Moreover, these data suggest a connection between an industry's advertising expenditure-to-sales ratio and market power, where market power is, in this case, measured by the extent to which sales are concentrated among just a few firms. One common statistic used to measure the concentration of sales among the largest firms is the industry's four-firm concentration ratio $CR_4$—which is the percentage of industry sales accounted for by the largest four firms. If there are ten firms in an industry and the largest four have market shares of 20 percent, 15 percent, 10 percent, and 5 percent respectively, then the industry's $CR_4 = 0.50$ or 50 percent. However, if the shares were instead 30 percent, 25 percent, 20 percent, and 15 percent, respectively, then $CR_4$ would be 90 percent. This second $CR_4$ would indicate a heavily concentrated market structure—one that seems much closer to a monopolized industry where $CR_4 = CR_1 = 100$ percent.[6]

Table 7.1 shows the relationship between industry advertising expenditure-to-sales ratios and $CR_4$ values for some selected industries in 2015.

The average advertising expenditure-to-sales ratio across all industries is roughly 3.5 percent. The evidence in Table 7.1 does suggest that the advertising-to-sales ratio is higher with higher measures of industrial concentration, whereas a low advertising-to-sales

**Table 7.1** Advertising expenditure and market concentration in selected industries

| Advertising expenditure industry | As % of sales revenue | $CR_4$ |
|---|---|---|
| Perfume, cosmetic, toilet prep | 20.9 | 49.9% |
| Distilled and blended liquor | 11.5 | 69.8% |
| Soap and detergent mfg. | 12.7 | 67.1% |
| Dolls and stuffed toys | 10.9 | 58.9% |
| Pharmaceutical and medicine mfg. | 19.6 | 29.5% |
| Grocery stores | 0.7 | 30.1% |
| Gas stations | 0.8 | 10.1% |

*Sources:* Schonfeld and Associates and US Census Bureau.

ratio appears to be associated with a relatively low $CR_4$ measure. Again, though, we do not know which way the causality runs.

The relationship observed in Table 7.1 between advertising expenditure and concentration is not new. The pioneering industrial economist Joseph Bain was one of the first economists to uncover it in his work on concentration and profitability in the mid-twentieth century. Bain (1956) brought together the results of his extensive interviews with industry executives in 20 US manufacturing industries and some key empirical facts about each industry. These data, along with his own informed judgment, were used to understand what were the fundamental forces that determine industrial structure and profitability.

Two general results stood out. First, Bain found that profits are especially high in those industries that had relatively few large firms and high barriers to enter the industry. Second, in Bain's view, the leading barrier to entry was related to product differentiation, and specifically, the building of powerful brand images by incumbent firms that made it difficult for new entrants to win customers. Bain (1956) suggested that the leading cause of such product differentiation, at least in the consumer goods industries, was advertising. His view was that advertising led to increased profitability by creating strong entry barriers that blocked new entrants from competing away those profits.

Bain's work in the 1950s motivated scholars to continue to investigate the relationship between market power and advertising using more quantitative techniques. Among the early studies investigating the role of advertising as a barrier to entry are Comanor and Wilson (1967, 1974) and Strickland and Weiss (1976). Comanor and Wilson (1967) collected data on 41 manufacturing industries producing consumer goods over the years 1954–57. For each observation, they constructed a measure of average profitability for the industry, the industry advertising-to-sales ratio, a measure of the capital required to achieve a plant size of minimum efficient scale in that industry, and $CR_4$ as a measure of industry concentration.[7] Their aim was to identify the size and statistical significance of the advertising-to-sales ratio as a source of market power and economic profit.

Comanor and Wilson (1967) then ran various OLS regressions in which the dependent variable was the average profit rate, while the advertising-to-sales ratio, the minimum capital requirements to run an efficient scale plant, and the dummy variables for the degree of concentration served as regressors (right-hand-side variables). There were two main findings. These are that the industry's profit rate is very significantly and positively related to both the industry advertising-to-sales ratio and the industry's capital requirement for a plant of the smallest size required to achieve the minimum average cost. Comanor and Wilson (1967) interpret these findings as evidence in support of Bain's (1956) conjecture that barriers to entry are the primary factor behind supra-normal profits and that advertising by established firms is a key source of those barriers.

Given our earlier discussion of the Dorfman-Steiner (1954) condition and the issue of endogeneity in regression analysis, it should be easy to see the problem with the Comanor and Wilson (1967) approach. Some of the right-hand-side variables such as the advertising-to-sales ratio are themselves clearly endogenous. We know from our derivation of the Dorfman-Steiner condition that it is precisely when firms can earn a high markup on their products that they are incentivized to try to shift their demand curve outward by means of advertising.[8]

In a second and much more extensive effort, Comanor and Wilson (1974) tried to respond to the endogeneity issue with an instrumental variable approach in which the advertising-to-sales ratio is explained by a first-stage regression. Their results continue to support the view that a high advertising-to-sales ratio is an important causal factor explaining the high profitability of some industries.

However, profitability and advertising intensity are not the only endogenous variables for Comanor and Wilson (1974). For instance, they also take structural features such as industrial concentration and minimum efficient plant scale to be exogenous. Yet concentration itself is again likely to depend on the advertising and pricing decisions that firms make. Indeed, the number of firms in an industry will very much reflect a market's size and the intensity of price competition as measured by the elasticity of demand.[9]

For example, suppose that as a result of advertising the products of the rival firms in an industry are now viewed by consumers as closer substitutes. This in turn will lead to smaller price-cost margins. Consequently, a firm in the industry can now cover its fixed costs only by earning this margin over a larger volume. Some firms may then exit while others grow, perhaps by merger, as the industry becomes one with fewer but larger firms. As this example makes clear, an industry's market structure is likely to be as endogenous as the advertising-to-sales ratio, and perhaps even influenced by that ratio.

When endogenous variables are used as regressors to explain another endogenous variable, such as in this case, profitability, the coefficient estimates are likely to be biased. The fact that the Comanor and Wilson (1974) analysis addressed only the endogeneity of the advertising-to-sales ratio but continued to treat industrial structure as exogenous, is one reason that it is likely flawed as their regression coefficient estimates are therefore very likely to be biased.

This reasoning helps to explain the approach taken by Martin (1979), which is one of the more careful studies following Bain's (1956) pioneering work on barriers to entry. Martin (1979) used data from 209 industries to estimate a three-equation model in which the advertising-to-sales ratio, the four-firm concentration ratio ($CR_4$), and the price-cost margin (PCM) are the three endogenous variables. Also included, are several exogenous $X_i$ variables such as the plant size needed to achieve minimum cost, a measure of geographic dispersion, whether the good produced is a durable, and the four-firm concentration ratio in the industry *four years earlier*.

Denoting the total number of exogenous variables by $k$, Martin's model (1979) is as follows:

$$AS_i = a_{10} + a_{11}CR4_i + a_{12}PCM_i + b_{11}X_1 + b_{12}X_2 + \ldots + b_{1k}X_k + \varepsilon_1$$
$$CR4_i = a_{20} + a_{21}AS_i + a_{22}PCM_i + b_{21}X_1 + b_{22}X_2 + \ldots + b_{2k}X_k + \varepsilon_2 \qquad (7.15)$$
$$PCM_i = a_{30} + a_{31}CR4_i + a_{32}AS_i + b_{31}X_1 + b_{32}X_2 + \ldots + b_{3k}X_k + \varepsilon_3$$

The impact of advertising (AS) on market structure ($CR_4$) and profitability (PCM) is measured by the coefficients $a_{21}$ and $a_{32}$, respectively. Given what we have learned about the bias in OLS regression coefficients arising from the inclusion of endogenous variables as regressors on the right-hand side, it should be clear that none of the equations in (7.15) can be estimated directly by OLS. Each of them includes some endogenous variables—$AS_i$, $CR4_i$, or $PCM_i$—as part of the set of factors explaining any one of the other outcomes. Is there again a "fix" along the lines of instrumental variables that can overcome this problem?

The first step in finding such a fix is to bring all the endogenous variables to the left-hand side so that (7.15) becomes:

$$
\begin{aligned}
AS_i - a_{11}CR4_i - a_{12}PCM_i &= a_{10} + b_{11}X_1 + b_{12}X_2 + \ldots + b_{1k}X_k + \varepsilon_1 \\
CR4_i - a_{21}AS_i - a_{22}PCM_i &= a_{20} + b_{21}X_1 + b_{22}X_2 + \ldots + b_{2k}X_k + \varepsilon_2 \\
PCM_i - a_{31}CR4_i - a_{32}AS_i &= a_{30} + b_{31}X_1 + b_{32}X_2 + \ldots + b_{3k}X_k + \varepsilon_3
\end{aligned}
\tag{7.16}
$$

The system of equations in (7.16) can be more succinctly described in matrix form as:

$$
AY = BX + \varepsilon
\tag{7.17}
$$

Here, $A$ and $B$ are coefficient matrices with dimensions $3 \times 3$ and $3 \times k + 1$, respectively; $Y$ and $X$ are variable matrices with dimensions $3 \times 1$ and $k + 1 \times 1$, respectively, $\varepsilon$ is a $3 \times 1$ error vector. If we assume that the matrix $A$ has an inverse $A^{-1}$, we may rewrite (7.17) as:

$$
IY = (A^{-1}B)X + A^{-1}\varepsilon = \Gamma X + A^{-1}\varepsilon
\tag{7.18}
$$

where $I$ is the identity matrix.

The initial set of equations (7.15) is known as the structural model describing the set of interactions that our understanding of the market implies. In contrast, equation (7.18) is known as the reduced form representation of the structural system. The reduced form expresses each endogenous variable as a function only of the exogenous $X_i$ variables and the random disturbances $\varepsilon$. Hence, the coefficients in each reduced form equation, the elements of $\Gamma$ in (7.18), can be estimated by OLS without any difficulty. In effect, the $X$ variables are the instruments for the endogenous variables of the model.

However, the reduced form coefficients are not the ones of chief economic interest. What we want to know is the impact of advertising ($AS_i$) on concentration ($CR4_i$) and profitability ($PCM_i$). These effects are measured respectively by the coefficients $a_{21}$ and $a_{32}$ in the structural system (7.15). The question then becomes whether we can work backwards to retrieve these structural coefficients of interest from the reduced form in (7.18).

The issue of recovering the key structural coefficients is known as the identification problem. This name reflects the difficulty that while the $X$ variables can be thought of as instruments that permit the estimation of every equation in its reduced form, the precise identification of the coefficients of a structural equation may be problematic. Such identification is assured, however, if the exogenous variables in a specific structural equation satisfy the "rank condition." Put simply, the rank condition requires that we do not use the same instruments for each endogenous variable. Basically, identification of the coefficients in one structural equation explaining the endogenous variable $Y_i$ requires that there be some exogenous $X$ variables in the model that are *not* important for explaining $Y_i$, but that are important for explaining the other endogenous variables.

In Martin's (1979) three-equation model, one of the exogenous $X$ variables explaining the advertising-to-sales ratio $(AS_i)$ is a variable indicating whether the product is a durable good. Similarly, one of the exogenous variables explaining the current industry concentration $CR4_i$ is concentration ratio four years earlier. Neither of these exogenous variables, however, appears in the structural equation explaining the price-cost margin. By changing either of these two exogenous variables, it is possible to induce a change in either $AS_i$ or $CR4_i$ alone without affecting the equation for $PCM_i$ except to the extent that such changes induce a change in either $AS_i$ or $CR4_i$. These last effects of course are precisely what are measured by the structural coefficients $a_{31}$ and $a_{32}$. So, the PCM equation in Martin's (1979) framework does meet the rank condition and is therefore fully identified.

All the equations in Martin's (1979) model are fully identified and the key findings are shown in Table 7.2.

The results in Table 7.2 imply that the advertising-to-sales ratio has a strong positive and significant impact on the industry's profitability as measured by its price-cost

**Table 7.2** Martin's (1979) estimated interactions among advertising, profitability, and industrial concentration

| Effect of advertising-to-sales ratio on: | | | |
| --- | --- | --- | --- |
| PCM | | CR$_4$ | |
| Consumer goods | Producer goods | Consumer goods | Producer goods |
| 0.611 | 3.891 | 0.005 | −0.438 |
| (2.51)*** | (5.80)*** | (3.39) | (0.73) |
| **Effect of profitability on:** | | | |
| A/S | | CR$_4$ | |
| Consumer goods | Producer goods | Consumer goods | Producer goods |
| 0.276 | 0.038 | −0.068 | −0.046 |
| (2.81)*** | (4.07)*** | (0.62) | (0.76) |
| **Effect of concentration on:** | | | |
| PCM | | A/S | |
| Consumer goods | Producer goods | Consumer goods | Producer goods |
| 0.078 | 0.041 | 0.365 | 0.017 |
| (0.90) | (1.34) | (2.20)** | (1.55)* |

*Notes:* $t$-Statistics in parentheses: *Significant at 10% level; **Significant at 5% level; ***Significant at 1% level.

margin. It does not appear to have much impact on industrial structure. However, the results do imply that more concentrated industries do significantly more advertising. There is also a significant effect running from profitability to advertising parallel to that running from advertising to profitability. That is, the causal relationship between profitability and advertising is bidirectional.

To sum up, the early investigations of the impact of advertising on market performance uncovered a persistent positive relationship between advertising and profitability. On its face, this empirical regularity, especially the evidence offered by Martin's (1979) study, would seem to be relatively strong evidence that advertising is an anti-competitive strategy that protects profitability and market power. Despite these findings, it is fair to say that this view is not the modern economic consensus. It is important to understand why.

## 7.5 ADVANCES IN ECONOMIC THEORY AND THE RISE OF FIRM-BASED STUDIES

The early empirical work on advertising done in the 1960s–1970s was based on data built from a cross-section of industries. In constructing the data, there was no consideration of how firms in any one of the industries competed. The nature of competition among the firms in an industry was suppressed. In those same years, however, the way economists thought about how to model competition or the strategic interaction among firms was changing. Specifically, a new game theoretic understanding of the nature of competition was taking hold, and it called into question empirical work based on cross-industry studies. Game theory made it clear that the "rules of the game" matter to how firms compete in a market. Essentially, these earlier studies, by ignoring how firms competed, ignored how the "rules of the game" varied from industry to industry.

For example, the technology of production in some industries, such as the automobile industry, requires firms to set their production schedules in advance of knowing what price will clear the markets. In these industries, the key strategic variable according to which firms compete is the volume of production. In other industries, such as passenger airlines, firms can adjust their production schedules more quickly. In these industries, they are more likely to compete in terms of the price set. The "one-size-fits-all" approach to how firms compete in the earlier cross-sectional industry studies suppresses the differences in how firms compete across different industries. As a result, there are likely features about how competition plays out in an industry that are omitted from the cross-industry studies and, more importantly, features that are perhaps unobservable.

When important variables, even those that are non-observable, are omitted from a regression, the resulting coefficients are again biased. To see how, consider a simple example of non-observable variables. Suppose a researcher is interested in how a student's academic preparation affects the student's score on a standardized math test. The student's score likely depends on the student's academic preparation, as measured by whether the student has taken an Honors Math class, and on the student's inherent mathematical ability, as well as some random factors $\varepsilon$; that is:

$$Test\ Score = \alpha_0 + \alpha_1(HonorsMath) + \alpha_2(Ability) + \varepsilon \tag{7.19}$$

A student's innate ability is, however, unobservable and therefore will be omitted from the study, resulting in an estimated regression:

$$Test\ Score = \hat{\alpha}_0 + \hat{\alpha}_1(HonorsMath) + v \tag{7.20}$$

where $v = \alpha_2(Ability) + \varepsilon$.

In this case, the regression coefficient $\hat{\alpha}_1$ will be a biased estimate of the true effect $\alpha_1$ of having taken an Honors Math class. Why? Because it is very likely the case that students with high mathematical ability are also more likely to take Honors Math classes. Because of their high ability, these students would have done reasonably well on the standardized test even without taking Honors Math. When the key unobserved *Ability* measure is omitted from the regression, its effects are now mixed in with the effects of taking an Honors Math class. So, the error term $v$ in (7.20) is almost certainly correlated with the Honors Math class variable and the coefficient estimate for this variable is biased upward—some of the positive effects of *Ability* will be attributed to taking an Honors Math class.

Analogously, the game theoretic understanding of competition led economists to worry that cross-sectional industry studies such as Comanor and Wilson (1967, 1974) and Martin (1979) left out important and perhaps unobservable variables. Owing to the many different "rules of the game" that might apply in each industry, an approach that was based on the same "rules of the game" across many different industries became increasingly suspect. It was likely that something important was missing in many of the industries, though it was not always possible to know what that was.

In addition, it became increasingly recognized that, at the industry level, many of the variables in the equations used by Comanor and Wilson (1967, 1974) and Martin (1979) would be endogenous—not just profitability, advertising intensity, and structure measures, but others as well. Cross-industry studies were therefore likely to yield biased coefficient estimates even if the source and direction of the bias were unclear.

There are potential fixes for the omitted variables problem. An instrumental variables (IV) approach could be used. In our student test example, the solution again would be to find an instrument that is useful for explaining a student's decision to take an Honors Math class that is not correlated to the student's innate ability. In the case of industry studies, the solution could be to use panel data that includes observations across industries and over time, using a separate dummy intercept for each industry—a so-called *fixed effect*—that will pick up the effects of unobservable factors so long as these unobservable factors do not change over time.[10]

However, the assumption of time-invariant factors in an industry will not always be justified. More generally, the difficulty in finding good instruments for the numerous endogenous variables, and the increasing recognition that one model will not work for any broad cross-section of industries, motivated economists to turn to empirical studies based on individual firm data within an industry or industries.

The game theoretic approach also led to new insights on advertising. Grossmann (2008), for example, developed a game theoretic model in which firms in an industry compete not only in prices, but also in R&D and in advertising. Firms in his model must choose how to allocate funds between these two strategic activities. In making their decisions, Grossmann (2008) assumed that firms recognize that advertising is largely combative, i.e., it shifts demand between firms, but does not increase it overall.

Somewhat paradoxically, Grossmann's (2008) model implies that advertising has positive long-run effects for *both* firms and consumers despite its combative nature. Why? Because the costs of advertising are largely sunk. That is, they amount to a lump-sum cost that a firm must cover in the long run. As a result, an increase in combative advertising *decreases* the number of firms that can survive in the market. However, the returns to R&D increase as any firm surviving in the market is larger and gains market share. This leads to an increase in the returns to R&D and therefore the rate of product improvement increases. In short, the more intense is advertising the more concentrated is the market *and* the higher is the rate of product improvement—benefiting both firms and consumers.

Grossmann (2008) is of course not the only model of advertising in imperfectly competitive markets. It does serve, however, to call attention to the fact that advertising can be a tool for more efficient firms to promote higher-quality (or lower price) products and gain market share. In turn, this can establish a link between a firm's advertising, market share, and profitability that is not based on advertising being anti-competitive, as implied by the earlier work of, say, Comanor and Wilson (1967, 1974).

Dinlersoz and Yorukoglu (2012) also explore the dynamics of firm entry and growth in a product differentiated industry over time. In their model, firms experience random productivity shocks over time, and as shocks accumulate, some firms become very cost efficient while some become very inefficient and exit. More efficient firms, therefore, become relatively large and are more likely to survive in the long run. There is also a positive feedback effect on the demand side because consumers who buy from a firm in one period will know that firm's product but have only imperfect information about other firms, especially about new entrants. This permits large firms to charge a relatively high price (relative to their low marginal cost) and because of their low cost, these more efficient firms will have an incentive to advertise heavily.[11]

The dynamic model in Dinlersoz and Yorukoglu (2012) yields many interesting predictions. One is that the bigger, more efficient firms will do more advertising and, second, that the bigger, more efficient firms will charge a higher markup over price. Together, these two predictions again imply that advertising will be positively associated with firm size and profitability but again, without implying that advertising itself will *cause* market power. Dinlersoz and Yorukoglu (2012) test the two predictions, using data from the US Census Bureau's Census of Manufactures (CM), which is a survey of manufacturing establishments taken every five years.

In the first regression, the 1997 advertising level (*AE*) of each firm in an industry is regressed on a measure of firm size in 1992 (*SizeLagged*), a measure of the firm's current productivity (*Current Productivity*), and a dummy variable indicating whether manufacturing establishment was one of many establishments run by the company, or was its only plant (*MultiUnit*).

As Dinlersoz and Yorukoglu (2012) recognize, the advertising expenditures that are reported in 1997 will not include any expenditures of those production establishments that exited or failed between 1992 and 1997. This means that their sample is biased in so far as it includes only 1997 data from those establishments that were around in 1992 and that survived for the next five years. This problem is sometimes called *survivor bias* but is more generally known as *selection bias* reflecting the fact that the sample upon which the regression is based is not truly random. In particular, information about those firms that exited has been left out. Omitting such observations in a non-random fashion is not quite the same thing as omitting a key variable, but it does give rise to a similar problem of correlation between the right-hand-side variables and the error term. In other words, *selection bias* also gives rise to biased coefficient estimates.

Heckman (1979) proposed a correction for selection bias by including an additional variable in the regression created by a two-stage procedure. The first stage is to estimate a probit equation to determine the probability that an establishment in the sample in 1992 will still be in the sample in 1997. For this stage, Dinlersoz and Yorukoglu (2012) use not only the exogenous variables that we listed above (*SizeLagged, Current Productivity, MultiUnit*), but they also add in other variables that are likely to be related to the firm's survival but not related to the firm's advertising expenditure (*AE*). These variables include whether the firm exported and also its size relative to all the establishments the firm operated in 1992. This stage allows us to compute what is known as the Inverse Mills Ratio (*IMR*), which is essentially a measure of the likelihood that a production establishment survived from 1992 to 1997, again conditional on its size, productivity, export activity and so on. *IMR* then serves as a sort of instrument in the second regression to capture the effects of leaving out the non-surviving firms. If selection bias is a problem, not including *IMR* would mean leaving out a key variable, which underscores the intuitive similarity between omitted variables and selection bias problems.

The Dinlersoz and Yorukoglu (2012) advertising and price equation estimates are shown in Table 7.3.[12]

Observe that the coefficient on productivity (which is inversely related to unit cost) is significant and positive in the advertising equation, as is the coefficient on firm size. Thus, advertising expense is particularly high for large, efficient firms, just as the dynamic model in Dinlersoz and Yorukoglu (2012) implies. The positive and significant coefficient on *IMR* indicates that whatever unobserved factors make survival more likely also raise advertising expenditures.

Consider now the estimated price equation. Here, the key insight comes from the coefficient on *Current Productivity*, which is negative, but less than one in absolute value. This estimate implies that more efficient firms do charge lower prices, but their

**Table 7.3** Firm advertising and price decisions*

| | Dependent variable Current advertising expenditure ($AE$) | | Dependent variable Current price ($P$) | |
|---|---|---|---|---|
| Independent variable | Coefficient | Standard error | Coefficient | Standard error |
| *SizeLagged* | 0.017*** | 0.004 | 0.015** | 0.007 |
| *Current Productivity* | 0.237*** | 0.071 | −0.537*** | 0.050 |
| *MultiUnit* | 278.500** | 122.0 | 0.122*** | 0.030 |
| *IMR* | 0.168*** | 0.033 | — | — |

*Notes:* *The Advertising equation includes fixed industry effects. The Price equation includes fixed product effects. ***Indicates significance at the 1% level. **Indicates significance at the 10% level.

price does not fall one-for-one with their productivity, indicating that these firms do earn a higher margin.

In sum, Dinlersoz and Yorukoglu (2012) offer firm-level evidence that advertising is a complement to productive efficiency in so far as it is more cost-efficient firms that advertise more heavily. As these firms tend to charge lower prices while still earning higher markups, they also tend to be larger and more profitable. If the efficiency advantages are large enough, the most efficient firms will dominate their industries. In that case, the Dinlersoz and Yorukoglu (2012) findings imply that these firm outcomes will combine to produce a correlation at the industry level between concentration, profitability, and advertising just as the earlier studies of Comanor and Wilson (1967, 1974) and Martin (1979) found. Again though, the underlying mechanism will be different—far less anti-competitive—than Comanor and Wilson (1967, 1974) suspected.[13]

## 7.6 EMPIRICAL EVIDENCE ON ADVERTISING AND ENTRY DETERRENCE

Bain (1956) put forth the argument that the advertising done by incumbent firms created a key barrier to enter a market, permitting incumbent firms to earn high profits in a concentrated industry and to be insulated from the threat of entry. In the absence of an entry barrier, the high profits earned by the incumbent firms would have lured new entrants into the market, thereby expanding market output, leading to lower prices and profits. Any sustained profitability of incumbent firms must reflect, in part, the inability of new entrants to compete in this market.

Brand name identity is an important advantage, or asset, enjoyed by an incumbent firm that gives the firm a competitive edge when competing with a new entrant. Bain (1956) saw advertising as the way that a firm creates brand identity, and so advertising, viewed in this light, could be a strategy used to deter other firms from entering the market. The fact that PepsiCo, when it acquired the orange juice firm Tropicana, continued to market juice products under the Tropicana name, or that Molson-Coors continued to market Miller, Coors, Molson, and Blue Moon under their original brand names after acquiring these labels does indeed suggest that established brand names are an important advantage for incumbents and an important challenge for new entrants.

As we have presented it, the view behind the initial work of Bain (1956), Comanor and Wilson (1967, 1974) and others was that advertising was largely a persuasive effort that reduced the price elasticity of a firm's demand and thereby inhibited competition. However, if advertising is mostly informative about a product's characteristics and if a new entrant's product is a close substitute to the incumbent's product, then an incumbent firm's advertising could spill over to the entrant's product and ultimately benefit it thereby promoting competition. It follows that one would expect the nature of strategic advertising to differ depending on which of these two cases applies.

Ellison and Ellison (2011) investigate this issue using data from the market for patented drugs. Since the mid-1980s, the expiration of a drug patent has opened the door to entry by generic (i.e., perfect) substitutes, partly as the result of changes in federal and state laws that either mandate or at least permit pharmacies to use the cheapest equivalent medication when filling prescriptions. Ellison and Ellison (2011) use data for 63 different patented drugs that lost their patents between 1986 and 1992 to investigate what were the advertising choices the patent-holding firms made in anticipation of the patent loss and the threat of entry by new, generic rivals.

An important point that Ellison and Ellison (2011) make is that, however advertising might deter ($D$) or not deter ($ND$) entry, employing such a strategy may well depend on the size of the market. For example, some drugs treat only very rare illnesses. The market for such a drug may be too small for a generic entrant to compete for customers. In this case, the incumbent losing its patent does not need to engage in strategic entry-deterring behavior. The size of the market coupled with the technology of production make it unattractive for entry. Conversely, other markets are so large that entry by one or more generics is likely to be inevitable. Here again, we would not expect an incumbent to try to deter entry as the cost of such efforts is not worth the potential gain.

Ellison and Ellison (2011) show that when markets are ranked by size, those in the top three quintiles had at least one generic rival within three years of patent expiration roughly 86 percent of the time on average. By contrast, markets in the smallest quintile had no generic entrants over the comparable three-year period. They also estimate a probit equation predicting generic entry ($Y_i = 1$) in three years following patent expiration or no such entry ($Y_i = 0$). They find that market size is in fact the most important and statistically most significant factor influencing such entry.

To be specific, Ellison and Ellison (2011) find that the largest 60 percent of markets are sufficiently large that entry is inevitable, and that the smallest 20 percent of markets are so small that entry is very unlikely. The question then becomes whether we can detect any deterrent effort in that remaining 20 percent of markets where entry would, in the absence of deterrence, be likely but not certain.

For prescription drugs, regular visits of a company's sales representatives to doctors, called detailing, is how doctors are encouraged to prescribe that drug. It is perhaps the most important form of drug promotion that drug companies employ given the key role physicians play in choosing patient medications. In the absence of any strategic actions aimed at deterring entry, we would expect to see the firm's advertising intensity, as measured by its advertising expenditure-to-sales ratio in the pre-entry periods either steadily rise with market size or steadily fall, depending on the nature of the informative and persuasive role of detailing. In other words, we would expect a monotonic relation between advertising intensity and market size of the drug.

In light of the above expectation, evidence of using advertising strategically to deter entry would be a finding that the advertising-market size relation is non-monotonic—rising and then falling sharply instead of always rising or falling and rising sharply instead of always falling. This implies that in considering the Ellison and Ellison (2011) preliminary findings on entry, we should look for evidence of non-monotonicity in those markets where entry is likely, i.e., those lying in the 20–40 percent range of market size.

Ellison and Ellison (2011) look for the evidence just described. Table 7.4 shows their results in terms of how detailing expenses, relative to revenues, vary across the five market size quintiles running from the smallest to the largest 20 percent of markets—in the three years prior to patent expiration.

Recall that Quintile 2 is the market range in which we would most likely see deterrent efforts. Table 7.4 shows that while detailing expenses in years just prior to patent expiration tends to increase by about $5 or more for every $1,000 increase in revenues in other markets, this effect *drops* to $1 in those markets where generic entry is likely. This action would be consistent with a deterrent strategy if drug advertising by the incumbent firm spills over to a significant degree to the demand for a generic drug. Ellison and Ellison (2011) believe that this is in fact the case, in part due to the mandate many states give to pharmacies to find low-cost generic alternatives in filling prescriptions.

There remains the question of whether the decline in detail advertising in entry-threatened markets is statistically significant. A test for significance is provided by the monotonicity tests developed by Hall and Heckman (2000). The basic idea is straightforward. Suppose that detailing increases steadily with market size as it would in the absence of a deterrent strategy. This implies that in a regression of detail spending on market size, i.e., $Detailing_i = \alpha_0 + \alpha_1 Size_i + \varepsilon_i$ the estimated value for $\alpha_1$ ought to be positive. The Hall and Heckman (2000) procedure is based on running this regression many times over subsamples of the data set of size $m$, and forming a statistic based on the maximum negative value of $\alpha_1$ across all such regressions. If one uncovers a large, negative estimate of $\alpha_1$ for one of these regressions, the Hall and Heckman (2000) statistic will tend to be large as well, casting doubt on the hypothesis that the relationship is monotonically positive.

**Table 7.4** Detail advertising intensity and market size (by quintile)

| Quintile 1 | Quintile 2 | Quintile 3 | Quintile 4 | Quintile 5 |
|------------|------------|------------|------------|------------|
| 0.0051 | 0.0013 | 0.0055 | 0.0084 | 0.0042 |

Ellison and Ellison (2011) set $m = 15$ for their subsample regressions and compute two variants of the Hall and Heckman (2000) measure. One of these allows them to reject the null hypothesis of monotonicity at the 20 percent level while the other is significant at the 5 percent level. Thus, there is some evidence that pharmaceutical firms choose advertising strategically to deter generic entry. Yet they do so by *depressing* advertising efforts because these spill over to benefit generic entrants.[14]

Interpreting the above result, however, requires care as demonstrated by King (2002) in his study of the market for anti-ulcer drugs, e.g., Tagamet, Zantac, Pepcid, and Axid. Tagamet initially had a monopoly in this market. So, the emergence of strong rivals shows that entry barriers were not insurmountable. King's (2002) unraveling of the relation of those barriers to advertising efforts though is particularly interesting. Later entrants did have to spend more on advertising (relative to sales) to compete. However, King (2002) finds that advertising by all firms *lowered* consumers' perception of product differentiation and, therefore, increased price competition. The resulting fall in price-cost margins then worked to discourage entry. In other words, advertising by incumbent firms can deter entry by new firms precisely because it intensifies competition among existing ones and, therefore, makes entry less profitable. However, advertising makes the industry less profitable as well.

A prudent interpretation of King's (2002) evidence is that, like any successful investment, advertising and other promotional efforts that go into the development of well-known brand names do yield some return. Yet while the benefit of accumulated advertising and brand identity may make later entry by new firms more difficult, strategic entry deterrence was not likely the goal of those advertising decisions. Advertising expenses would have been incurred as part of a firm's efforts to market its product and compete effectively with rivals.

## 7.7 EMPIRICAL EVIDENCE ON ADVERTISING AND PRICES

We now turn to the empirical evidence on how advertising affects market prices. A pioneering and well-known study on this topic is Benham's (1972). His study found that the average price of eyeglasses was about 25 percent higher in states that prohibited advertising by optometrists compared with the average price in those states that permitted such advertising. This evidence suggests that advertising, particularly informative advertising that facilitates price comparisons, enhances price competition to a significant degree.

Building on Benham (1972), Kwoka (1984) finds that advertising also lowers the prices charged for optometric services. However, the study also finds that in those states or markets where advertising is legal, optometrists who do not advertise compete in part by raising the time spent with patients. This finding partly dispels the fear that any advertising-induced increase in price competition will lead to lower quality. However, like the cross-sectional industry studies reviewed above, the question of endogeneity and omitted variables in cross-sectional state studies undermine the significance of these results.

Nevertheless, later studies echo Benham's (1972) findings. Glazer (1981) compared food prices in Queens with those in nearby Nassau County during New York City's newspaper strike in the late summer of 1978—a strike that simultaneously shut down all three of the city's major newspapers. In those days, the availability of grocery coupons and food price specials were communicated through the newspapers. However, while Queens relied on the major three newspapers for this service, Nassau County residents had access to local, community-based papers and these did not go on strike. Glazer (1981) found that food prices rose significantly higher in Queens during the first part of the strike, but then fell relative to Nassau food prices once the strike was over.

Milyo and Waldfogel (1999) use what we call a "natural" experiment to study the effect of advertising on prices. In 1996, the US Supreme Court ruled in the *Liquormart* case that Rhode Island's ban prohibiting liquor retailers from advertising their prices was unconstitutional. From that moment on, Rhode Island liquor stores were free to advertise what products they had and what prices they were charging. Milyo and Waldfogel (1999) investigate what effect this change in the law, an exogeneous event, had on Rhode Island liquor prices over the next 15 months, using quarterly data.

However, Milyo and Waldfogel (1999) cannot test the impact of ending the ban just by looking at whether Rhode Island liquor prices rose or fell after the Supreme Court ruling. There may be many reasons why Rhode Island liquor store prices would move in either direction following the end of the advertising ban, e.g., there could at the same time be changes in wholesale prices, changes in labor costs, changes in demand, and so forth. We need to control for all of these to isolate the effect of the ban's ending itself. In medical research this can be done by comparing the outcomes of a group that receives the treatment with those of a control group that is not treated. A "natural" experiment uses the same kind of approach, but with real-world as opposed to laboratory data.

Milyo and Waldfogel (1999) use the neighboring state, Massachusetts, as a control group for Rhode Island, the treatment group where the ban on advertising of liquor prices was lifted. Liquor store advertising in Massachusetts had been legal since well before the *Liquormart* decision. Of course, we should not expect the prices of alcoholic beverages to be the same in both states either before or after the advertising ban was struck down. Unobservable random factors may push prices up or down in one state and down or up in another. In general, we expect that retail liquor prices in Massachusetts prices will differ from those in Rhode Island for several reasons besides differences in advertising laws.

The question that we are interested in is whether the pattern of difference in retail liquor prices in the two states that existed before the *Liquormart* decision changes in any significant way after it. That is, Milyo and Waldfogel (1999) look for a *difference* in the differences in liquor prices that emerged after the Supreme Court's ruling. In particular, if advertising is pro-competitive as Benham (1972), Glazer (1981), Kwoka (1984) and others have found, then we would expect that Rhode Island retail liquor prices would fall *relative* to Massachusetts prices *after* the *Liquormart* case.

To implement a *difference*-in-difference test on the impact of retail liquor store advertising on prices, Milyo and Waldfogel (1999) visited 58 stores in Rhode Island and 57 stores in Massachusetts to record the prices of 33 alcoholic beverages over each of eight, roughly quarterly periods from June 1995 through June 1997. Note that the last five of these periods took place after the May 1996 *Liquormart* ruling, legalizing the advertising of liquor prices. They use these panel data to estimate the following equation:

$$p_{dst} = \theta_s + \gamma_d + \gamma'_d \delta^{RI} + \sum_{t=1}^{8} \alpha_t QTR_t + \sum_{t=1}^{8} \alpha'_t \delta^{RI} QTR_t + \varepsilon_{dst} \tag{7.21}$$

Here, $p_{dst}$ is the price of beverage $d$ at store $s$ in quarter $t$. Because Milyo and Waldfogel (1999) also have data on wholesale prices, they also estimate a version of equation (7.21) with the dependent variable being the markup of retail over wholesale price.

The $\theta_s$ term is a fixed effect variable that recognizes that different stores might differ in costs or other factors that do not vary over time and estimates a different constant term for each state. The $\gamma_d$ term is a similar fixed effect that recognizes that there may be similar, time-invariant factors affecting the price of each liquor beverage. The $\delta^{RI}$ term is a dummy variable equal to 1 if the store is in Rhode Island and 0 if not. This dummy variable allows for some difference in the product fixed effect depending on whether the store is in Rhode Island or Massachusetts.

The test for the impact of alcohol price advertising in Rhode Island is found in the last two summation terms. In each of these, $QTR_t$ is a dummy variable equal to 1 if $QTR_t = t$, and 0 otherwise. That is, $QTR_t$ is 1 if an observation comes from the first of the eight periods, i.e., $QTR_1 = 1$, and $QTR_2 = QTR_3 = QTR_4 = QTR_5 = QTR_6 = QTR_7 = QTR_8 = 0$. Similarly, if the observation comes from the second period, only $QTR_2 = 1$, and all the remaining $QTR_t$ variables are zero, and so on. These time dummies are a way of capturing changes in alcohol prices that are due to timing effects common to stores in both states.

There is also a second set of time dummies that are interacted with the Rhode Island dummy $\delta^{RI}$. Including these dummies therefore permits us to check if there is a *difference* in the time path of prices between Rhode Island and Massachusetts after the *Liquormart* decision. In particular, if advertising is pro-competitive, we would expect the coefficients $\alpha'_1 = \alpha'_2 = \alpha'_3 = 0$, indicating no difference in the relative movements of Rhode Island and Massachusetts prices in the three periods before the Supreme Court ruling, but that the overall effect of $\alpha'_4$ through $\alpha'_8$ would be negative, indicating a fall in Rhode Island liquor prices *relative* to those in Massachusetts after the ruling.

Table 7.5 shows the results of two separate tests, each having both the price and markup as the dependent variable. The first is that $\alpha'_1$ through $\alpha'_3$ are zero, i.e., that Massachusetts and Rhode Island retail alcohol prices and markups moved together *before* the *Liquormart* decision. The test statistic for this case has an $F$ distribution. The second test examines whether we can reject the null hypothesis that $\alpha'_4$ through $\alpha'_8$ are all equal to a common and presumably negative value indicating that Rhode Island prices and/or markups fell relative to their Massachusetts counterparts after the advertising

**Table 7.5** Difference-in-difference test of effect of advertising on retail liquor prices in Rhode Island (RI)

| Test that RI liquor prices and markups moved similarly to those in Massachusetts when advertising was banned in RI | | Test that RI retail liquor prices and markups moved differently from those in Massachusetts after the RI advertising ban ended | |
|---|---|---|---|
| Prices* | Markups** | Prices* | Markups** |
| $F = 0.45$ | $F = 0.77$ | $t = -0.39$ | $t = -0.80$ |

*Notes:* *Prices are measured in logarithms. **Markups are measured as log price less log wholesale cost.

ban was removed. Because we are holding the effect to be the same in all periods, it can be represented by one coefficient so that this hypothesis can be evaluated using a standard *t*-test.

Table 7.5 presents both good news and bad news. The good news is that we cannot reject the hypothesis that, after controlling for store and product effects, Massachusetts and Rhode Island prices and markups moved similarly prior to the *Liquormart* decision. Massachusetts is, therefore, a good control group for Rhode Island. The *F*-statistic in either case is not significant at even the 10 percent level. The bad news is that we cannot reject the hypothesis that alcohol prices in the two states continued to move similarly *after* that court decision. The estimated common coefficient for the post-*Liquormart* periods is negative, but far from significant. In sum, it appears that Massachusetts serves as a good control for Rhode Island in this case, but that there is not an overall significant difference between the control group (Massachusetts liquor stores) and the group receiving a "treatment" (Rhode Island liquor stores) after the "treatment" of removing Rhode Island's advertising ban was administered.

Using data with more periods after the *Liquormart* decision could perhaps yield more definitive results. Some evidence for this is found in Figure 7.1 showing average retail liquor prices in both states over the roughly eight quarters that the Milyo and Waldfogel (1999) data cover.

Observe that over the first three observation periods, the two series of prices move similarly. This observation supports the use of Massachusetts liquor stores as a control group comparison for liquor stores in Rhode Island just as found in the regression analysis. However, the similarity in movement continues (in a rough way) over the remaining periods after the ban was lifted. This suggests that the *Liquormart* decision had little impact on Rhode Island retail liquor prices. Again, this is what the regression results implied.

However, note that in the very last period observed, Rhode Island liquor prices do decline sharply relative to those in Massachusetts. Because the Milyo and Waldfogel (1999) data does not extend beyond this point, we cannot know if this decline was sustained. If it was sustained, then it would suggest that permitting alcohol price adver-

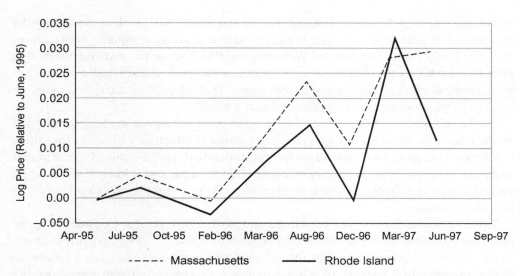

*Note:* The path of retail liquor prices in Massachusetts and Rhode Island before and after retail advertising was legalized in Rhode Island.

**Figure 7.1 Empirical evidence on the effects of retail liquor store advertising**

tising in Rhode Island did intensify price competition resulting in relatively lower state's retail prices—it just took time.

Milyo and Waldfogel (1999) also find that after the ban was lifted it was the low-price liquor stores in Rhode Island that most aggressively took up advertising. Specifically, the Rhode Island stores that began advertising their prices in storefront windows were those that prior to the *Liquormart* decision charged prices 5.56 percent lower than stores that did not take up advertising at all. For those Rhode Island stores that advertised their prices in local newspapers, this difference was an even greater 7.71 percent. This is important. It means that while the end of the advertising ban may not have led to an overall average level of market prices that was lower it may have enabled low-price stores to attract more customers. If so, the average price *paid* by consumers overall would have dropped following the end of Rhode Island's advertising ban.[15]

A third finding in Milyo and Waldfogel (1999) is that when a store advertises a product, the store also drops its price dramatically—by anywhere from 10.5 to 24 percent. Equally interesting, different stores respond differently to a rival store that adopts an advertising-with-price-cut strategy for a product. Stores that do not advertise, do not, in response, lower their prices significantly on that product. However, advertising stores do lower their prices on that product significantly—especially if they are advertising that product themselves. This suggests that price dispersion can persist, and we can have a market equilibrium in which some stores charge high prices and others charge low ones.[16]

Pinske and Slade (2007) also study advertising and pricing in a specific product market. Their results echo the findings of Milyo and Waldfogel (1999), although the econometric approach is quite different. Pinske and Slade (2007) look at the advertising and price decisions of three major brands of saltine crackers competing in ten stores over 101 weeks in the area around Williamsport, PA. Each week, manufacturers set a price to the retailers who in turn set retail prices for the week. Retailers also decide each week about whether to advertise in a local paper. That advertising decision is therefore a 1,0 variable, modeled using a probit regression model.[17]

Pinske and Slade (2007) assume that the advertising decision is made first, followed by the pricing decision. Specifically, retailer $i$'s choice of advertising in week $t$ for saltine crackers sold in store $s$ will depend on its expectation that its rivals will advertise in that week. An expectation is, of course, an unobserved variable, but it likely depends upon variables such as the rival's decision to advertise in the previous period and other factors that are observable.

Table 7.6 shows some of the key Pinske and Slade (2007) results. Consider the price equation estimates shown in the second column of Table 7.6. The first row estimate in this column indicates that a positive decision to advertise locally leads a retailer to reduce the price of a package of saltines by nearly 26 cents. As the average price per package over the sample is on the order of one dollar, this is a roughly 26 percent price reduction. The estimated coefficients on the firm's own advertising in the prior week and on its own price in the previous week, indicate that the bulk of the initial price cut is rescinded in the following week (so long as no more ads are placed). Nevertheless, the

**Table 7.6** Retail price and advertising decisions model for Saltine cracker producers

| Independent variable | Dependent variable | | |
|---|---|---|---|
| | Prices$_{s,t}$ | Advertising$_{s,t}$ | Advertising$_{s,t}$ |
| Advertising$_{s,t}$ | −0.257 | | |
| | (−39.1) | — | — |
| Advertising$_{s,t-1}$ | 0.087 | −0.361 | −0.218 |
| | (10.8) | (−1.90) | (−1.50) |
| Rival Advertising$_{s,t}$ | | −2.474 | −1.320 |
| | — | (−3.30) | (−1.40) |
| Rival Advertising$_{s,t-1}$ | −0.015 | −0.616 | −0.623 |
| | (2.80) | (−4.00) | (−6.00) |
| #Weeks No Ads | 0.004 | 0.031 | 0.030 |
| | (3.30) | (6.80) | (11.40) |
| Price$_{t-1}$ | 0.521 | −1.719 | −1.585 |
| | (33.2) | (−4.40) | (−12.00) |
| Mean Rival Price$_{s,t-1}$ | | −1.672 | −2.841 |
| | — | (−1.40) | (−4.00) |
| *Estimation method:* | OLS | Ordinary Probit | Spatial Probit |

clear implication is that having made the decision to advertise, these firms also decide to make substantial price cuts—a similar finding to Milyo and Waldfogel (1999).

Table 7.6 also shows two versions of the probit advertising equation. One is the straightforward probit approach linking firm $i$'s decision to buy local advertising at store $s$ in week $t$ to its own advertising in the previous week, its rivals' advertising in both the current and past weeks, the number of weeks since firm $i$ has run an ad in that local market, and both firm $i$'s price and the average price set by its rivals in the previous week.

The second is also a probit equation, but it is estimated using a spatial econometrics approach, which recognizes commonalities in firms that are "close" to each other. For example, part of what is in the disturbance term at store $s$ in week $t$ may be something that to some extent is known by all the firms selling in that market even if it affects each firm differently. Similarly, one firm's knowledge that a rival advertised last week will likely affect the likelihood that the same rival advertises this week which, in turn, influences the current advertising decision of the first firm. Spatial econometrics is a way of imposing some structure on these inter-firm relationships such that the coefficient estimates will reflect such interactions.

Three findings are revealed in the probit advertising estimates of Table 7.6. First, recent (i.e., prior week) price cuts tend to lower the probability that a firm chooses to advertise this week. This implies that a firm's decision to advertise leads it to lower its price, but that the low price reduces the likelihood of advertising in subsequent periods. Second, a firm that foresees that its rivals will advertise in the current week is less likely to advertise itself. This suggests that the saltine producers prefer to avoid advertising "wars."

The third finding is that we observe that the magnitude of the probit equation results, although significant, is found to be much smaller when using a spatial probit rather than an ordinary one. The reason is that the spatial estimation procedure recognizes that firms that are "close" to each other are likely to have much in common. In turn, this approach allows for cross-equation relationships that permit using the $X$ variables from one "close" firm to be instruments to deal with any endogeneity issues of the $X$ variables for the other firm and vice versa. If we put some structure on these spatial relations, the spatial approach can be used to deal with such issues as the omitted variable problem.

Pinske and Slade (2007) believe that an important omitted variable for which they do not have data is a store's inventories. Presumably, firms tend to advertise (and set a lower price) when their inventories are high in order to clear them. Moreover, if overall demand in the market is constant and most variability is due to week-to-week changes in which brands are bought, then when a rival's inventories are high, the firm's own inventories are more likely low. When the inventories variable is left out, the effect is likely captured, in a biased way, by the coefficient on rival advertising, making its estimate much larger in absolute terms than is the actual case.

The bias that comes from omitting a key variable can be addressed using some variant of an instrumental variables (IV) approach. The spatial probit equation in Table 7.6 implicitly does this because for each firm, it effectively uses the observable $X$'s chosen by "nearby" rivals as instruments for the $X$'s of that firm. Moreover, as Table 7.6 shows, this IV correction is important. The evidence in Table 7.6 tells us that the effect of the rival firm's current advertising on a firm's own advertising is smaller when the spatial approach is used, and this suggests that there is likely a bias due to an omitted variable.

Milyo and Waldfogel (1999) and Pinske and Slade (2007) focus on narrow product categories, i.e., alcoholic beverages and saltine crackers. However, similar evidence is provided by Chevalier et al. (2003) in an empirical study that looks at weekly evidence over nearly eight years on price and advertising behavior covering 29 different product categories at 100 grocery stores in the Chicago area. Because advertising is expensive, stores must choose which goods to advertise. Chevalier et al. (2003) find that firms simultaneously advertise and cut the prices of a product line during periods of peak demand specific to the product, e.g., holidays, especially those in summer, for beer, and tinned tuna during Lent. They also note that the brand identification created by advertising can help consumers compare prices more easily. A firm's advertising commits the firm to low prices on products precisely when those goods are most salient in consumers' shopping plans. Such price cuts and the advertising that announces them are what gets customers "through the door."

The empirical evidence covered here suggests that advertising and price reductions at the retail level are complementary strategies.[18] At the retail level, advertising, which is by and large informative, is more likely to lower prices. Retailers that tend to offer low prices regularly are the retailers that advertise the most.[19] Whether a retailer advertises frequently or not, when it does advertise a specific product the retailer also tends to reduce the price of that product. These and other findings from the retail sector suggest that advertising intensifies price competition. However, retail price advertising does not lead to the "law of one price" as argued by Stigler (1961).[20]

## 7.8 SUMMARY

In this chapter, we have investigated the impact that advertising has on market outcomes such as firm profitability, entry, and prices. We began by first considering how much a profit-maximizing firm chooses to spend on advertising, and the implied relationship between advertising expenditure and profitability. This set the groundwork for understanding the empirical challenges of identifying causal links between advertising, profitability, and market efficiency.

A correlation between profitability and advertising intensity is often found in real-world data. However, that correlation should not lead us to conclude that greater advertising intensity makes firms more profitable. The Dorfman-Steiner result makes clear that firms with a greater markup of price over cost will advertise more intensely. The causality behind the correlation found in the data may well run from profitability to advertising and not the other way around. This highlights a general difficulty with determining a clear causal relationship in empirical work. Advertising expenditure, like many other dimensions of market performance, is an endogenous variable. Such endogeneity requires the use of instrumental variables or other techniques to ensure that regression analysis is not biased. Similar difficulties arise if a key variable is omitted from the regression, or if there is a selection bias in the data that systematically excludes observations.

It is fair to say that early empirical research into the market impact of advertising was not able to overcome these challenges. Most of those studies were based on cross-industry comparisons and found a positive relation between advertising and profitability, as well as between advertising and market concentration (Comanor and Wilson, 1967; Strickland and Weiss, 1976). These results were undermined by the problems of bias and identification. Perhaps more importantly, the game theoretic approach to competition, that became widespread in the 1980s, cast doubt on whether cross-industry studies could ever overcome problems related to omitted variables.

Empirical research in recent decades is based on data collected at the firm level where the assumption of exogeneity for several variables has been more easily justified. In general, the firm-level studies have found that advertising can play a more pro-competitive role than the older, industry-based studies did. The firm-level research has also shed new light on the positive correlations between advertising and profitability (or concentration). There is evidence to suggest that innovative, cost-efficient firms will advertise heavily to exploit their advantages more fully as in Grossmann (2008) and Dinlersoz and Yorukoglu (2012). As a result, these firms will earn above-normal profits and gain considerable market share.

Evidence that firms strategically use advertising to deter entry is much weaker (Scott Morton, 2000; Ellison and Ellison, 2011). When advertising spills over to rivals it is plausible that the entry-deterring advertising level is *less* than the non-deterrent level. Entry deterrence seems unlikely to be the reason why advertising is excessive from a welfare or efficiency perspective.

There is abundant evidence from the early 1970s that retail advertising is associated with more aggressive price competition. Grocery stores and other retailers use advertising to announce price cuts on specific items and to signal that they are low-price firms in general. This is not to say that advertising leads to the law of one price, as predicted by Stigler (1961). Price dispersion seems to be widespread.

## NOTES

1   See *WebpageFX*, a national web development and marketing company for production expenses of TV campaigns.

2   If the firm was not a monopolist but instead competed with other firms for customers, then its demand function would depend as well on the other firm's prices and advertising strategies.

3   Some analysts transform the elasticity into a positive number by defining it as: $E_P = -\dfrac{\partial Q}{\partial P} \dfrac{P}{Q}$.

4   This assumption may not always hold. Often there is considerable quantity discounting when airtime, network time, or magazine space is purchased by a firm for advertising.

5   This data comes from government filings and published financial records. The companies are classified into industries and the industry advertising-to-sales revenue level is reported each year at: http://www.

rab.com/research/10014.pdf and at http://digitalgabe.com/wp-content/uploads/2018/06/Top-200-Media-Spenders.pdf.

6 Today, we use a more complete measure of industrial structure, the Herfindahl Index $HI = \sum_{i=1}^{n} S_i^2$, where $s_i^2$ is the market share of the $i$th firm squared. For a monopoly, $H_I = 1$ if we measure shares in percent, or 10,000 if we measure them as percentages $\times 100$. For a duopoly of two equal size firms, $H_I = 0.5$ or 5,000, respectively. However, for an asymmetric duopoly in which one firm has an 80 percent market share and the other has only 20 percent, the $H_I = 0.68$ (or 6,800). This contrasts with $CR_4$ (or more appropriately for this case $CR_2$), which would be the same (namely 100 percent) in either of these two examples.

7 Comanor and Wilson (1967, 1974) tend to reach the same conclusion whether $CR_4$ or $HI$ is used.

8 We note that Comanor and Wilson (1967) explicitly discuss the potential endogeneity of advertising and reject it as a confounding factor in their analysis.

9 Manuszak and Moul (2008) also provide evidence that market size is a key determinant of market structure.

10 Alternatively, one can use differenced data (the change in variables from one period to the next) that will wash out those "fixed effects." Chen and Waters (2017) use a dynamic, differenced-data approach that confirms some of the findings in Martin (1979).

11 An important paper by Johnson and Myatt (2006) eschews the persuasive-informative-complementary categorization of advertising in favor of a simple dichotomy: hype and real information. Hype refers to basic features such as availability, durability, low price and other characteristics that appeal to all consumers. Real information refers to particular features such as a small car size or wool clothing material that indicate whether the product matches with an individual's tastes. The impact of advertising depends, in part, on which of these two types firms have an incentive to provide.

12 No selection bias correction is needed in the price equation as the data only includes firms active in both periods.

13 Doraszelski and Markovich (2007) explore how the effects on consumers of advertising in period $t$ fall as period $t$ becomes further in the past. However, there is randomness in this decay. As a result, advertising becomes prohibitively expensive for small firms, especially in small markets. This can lead to an asymmetric equilibrium market structure in which large firms dominate the market and are the only ones to advertise. That is, industry dynamics will naturally yield an equilibrium in which a few, very large firms dominate the market and do the vast bulk of the advertising.

14 Ellison and Ellison (2011) find roughly similar results for advertising in medical journals. An earlier study by Scott Morton (2000) also found only weak evidence that brand name advertising in the pharmaceutical industry acted as an entry barrier for generic drugs. Schmalensee (1983) provides an earlier theoretical model in which an incumbent may *under*invest in advertising to deter entry, an outcome consistent with the evidence in Ellison and Ellison (2011).

15 Retail liquor markets have been the focus of other empirical studies, many of which reinforce the Milyo and Waldfogel (1999) findings. Sass and Saurman (1995), for example, find that alcohol sales are much more concentrated among just a few brands in states that prohibit alcohol advertising.

16 We discussed a two-price equilibrium outcome in Chapter 3.

17 The probit regression model was discussed in Chapter 6.

18 Not all empirical work reaches this conclusion. Iwasaki et al. (2008) provide evidence that advertising has generally raised alcohol and tobacco prices in the US. However, Iwasaki et al. (2008) treat industrial structure as exogenous and increased concentration has a significantly *negative* effect on

prices. If advertising leads to greater concentration this would imply a countervailing price-reducing effect. Somewhat similarly, the tobacco-product price equation estimated by Iwasaki et al. (2008) finds a positive price-effect not only for advertising in general, but also for legislation prohibiting broadcast advertising.

19  Simester (1995) offers evidence that advertised prices are also informative about unadvertised prices when low-cost firms are the ones that advertise very low prices.

20  Ellison and Ellison (2009) provide evidence that Internet advertising often uses obfuscation techniques that can increase effective price dispersion. Such techniques can include offering a very low price but adding on high shipping fees and advertising a low price but later revealing that this is only for a low-quality product or one with a high product-return fee. Anderson and Renault (2006) provide a model in which firms deliberately reduce the detailed information content of their advertising to attract a larger group of consumers with less specialized tastes to their stores.

## 7.9 REFERENCES

Anderson, S., and R. Renault. 2006. "Advertising Content." *American Economic Review* 96 (January), 93–113.

Bain, J. S. 1956. *Barriers to New Competition*. Cambridge, MA: Harvard University Press.

Benham, L. 1972. "The Effect of Advertising on the Price of Eyeglasses." *Journal of Law & Economics* 15 (October), 337–52.

Chen, J., and G. Waters. 2017. "Firm Efficiency, Advertising, and Profitability: Theory and Evidence." *Quarterly Review of Economics and Finance* 63 (February), 240–48.

Chevalier, J., A. Kashyap, and P. Rossi. 2003. "Why Don't Prices Rise During Periods of Peak Demand? Evidence from Scanner Data." *American Economic Review* 93 (March), 15–37.

Comanor, W. S., and T. A. Wilson. 1967. "Advertising, Market Structure and Performance." *The Review of Economics and Statistics* 49 (November), 423–40.

Comanor, W. S., and T. A. Wilson. 1974. *Advertising and Market Power*. Cambridge, MA: Harvard University Press.

Dinlersoz, E., and M. Yorukoglu. 2012. "Information and Industry Dynamics." *American Economic Review* 102 (April), 884–913.

Doraszelski, U., and S. Markovich. 2007. "Advertising Dynamics and Competitive Advantage." *Rand Journal of Economics* 38 (Autumn), 557–92.

Dorfman, R., and P. Steiner. 1954. "Optimal Advertising and Optimal Quality." *American Economic Review* 44, 826–36.

Ellison, G., and S. F. Ellison. 2009. "Search, Obfuscation, and Price Elasticities on the Internet." *Econometrica* 77 (March), 427–52.

Ellison, G., and S. F. Ellison. 2011. "Strategic Entry Deterrence and the Behavior of Pharmaceutical Incumbents Prior to Patent Expiration." *American Economic Journal: Microeconomics* 3 (February), 1–36.

Glazer, A. 1981. "Advertising, Information and Prices: A Case Study." *Economic Inquiry* 19 (October), 661–71.

Grossmann, V. 2008. "Advertising, In-House R&D, and Growth." *Oxford Economic Papers* 60 (January), 168–91.

Hall, P., and N. Heckman. 2000. "Testing for Monotonicity of a Regression Mean by Calibrating for Linear Functions." *Annals of Statistics* 28 (February), 20–39.

Heckman, J. 1979. "Sample Selection Bias as a Specification Error." *Econometrica* 47 (January), 153–61.

Iwasaki, N., Y. Kudo, C. Tremblay, and V. Tremblay. 2008. "The Advertising–Price Relationship: Theory and Evidence." *International Journal of the Economics of Business* 15 (July), 149–67.

Johnson, J., and D. Myatt. 2006. "On the Simple Economics of Advertising, Marketing, and Product Design." *American Economic Review* 96(3), 756–84.

King, C. 2002. "Marketing, Product Differentiation and Competition in the Market for Antiulcer Drugs." HBS Working Paper No. 01-014.

Kwoka, J. 1984. "Advertising and the Price and Quality of Optometric Services." *American Economic Review* 74 (March), 211–16.

Manuszak, M., and C. Moul. 2008. "Price and Endogenous Market Structure in Office Supply Stores." *Journal of Industrial Economics* 56 (March), 94–112.

Martin, S. 1979. "Advertising, Concentration, and Profitability: The Simultaneity Problem." *The Bell Journal of Economics* 10 (Autumn), 639–47.

Milyo, J., and J. Waldfogel. 1999. "The Effect of Price Advertising on Prices: Evidence in the Wake of *44 Liquormart.*" *American Economic Review* 89 (December), 1081–96.

Pinske, J., and M. Slade. 2007. "Semi-Structural Models of Advertising Competition." *Journal of Applied Econometrics* 22 (December), 1227–46.

Sass, T., and D. Saurman. 1995. "Advertising Restrictions and Concentration: The Case of Malt Beverages." *Review of Economics and Statistics* 77 (February), 66–81.

Schmalensee, R. 1983. "Advertising and Entry Deterrence: An Exploratory Model." *Journal of Political Economy* 91 (August), 636–53.

Scott Morton, F. 2000. "Barriers to Entry, Brand Advertising, and Generic Entry in the US Pharmaceutical Industry." *International Journal of Industrial Organization* 18 (October), 1085–1104.

Simester, D. 1995. "Signaling Price Image Using Advertised Prices." *Marketing Science* 14 (May), 166–88.

Stigler, G. 1961. "The Economics of Information." *Journal of Political Economy* 69 (June), 213–25.

Strickland, A., and L. Weiss. 1976. "Advertising, Concentration, and Price Cost Margins." *Journal of Political Economy* 84 (October), 1109–21.

US Supreme Court. 1996. *44 Liquormart, Inc. v. Rhode Island*, 517 U.S. 484.

# 8
# Deceptive Advertising and Puffery

## 8.1 INTRODUCTION

Informative advertising is a way that firms can promote the attributes of their products and compete for consumers. But how informative is any advertising? Some advertising contains very little information at all. Moreover, when it does, it seems likely that the informative content will be biased in favor of the firm that creates and pays for such advertising. For example, publishers of this book could advertise that our book "is one of the most important and relevant books published in a long time." This strikes even the authors as a biased view but, at the same time, we cannot say that the advertising is false! Such a statement is in fact hard to prove or disprove as it is more of an opinion than a verifiable claim.

Advertising that is an exaggerated claim about a product is known as "puffery." Puffery is essentially a vague or subjective claim that cannot be verified. Puffery is not illegal. However, advertising that crosses the line between stating an exaggerated point of view and creating false expectations in the minds of consumers can be found to be deceptive and that is unlawful. One challenge that policy-makers face is the difficulty of identifying that line. Different individuals and different government agencies may draw it quite differently.

Puffed up claims such as "we are better than the competition" may strike some as a claim that could be tested for its truthfulness. If that is the case, the firm making such a claim could be sued if it can be shown that the claim misled consumers. As we shall see, this is exactly what happened in a dispute between Pizza Hut and Papa John's when Papa John's ran an advertising campaign in which each ad ended with the slogan "Better Ingredients. Better Pizza." Pizza Hut viewed this claim as verifiably false. Accordingly, it sued Papa John's for deceptive advertising.

Our goal in this chapter is to understand the economic implications of deceptive advertising however it is defined as well as the impact of efforts to protect consumers against such advertising including how these may alter market outcomes. We begin the next section with a quick review of the regulatory framework that has evolved regarding commercial speech. We then explore the blurred line between outright deceit and puffery as exemplified by the Pizza Hut and Papa John's dispute and the role that policy can play in preventing false claims.

In section 8.4, we examine the incentives that may lead firms to engage in deceptive advertising and the behavior of consumers who recognize that some of the ads they receive may be untruthful. Considering these two elements together allows one to develop and test hypotheses regarding the market impact of deceptive advertising.

## 8.2 ADVERTISING REGULATION

In the US, speech is generally protected by the First Amendment, even speech that some may view as hateful and obnoxious.[1] Almost from the beginning, however, the federal and state legislatures and courts treated commercial speech differently and not as free from government regulation. Many states have imposed legal bans on advertising the price and availability of various products, such as prescription eyeglasses and alcohol.

At the federal level, a number of US agencies are involved in the regulation of commercial speech. The Federal Communications Commission (the FCC) oversees all content on mass-media including radio, television, cable television, and direct broadcast satellite with the goal to either limit the audience exposed to or prevent altogether obscene, indecent, or profane material. In recent years, however, the rapid spread of customized digital advertising targeted to specific customers based on extensive information regarding buying habits, location, and other personal data has raised deep concerns over consumer privacy. The FCC has also been the primary agency assigned to regulate such practices with a view to protect consumer data.[2]

A very different role is performed by the Food and Drug Administration (FDA), which is concerned with the content of advertising for drugs and supplements. For many, if not most consumers, such medications are often referred to as credence goods because it is very difficult, if not impossible, for the typical consumer to know the quality or efficacy of the therapy. For example, a patient taking medication to reduce blood pressure may not be able to judge whether the medication is working any better than would a treatment based on exercise and diet modification—even after taking the drug for some time.

In this and similar cases, experience is not informative and the patient either has to believe that the medication works (or not) as well as that it is safe. The FDA regulations are mainly meant to ensure that advertising for drugs does not mislead consumers regarding the conditions for which a drug is appropriate and effective, and to alert consumers both to possible side-effects and to those medical conditions that would make taking the drug dangerous.

The primary federal agency charged with preventing deceptive advertising, however, is the Federal Trade Commission (FTC). While the FTC was established largely to enforce the antitrust laws, the 1914 Act that created the agency explicitly viewed deceptive practices as a form of unfair competition that hurt consumers. It therefore empowered the FTC to issue "cease and desist" orders to corporations deemed to be employing such tactics.

Yet despite such authorization, it is generally fair to say that the FTC did very little policing of advertising until after two, very critical reports emerged in 1969. These were the Nader Report (Cox et al., 1969) and the closely associated report of the American Bar Association. Both reports found that the FTC had done little to protect consumers against fraudulent advertising. They found that this was particularly true for advertising targeted to those unable to detect misrepresentations before buying and also the least able to obtain an effective remedy after making a purchase and discovering the deception. Such groups included, in particular, the elderly, the poor, and children.

As documented by Clarkson and Muris (1981), the 1969 reports led to major changes at the FTC. Whole divisions were reorganized, and more than half of the top staff members were discharged. Most importantly of all, a new policy often referred to as the Advertising Substantiation Program (ASP) was initiated. In brief, the ASP required that claims of a verifiable nature must have prior, fully documented, and adequate substantiation. Effectively, this new approach shifted the legal burden from the FTC's having to prove a claim false to one in which the advertising firm had to prove that its claim was substantiated by clear evidence. This made it much less costly for the FTC to pursue deceptive claims more vigorously.

The signs that the regulatory wind had changed came quickly. In 1970, the FTC asked several companies to provide substantiation for many of their product claims. Subsequently, several firms were issued cease and desist orders, e.g., Firestone was required to stop claiming that its tires stopped a car "25 percent faster" than rival tires did. The central case though was the FTC complaint against the Pfizer pharmaceutical company regarding advertising for its tanning lotion product, *Unburn*. The ads in question claimed that *Unburn*'s ingredients (which included alcohol) not only aided tanning, but relieved sunburn pain because they anesthetized nerves in sunburnt skin. While the charges against Pfizer were ultimately dismissed, the FTC's ruling in the case made it clear that the litmus test for deception now included the need for clear supporting evidence of any verifiable claim *prior* to running the advertisement. Absent such a requirement, the FTC argued, deceptive advertising would unfairly advantage the firms who engaged in it and unfairly burden consumers with the risk that the product might not work as described, if at all.[3] Many state agencies have since adopted ASP policies.[4]

In addition to the government agencies discussed above, there are also several non-governmental organizations that play an important role in advertising regulation, or more specifically in advertising self-regulation. These include the Better Business Bureau (BBB) which sets standards for business practices, including advertising practices. Together with the American Association of Advertising Agencies, and the American Advertising Federation and the Association of National Advertisers, the BBB has formed the National Advertising Review Council (NARC) to foster a culture of truthfulness and accuracy in advertising through voluntary self-regulation. NARC programming provides an alternative to the federal and state regulations for settling disputes about advertising claims. There is also the Interactive Advertising Bureau (IAB), which includes the major media and technology companies responsible for selling the vast majority of online advertising in the US. Their purpose is to educate marketers and, more generally, the business community about advertising standards and practices. The

ADVERTISING AND THE MARKETPLACE

IAB tries to work with federal agencies to help shape legislation and maintain effective self-regulation of advertising, including online digital advertising practices.

The network of federal, state and local government, and non-government offices provides important avenues for consumer protection against deceptive advertising practices. But what about a firm's protection—specifically, protection against misleading claims that are made by a rival competitor? If a rival firm's advertising is false or misleading, the plaintiff firm may bring a legal case under the Lanham Act. The Lanham Act is the main federal trademark statute that prohibits trademark infringement, trademark dilution, and false advertising. Specifically, section 43(a) of the Act states that: "Any person who, in commercial advertising or promotion, misrepresents the nature, characteristics, quality, or geographic origin of his or another person's goods, services, or commercial activities, shall be liable in a civil action by any person who believes that he or she is likely to be damaged by such act."

The plaintiff firm seeking remedy via the Lanham Act must establish: (1) that a false or misleading statement of fact about a product has been made; (2) that such statement either deceived, or had the capacity to deceive, a substantial number of potential consumers; (3) that the deception is material, in that it is likely to have notably influenced the consumer's purchasing decision; (4) that the product is in interstate commerce; and (5) that the plaintiff has been or is likely to be injured as a result of the statement at issue. A plaintiff that prevails on a Lanham Act claim can obtain an injunction against the false or misleading advertising, as well as damages and, in certain cases, attorneys' fees.

The Lanham Act is the principal way for firms to discipline advertising practices in the marketplace. A firm's rivals become the enforcement mechanism. The Supreme Court made this point clear in their argument in the 2014 case of *POM Wonderful LLC v. Coca-Cola* where they state that "Competitors who manufacture or distribute products have detailed knowledge regarding how consumers rely upon certain sales and marketing strategies. Their awareness of unfair competition practices may be far more immediate and accurate than that of agency rule makers and regulators."[5]

Under the Lanham Act, the plaintiff firm must demonstrate that the defendant firm's advertising is either literally false or is likely to mislead consumers. Advertising claims of superiority that are subjective and vague are, on the other hand, considered to be non-actionable claims or puffery. Non-actionable puffery is exaggerated, blustering, and/or boasting statements upon which *no reasonable* buyer would be justified in relying. Puffery is a general claim of superiority over comparable products that is so vague that it can be understood as nothing more than a mere expression of opinion. We review in the next section an interesting case that revolved around the line between puffery and deception.

## 8.3 THE EXTENT OF FALSE ADVERTISING CLAIMS

How extensive is false advertising? Answering this question accurately requires considerable care. There is a difference between puffery or exaggeration and outright deception, which is false.

Savvy consumers will recognize a firm's incentive to exaggerate. They will, therefore, not believe excessive claims even when the firm engages in them. In short, exaggerated claims are not deceptive. Deception is a false statement and falsification may be demonstrated, and therefore legally actionable, only when a firm makes a claim about something that can be tested against real evidence.

There are, however, some reasons to think that the market itself provides protection against outright fraudulent or deceptive advertising. First, to the extent that experience reveals the truth about a product, firms will be reluctant to develop a reputation for dishonesty. Firms that lie will not be believed even when telling the truth, and firms with shaky reputations will need to sell at a lower price to attract customers. Moreover, in the case of outright fraud, consumers can seek legal action that can prove very costly for a firm regardless of the impact that this may have on its reputation. In addition, firms that win business by deceptive advertising almost always do so at the expense of their rivals. So, there is also an incentive for these competitors to blow the whistle on fraudulent advertising.

However, there is reason to doubt that such forces will work to eliminate all deception from the marketplace. To begin with, reputation effects may not emerge in the short run. In that case, the immediate profit gain from deception may well outweigh the discounted value of losses that a reputation for deception ultimately brings. Second, while it is true that customers may be able to seek legal relief from a firm that deceived them, such relief can be prohibitively costly to pursue, especially for consumers with limited incomes and limited abilities to understand the nature of the deception.

This is also the main reason why the threat of legal action by a rival may not be a very effective deterrence against a firm engaging in fraudulent advertising. Legal action by rival firms cannot be counted on to dissuade a corporation from advertising deceptively if in fact it can be very difficult to win such cases. Advertising is an essential part of competition. Hence, courts and government agencies must be careful not to suppress one firm's advertising simply because it causes another firm to lose business. Second, the line between exaggeration or puffery, on the one hand, and outright fraudulent complaints, on the other, is very blurred. In practice, it can be very difficult to determine that a firm crossed that line with an illegal claim. The *Pizza Hut/Papa John's* case, which we cover next, illustrates these points.

## 8.3.1 The Pizza Wars: Puff, Puff, or Lies?

In 1995, Papa John's pizza stores launched a new, national advertising campaign. At the heart of this effort was the claim that Papa John's used better ingredients than its rivals and, therefore, produced better pizza. Hence, each TV and radio ad ended with the phrase: "Papa John's—Better Ingredients. Better Pizza." As Papa John's campaign grew, it began to broaden its claims of superiority. In some ads, it named unpleasant ingredients allegedly found in some Pizza Hut recipes. It ran ads stating that while Papa John's used fresh tomatoes and filtered water to make its sauce and dough, it did not use "hydrolyzed soy protein" or similar additives and "whatever water came out of the tap" used by other pizza stores.

In another ad, Papa John's claimed that it won "big time" in a taste test against Pizza Hut. Perhaps the most effective ad used by Papa John's was one that featured the co-founder of Pizza Hut, Frank Carney. Carney had left Pizza Hut and the pizza business altogether, but then was lured back to become a major franchise operator of Papa John's stores. The ad claimed that this was because "he liked the taste of Papa John's pizza better than any other pizza on the market."

In the mid-1990s when Papa John's initiated its ad campaign, Pizza Hut (and Domino's) were far bigger companies operating perhaps four times as many stores as Papa John's. However, as the ad campaign unfolded, it seemed to have some effect as Papa John's market share began to rise. The then-CEO of Pizza Hut, David Novak, decided to take action. Pizza Hut filed a civil action in the US District Court for the Northern District of Texas charging Papa John's with false advertising in violation of Section 43(a)(1)(B) of the Lanham Act.[6]

Initially, a jury sided with Pizza Hut, agreeing that Papa John's claims of better sauce and dough were false and misleading as defined by the Act. The judge ordered Papa John's to stop using the "Better Ingredients. Better Pizza" slogan in any future ads and to pull all current ads that used that slogan. In addition, Papa John's was ordered to pay Pizza Hut more than $12.5 million in damages.

However, Papa John's appealed the decision. The firm argued that the "Better Ingredients. Better Pizza" slogan was simply a matter of opinion, not to be taken as literal fact. It was, the company argued, the actual belief of Papa John's management and therefore involved no falsification or deception. Papa John's turned the tables a bit by arguing that its claims were no more exaggerated than the one made by Pizza Hut that it had "the best pizza under one roof."

In September 2000, the 5th US Circuit Court of Appeals sided with Papa John's and reversed the decision of the lower court jury. In justifying this ruling, the appeals court said that the jurors were never asked if consumers relied on Papa John's "better" claims when deciding what pizza to buy. The court further ruled that describing a "pizza" as "better" is an unquantifiable claim. Hence, the "Better Ingredients. Better Pizza" slogan is a statement of non-actionable opinion. In the end, Papa John's was allowed to continue use the "Better Ingredients. Better Pizza" slogan, and the award of damages was vacated.

We can draw three conclusions from this "pizza wars" case. First, the line between mere exaggerated puffery and actually deceptive advertising is a blurred one. Reasonable people—including reasonable judges—will disagree about when that line has been crossed. Second, the threat of legal action by either firms or consumers will not likely be enough to eliminate deceptive advertising. Pizza Hut is a large corporation with enormous legal resources, yet it still lost the case. A smaller pizza company would find the cost of a legal challenge to be a tough barrier to overcome. Similarly, the case also casts doubt on the ability of consumers to win or even to pursue such claims given that their resources are typically much fewer than those of Pizza Hut.

Finally, there is the danger that established, well-known firms (e.g., Pizza Hut) may charge rivals with false advertising to suppress competition and entry. Recall that Papa John's was about one quarter of the size of Pizza Hut at the time that the "Better Ingredients. Better Pizza" campaign was launched. It is now on the order of half as large. It is plausible that Pizza Hut's filing suit was motivated by the hope that extensive legal action could limit the success and growth of a vigorous new rival. Again, advertising is one of the competitive tactics firms employ, and policy must take care to avoid making it easy for established firms to abuse their power by using this tactic to suppress competition.

## 8.3.2 Evidence on the Existence of Deceptive Advertising

Consumer rationality and access to legal remedies are not likely to eliminate deceptive advertising altogether. Economists suspect therefore that some deceptive advertising will happen. Finding evidence though that may guide us in understanding both the impact of such deceptive practices and how policy might best respond requires some thought. For economists, it is natural to look to settings in which the incentives for making false or misleading claims are strong. One characteristic that may make such advertising particularly attractive is the presence of high "switching costs." By this, we mean a situation in which the consumer finds it difficult to switch to an alternative company once the consumer has selected one in particular.

For example, once a consumer brings a car to a repair shop, it is not easy to begin searching for alternative services. Similarly, once a consumer makes a reservation and then arrives at a hotel, it can be quite difficult to find different lodgings if the hotel amenities are not as promised or if hidden fees push the price much higher than advertised.[7]

Another possible setting in which consumers may have difficulty switching is a ski resort. Ski lift operators typically report conditions and the amount of fresh snow on a daily basis. However, once a skier drives to a particular ski mountain in a particular area, the cost of traveling to an alternative ski site if conditions at the first are not as advertised can be prohibitive. Not surprisingly, ski resorts consequently have an incentive to exaggerate the amount of new snow that has fallen. This incentive is likely to be particularly strong on weekends when there are many one- or two-day skiers. Those who ski during the workweek include many who likely booked far in advance before any current information on snow conditions could be known.

This heuristic thinking lies behind the simple econometric investigation of Zinman and Zitzewitz (2016). Essentially, they look for a "weekend" effect in fresh snow reported by ski resorts. Using daily snow report data from roughly 400 different resorts over the four consecutive ski seasons running from 2004–2005 to 2007–2008 (over 56,000 observations), they estimate the following simple regression:

$$S_{R,t} = \alpha_W + \beta_R + \gamma * Weekend_t + \varepsilon_{R,t} \tag{8.1}$$

Here, $S_{R,t}$ is the new snow reported by resort $R$ on day $t$. $\alpha_W$ is a fixed effect that controls for the week of that report (weeks in January are naturally snowier than weeks in

March), and $\beta_R$ is a fixed effect for each resort (some resorts may consistently claim more snow than others). The key variable is *Weekend$_t$*, which is a 1,0 dummy variable indicating whether or not the day of the report is a Saturday or Sunday. $\varepsilon_{R,t}$ is of course a random error term.

The key parameter of interest of course is the *Weekend$_t$* coefficient $\gamma$. If this is significantly positive, it offers evidence that ski resorts engage in deceptive advertising precisely when it is most likely to pay off. This is exactly what Zinman and Zitzewitz (2016) find. Specifically, they find that $\gamma$ is positive and significant. On average, they find that ski resorts report about 22 percent more new snow on Saturday and Sunday mornings as opposed to other days of the week. When these reports are compared with actual weather data for the local area, it translates into 12–23 percent more snow than official government sources record, depending on which source is used. They also find that such exaggerations are more likely at resorts that do not offer a money-back guarantee. The nature of the exaggeration is also interesting. Resorts are more likely to round a fractional inch of snow up to a full inch on weekends. They are especially prone to exaggerate when a large amount of snow has fallen and received press attention.[8]

Exaggerating the quality (or misrepresenting the price) of a product is one form of puffery and, possibly, deception. However, as the Papa John's case illustrates, firms may also engage in false practices by disparaging rival products. The Internet has made it easier for consumers to gather information and make more price and quality comparisons. However, the anonymity of the web may permit individuals and firms to make false statements with less fear of being caught.

Mayzlin et al. (2014) explore false advertising on the web by looking at the difference between hotel reviews posted on *TripAdvisor* and *Expedia*. Both sites provide reviews of individual hotels (among other services). A key difference though is that *TripAdvisor* effectively allows anyone to post a review of a particular hotel. In contrast, *Expedia* only permits a consumer to post a review if the consumer booked through its website and stayed at least one night at the hotel in the past six months. This means not only that the reviewer actually used the hotel's services, but also that *Expedia* has information on the reviewer from their credit card. The cost of posting a fake review on *Expedia* is quite high relative to the cost of posting a fake review on *TripAdvisor* in part because the risk of getting caught is much higher.

A hotel that posts positive reviews about itself or negative reviews about a rival, falsely presenting those reviews as authored by an actual consumer, faces significant penalties if caught. This is especially the case if the hotel is one of many operated by large chains such as Hilton or Marriott. This is because if, say, a specific Hilton hotel is found to be posting fake positive reviews about itself or fake negative reviews about a rival, the penalties derived from government actions, private lawsuits, and either *TripAdvisor* or *Expedia* apply to the entire company. Note that even within a hotel chain there can be a further organizational difference in that the hotel may be operated either by an independent owner-operator who claims a direct share of that specific hotel's profits or by an employee-operator who is paid by the hotel chain.[9]

The foregoing considerations led Mayzlin et al. (2014) to develop a model with clear predictions. To begin with, we would expect more fake reviews on *TripAdvisor* than on *Expedia*. Second, this difference should be especially large when the hotel has a nearby rival because such local competition is what may incentivize this deceptive behavior. However, all neighbors are not equal. When the tables are turned and it comes to being the victim of fake bad reviews posted by a nearby rival, the arguments presented above suggest that this will be less likely when that rival is part of a multi-hotel chain and more likely when that rival is an independent operator.

Of course, it is difficult to identify fake bad reviews. Yet, if we can control for all the objective factors that affect a review, the total number of bad reviews a hotel receives will be artificially inflated on *TripAdvisor* relative to *Expedia*, particularly when that hotel has a geographically close rival that is *not* part of a multi-unit chain and that is run by an independent operator. Mayzlin et al. (2014) gather data on the reviews of 2,931 hotels across the US. For each hotel $i$ in each city $j$, they compute the fraction of "bad" reviews (one or two stars out of five) on both *TripAdvisor* and *Expedia*, $FTA$ and $FEX$, respectively. They then estimate a regression of the following form:

$$FTA_{i,j} - FEX_{i,j} = \alpha_j + \beta_1 NMU_{i,j} + \beta_2 NIND_{i,j} + \ Other\ Factors + \varepsilon_{i,j} \qquad (8.2)$$

Hence, the dependent variable is the difference in the fraction of poor (one or two out of five stars) reviews found on *TripAdvisor* versus *Expedia* for hotel $i$ in city $j$. The $\alpha_j$ are a fixed effect allowing for a different mean evaluation in each city. $NMU_{i,j}$ is a 1,0 dummy variable indicating whether the hotel faces a nearby rival hotel that is part of a multi-unit chain. $NIND_{i,j}$ is a 1,0 dummy variable indicating whether the hotel faces a nearby rival that is run by an independent operator. The other factors include such variables as the age of the hotel building, whether it is near a restaurant or near a convention center, whether it offers only guest suites, and other controls. The $\varepsilon_{i,j}$ term of course captures all other random influences on a hotel's rating.

In general, we expect a greater proportion of negative reviews on *TripAdvisor* than on *Expedia* because on the former site it is easier for hotels to post fake negative reviews of their neighbors. More specifically, the earlier discussion of the costs and benefits of posting a fake review implies that $\beta_1$ should be less than zero and $\beta_2$ should be greater than zero. A hotel with a nearby rival is less likely to be the victim of a fake negative review posted by that rival if the rival is part of a multi-unit chain, but more likely to be targeted by a nearby rival run by an independent owner.

These are exactly the outcomes that Mayzlin et al. (2014) find. Specifically, they find that 25 percent of the *TripAdvisor* reviews fall in the one- or two-star category while only 15 percent of *Expedia* reviews do. In addition, their coefficient estimates are: $\beta_1 = -0.0252$ and $\beta_2 = 0.0173$. The former is significant at the 1 percent level and the latter is significant at the 10 percent level. Thus, the Mayzlin et al. (2014) findings are quite consistent with the hypothesis that a hotel with a nearby rival should expect to receive a greater percentage of negative reviews than it would otherwise especially if that rival is run independently, but less so if the rival is one hotel in a sizable chain.

Of course, if a hotel does expect such review manipulation, we might expect it to respond with some puffery of its own by posting *fake positive* reviews. Again, as *TripAdvisor* is more vulnerable to such deception than is *Expedia*, such responses should be more prevalent on the *TripAdvisor* site. Mayzlin et al. (2014) report a regression in which the dependent variable is the difference in the fraction of five-star reviews awarded a hotel on *TripAdvisor* and *Expedia*, respectively.

The results again confirm the underlying hypothesis. A hotel that has a nearby rival that is part of a multi-unit chain (and is therefore less likely to post a fake negative review) has proportionally fewer five-star reviews on *TripAdvisor* than on *Expedia* than one would otherwise expect. Similarly, a hotel with a nearby, independently operated rival (that is more likely to post fake negative reviews) has proportionally more five-star reviews on *TripAdvisor* than on *Expedia* than would otherwise be the case. Both effects are significant at the 10 percent level.[10]

## 8.4 DEMAND AND PROFIT EFFECTS OF DECEPTIVE ADVERTISING

Economists typically assume that consumers are rational. For a variety of reasons including a widespread reluctance to substitute government judgments for those of private individuals, policy-making often makes this same assumption. Consumers are taken to be rational or at least "reasonable." This is perhaps the central reason why FTC regulations do not restrict puffery claims such as "world's best coffee" or "America runs on Dunkin." Implicit in this policy is the view that *no reasonable* consumer would be deceived to think that the firm in question has been officially claimed to sell the best coffee in the world or that all activity in the US would stop if Dunkin' Donuts suddenly ceased operations.

However, there is an equally widely held view that consumers should be able to trust a firm that makes an empirically verifiable claim. In 2013, L'Occitane sold and advertised two costly body creams—Almond Shaping Delight and Almond Beautiful Shape—that it claimed were clinically proven to "visibly refine and reshape the silhouette" and "trim 1.3 inches in just four weeks." As you might suspect, the truth was that no such clinical evidence existed. Hence, the FTC filed suit because, again, the law reflects the general view that consumers should be able to trust that a firm making such an explicit and testable claim will not lie. In January 2014, L'Occitane settled by paying a modest $450,000 fine and agreeing to cease making such a claim.

Of course, the L'Occitane case is neither the first nor the last case of such deceptive advertising. It was one of four companies that the FTC successfully sued in early 2014. Many other such suits have been prosecuted since. Given that deceptive advertising happens, it is natural to ask what the actual impact of such advertising is both for consumers and for the firms engaging in such practices.

In the case of hotel reviews, this is not a completely straightforward issue. In a competitive environment, a firm that engages in deceptive advertising may face rivals who do the same. In such cases, the net effect on consumers' purchasing may be negligible.[11] This implies that the firms would be better off if all could refrain from deception. In other cases, however, we may be able to identify actual gains in sales and profits—at least for the short run—that a firm's deceptive advertising may induce. We briefly consider two empirical studies that offer evidence on this issue.

Cawley et al. (2013) examine the impact of deceptive advertising in a market where deceptive advertising may be expected to occur with some frequency, namely, the market for over-the-counter (OTC) weight-loss supplements. Because such products are regulated as food, and not as drugs, the constraints on their advertising are much looser than those imposed by the FDA. This is likely the reason that the OTC weight-loss market is one in which exaggeration and deception are relatively common. Indeed, so frequent were such excessive claims that in 2002, the FTC issued a lengthy report identifying seven distinct types of deceptive statements common to OTC weight-loss products. Examples include statements that the use of the product will lead to a weight loss of two pounds or more per week for a month or longer without any dieting or exercise, or that using the product will cause permanent weight loss even after its use is discontinued.[12]

Cawley et al. (2013) use data from the Simmons National Consumer Survey covering about 27,000 women and 14,000 men over the 2001–2007 period. The Simmons data are based on a survey of American households across income levels and provide information on consumption behavior, magazine reading, and television viewing. This information is gathered using both face-to-face interviews and subsequent written questionnaires with those interviewed. These interviews specifically include questions such as whether the subject is watching their weight, whether they have taken OTC supplements, and whether they have engaged in any physical fitness programs such as an aerobics or Pilates class over the last several weeks.

Cawley et al. (2013) then analyze all OTC ads in the consumer magazines and television outlets that the respondents either read or watched and classified these as deceptive if they contained any of the statements identified by the FTC as deceptive in its 2002 study. This allows for identification of each subject's exposure to both total OTC advertising and the percentage of that total which is considered deceptive.

With these data, Cawley et al. (2013) estimate a separate logit regression for men and women in which the dependent variable is 1 if the subject used an OTC supplement over the past year and 0 if not. Among the various variables used to explain this choice are: (1) the total amount of advertising to which the subject was exposed; and (2) the percentage of those ads that included a deceptive statement—both for print and for television advertising, separately—defined as advertising that included at least one of the FTC criteria noted above.

The results are decidedly mixed. For women, they find that advertising OTC products has little overall effect whether it is deceptive or not. Depending on the precise specification, they find that either the positive impact of deceptive ads on TV, which tends to increase women's use of OTC weight-loss products, is offset by the negative impact of deceptive ads in print media that tends to decrease such use, or the net overall effect of deceptive ads is negative for women.

Perhaps somewhat surprisingly, Cawley et al. (2013) find that it is men who are more susceptible to advertising for OTC products. In particular, raising the fraction of deceptive weight-loss advertisements that male respondents typically view significantly raises the likelihood that they will use an OTC weight-loss product. The effect though is not large. Even a 50 percent increase in the fraction of print ads viewed that are deceptive results in only a little over a 1 percent increase in the likelihood of using an OTC weight-loss product.

Overall, the Cawley et al. (2013) findings suggest that deceptive advertising does not have a consistently large effect in the OTC weight-loss product market. Such advertising may slightly increase the use of such products by men, but it has either no effect or a negative effect on women's use of such products. This overall lack of any strong effect may be because rational consumers do ignore deceptive advertising.[13]

Alternatively, the lack of any strong effects in the Cawley et al. (2013) study may reflect that a deceptive advertisement for brand X of an OTC weight-loss drug increases the likelihood one uses the Brand X product, but decreases the likelihood of using an alternative brand with little net increase in the probability of using an OTC weight-loss product overall. Their study is not particularly well-suited to identify the gains to any *one firm* from deceptive advertising.

Rather than focusing on how deceptive advertising affects consumer's behavior, Rao and Wang (2017) examine the effect of deceptive advertising on a firm's market share and profitability. Consider a duopoly comprised of two firms, denoted by superscripts 1 and 2, respectively. Assume as well that each consumer buys exactly one unit each period and that the population of consumers is given at $\bar{Q}$. Hence, $\bar{Q}$ units are sold each period.

Let $Q_t^i$ be the units sold by firm $i$ in period $t$. Because there are only two firms, we must have $Q_t^1 + Q_t^2 = \bar{Q}$. Let $s_t^{i,j}$ be the fraction of firm $i$'s customers in period $t-1$ that switch to rival firm $j$ in period $t$. Similarly, let $r_t^i$ be the fraction of firm $i$'s customers in period $t-1$ that continue to purchase from firm $i$ in period $t$. Then the following must hold for firm 1:

$$Q_t^1 = s_t^{2,1} Q_{t-1}^2 + r_t^1 Q_{t-1}^1 \tag{8.3}$$

Firm $i$'s market share at time $t$ is $m_t^i = Q_t^i / \bar{Q}$. Again, the duopoly assumption implies that the two market shares must always sum to unity. Hence, we may rewrite equation (8.3) as:

$$m_t^1 = s_t^{2,1}(1 - m_{t-1}^1) + r_t^1 m_{t-1}^1 \tag{8.4}$$

Of course, symmetric equations similarly describe the output and market share of firm 2.

Because a firm's customers in period $t-1$ must either remain with it in period $t$ or switch to a rival, it should also be clear that $r_t^i + s_t^{i,j} = 1$. In a long-run equilibrium without deceptive advertising, we will assume that $r_t^i = \bar{r}$ and $s_t^{i,j} = \bar{s}$ for both firms,

$i = 1,2$. It is then easily verified that in such a long-run equilibrium, the market share of each firm will be:

$$m_t^1 = m_t^2 = \frac{\overline{s}}{1 - \overline{r} + \overline{s}} = \frac{\overline{s}}{2\overline{s}} = \frac{1}{2} \tag{8.5}$$

However, deceptive advertising by, say, firm 1 can disturb the equilibrium of equation (8.5). Imagine for example that firm 1 engages in deceptive advertising in period $t-1$ and that its advertised claims, e.g., *Frosted Mini-Wheats* increases children's attention ability by 20 percent, are not known to be unfounded by consumers. Then in the subsequent period $t$, we would expect not only that many of its existing customers stay with the firm ($r_t^1, r_t^2$ unusually high), but also that many of firm 2's customers would switch to firm 1 ($s_t^{2,1}$ unusually high). On both counts, firm 1's market share rises and firm 2's declines. However, once the deception is realized and consumers understand that firm 1's claims are not valid, the market should start to revert back to the initial equilibrium.

The foregoing analysis is essentially the argument that Rao and Wang (2017) test. To be precise, they consider four cases in which the FTC eventually forced firms to discontinue deceptive product claims. One of these, in fact, involved the claim by Kellogg's that its *Frosted Mini-Wheats* had been shown to increase children's attentiveness by nearly 20 percent. This message ran for over a year until April 2009 when the FTC issued a consent decree forcing Kellogg's to stop these advertisements because they were not valid. Not only were the television ads and package labeling changed, but major newspapers and news services covered the announcement of the settlement, including the fact that the company also agreed to pay a $4 million settlement in a related class-action lawsuit.

The second and third cases both involve the yogurt products produced by Dannon. In one case, Dannon falsely advertised from February 2006 to December 2010 that *Activia* yogurt could improve intestinal digestion. In the other case, the company's advertisement from January 2007 to December 2010 claimed that its yogurt drink *Dan Active Yogurt* strengthened the body's immune defenses. As the termination date of each advertising campaign suggests, December 2010 was the date at which the FTC announced its settlement in each case. Again, these announcements and the accompanying cease and desist requirements were also reported in the public media.

Rao and Wang (2017) also consider the case of the health supplement, *Airborne*, whose pills are a mixture of vitamins and minerals. *Airborne* had been launched in 2004 accompanied by the claim that it had "guaranteed cold-fighting properties," and that "if taken at the first sign of a cold symptom, its herbal formulation [was] clinically proven to nip most colds in the bud." The FTC decision that Airborne's claims were not supported by evidence was released in 2008 along with a consent by Airborne to stop making such claims.

Rao and Wang (2017) use home scan data from Nielsen to measure monthly purchases among sample households and thereby construct market share estimates both for the firms engaged in deceptive advertising, Kellogg's, Dannon, and Airborne, respectively, and also for their major rivals. They then estimate the following two regressions for each of the four cases.

$$m_{jt}^{D} = \beta_{0j} + \beta_{1j}D_{jt} + \beta_{2j}FTC_{jt} + \varepsilon_{jt} \qquad j = 1, 4 \tag{8.6a}$$

and

$$m_{jt}^{R} = \lambda_{0j} + \lambda_{1j}D_{jt} + \lambda_{2j}FTC_{jt} + u_{jt} \qquad j = 1, 4 \tag{8.6b}$$

Here, $m_{jt}^{D}$ and $m_{jt}^{R}$ are the time $t$ market share of the deceptive advertising firm and the combined market share of its major rivals, respectively. $D_{jt}$ is the number of months that the deceptive advertising campaign has been running up to time $t$. Similarly, $FTC_{jt}$ is the number of months since the FTC sent its cease and desist request.

The logic of the simple model that we discussed above is that the market share of the deceptively advertising firm should rise during the periods before the FTC reveals the deception and fall thereafter. Just the opposite pattern should hold for the market share of that firm's rivals.

If the hypothesis is correct, we should find $\beta_{1j} > 0$ and $\beta_{2j} < 0$ in equation (8.6a). Just the opposite pattern should hold for $\lambda_{1j}$ and $\lambda_{2j}$ in equation (8.6b). The estimated coefficients for each industry are shown in Table 8.1.

The first two columns in Table 8.1 show, for each of the four deceptively advertised products, estimates of the product's monthly gain in market share during the time the deceptive ad ran, i.e., the coefficient $\beta_{1j}$ in equation (8.6a) and its associated $t$-statistic. With the exception of *Airborne*, these estimates are all strongly and significantly positive. For example, the estimate is that Kellogg's *Frosted Mini-Wheats* gained seven one-hundredths of a market share point in each of the roughly 15 months its deceptive ads aired. While this may not seem large, it adds up to a sizable market share rise of over one full percentage point as the ad campaign's cumulative effect, which is substantial given that the *Mini-Wheats* share of the ready-to-eat cereal market was never more than 7 percent and averaged closer to 4 percent during this time. Similarly, strong effects are found for Dannon's *Activia*, and to some extent for its *Dan Active* product as well.

The next two columns show estimates of $\beta_{2j}$ from equation (8.6a) indicating how the FTC's announcement that the advertising claims will be discontinued affects sales of the deceptively advertised good. In part, this serves as a guard against endogeneity issues as all firms typically discontinue any specific advertising campaign once its sales effects begin to wane. In the present cases, however, Rao and Wang (2017) are looking explicitly at the terminations of ad campaigns that presumably are still effective and are only being discontinued because of the FTC. Hence, any loss in sales should reflect losses due to this enforced discontinuance. In this respect, the evidence in Table 8.1 indicates that the abrupt ending of the deceptive advertising was associated with a significant fall in market share for each of the firms whose ad campaign was discontinued.

The second half of Table 8.1 shows the impact of the same two variables—the cumulative time that the deceptive ad has run and the time since the FTC desist letter—on the

**Table 8.1 Effect of deceptive advertising on product's market share**

| Deceptively advertised product | Dependent variable: Market share of deceptive advertiser | | | | Dependent variable: Market share of major rival(s) | | | |
|---|---|---|---|---|---|---|---|---|
| | Cumulative false ad effect | | Cumulative effect of FTC order | | Cumulative false ad effect | | Cumulative effect of FTC order | |
| | Coefficient | t-statistic | Coefficient | t-statistic | Coefficient | t-statistic | Coefficient | t-statistic |
| *Mini-Wheats* | 0.0007 | 7.34 | −0.0005 | −6.03 | −0.0005 | −1.52 | −0.0001 | −0.31 |
| *Activia* | 0.0008 | 19.32 | −0.0022 | −7.64 | −0.0001 | −11.48 | 0.0000 | 0.54 |
| *Dan Active* | 0.0002 | 7.16 | −0.0011 | −5.84 | −0.0001 | −10.38 | 0.0000 | 0.75 |
| *Airborne* | 0.0002 | 1.98 | −0.0006 | −3.06 | −0.0001 | −4.21 | 0.0000 | 0.20 |

market shares of those products that were the major rivals to the deceptively advertised goods. These correspond to the coefficients $\lambda_{1j}$ and $\lambda_{2j}$, respectively, in equation (8.6b). As we would expect, these results imply that rival products suffered a significant loss in market share as a result of Kellogg's, or Dannon's, or Airborne's deceptive advertising. While the estimates of rivals' market share losses do not precisely offset the gains estimated for the deceptively advertising firm, they do generally indicate that a firm's gain in market share from deceptive advertising comes largely at the expense of its rivals.

Rao and Wang (2017) also use their Nielsen data on individual consumers to estimate demand curves for the products using the multinomial approach that we described in Chapter 5. These results are consistent with the market share analysis described above. Together, this evidence indicates that Kellogg's deceptive advertising generated between $59 and $144 million in revenue during the 12 to 32 months that the campaign was aired on television and used in the box cover design.[14]

## 8.5 THE IMPACT OF ADVERTISING REGULATION

Taken together, Cawley et al. (2013) and Rao and Wang (2017) provide mixed evidence regarding the impact of deceptive advertising. The first suggests an outcome where there is considerable deception in the advertising, but that this has only a small impact on consumer decisions. In contrast, the second study finds sizable short-run gains from such deception, although these do tend to disappear as soon as the fraud is revealed. However, if Kellogg's price-cost margin is 7 percent or more, the Rao and Wang (2017) estimates imply that Kellogg's deceptive advertising was profitable even after its payment of $4 million as part of its settlement.

We suspect that such ambiguity about the impact of deceptive advertising is likely to be unresolved for some time. From the consumer's perspective, even the cases described by Rao and Wang (2017) may provide some benefits. The response of the rival firms competing with Kellogg's *Mini-Wheats* may be to set lower prices, and so deceptive advertising could intensify price competition. Even in a world where competition is weak, e.g., a monopoly, the fact that firms are known to often exaggerate the quality of their products may lead savvy consumers to be less willing to pay for products and thereby force firms, even those with a relatively high-quality product, to set a lower price than they otherwise would have done.[15]

In light of the above, the policy issue that emerges is the impact of and the role for advertising content regulation. Can it be effective? If so, how strong should enforcement be?

As for effectiveness, the evidence available is that regulation does have some, if limited, effect. Recall that the FTC launched its Advertising Substantiation Program (ASP) in the early 1970s. Working with very restricted data, Peltzman (1981) finds that firms that were forced to cease and desist their advertising after an ASP-based investigation do less advertising (relative to sales) after such cases. He also finds that firms forced to cease and desist after an ASP-based investigation suffer a significant stock price decline implying a further incentive to forgo deceptive advertising in the first place.

Somewhat more thoroughly tested evidence that the ASP reduced deceptive advertising is provided by Sauer and Leffler (1990). Their approach is a simple yet insightful one. They divide goods into two classes that might be classified as search and experience, but we will adopt their framework here and call them either Type 1 or Type 2. Type 1 goods are ones for which consumers can readily observe or otherwise know key features such as taste or color. Food, soft drinks, and cosmetics could fit within this definition. In contrast, Sauer and Leffler (1990) define a second category of goods that consumers buy infrequently and for which they have little ability to judge the quality except after purchasing and gaining experience with the product. Such Type 2 goods include appliances, furniture, and automobiles.

Sauer and Leffler (1990) argue that deceptive advertising will be concentrated in the Type 2 goods category. The underlying logic is that deception will not be very effective in their Type 1 goods category as it is more difficult to fool consumers about these products. Advertising for these kinds of search goods will, therefore, generally provide information on availability and price. Instead, it is the Type 2 goods category where we should expect deceptive advertising to play a larger role, at least in the absence of any regulation. Because a buyer of such goods typically makes a purchase infrequently, e.g., purchases a car or major appliance only once every five years or so, the profit gain of inducing the consumer to buy the good by way of a false claim that the consumer can only discover *after* the purchase has been made is relatively large. Such a practice makes a profit today and loses little repeat business because consumers do not make many repeat purchases in any case.

The above argument does *not* imply that Type 2 goods will be more heavily advertised overall—only that the fraction of deceptive advertising for such goods will be higher than for Type 1 goods in the absence of any regulation. In this regard, it is important to understand that rational consumers also recognize the above logic. They will recognize that the ads for large-ticket items such as washing machines, dishwashers, and automobiles will contain a large element of hype or deception if there is little enforcement that such ads be accurate. They will therefore tend to discount such ads.

It is in this setting that regulation such as the ASP can have impact. If such regulation reduces the proportion of ads for Type 2 goods that are deceptive—and if this is recognized by consumers—then the credibility of ads for Type 2 goods increases. In turn, this would make them more useful, thereby inducing Type 2 firms to increase their advertising relative to Type 1 as it is now more effective.

To test this hypothesis, Sauer and Leffler (1990) run a very simple regression described by:

$$\text{ADINT}_{it} = \alpha_i + \beta_1 ASP_t + \beta_2 \text{ASP}_t \text{TYPE}_i + \varepsilon_{it} \qquad (8.7)$$

where $\text{ADINT}_{it}$ is firm $i$'s advertising-to-sales ratio in time $t$; $ASP_t$ is equal to 1 if the time period is after the onset of the ASP, and 0 otherwise; $\text{TYPE}_i = 1$ if firm $i$ is a Type 2 firm, and 0 otherwise; and $\varepsilon_{it}$ is a random disturbance term. The estimate of $\beta_1$ will capture how factors which influence advertising intensity changed after the ASP

**Table 8.2** Estimated effect of FTC's ASP on relative advertising intensity across firm types

| Independent variable | Estimated coefficient | t-statistic |
| --- | --- | --- |
| $ASP_t$ | −0.0187 | (7.18) |
| $ASP_t TYPE_i$ | 0.0177 | (4.68) |

policy went into effect. It is the estimate of $\beta_2$ that is of particular interest. This indicates how the advertising intensity of Type 2 firms changed *relative* to that of Type 1 firms with the onset of the ASP. Table 8.2 shows the basic results found by Sauer and Leffler (1990) using a sample of 152 observations from years just before and just after the ASP started.

Both coefficient estimates in Table 8.2 are highly significant. The first coefficient indicates that advertising intensity in general fell after the introduction of ASP—an outcome that Sauer and Leffler (1990) ascribe not to the ASP itself, but to a widespread and sizable increase in the prices media charged for advertising. The second coefficient though says that advertising intensity at Type 2 firms *rose* relative to Type 1 firms once ASP was introduced. In other words, while advertising intensity may have dropped at all firms in the post-ASP era, it fell *significantly less* at firms producing Type 2 or essentially experience goods. This finding is consistent with the hypothesis that Sauer and Leffler (1990) put forward, namely, that by restricting firms' gains from deceptive advertising, the ASP raised the credibility of advertising for Type 2 goods. In turn, this gain in credibility made advertising for such goods more productive and so led Type 2 firms to increase their advertising intensity relative to Type 1 firms.

Some further evidence on the impact of the FTC's ability to limit fraudulent advertising is provided by Avery et al. (2013). We earlier noted the FTC's 2002 report identifying deceptive advertising practices in the OTC weight-loss market. This was followed by a campaign—the Red Flag Initiative—to get industry members to self-screen and self-police so as to avoid such fraudulent statements. Avery et al. (2013) find that this initiative led to a significant reduction in false and potentially misleading statements. The number of ads containing at least one of the seven deceptive statements noted by the FTC fell from nearly 50 percent to about 15 percent. They also found that this reduction was partially, but not fully, offset by a substantial increase in so-called "orange flag" statements that are potentially misleading, but not explicitly deceptive.

In sum, there is clear evidence that FTC policies can limit deceptive advertising. It is equally clear that such deception has not been eliminated entirely. This is probably inevitable given the cost and benefit of efforts to eliminate such fraudulent practices. Moreover, the negative impact of fraudulent advertising may be partially offset by its pro-competitive effect on prices. The bottom line is that while there is evidence that the FTC's policies to limit deceptive advertising have had some success, there is much less evidence on whether the level of such efforts has been optimal.[16]

## 8.6 A NOTE ON "NATIVE ADVERTISING"

In the early 1950s, *The Atlantic Monthly* introduced a new format for advertising known as the "advertorial." An advertorial is an advertisement written in the form of an editorial, which is a form and style consistent with the format of the magazine medium. The first advertorials to appear in *The Atlantic Monthly* were five pages of advertorials paid for by the American Iron and Steel Institute, each labeled "An Atlantic Public Interest Advertisement."[17] The advertorial was an innovation that blurred the line between editorial and advertising. This kind of advertising is now more generally known as native advertising.

Native advertising is advertising that tries to match the form and function of the media platform on which the advertising appears. We focus on media as platforms in the final three chapters of this book. However, it should be recognized here that the rapid rise of such platforms—whether as news media, social networks, or other services—has been accompanied by a rapid rise in digital advertising to the point that in 2018 such advertising comprised roughly 60 percent of expenditures in the US for digital display.[18] An increasing share of this advertising has been native advertising, which actually has a long history that predates the digital media platforms even though it may seem like a new phenomenon.[19]

The distinctive feature of native advertising, and the one from which its name derives, is that the promotional material is presented in a format that closely replicates the hosting site. As a result, it may be difficult for even a reasonable consumer (as defined by the FTC) to distinguish between the host and the advertiser. Without that distinction, however, the commercial may be taken to carry the endorsement or backing of the media host. Thus, an ad posted to the *New York Times* website may take on the look and feel of a *New York Times* article, much the way that the *Atlantic*'s printed advertorial mimicked an *Atlantic* opinion piece (and much the way that TV "infomercials" of the late twentieth century looked a lot like actual network documentaries).

Because the FTC has been, since its inception, charged with the task of preventing commercial deception, it has had to address native advertising explicitly. As a result, the FTC released in 2015 its first extended statement regarding its Enforcement Policy on native advertising. In that statement, it made clear that it would apply the same truth-in-advertising principles that it follows in determining deceptive advertising practices in general when determining whether a native advertisement on digital media platforms is deceptive.[20] In particular, the FTC's announced approach will again be based on whether a "reasonable consumer" would recognize the commercial nature of any ad considered as well as the identity of the advertising firm as distinct from that of the medium host. The FTC's statement took special effort to make clear that among the sources of deception it would consider would be efforts to present the advertisement in a setting and format that closely replicated the consumer's experience with other, non-commercial material on that site.[21]

The FTC's Enforcement Policy statement was quickly followed by a cease and desist order against retailer Lord & Taylor concerning its native advertising. Consequently, many companies have now taken steps to identify their native advertising more clearly. Online news sites, for example, attempt to do this by differentiating what is sponsored content by some visual techniques and/or labels. Buzzfeed now shades sponsored content and inserts the words "Presented by" with the advertised brand's logo. Similarly, the *Wall Street Journal* online labels sponsored content "Content from our Sponsors," and the online magazine *Slate* puts sponsored content in a box explicitly labeled as such.

Yet despite steps like those taken above, concern over native advertising persists. This is in part because increasingly sophisticated digital media techniques may make it hard for even a reasonable consumer to identify the true source of an ad.[22]

The FTC has also recently published a guide for businesses on native advertising on digital media platforms, giving various case studies of when native advertising crosses the line into deception on the basis of the reasonable consumer test.[23] Consider, for example, an app that engages the player in a wilderness survival game. At various steps of the game the player is offered a choice of supplies and equipment, each one accompanied by a short message. Suppose that a player taps on a bar of a brand name soap, with the message "Clean up," and that the player is then taken out of the game and into the soap manufacturer's branded game app. Because the soap icon is similar to other items players can choose in the game, a player might not "reasonably" recognize the icon as an ad before tapping and being taken out of the game.

Alternatively, consider a game app in which the characters wear or use branded products in the game. Such product placement (for which the maker of the branded item may or may not have paid) is not communicated to the player before they start the game. Do either or both of these presentations constitute deception?

The FTC has in fact discussed such cases. It has stated the first case amounts to deception unless the full commercial implications of pressing the branded soap icon are made known to the consumer in advance. However, it has ruled that the second case does not entail deception. In the FTC's view, disclosure of a paid product placement, whether in a game or a film, is not necessary to prevent consumer deception because the branded product could be there even in the absence of any payment as its use can reflect the creative judgment of the game or film creator as to what is realistic and engaging. In the FTC's view, a reasonable consumer will understand that the second explanation is just as likely as the first and, therefore, such a consumer's purchase decision will be unaffected.

As our earlier discussion of deceptive print and television advertising makes clear, the extent and impact of truly deceptive advertising has never been easy to identify. However, policing the deception associated with native advertising is an even more difficult task. This is because it is no longer a question of making a demonstrably false or verifiable claim. With native advertising, the issue is not the claim that is being made, but rather the identity of who is making it and the ability of a consumer to know that a game or app is also (or mainly) a commercial presentation. There is some reason to be concerned that this blurring of endorsement and authorship, function and promotion, is likely to worsen as the digital age progresses.

## 8.7 SUMMARY

In this chapter, we have recognized the fact that some advertising is blatantly deceptive. A ski resort claiming to have four inches of new snow (when it really has just two) or an OTC weight-loss product claiming to induce more weight reduction than fasting are both real-world examples of such fraudulence. In noting this, however, one must recognize that what makes such claims clearly deceptive is that they can be objectively evaluated. Such verification is not possible in the case of many somewhat exaggerated advertising claims such as "the world's best coffee" or the "most original design." Hence, these non-testable claims are not considered deception, but mere puffery.

If all consumers are highly informed and rational, they may not be directly hurt by deceptive advertising. They will see through the false claims and still make correct purchasing decisions. Even in this world, however, false advertising may be harmful because, while consumers see through it, firms may find themselves in a prisoner's dilemma where each firm finds that, given that its rivals are advertising deceptively, it must do the same despite the fact that when all firms do this, no firm gains any advantage. Consequently, each just ends up wasting money on the deceptive advertising expense as in the model suggested by Mayzlin et al. (2014).

However, even reasonably savvy consumers can be hurt when considerable expense has to be incurred in evaluating a claim and when there are important switching costs that make it difficult to switch to another product if a claim is discovered to be false. For example, skiers who make a long trip to an advertised ski resort may find it very hard to turn to an alternative resort even if, upon arrival, they find that the initial resort falsely reported its skiing conditions. Nagler (1993) shows that consumers may also be hurt if they exhibit cognitive dissonance and so are reluctant to switch brands because it is an admission that they made a mistake.

In our view, the evidence is clear that deceptive advertising does happen. Whether it is an unfounded claim by Firestone that its tires stop a car faster, a brazenly exaggerated ski conditions report, a fake review on *TripAdvisor*, or a false claim about an OTC product's ability to induce weight loss, the evidence seems clear that some firms do make some fraudulent product claims.

What is less clear is the ultimate impact of deceptive behavior. Without a doubt, some consumers and some rival firms are hurt by fraudulent advertising. Yet the balance between the gains of preventing such losses and the costs of that effort have yet to be fully addressed. Indeed, some false advertising likely has a pro-competitive effect that brings consumers the benefits of lower prices even as it may mislead them in the choice of goods they purchase at those prices. Rhodes and Wilson (2018) provide a formal model in which such an outcome is quite likely. Petty (1991) provides evidence that in 125 Lanham Act cases considered, one quarter of them involved large firms or trade associations suing new, small entrants. Fears that laws against deceptive advertising may be used to suppress competition are not unfounded.

In short, evidence on the optimal amount of commercial deception and/or enforcement efforts is in short supply. The recent rise of a rather different form of deception, native advertising, is likely to make determination of that optimum even more difficult.

## NOTES

1  The US Constitution's first amendment forbids any law that abridges "the freedom of speech, or of the press."

2  However, legislation in the area of consumer privacy has been difficult and controversial to enact, in part, due to fears that extensive regulation in this area could stifle innovation.

3  See Cohen (1980) for an extensive discussion of the adoption of the ASP standard.

4  As noted earlier, states historically banned many professional groups from any advertising. The landmark US Supreme Court decision (*Bates v. State Bar of Arizona 1977*) effectively ended all such prohibitions.

5  https://www.theantitrustattorney.com/files/2014/06/POM-Wonderful-Case.pdf (accessed 1 October, 2020).

6  http://www.notaromichalos.com/wp-content/uploads/2014/04/LanhamAct43a.pdf (accessed 4 April, 2020).

7  In the late summer of 2019, Attorneys General from Nebraska and Washington, DC filed deceptive advertising lawsuits against the Marriott and Hilton hotel chains. The suits charged the hotel chains with engaging in "drip pricing" by which customers were charged various fees for such things as Wi-Fi service, gym access, in-room safes (whether they use them or not), newspapers and the availability of bottled water not included in the price advertised with the initial booking (Carrns, 2019).

8  Zinman and Zitzewitz (2016) also note that in 2009, the website *skireport.com* introduced a new feature that made it easier for skiers to use their iPhones to report actual conditions directly from a ski run in real time. They offer suggestive evidence that this curbs resorts' exaggerations.

9  Of course, every single, independent hotel is run by an owner-operator.

10  Note that the Mayzlin et al. (2014) analysis implies essentially combative and, therefore, wasteful advertising competition. Firms post fake negative reviews about rivals and fake positive reviews about themselves that tend to cancel each other out. In equilibrium, consumer choices are the same as they would have been without such deception, but no firm can unilaterally stop making these efforts as it would then be at a significant competitive disadvantage.

11  This is implicit, for example, in the theoretical model in Mayzlin et al. (2014).

12  For a full list of the specific deceptive claims commonly made in the OTC weight-loss market see FTC (2002).

13  This is the case in the formal model that underlies the paper by Mayzlin et al. (2014).

14  The authors point out that these numbers should be regarded as an upper bound because the company might have launched other marketing activities independent of the false-claims campaign during this period.

15  This is precisely the point made by Rhodes and Wilson (2018).

16  See Darby and Karni (1973) for an informative discussion of the optimal amount of fraud.

17  D. Snyder, "Business Is the Public's Interest," *The Atlantic Monthly* (1951).

18  https://www.emarketer.com/content/us-native-digital-display-advertising-forecast (accessed 10 April, 2020).

19  For some historical background to native advertising refer to https://www.ftc.gov/system/files/documents/public_statements/896923/151222deceptiveenforcement.pdf (accessed 22 December, 2019).

20 https://www.ftc.gov/system/files/documents/public_statements/896923/151222deceptiveenforcement.pdf. For background research informing their statement see https://www.ftc.gov/reports/blurred-lines-explora tion-consumers-advertising-recognition-contexts-search-engines-native (accessed 27 May, 2021).

21 https://www.ftc.gov/system/files/documents/public_statements/896923/151222deceptiveenforcement.pdf, p. 11 (accessed 22 October, 2020).

22 See Shirooni (2018).

23 These examples are taken from the FTC Guide for Businesses on Native Advertising: https://www.ftc.gov/ tips-advice/business-center/guidance/native-advertising-guide-businesses (accessed 1 December, 2020).

## 8.8 REFERENCES

Avery, R., J. Cawley, M. Eisenberg, and J. Cantor. 2013. "Raising Red Flags: The Change in Deceptive Advertising of Weight Loss Products after the Federal Trade Commission's 2003 Red Flag Initiative." *Journal of Public Policy and Marketing* 32 (April), 129–39.

Carrns, A. 2019. "Marriott and Hilton Sued Over 'Resort Fees,' Long a Bane for Travelers." *New York Times*, August 23, B5.

Cawley, J., R. Avery, and M. Eisenberg. 2013. "The Effect of Deceptive Advertising on Consumption of the Advertised Good and its Substitutes: The Case of Over-the-Counter Weight-Loss Products." NBER Working Paper 18863.

Clarkson, K., and T. Muris. 1981. *The FTC Since 1970*. New York: Cambridge University Press.

Cohen, D. 1980. "The FTC's Advertising Substantiation Program," *Journal of Marketing* 44 (Winter), 26–35.

Cox, E., R. C. Fellmeth, and J. E. Schulz. 1969. *The Nader Report on the Federal Trade Commission*. New York: Grove Press.

Darby, M., and E. Karni. 1973. "Free Competition and the Optimal Amount of Fraud." *Journal of Political Economy* 16 (April), 67–88.

FTC. 2002. "Weight Loss Advertising: An Analysis of Current Trends." https://www.ftc.gov/sites/default/ files/documents/reports/weight-loss-advertisingan-analysis-current-trends/weightloss_0.pdf (accessed 28 May,2021).

Mayzlin, D., Y. Dover, and J. Chevalier. 2014. "Promotional Reviews: An Empirical Examination of Online Review Manipulation." *American Economic Review* 104 (August), 2421–55.

Nagler, M. G. 1993. "Rather Bait Than Switch: Deceptive Advertising with Bounded Consumer Rationality." *Journal of Public Economics* 51 (July): 359–78.

Peltzman, S. 1981. "The Effect of FTC Advertising Regulation." *Journal of Political Economy* 24 (December), 403–81.

Petty, R. 1991. "Competitor Suits Against False Advertising: Is Section 43(a) of the Lanham Act a ProConsumer Rule or an Anticompetitive Tool?" *Baltimore Law Review* 20 (Spring), 381–427.

Rao, A., and E. Wang. 2017. "Demand for 'Healthy' Products: False Claims and FTC Regulation." *Journal of Marketing Research* 54 (December), 968–89.

Rhodes, A., and C. Wilson. 2018. "False Advertising." *RAND Journal of Economics* 49 (Summer), 348–69.

Sauer, R., and K. Leffler. 1990. "Did the Federal Trade Commission's Advertising Substantiation Program Promote More Credible Advertising?" *American Economic Review* 80 (March), 191–203.

Shirooni, C. 2018. "Native Advertising in Social Media: Is the FTC's 'Reasonable Consumer' Reasonable?" *Washington University Journal of Law and Policy* 56 (April), 219–308.

Zinman, J., and E. Zitzewitz. 2016. "Wintertime for Deceptive Advertising?" *American Economic Journal* 8 (January), 177–92.

# 9
# Advertising, Signaling, and Product Quality

## 9.1 INTRODUCTION

In this chapter, we again explore the idea of advertising as information, but do so in a different way. Specifically, we examine how advertising can be informative even when it does not mention price, location, specific product details, or any other explicit information. This is because advertising's visual and auditory cues often communicate implicitly, as a signal, to consumers.

By way of analogy, consider the peacock's magnificent tail. This very showy and cumbersome plumage is somewhat baffling from an evolutionary viewpoint. It would seem to make the peacock vulnerable to predators and hinder its survival. Yet while peacocks (males) with showy tails share these disadvantages, some may have other potential genetic advantages such as resistance to disease, ability to recognize danger early on, or other positive survival features. Then among those males with magnificent plumage, it will be these genetically advantaged peacocks that are most likely to survive to courtship age. As a result, the peahen (female) that observes a peacock with a particularly beautiful set of tail feathers can infer that this must be one of those males with these other genetic advantages—otherwise, he would not have survived. Accordingly, the magnificent tail becomes a *credible* signal of genetic fitness precisely because only those peacocks with such strengths can absorb the *high cost* the tail brings in terms of survival risk.

Advertising can be creative, eye-catching, elaborate, and, of course, expensive. Its production can include costly celebrities filmed or photographed in luxurious surroundings. Our analogy suggests that it is exactly these features that may enable advertising similarly to serve as a signal of quality, much like the peacock's tail. However, we need to understand just when this signaling role will be sustainable in a market equilibrium. In turn, this means that we need to work out what kind of information about product quality consumers may not have before purchase and the conditions under which advertising could be a reliable *and* credible signal that resolves the uncertainty that consumers still have. In other words, when can advertising permit consumers to figure out whether the seller of an experience good is selling a high-quality or low-quality good? These are the issues that we examine in this chapter.

## 9.2 ADVERTISING SIGNALS: EXPERIENCE GOODS, REPEAT PURCHASES, AND PRODUCT QUALITY

While the work of Nelson (1970, 1974) is some of the earliest work on market signaling, and specifically, advertising as a signal of quality, the work of Spence (1973) is generally regarded as the standard signaling model, and is most helpful in identifying what the critical conditions are for signaling to be effective. In this regard, three requirements stand out. First, consumers must face some uncertainty in the market in the absence of any signal. Signaling can only provide useful information if there is an information gap in the first place.

Second, while consumers have some *ex ante* uncertainty about a product pre-purchase, they can learn about the product's quality with experience. In other words, consumers will be able to verify the signal *ex post* or after purchase. If consumers, not knowing the quality of a product pre-purchase, have a belief that a certain kind of advertising is a signal of high quality then there must be a way to verify that belief. This can only happen if after consumption consumers learn a product's true quality.

Third, there must be some difference between a firm that sells a high-quality product and a firm that sells a low-quality one in the ability of the high-quality one to bear the signaling expense. In Spence's (1973) framework, it is more costly for a low-quality seller to mount a compelling advertising campaign than it is for a seller of high-quality goods.[1] However, there are other mechanisms by which this difference between the two types of firms comes about.

### 9.2.1 A Simple Signaling Example

The initial insight that advertising could play a signaling role is attributed to Nelson (1970, 1974).[2] Nelson understood that firms who produce high-quality experience goods[3] are disadvantaged in the marketplace when consumers cannot distinguish between their products and the goods from firms producing low-quality versions. Nelson (1970, 1974) understood that high-quality firms will therefore have an incentive to find ways to reveal to consumers the better value of their product. Advertising, which is difficult for low-quality producers to imitate, provides such a way.

Nelson (1970, 1974) applies his reasoning to *experience* goods: those goods for which the true quality can only be verified by experience. To this Nelson (1970, 1974) adds the idea that there is value in *repeat sales*. In particular, he assumes that customers who bought a product expecting it to be of high quality and whose experience confirms that expectation will return to buy the product in the future. In contrast, consumers who find out that they purchased, in fact, a low-quality or sham product do not return.

For example, consider the market for a software product in which there is just one firm and it is selling a license to use a program or app that could be either high- or low-quality, each with probability ½. Nature determines which way this chance falls and then the firm knows what kind of app it has. However, the 100 consumers in the market do not. Instead, each simply knows that the probability of either a high- or low-quality app is ½. These consumers are identical. Each is willing to pay $20 for a high-quality app, but only $2 for a low-quality one. There are two market periods, but for simplicity, no discounting between periods.[4] Each consumer buys at most one app today or in the current period. Only if the app proves to be of high quality does a consumer renew it again tomorrow or in the next period. Because it is a software good, the bulk of costs are in the design stage. Therefore, the marginal cost of producing and maintaining the app is relatively low and equal to $5, regardless of its quality.

In the absence of any other information, each consumer, thinking only of today,[5] would be willing to pay ½ ($20 + $2) = $11, or the average expected value for the app in the current period. Once a consumer purchases, the quality of app the firm is licensing will be known. If it is a high-quality app, the consumer will willingly pay $20 to renew the license in the future. If the consumer discovers it is low-quality, then in the future the consumer would be willing to pay only $2, which is lower than the $5 production cost.

Suppose consumers view advertising as a signal. In particular, consumers believe that if advertising reaches a certain level $\hat{A}$, then the app is high quality, whereas if advertising is less than $\hat{A}$, then consumers believe that the app is low quality. A firm that is licensing a high-quality app can work out the following strategic choice. If the firm expends $\hat{A}$ on advertising today then, given consumers' beliefs, the firm can sell at a price of $20 today as well as sell at a price of $20 tomorrow to the repeat consumers who will renew. If the firm with the high-quality app does not spend $\hat{A}$ on advertising, then consumers will believe the product is low quality and will only buy at a price of $2 in the first period. Afterwards, the consumers who initially bought the product at $2, will discover it is a high-quality product and then will renew at a higher price of $20. Hence, the firm can either earn a total profit of ($20 – $5) × 100 + ($20 – $5) × 100 – $\hat{A}$ = $3,000 – $\hat{A}$, or can earn ($2 – $5) × 100 + ($20 – $5) × 100 = $1,200. So, as long as $\hat{A}$ < $1,800, it pays to advertise.

If the firm has low-quality software, what is the incentive to advertise? If the firm expends $\hat{A}$ on advertising, then given consumers' beliefs they will infer that the product is high quality and will be willing to spend $20 to purchase. However, once purchased, consumers will discover the product is low quality and will not buy again. A firm with a low-quality good that advertises would earn in that case ($20 – $5) × 100 – $\hat{A}$ = $1,500 – $\hat{A}$ in the first period. This is all the profit it can earn because once the truth is known, the low-quality firm cannot profitably sell to repeat consumers. The low-quality firm's choice is therefore between incurring the advertising expense and earning a total profit of $1500 – $\hat{A}$, or staying out of the market; i.e., not advertising and not selling its app at all. So, as long as $\hat{A}$ > $1500, staying out is the preferred option.

In short, in this simple example, if the advertising threshold $\hat{A}$ in consumer beliefs is such that $1800 > $\hat{A}$ ≥ $1500, then a separating equilibrium results. The high-quality firm will identify itself as such by spending $\hat{A}$ for advertising, while the low-quality one will not be in the market. To be sure, spending even the lowest threshold of $\hat{A}$ = $1,500 is a costly signal, and the high-quality firm would rather not incur that cost. Again though, it is precisely that cost that allows the advertising to signal credibly that the firm is indeed selling a high-quality app.

## 9.2.2 Advertising as a Signal of Quality

Our example based on Nelson (1970, 1974) is suggestive. However, the equilibrium outcome in the example is sensitive to the parameter values that we choose. For example, if the marginal cost of the low-quality product falls to $2, then the low-quality firm could spend as much on advertising ($1,800) as a high-quality one and masquerade as a high-quality firm. In that case, consumers would soon learn that advertising does not mean high quality and they would change their beliefs.

Note as well that the critical difference between the high-cost and low-cost seller in the example stems not from the *cost* of advertising, but from the *return* to advertising by way of repeat sales. Yet there may be many markets, e.g., those for infrequent purchases such as household appliances, in which repeat sales of the firm are heavily discounted.

Nevertheless, there is an important insight here about advertising. The ability of a high-quality producer to use advertising to change a consumer's belief about what is a high-quality product can perhaps give the firm an incentive to produce high quality. After all, if all consumers believe that all cars are as good as a BMW, then why should BMW produce a higher-quality car?

We want to explore the signaling rationale for advertising more formally. To do this, we begin with a simple price-setting monopoly firm that is selling a product that may be either high ($H$) or low ($L$) quality.[6] Firms can differ in their likelihood of selling high quality. Specifically, the firm can be one of two types. It is either a type 1 firm, in which case it produces a high-quality product with probability $\gamma$, or it is a type 0 firm, in which case it produces a low-quality product with certainty.

A type 1 firm wants to market a high-quality good, but the firm is unsure whether its product will make the grade and turn out to be high quality. An example might be a fashion company marketing a fashion accessory. *A priori*, there is clearly some uncertainty about whether the design and workmanship will be popular. Another example could be a firm marketing a health or beauty product. Again, the firm cannot know for certain whether the product will generally work well for those who buy it. Indeed, the performance of the product may be difficult to prove scientifically.

We assume that whether a firm is type 1 or 0 is determined exogenously, or alternatively by Nature, as a random draw. That is, Nature draws a type 1 firm $\lambda$ of the time. After Nature makes its draw, the firm learns its type and so the firm knows whether it is a type 1 or a type 0 firm. As in our earlier numerical example, we again assume that the firm's variable production cost does not depend on either firm type or product quality.[7] For convenience, we set the production cost, assumed the same for both types of firm, equal to 0.

Before making a purchase, consumers know neither the quality of the product nor the type of the firm marketing the product. Consequently, consumer demand for the product depends on what the consumer believes or expects the quality of the product to be, and/or what type of firm is selling in the market. If a consumer was informed and knew before purchase that the product was high quality, then consumer demand would be $D_H(p)$. Alternatively, if the consumer knew the product was low quality, consumer demand would be $D_L(p)$. If the consumer knew instead that a type 1 firm is selling the product, then demand would be $D_1(p) = \gamma D_H(p) + (1-\gamma)D_L(p)$, whereas if the consumer knew that the firm was a type 0 firm then demand would be $D_0(p) = D_L(p)$.[8] Finally, if the consumer knows neither the quality of the product nor the type of firm selling in the market then demand is $D_P(p) = \lambda D_1(p) + (1-\lambda)D_0(p) = \lambda\gamma D_H(p) + [\lambda(1-\gamma) + (1-\gamma)]$ $D_L(p)$.

If we assume that demand and cost functions are well-behaved, then the firm's profit function will be a concave function in price. The firm will choose that price which maximizes its expected profit, given the demand that the firm faces. We assume expected profits are such that: $\pi_H > \pi_1 > \pi_P > \pi_L = \pi_0 > 0$.

To make the analysis clearer to see, let's consider a demand function where the consumer buys at most one unit of the product.[9] The consumer values a high-quality product at $V_H$ and a low-quality one at $V_L$ with $V_H > V_L$. This means that the profit-maximizing price will always be the one that extracts all surplus for the monopolist.

In principle, there are three types of equilibrium outcomes that may occur: (1) *pooling*, (2) *strong* separation, and (3) *weak* separation. In a *pooling* equilibrium each type of firm, type 0 and type 1, sell their product at the *same* price and the consumer does not know the type of the firm that is selling in the market. The firm will set a price equal to the consumer's maximum willingness to pay in this case:

$$p^{Pooling} = \lambda\gamma V_H + [\lambda(1-\gamma) + (1-\lambda)]V_L \tag{9.1}$$

As each firm knows its own type if not the quality of its product, a firm can try to signal to consumers its type. Signaling depends on some cost differential between the firms that allows the signal to be credible. Before we examine how advertising could be such a signal, it is helpful to note what prices would be set in a *weak* separated equilibrium in which the firm's type (but not product quality) is known by the consumer before purchase:

$$p_1^{Weak} = \gamma V_H + (1-\gamma)V_L \text{ if the firm is type 1}$$

$$p_0^{Weak} = V_L \text{ if the firm is type 0} \tag{9.2}$$

In a *strong* separating equilibrium, on the other hand, a consumer knows exactly the quality of product before purchase. In this case, it is reasonable to assume the firm knows the quality of its product as well. Hence, the equilibrium price will depend on the quality of the good as follows:

$$p_H^{Strong} = V_H \text{ if the firm is selling a high-quality good}$$

$$p_L^{Strong} = V_L \text{ if the firm is selling a low-quality good} \tag{9.3}$$

For a *strong* separating equilibrium to hold, additional information must be acquired about the quality of a type 1 firm's product. We consider that case in the next section.

Let's begin here with the case that a type 1 firm does not know and cannot easily find out what sort of product it is producing.

In order for a *weak* separating equilibrium to hold there must be some way that a type 1 firm can differentiate itself in the eyes of the consumer from a type 0 firm *and* some reason for it to do so. Advertising can play this signaling role if there is something different about the way advertising works at different types of firms. For example, perhaps a certain kind of advertising is more expensive for the type 0 firms than it is for the type 1 firms.

Why should advertising be more expensive for some firms than for others? Specifically, why should it be more expensive, at least at some threshold level, for a type 0 firm than for a type 1? A little thought quickly suggests some possible answers.

One explanation stems from the fact that for certain types of goods, such as fashion, entertainment, and luxury products, advertising campaigns will typically use costly endorsements from celebrities, or the ads will be filmed at resort locations that are both dramatic and luxurious. However, celebrities, resorts, and other ad inputs have their own market to protect as well. Promoting the products with low quality, which is the only quality of product type 0 firms sell, is bad for their business. Accordingly, one reason that type 0 firms might find it relatively expensive to advertise a lot is that they must pay celebrities a sizable premium to compensate them for being associated with firms generally seen as pushing low-quality goods.

Another explanation may simply be that a type 0 firm is not very good at organizing its advertising efforts. After all, a type 0 firm has no intention of producing a high-quality product. That may reflect attitudes and abilities that also make it difficult to produce high-quality ads. Think of the kinds of products that often advertise on late night television when airtime is relatively cheap. It may well be the case that such firms simply do not have the capacity to engage in the high-production value commercials.

Let $C_0(A)$ denote the cost for a type 0 firm of sending $A$ amount of advertising and $C_1(A)$ be advertising cost for firm 1. We assume that beyond some level $\hat{A}$, the cost of advertising for a type 0 firm is higher than for a type 1. Specifically, if:

$$C_0(A) = kA^2$$
$$C_1(A) = \beta A$$

(9.4)

then for $A > \hat{A} = \frac{\beta}{k}$, we have that $C_0(A) > C_1(A)$.

How could consumers use the amount of advertising $A$ to form beliefs about the likelihood that the firm in the market is a type 1 or a type 0 firm? Each firm must conjecture about what consumers would believe if they saw a costly advertising promotion. This conjecture is often called an "out of equilibrium" belief because in any separating equilibrium a consumer does not observe each firm advertising—so the conjecture is what would a consumer believe if they should ever see such advertising, i.e., would such advertising change a consumer's willingness to pay?[10] It seems reasonable to assume that a consumer would believe that if the amount of advertising done by the firm in the market is $A > \hat{A}$, then the firm is a type 1 firm.

Now consider the choice of a type 1 firm. If consumers are using $\hat{A}$ as a threshold, then the firm could advertise at level $\hat{A} + \epsilon$ and, given consumers' beliefs be identified as a type 1 firm. It would then be able to set the price $p_1^{weak} = \gamma V_H + (1 - \gamma)V_L$, and earn profit.

$$\pi_A^1 = [\gamma V_H + (1-\gamma)V_L - C_1(A)] = [\gamma V_H + (1-\gamma)V_L - \beta(\hat{A}+\epsilon)] \tag{9.5}$$

What does a consumer believe if they observe advertising $A \le \hat{A}$? Suppose a consumer believes that in this case the firm is a type 0 firm. This means that a type 1 firm that does not advertise would be considered by a consumer to be a type 0 firm marketing a low-quality good and would earn in this case $\pi_{NA}^1 = V_L$.

Given consumer beliefs what is the choice facing a type 0 firm? If it advertises, then it could masquerade as a type 1 firm and set a higher price, but it would incur the cost of advertising. If it does not advertise, its type and lower-quality good would be revealed to the consumer. The type 0 firm faces the choice between the profit earned by advertising and pretending to be a type 1 firm, which we denote by $\pi_A^0$, and that earned by not advertising and revealing its type, $\pi_{NA}^0$:

$$\pi_A^0 = [\gamma V_H + (1-\gamma)V_L - C_1(A)] = [\gamma V_H + (1-\gamma)V_L - k(\hat{A}+\epsilon)^2] \tag{9.6}$$
$$\pi_{NA}^0 = V_L$$

For the consumer's beliefs to be confirmed by market experience, i.e., only type 1 firms advertise, and for the equilibrium to exhibit *weak* separation, two conditions must hold. First, type 1 firms must find it more profitable to advertise at $\hat{A} + \epsilon$ than not to advertise, or:

$$\pi_A^1 - \pi_{NA}^1 = [\gamma V_H + (1-\gamma)V_L - \beta(\hat{A}+\epsilon)] - V_L > 0 \tag{9.7}$$

Second, a type 0 firm must find that it is more profitable not to advertise than to advertise at $\hat{A} + \epsilon$, or:

$$\pi_A^0 - \pi_{NA}^0 = [\gamma V_H + (1-\gamma)V_L - k(\hat{A}+\epsilon)^2] - V_L \le 0 \tag{9.8}$$

These two conditions may be expressed equivalently as:

$$\gamma(V_H - V_L) > \beta(\hat{A}+\epsilon) \tag{9.9}$$
$$\gamma(V_H - V_L) \le k(\hat{A}+\epsilon)^2$$

For the equilibrium to be *weakly* separated, a type 0 firm must be deterred from advertising. The minimum amount of advertising that would deter a type 0 firm is:

$$A^* = \hat{A} + \epsilon = \sqrt{\frac{\gamma(V_H - V_L)}{k}} \tag{9.10a}$$

However, this level of advertising must be such that it is more profitable for a type 1 firm to advertise than not to advertise, that is:

$$\gamma(V_H - V_L) > \beta A^* \rightarrow \gamma(V_H - V_L) > \frac{\beta^2}{k} \tag{9.10b}$$

If both (9.10a) and (9.10b) hold, then the consumer beliefs will be confirmed by their market experience. Only type 1 firms advertise at a level $A^*$ and neither type of firm has an incentive to change their strategy.

A numerical example may help. Suppose that consumer willingness to pay for a high-quality product is $V_H = 22$, whereas it is $V_L = 6$ for a low-quality product. Suppose as well that the likelihood that a type 1 firm sells a high-quality product is $\gamma = \frac{3}{4}$, so that it sells a low-quality product with probability $1 - \gamma = \frac{1}{4}$. Let the unit production cost of either a high- or low-quality good be the same and constant, and equal to 0. Finally, let the type 1 and type 0 advertising cost functions be: $C_1(A) = \frac{19}{10}A$ and $C_0(A) = \frac{1}{3}A^2$, respectively (i.e., $\beta = \frac{19}{10}$ and $k = \frac{1}{3}$ in equation (9.4)). Accordingly, the two cost functions are equal at $\hat{A} = \beta/k = \frac{57}{10}$.

In a *weakly* separated equilibrium, a firm that advertises at level $A^*$ identifies itself as a type 1 firm. Given consumer demand, a type 1 firm charges a price $p_1^w = \gamma V_H + (1 - \gamma)V_L = \frac{3}{4} \times \$22 + \frac{1}{4} \times \$6 = \$18$. A firm that does not advertise is identified as a type 0 firm and for its product the consumer is willing to pay $p_0^w = V_L = \$6$. A type 0 firm will find advertising at level $A^*$ unprofitable if $p_1^w - \frac{1}{3}(A^*)^2 < p_0^w$, which implies that $12 < \frac{1}{3}(A^*)^2$, and that $A^* > 6$.

Incurring an advertising expenditure of $A^* \approx \$6$ and, given consumer beliefs, a type 1 firm earns a profit roughly equal to [$\$18 - \frac{19}{100}\$6$]. This is greater than earning $6, the profit the firm would earn if it did not advertise and was viewed by consumers as a type 0 firm. By spending a little more than $6, a type 1 firm can ensure that a type 0 firm will not advertise, and it will be able to reveal its identity to consumers through its advertising.

As with Nelson (1970, 1974), advertising signals information regardless of whether the ad messaging provides any explicit information. In addition, the signaling role of advertising suggests that in a longer run framework, the expense of advertising acts as a mechanism to commit the firm to seek higher quality.

It is also worthwhile noting that in the quality signaling framework, advertising expenditures are not efficient. They do not add any economic value, but instead impose additional costs. To see this, consider again the market example with the additional factor that we assume that Nature draws the type of firm with equal probability; that is $\lambda = \frac{1}{2}$.

Suppose there is no signaling and as a result the market outcome is a pooling equilibrium. In that case, the rational consumer expectation is that half of the time the firm is type 0, in which case the good is low quality. The other half of the time the firm is type 1, in which case the good is low quality with probability $\frac{1}{4}$ and high quality with probability $\frac{3}{4}$. Putting these probabilities together, the expected value of the good marketed by a firm whose type is unknown to the consumer determines the price:

$$p^{Pooling} = (1 - \lambda)V_L + \lambda[\gamma V_H + (1 - \gamma)V_L] = \frac{1}{4}\$6 + \frac{3}{8}\$22 + \frac{1}{8}\$6 = \$12 \tag{9.11}$$

As there is no production cost, the total surplus in this case is $12 and all of this goes to the firm.

Now consider a *strongly* separating equilibrium that is somehow achieved without advertising. In this case, consumers somehow know both a firm's type and the quality of the product it is selling. Half the time they know that it is a type 0 firm selling a low-quality product worth and therefore priced at $6. Three-eighths of the time they know it is a type 1 firm selling a high-quality product worth and priced at $22. Finally, one-eighth of the time they know that the firm is of type 1 and its product is low quality. Hence, the expected price in this case is:

$$p^{Srong} = (1 - \lambda)V_L + \lambda\gamma V_H + \lambda(1 - \gamma)V_L = \frac{1}{2}\$6 + \frac{3}{8}\$22 + \frac{1}{8}\$6 = \$12 \qquad (9.12)$$

Again, this implies a total *ex ante* or expected surplus of $12.

Finally, consider the *weakly* separating equilibrium in which consumers know only the firm's type. A type 1 firm sells at a price equal to the expected value of its product, or $18. Likewise, a type 0 firm sells at a price equal to the expected value of its product, namely, $6. Because either type of firm occurs with probability 1/2, the average price is again $12, implying a total surplus again of $12.

What advertising accomplishes is to move the market outcome from, say, the *pooling* case to the *weakly* separating one. It does not in any way enlarge the surplus. In terms of our Chapter 4 discussion, advertising is clearly welfare-reducing in this signaling framework because the cost of the advertising *lowers* the total surplus. This by the way is true for our example illustrating Nelson's (1970, 1974) intuitive model as well.

To be sure, the lack of any positive benefits for advertising in our discussion of advertising is partly an artifact of the demand structure we have assumed. That structure implies that the same number of purchases happens regardless of the type of equilibrium that prevails. Because the expected value of a purchase in any equilibrium is the same ($12), the total surplus is also identical.

However, it could be that as the likelihood of a high-quality good increases market demand expands. This could occur if, contrary to our assumption that consumers are risk neutral, they are risk averse. In that case, a weakly separating equilibrium in which advertising reveals a type 1 firm and therefore a greater probability that a good purchased from that firm is high quality will lead to increased demand. Because in this case, advertising works as a signal that increases demand, it *can* raise the total surplus and be welfare enhancing.

## 9.3 REGULATION OF DECEPTIVE ADVERTISING AND QUALITY SIGNALING

We discussed many of the issues surrounding deceptive advertising in the previous chapter. One issue related to that topic that we did not discuss, however, is how regulation of deceptive advertising could play a role in incentivizing the use of advertising to signal quality. This is the topic to which we now turn.

Let's suppose that the *content* of advertising can act as a signal, just as we have now shown. Specifically, we consider the ability of firms to make *verifiable* claims in their ads, i.e., ones that are not puffery, with the additional feature that there is a regulator, e.g., the FDA or FTC, that can levy a penalty if such a verifiable claim is found to be false.

Of course, including a verifiable claim in an advertisement *does* potentially provide some information and blurs the line between signaling and informative advertising. However, making a verifiable claim is only informative if consumers can reasonably believe the claim is true. We saw in Chapter 8 that the over-the-counter market for health and wellness goods is full of "claims" that cannot be backed up with evidence.[11] We want to identify here the key conditions by which a legal penalty for making a false claim or advertising deceptively can help to make such claims informative.

Even if there is no penalty levied, there may be a financial cost to a false advertising campaign. This is because the authorities can issue a cease and desist order to stop the advertising campaign. As some of the campaign's costs are sunk, and therefore lost, such an order imposes costs even in the absence of a formal penalty.

### 9.3.1 Signaling Product Quality and Penalties for Deceptive Advertising

To illustrate how regulation of advertising claims that are in principle verifiable affects a firm's incentive we will continue with the previous model.[12] There is a firm selling a product that may be either high ($H$) or low ($L$) quality. The firm is one of two types, either a type 1 firm that produces a high-quality product with probability $\gamma$, or it is a type 0 firm that produces a low-quality product with certainty. Nature draws a type 1 firm $\lambda$ of the time, the firm learns its type and knows whether it is a type 1 or a type 0 firm.

The firm's variable cost function does not depend on either type or quality. In this scenario, however, we will assume that each firm has the *same* cost of advertising a verifiable claim, which is constant and equal to $\bar{A}$. The differential in cost between the two types of firm comes about because of the regulation of deceptive advertising. In terms of expected values, type 0 firms face a higher expected penalty than type 1 firms.

In the absence of any advertising a consumer does not know the type of firm that is in the market. A firm may advertise to the consumer and claim that it is high quality. This claim can be verified either by the consumption experience or by regulators.[13] If the claim is found to be misleading or deceptive, then the firm can be punished by the regulator; e.g., the FTC. We will denote by $\varphi$ the penalty or fine levied to a firm that makes a verifiable claim that is found to be false. We will denote by $\theta$ the probability that the regulator detects a claim when it is false and issues a penalty.

Remember a type 0 firm knows it sells a low-quality good, whereas a type 1 firm does not know for sure whether its good is high quality. A type 0 firm faces a higher penalty cost of making a verifiable claim than a type 1 firm because a type 0 firm always sells a low-quality good whereas a type 1 firm sells a low-quality good only $(1 - \gamma)$ of the time. This difference in the expected cost of penalties that each firm faces is a cost differential that may allow the type 1 firm to signal its type through verifiable advertising claims. Accordingly, we are interested in identifying the conditions for a *weakly* separated equilibrium where verifiable advertising can reveal the firm's type.

We return to our earlier numerical example in which each consumer values a high-quality good at $V_H = \$22$, and a low-quality one at $V_L = \$6$. Recall as well that while a type 0 firm always produces a low-quality good, and a type 1 firm produces a high-quality good with probability $\gamma = \frac{3}{4}$. Consumers know that the firm is either type 0 or type 1 with probability $\lambda = \frac{1}{2}$. We must check under what conditions it will be profitable for a type 1 firm to advertise a verifiable claim that its product is high quality but not be profitable for a type 0 to make the same claim.

From our earlier analysis we know that if a consumer believes that the firm selling in the market is type 1 then the consumer will pay $\$18 = \frac{3}{4} \times \$22 + \frac{1}{4} \times \$6$ for the product. If the consumer instead believes that the firm in the market is a type 0 firm, the consumer will pay only $6. It is the differential cost of making a verifiable claim in advertising that differentiates the two types of firms. Each type of firm bears the cost of advertising $\bar{A}$, but the two types of firms face different costs of being caught making a false claim and subsequently paying a penalty.

Given that the regulatory agency catches false claims with probability $\theta = \frac{1}{2}$, a type 1 firm that produces a low-quality product with probability $(1 - \gamma) = \frac{1}{4}$, has an expected penalty cost of $\theta(1 - \gamma)\varphi = \frac{1}{8}\varphi$ if it advertises its good as a high-quality one. For a type 0 firm that always produces a low-quality good, the expected penalty if its advertising includes a claim to be high quality $\theta\varphi = \frac{1}{2}\varphi$. Each firm also has the option of not advertising its good as a high-quality product, in which case each faces no prospect of penalty and incurs no advertising cost. Note though that there is no reason to spend money on advertising that makes no claim for high product quality, as we have assumed that without such a claim advertising will not be convincing.

If consumers believe that only a type 1 firm advertises a verifiable claim that the good is high quality, and only a type 0 firm does not advertise, then the expected profit for a type 1 firm to advertise or not to advertise is:

$$\pi_A^1 = [\gamma V_H + (1 - \gamma)V_L - \bar{A} - \theta(1 - \gamma)\varphi] = \left[18 - \bar{A} - \frac{1}{8}\varphi\right] \tag{9.13}$$

$$\pi_{NA}^1 = V_L = \$6$$

For a type 1 firm to find it profitable to advertise, it follows that:

$$\pi_A^1 - \pi_{NA}^1 = \left[\$12 - \bar{A} - \frac{1}{8}\varphi\right] > 0 \text{ or } \$12 > \bar{A} + \frac{1}{8}\varphi \tag{9.14}$$

The expected profit for a type 0 firm either advertising $\bar{A}$ that its product is high quality $\pi_A^0$ or not advertising at all $\pi_{NA}^0$ is:

$$\pi_A^0 = [\gamma V_H + (1-\gamma)V_L - \bar{A} - \theta\varphi] = \left[18 - \bar{A} - \frac{1}{2}\varphi\right]$$

$$\pi_{NA}^0 = V_L = \$6 \tag{9.15}$$

For a type 0 firm *not* to advertise and claim a high-quality product, we must have:

$$\pi_A^0 - \pi_{NA}^0 = \left[\$12 - \bar{A} - \frac{1}{2}\varphi\right] < 0 \text{ or } \$12 < \bar{A} + \frac{1}{2}\varphi \tag{9.16}$$

Putting (9.14) and (9.16) together, then leads to the following condition for a weakly separated equilibrium:

$$\frac{1}{2}\varphi > \$12 - \bar{A} > \frac{1}{8}\varphi \tag{9.17}$$

The first inequality in (9.17) says that for a *weak* separating equilibrium, the penalty $\varphi$ must be large enough to ensure that a type 0 firm does no advertising and so makes no false claims to having a high-quality product. The second inequality says that the penalty cannot be so large that a type 1 firm also forgoes any advertising of claims.

Suppose for example that the advertising cost of a verifiable claim of high quality is $\bar{A} = \$6$. The total expected cost of advertising this claim includes the expected cost of penalty as well. If the fine $\varphi > \$12$ then a type 0 firm will find it unprofitable to advertise (falsely) its product as high quality. If $\$48 > \varphi$, then the type 1 firm will find it profitable to advertise a verifiable claim and then incur the penalty $\frac{1}{8}$ of the time.

Because consumers respond to advertising that claims high quality, a penalty of \$12 plus a bit will deter a type 0 firm from doing this kind of advertising at all. The penalty will not, however, deter a type 1 firm from advertising high-quality product claims. With a penalty $\varphi = \$12$, a type 1 firm will find it profitable to advertise high quality and face the penalty in the event its product turns out to be a low-quality one.

The difference in the likelihood of deception across firm types introduces a differential penalty cost to the different types of firms. More generally the fine $\varphi$ will support a weakly separated equilibrium (denoted by superscript $W$) when the following two conditions on the profitability of type 1 and type 0 firms hold:

$$(1) \quad \pi_1^W - (1-\gamma)\varphi > \pi_0^W \tag{9.18}$$

$$(2) \quad \pi_1^W - \varphi < \pi_0^W$$

Together these conditions imply that to support a weakly separated equilibrium, the regulator must set a penalty such that: $\dfrac{\pi_1^W - \pi_0^W}{1-\gamma} > \varphi > \pi_1^W - \pi_0^W$.

Enforcement of false advertising penalties can support a weakly separated equilibrium even though both firm types have the same explicit advertising cost. Higher penalties (or higher rates of detection and enforcement) would lead to a lower threshold of advertising able to sustain a weakly separating equilibrium where consumers can learn a firm type from advertising. Raising the penalty may seem attractive if advertising has no positive social welfare benefits as discussed earlier. Raising the penalty too high, however, will force even a type 1 firm to stop advertising. This will undo the weakly separating equilibrium and push the market back into a pooling outcome in which consumers will be less certain of the quality of good they are buying. Again, this will have negative welfare consequences if consumers are risk averse.

If it is feasible for the regulator to verify whether the advertising claim of high quality is deceptive, then it seems reasonable to suppose that the firm itself could engage in some form of product testing to learn the quality of its product. Only a type 1 firm has the incentive to do testing. A type 0 firm does not need to engage in product testing as it knows that it has a low-quality product.

Engaging in product testing is a costly activity for the firm. Suppose that a type 1 firm incurs a cost $\tau$ to test its product and learn the quality of its product before marketing it. Of course, by doing the testing, the type 1 firm avoids incurring a fine when it has a low-quality product. When will a type 1 firm have an incentive to test, or not to test?

Consider a *weakly* separated equilibrium. Given the consumer's belief about what is the type of firm that advertises, i.e., the consumer is willing to pay $p_1^w$, a type 1 firm will not find it profitable to engage in testing when the following holds:

$$\pi_1^W - (1-\gamma)\varphi > \gamma\pi_1^W + (1-\gamma)\pi_0^W - \tau \qquad (9.19)$$

The left-hand side is the profit that the type 1 firm earns if it does not test and advertises high quality, in which case $(1 - \gamma)$ of the time its advertising is discovered to be deceptive and the firm pays a fine. The right-hand side is the expected profit that the firm earns if it incurs the testing cost and learns the product's true quality before marketing. When the firm learns that the product is high quality ($\gamma$ of the time) the firm advertises high quality, but because the consumer infers from this advertising only that it is a type 1 firm, the consumer is willing to pay the type 1 price. If after testing the firm learns that its product is low quality, then the firm will not advertise in order to avoid the cost of the fine.

For the consumer's beliefs to be validated in a weakly separated equilibrium, i.e., the consumer can only infer firm type but not product quality from advertising, it follows that the left-hand side of equation (9.19) must be greater than the right-hand side, otherwise the type 1 firm will engage in product testing and consumer beliefs would change. This inequality implies that for a weakly separated equilibrium the size of the penalty, relative to costly testing, must be such that:

$$\pi_1^W - \pi_0^W < \varphi < \pi_1^W - \pi_0^W + \frac{\tau}{(1-\gamma)} \qquad (9.20)$$

Of course, if testing were relatively inexpensive, i.e., if $\tau$ were relatively low, it would be difficult for (9.20) to be satisfied. A type 1 firm would always find it profitable to test and avoid the cost of being fined when its product is low quality. In this case, consumers would come to understand or infer from an ad verifiably claiming high quality that the product is in fact a high-quality product with complete certainty.

## 9.3.2 Private Quality Testing and Signaling

The market outcomes in the signaling equilibria we have so far examined have been weakly separating. The level and content of advertising has signaled the type of firm, but not the product quality itself. Is it possible that we can ever achieve a strongly separated market equilibrium such that consumers always know the type of product they are getting?

In many industries, such as pharmaceuticals, firms expend significant resources doing pre-market testing of the quality of their product. Of course, in the context of the model with which we have been working, only a type 1 firm will do any testing. A type 0 firm is by assumption fully informed about its product quality.

Suppose then the type 1 firm incurs a cost of $\tau$ to test its product and learn the quality of its product before marketing it. Its advertising can back up a verifiable claim with test results. Under what conditions will a type 1 firm choose to test? When will the availability of such testing allow advertising to play a stronger role and allow consumers to use it to identify product quality before purchase?

In a *strongly* separated equilibrium a consumer believes that advertising a verifiable claim means the good is high quality. This is a stronger belief than what a consumer believes in a weakly separated equilibrium. There a consumer believes advertising identifies a type 1 firm, but not necessarily a high-quality product. In a strongly separated equilibrium, a consumer's belief that advertising identifies a high-quality product must be validated by experience. For a *strongly* separated equilibrium, a type 1 firm advertises that its product is high quality only when product testing has shown it is. This occurs $\gamma$ percent of the time. For the other $1 - \gamma$ percent of the time the type 1 firm learns its product is low quality and does not advertise.

Given these beliefs, the expected profit of a type 1 firm that advertises is: $[\gamma(V_H - \bar{A}) + (1 - \gamma)V_L - \tau]$. It follows that for a type 1 firm to choose a testing option we must have:

$$[\gamma V_H + (1-\gamma)V_L - C(A^*) - \theta(1-\gamma)\varphi] < [\gamma(V_H - C(\bar{A})) + (1-\gamma)V_L - \tau] \tag{9.21}$$

Equation (9.21) may be simplified as follows:

$$\tau - [C(A^*) - \gamma C(\bar{A})] < \theta(1-\gamma)\varphi \tag{9.22}$$

The left-hand side of the equation is the net cost of testing. This is the cost of testing less the potential savings in advertising expense reflecting the fact that the firm now only advertises in that fraction $\gamma$ of cases that it knows it has a high-quality product. The right-hand side of the equation is the expected penalty when the type 1 firm does not test and has to pay a deceptive advertising cost of $\varphi$ the fraction $\theta(1-\gamma)$ of the time.

Recall our previous weakly separated equilibrium: $C(A) = \frac{1}{3}A^2$; $A^* = \sqrt{30}$; $C(A^*) = \$10$; $\gamma = 0.75$; $\theta = 0.5$; and $\varphi = \$4$. We will also assume $\bar{A} = \sqrt{18}$ so that $C(\bar{A}) = \$6$. We then have that testing and advertising the test results three-fourths of the time when they indicate high quality will be worthwhile so long as the testing cost (on a per consumer basis) satisfies: $\tau < \$4.50$.

The point is that a strongly separated equilibrium may be possible. What is required is some way, e.g., an independent testing service, for the type 1 firm to signal credibly that its product is high quality *and* that this service not be "too" expensive to make issuing that signal worthwhile. This can prove to be a tall order. Consumers have reason to doubt the independence of tests paid for by the firm whose product is being advertised. Even results reported by consumer services such as *Consumer Reports* or *J. D. Power & Associates* may not be considered definitive. In such cases, reporting test results is simply not enough to move the market to a strongly separating equilibrium.

Indeed, for a wide variety of experience goods, particularly those sold in the health and wellness sector, it can be difficult for consumers to assess the quality of the product even after consumption. These kinds of experience goods are what we call *credence* goods. Not surprisingly, it is often for credence goods that firms make verifiable claims about the product's performance, e.g., "scientifically proven to improve memory." These are claims which are often difficult for the consumer to evaluate both *ex ante* and *ex post*. It is up to the regulator to investigate the advertising claims of these goods and, if the evidence is not found to support the claim, to fine the firms. If there is no important advertising cost difference among the firms selling in these markets, a pooling equilibrium may be the only feasible market outcome.

Here again, it is worth noting that there may be some important welfare concerns in such markets. This is because the trading of low-quality goods in some health markets can lower social welfare. Especially for "credence goods" such as pharmaceuticals whose true quality may be impossible for the consumer to evaluate even after using it, a consumer's true willingness to pay for a low-quality product can be less than unit cost. In this case, total welfare under strong separation is greater than under weak separation, which is greater than the welfare that obtains in a pooling equilibrium. For these markets, there is a strong case to be made for regulation and setting the fine $\varphi$ in such a way to incentivize the type 1 firm to engage in product testing and use advertising to reveal high quality to consumers. This is of course why there is substantially more regulation in pharmaceutical markets than there is in, say, the market for food supplements.

## 9.4 EXTENSIONS OF THE QUALITY SIGNALING MODEL: EMPIRICAL EVIDENCE AND THE ROLE OF PRICES

We have seen that Nelson's (1970, 1974) conjecture that advertising can be informative as a signal of quality even if it contains no explicit product information can hold. Whether it is through repeat purchases or advertising cost differentials, firms more likely to market high-quality goods can, under certain conditions, use advertising to signal the superiority of their products. Indeed, as Milgrom (1981) and Farrell (1986) determined early on, this "quality revelation" likely extends to settings of multiple, but ranked, quality levels. Thus, if no firm in a multiple-quality market has signaled information about its product quality, the top-quality seller will likely have an incentive to do so and thereby identify itself. Once this happens though and the top-quality is known, the average quality of the remaining unidentified firms falls. This particularly hurts the second-highest quality firm and so that firm will likely want to identify itself as well. In short, the theoretical possibility of a separating equilibrium easily extends to a world of more than one quality level.

Whether the conditions necessary for a separating equilibrium are met in practice or whether firms use advertising volume to signal quality at all is, of course, a different matter. The problem is that any empirical testing of the advertising-as-quality-signal hypothesis runs into significant problems very quickly. To begin with, the researcher must identify a clear definition of quality and, in particular, one that the real-world firms know, but the real-world consumers do not. For example, data from public source such as *Consumer Reports* or, say, *Yelp* reviews will not satisfy this requirement.

Second, actual data typically includes both new and established products. Presumably, the quality of the latter groups is known. If, for instance, the established brand is known to be of poor quality, it may not take much advertising for a newcomer to win market share. Of course, the opposite will hold true if the established firm has a good reputation for quality. In empirical work, though, it is very difficult to take account of consumer experiences with established goods. Other differences among firms, such as their production costs, whether they produce other related products, and so on, also present confounding effects.

The above obstacles have not prevented researchers from testing the signaling theory, however. Early work by Kotowitz and Mathewson (1984) on the automobile and insurance markets did not find much support for the use of advertising as a quality signal. The same is generally true for the work of Caves and Green (1996) who tried to examine the advertising–quality relationship across 196 different industries. However, they did find a significant difference between advertising expense and product quality in markets comprised of mainly new goods.

Moorthy and Zhao (2000) offer perhaps the most supportive evidence in their study of ten product groups. They find that a measure of consumers' "perceived" quality is positively associated with the firm's advertising level. However, the relation between advertising and an objective measure of quality is only positive for durable goods. Overall then, the evidence regarding the use of advertising to signal product quality is probably regarded as mixed at best.

Of course, consumers have other ways of inferring product quality besides a firm's advertising level. Often, in fact, it is alleged that consumers use price as a signal of quality as well. Space does not permit a full examination of this argument, but we will point out a few aspects of using price to signal product quality.

First, as with advertising, the effectiveness of signaling quality via pricing must ultimately reflect some fundamental difference other than quality between high-quality and low-quality firms. Second, while it is relatively straightforward to construct such models in which price signals work, the predicted price movement will differ depending on the model chosen. For example, in a model with more than one period in which repeat purchases are important, as emphasized by Nelson (1970, 1974), we might expect high-quality firms to sell initially at a *low* price. This would get more consumers to try the product early on leading to a confirmation of the product's high quality and subsequent repeat purchases, possibly at a higher price.

However, in models based with only one market period such as those in the last section, firms with high-quality products may actually charge a high price to communicate that quality. The intuition behind this result is straightforward. Suppose that the marginal cost of a high-quality product is higher than it is for a low-quality product. In that case, the optimal price for a high-quality seller is higher than it is for a low-quality one, most obviously in the case of complete consumer information. If the high-quality firm raises its price above its optimal full-information level, it clearly loses profit from what it would earn in that case. However, for a low-quality firm to try to masquerade as a high-quality firm by matching that high price, the deviation from its optimal, full-information price is even greater and the profit loss larger. So, it is possible that the high-quality firm can set a price sufficiently high that the low-quality firm cannot profitably match it. In this case, the high-quality firm distinguishes itself by *raising* its price.

It is also possible that advertising and price may be used together to signal quality acting as a two-dimension signal. This is most likely in a setting in which repeat purchases are important, so getting more buyers early on is valuable. Add to this the assumption that, in contrast to the models of the previous section, consumers have elastic demands and will buy more than one unit if the price falls. In that case, one way to get those early customers is to set an initially low price. However, that is costly in terms of forgone profit. Hence, rather than relying solely on a strategy of moving down the demand curve by charging a low price, the firm might want instead to use advertising to push that demand curve out. Because advertising is expensive and cutting the price decreases revenue, this combination also incurs a cost. That though is partly the point. Indeed, the firm's hope is that it is a sufficiently high-cost tactic that a low-quality firm cannot mimic it. Thus, assuming that the high-quality good costs more to produce, a high-quality producer may use a low price and advertising together to signal its type.

## 9.5 ADVERTISING, MATCH QUALITY, AND INFORMATION PROVISION

Our analysis of advertising to signal quality is partly motivated by the observation that much real-world advertising appears to have little informational content. In the absence of such explicit data regarding a product's price, availability, key features and so on, it may still be the case that the volume of advertising effort or advertising expense serves to signal to consumers the kind of firm selling the product or perhaps the quality of the product being sold. This insight is valuable, but still, the question remains as to why firms often use such a signal instead of providing actual information.

### 9.5.1 Choosing How Much Information to Provide

A number of scholars including Lewis and Sappington (1994), Anderson and Renault (2006), and Johnson and Myatt (2006) have addressed this question.[14] Unfortunately, we do not have enough space to review all of these analyses here. Instead, we present a simplified version of the Lewis and Sappington (1994) model that serves to illustrate some key points.

Consider a monopoly marketing a particular version of some good, whose precise value is unknown to each consumer. Once again, we simplify matters by assuming that each of $N$ potential consumers buys at most one unit. Denote by $v_i$ consumer $i$'s true valuation of the monopolist's product. We will assume that $v$ is a random variable, uniformly distributed on the interval [0,1]. Initially $v$ is unknown to each consumer and to the firm, but its uniform distribution is known. Thus, in the absence of any additional information, each consumer's best guess is that their valuation is the expectation or mean of this distribution, namely, $E(v) = \frac{1}{2}$.

As for the firm, we will assume that it has to incur a minimal fixed amount of advertising cost $\bar{A}$. Such advertising has, however, no product information. If the firm wishes, it can include much information in its advertising $\bar{A}$, though this may incur some additional cost. In any event, such information reveals to consumer $i$ with probability $\mu$ their true valuation of the good $v_i$, but with probability $(1 - \mu)$ reveals nothing. Hence, after receiving such information, consumer $i$ updates their expected value of the good from $\frac{1}{2}$ to $v_i' = \mu v_i + (1 - \mu)\frac{1}{2}$. In other words, consumer $i$'s updated valuation $v_i'$ is a weighted average of their true valuation $v_i$ (which they still do not know) and their initial guess or prior belief that $E(v) = \frac{1}{2}$. If the advertising is very informative, i.e., if $\mu = 1$ consumer $i$'s updated valuation $v_i'$ is exactly right and equal to their true valuation. If though the advertising has zero informational content, then each consumer $i$'s best guess remains that their value for the good is $\frac{1}{2}$. Each consumer $i$ will buy one unit if their updated valuation matches or exceeds the price, i.e., if $\mu v_i + (1 - \mu)\frac{1}{2} - p \geq 0$.

For now, we will assume that there is no cost of adding informational content to the firm's advertising. We will also initially assume that the production cost per unit $c$ is constant. Hence, the firm's total cost is: $\bar{A} + cQ$. In fact, it is useful to assume at the outset that $c = 0$. In such circumstances, how much information should the firm provide? What value of $\mu$ should it choose?

A little thought reveals that if $c = 0$, the optimal value of $\mu = 0$ as well. The reason is straightforward. Suppose by contrast that $\mu = 1$, i.e., that each consumer was perfectly informed of her true valuation $v_i$. Recall that these valuations are uniformly distributed over the interval [0,1]. Hence, the optimal price for any value of $p$ must also lie in that same interval. A price of $1 though is so high that it would effectively rule out all consumers. The markup would be high, but virtually no one would be buying. Symmetrically, a price of 0 would attract all $N$ consumers, but generate essentially zero revenue.

If it were possible to price discriminate and if $\mu = 1$, then the firm would charge $1 to that customer with the greatest willingness to pay and then work down the demand curve by reducing the price a bit more to each additional customer so as to charge each their maximum willingness to pay. Effectively, the price would range from \$0 to \$1 over the mass of $N$ consumers, implying an average price of \$0.50 and, therefore, a total revenue of \$$N/2$. Clearly, this is the greatest total revenue that can be derived as the revenue from each individual consumer is, by assumption, being maximized. Of course, if the production cost is $c = 0$, then maximizing revenue would also be the same as maximizing profit given that the firm's only cost is the lump-sum advertising expense $\bar{A}$.

We are, however, ruling out price discrimination. By assumption, the firm has to charge the same price to each consumer. So, if it provides full information such that $\mu = 1$, it will not be possible to sell to all consumers in the market at a positive price. At any $p > 0$, there will always be some consumers who, if $\mu = 1$, know that their valuation is less than that price.

Now consider what happens if the firm includes no information in its advertising and $\mu = 0$. As noted, each of the $N$ consumers in that case falls back on their prior belief that their own valuation of the good is $v_i = \frac{1}{2}$. As a result, each consumer is willing to pay a price of $p = \frac{1}{2}$. With all $N$ consumers willing to pay this amount, the firm sets $p = \frac{1}{2}$, and again earns $N/2$ in revenue, which we know is the maximum possible and the outcome that maximizes profit given that $c = 0$.

The deeper insight that lies beneath the foregoing result is that providing information is a double-edged sword. This is because as individuals become informed about the quality of the match, some learn that they like the good more than they initially thought but some learn that they like it less.

Consider again consumer $i$'s updated valuation $v_i' = \mu v_i + (1 - \mu)\frac{1}{2}$. The derivative of this expression with respect to the amount $\mu$ of information provided is: $\frac{dv_i'}{d\mu} = v_i - \frac{1}{2}$. In other words, as consumers become informed, the updated valuation $v_i'$ *falls* below the initial guess of $\frac{1}{2}$ for those consumers whose true valuations $v_i$ are also below $\frac{1}{2}$. However, for those whose true valuation is above $\frac{1}{2}$, their updated valuation $v_i'$ *rises* above the initial guess of $\frac{1}{2}$ as more information of the quality of the match is obtained. That is, starting with all consumers uninformed and guessing that their true valuation of the product is $\frac{1}{2}$, the provision of any information makes half the consumers realize that this initial guess is too high—they do not really like the product that much. This, of course, reduces their willingness to pay for it.

Matters change a good bit though as the cost of production rises. The easiest way to see this is to recognize that if $c = 0.5$ or higher, the strategy of setting $p = \frac{1}{2}$ and $\mu = 0$ no longer earns any profit. All consumers will still buy a unit, but the price now permits no markup at all, $p = c$. Surely it would be better to inform some customers and lose the business of those whose updated valuation $v_i' < 0.5 < p$, but charge a higher price (and earn some profit) from those who now know that they are willing to pay more.

We can be precise about the role of the production cost $c$ in determining the optimal degree of information provision $\mu$. For any level of information provision $\mu$ and any price $p$, define a critical true valuation value $\hat{v}_i$ such that the updated valuation after receiving informative advertising is: $\mu\hat{v}_i + (1 - \mu)\frac{1}{2} = p$. That is, the marginal valuation $\hat{v}_i$ is the valuation of that consumer such that they are just willing to purchase the product at the price $p$. As that price rises, so does the value $\hat{v}_i$ of the marginal valuation. Solving explicitly for $\hat{v}_i$ yields:

$$\hat{v}_i = \frac{1}{2} + \frac{p - \frac{1}{2}}{\mu} \qquad (9.23)$$

Each consumer with a true valuation $v_i$ above $\hat{v}_i$ will also have an updated valuation $v_i'$ that is greater than $\mu\hat{v}_i + (1 - \mu)\frac{1}{2}$. Hence, each of these will be willing to buy the product at price $p$, as well. In contrast, all those whose true valuation falls below $\hat{v}_i$ will not be willing to buy at price $p$. As the distribution of true valuations spans the interval $[0,1]$, this implies that the fraction of the $N$ consumers who will buy at price $p$ is $N(1 - \hat{v}_i)$. This, of course, is just the total demand, $Q(\mu, p)$, for the product for a given degree of information $\mu$ and a given price $p$. That is:

$$Q(\mu, p) = N(1 - \hat{v}_i) = N\left[1 - \frac{1}{2} - \frac{p - \frac{1}{2}}{\mu}\right] = N\left[\frac{1}{2} + \frac{1 - 2p}{2\mu}\right] \qquad (9.24)$$

In turn, this implies that the firm's profit $\pi$ is:

$$\pi = (p - c)N\left[\frac{1}{2} + \frac{1 - 2p}{2\mu}\right] - \bar{A} \qquad (9.25)$$

There are two fronts on which the firm must optimize. It must choose optimal values for its price $p$ and its information provision $\mu$. These first-order necessary conditions are found by taking the derivative of the profit function with respect to each decision variable separately and setting these equal to 0. The optimal price is then found to be:

$$p = \frac{c}{2} + \frac{1 + \mu}{4} \qquad (9.26)$$

However, the derivative of the profit function with respect to $\mu$ is:

$$\frac{\partial \pi}{\partial \mu} = N(p - c)\left[\frac{2p - 1}{2\mu^2}\right] \qquad (9.27)$$

This is clearly positive for any $p > 0.5$ implying that, once the optimal unit production cost $c$ gets to a level where the optimal price exceeds 0.5, continued increase in $\mu$ up to its maximum value of 1 is warranted. In short, the model has a knife-edge equilibrium in which the firm either provides no information, so that $\mu = 0$, or provides complete information, so that $\mu = 1$. In the first case, it sets $p = \frac{1}{2}$. In the second, it sets a price of $p = \frac{1+c}{2}$.[15]

Matters would change a bit more if it were costly to include information in the advertising. For example, we might have $C(A) = \bar{A} + k\mu$. This, of course, will limit how much information the firm provides. For example, if $c = 0.55$ and $k = 0.05$, the strategy of setting $\mu = 0$ and $p = \frac{1}{2}$ is clearly no longer attractive. However, this will not lead the firm to set $\mu = 1$, and $p = \frac{1.55}{2} = \$0.775$. Its optimal choice will now be to set $p = \$0.675$

and $\mu = 0.6$, well below 1. The basic result that the firm is incentivized to provide no or incomplete information for low and even intermediate levels of $c$ is thus strengthened in a setting in which providing such information is costly.

As noted, the Lewis and Sappington (1994) model is one of a number exploring a firm's decision regarding how much information to provide in its advertising. Anderson and Renault (2006), for example, explore the informational content of advertising when consumers incur a search or travel cost to buy the good. Upon reaching a seller, that cost is sunk and the strategic interaction this implies has implications for the firm's information choice.

Suppose that some consumers have a strong preference for Bosch dishwashers and would pay, say, $1,500 for the Bosch 800 model. Assume further that an appliance store only has Bosch dishwashers. If the store advertises those dishwashers explicitly as Bosch, the ad will mainly attract the Bosch-loving consumers. Knowing that, the store may be tempted to charge a high price, e.g., $1,500, to whoever comes through the door because it is most likely a Bosch fan. Yet the consumers are sophisticated, too. They can see that if they incur the travel/search cost of X to get to the store, then paying a price of $1,500 for a Bosch 800 model will actually leave them worse off. As a result, an ad announcing that the firm has Bosch dishwashers for sale may not get any customers.

However, an ad just announcing that the firm has dishwashers for sale without mentioning any specific brand may attract many customers. Because the firm will not know what type of consumer it is facing, it will have to lower its price to sell to those who are not crazy about the Bosch brand. This of course means that those who strongly prefer Bosch will also get a price break relative to their willingness to pay. Thus, the firm has an incentive in this setting to suppress or not reveal some specific information about its stock of appliances. Note too that such suppression leads to improved market outcomes.

More recently, Kamenica and Gentzkow (2011) offer a novel variation on the issue of information suppression. Suppose consumers know that a firm produces a high-quality good only 30 percent of the time. The other 70 percent of the time its good is low quality. Before marketing the product, the firm can run one of two product tests and it has to release the results of the test to consumers. One test is always correct. If the good is low quality, the test always identifies it as such. Similarly, if the good is high quality, the test always gets that correct, too.

The second quality test procedure is not so accurate. It does always get it right if the good has high quality. However, if the good is low quality it correctly identifies it as such only four-sevenths of the time. The other three-sevenths, the test misidentifies the good as a high-quality type. The first, totally accurate test will report a high-quality product exactly 30 percent of the time. The second test though will report a high-quality product 60 percent of the time. It will not only accurately identify the 30 percent of the time that the product *is* high quality, but also mistakenly report three-sevenths of the 70 percent low quality events (another 30 percent) as high quality as well. Unless consumers know about the alternative, unused test, the firm has a clear incentive to use and report the second test. Here again, the firm selectively reports only *some* information.[16]

### 9.5.2  A Note on the Impact of Competition

Our discussion of how much information a firm will choose to provide has been cast in a setting of a monopoly. This does not mean that it is invalid. Some of the insights surely carry over to a more competitive market environment. At the same time, it is clearly worth considering how competition might change the analysis.

Schmalensee (1978) showed early on that Nelson's (1970, 1974) intuitive results might play out in a number of ways in a setting of imperfect competition. In particular, depending on the values of a few key parameters, the equilibrium could be one in which the *lowest* quality good has the largest market share, the greatest profit, and the biggest advertising budget. The intuition behind these findings is straightforward. A firm selling a low-quality product may not get many repeat sales. However, if the low-quality good is much cheaper to produce, such a firm can still earn considerable profit by advertising heavily to signal (falsely) that it has a high-quality product that commands a high price. With a high price and low cost, such a firm can earn considerable profit from its first round of sales so that the loss of repeat sales is much less important.

Both Meurer and Stahl (1994) and Anderson and Renault (2009) consider the role of competition in the context of our current discussion regarding the explicit choice of information provision. They show that such competitive pressures make it much more likely that product information will be fully disclosed. Their insight is that information disclosure can be used as a way to identify product differences and so, to soften price competition.[17] Anderson and Renault (2009) also show that the market outcome depends on the extent of the differences among firms in terms of product attributes and costs. In particular, they find that information provision motivated by competition has a disproportionate (and negative) impact on the firm with the largest market share.

## 9.6  SUMMARY

Advertising can be informative—telling consumers about the good's price, where to buy it, how well it works and so on. Yet it is commonly observed that much advertising, e.g., television and radio commercials, often has very little if any such informative content. Hence, this observation is a challenge to models that treat advertising as informative.

Nelson's (1970, 1974) work argued that advertising could be informative regarding a product's quality even if it contained no product information explicitly. His argument posits a difference between firms selling high-quality products and those selling low-quality ones in that the cost of advertising is either lower or the returns to advertising higher for the former. Hence, firms offering high-quality products can afford to do more advertising than those selling low-quality goods. Consequently, consumers can identify a high-quality seller by the (large) volume of advertising it does even if that advertising has little explicit information.

In practice, rigorous empirical tests of Nelson's (1970, 1974) hypothesis are difficult to construct. The studies that have been conducted are generally not supportive or inconclusive at best.[18] Moreover, as Schmalensee (1978) and others have shown, the market equilibrium can be very different from that predicted by Nelson's (1970, 1974) analysis once a degree of competition is introduced. Specifically, low-quality firms can have the largest advertising budget and the greatest profit.

In light of the foregoing difficulties with the advertising-as-signal approach, economists have turned to explicit consideration of the firm's decision regarding how much, if any, information to provide consumers. Lewis and Sappington (1994) present a model in which more information is provided for goods that are costly to produce. Anderson and Renault (2006) argue that firms may suppress some information to attract a more diverse and larger group of consumers, suggesting that in some cases at least, information suppression can raise overall social welfare. Here again, empirical testing is not easy. Yet there is little doubt that the theoretical models have been instructive even if much more work needs to be done.

## NOTES

1 Spence's (1973) classic paper was of course about signaling in the job market where imperfectly informed firms comprised the buying side of the market and workers of different quality incurred expenses to signal their value as potential employees.

2 The argument developed in Nelson (1974) was formally modeled by Kihlstrom and Riordan (1984) and Milgrom and Roberts (1986).

3 Recall an experience good is one whose quality can only be ascertained by consumers after they have tried the good.

4 With no discounting, a dollar "today" is worth the same as a dollar "tomorrow."

5 This is a less formal way of saying that consumers are myopic and not thinking about their purchasing in the next period.

6 The model in this section is based on Corts (2014).

7 We discuss price signaling later in this chapter. However, the fact that the firm does not initially know its product's true appeal or quality along with the one-market-period this model assumes, rules out the use of price to signal quality in this analysis.

8 Consumers know that a type 0 firm always produces low quality and a type 1 firm produces high quality with probability $\gamma$ and low quality with probability $(1 - \gamma)$.

9 Similarly, we could assume $N$ consumers that are all identical and each consumer buys one unit of the product. In what follows, we have set $N = 1$.

10 For example, recall that prior to 1982 there was no advertising of legal services. When the implicit ban on advertising was lifted, what did consumers believe about the type of legal firm advertising?

11 Many firms that market products in the health and wellness markets make verifiable claims about their products and often these claims are found to be false. See FTC: https://www.ftc.gov/news-events/press-releases/2017/11/internet-marketers-dietary-supplement-skincare-products-banned (accessed 29 April, 2020).

12 This section is adapted from Corts' (2014) model.

13 That the consumer can identify the quality of the good upon consumption means the product is an experience good, and not a credence good.

14 An earlier contribution is Jovanovic (1982).

15  Some care is necessary here in determining the optimal strategy because in thinking of the optimal price, one must consider the option of $\mu = 0$, in which case the optimal price is exactly ½. The threshold value is $c = 0.414$. In that case, setting $\mu = 0$ and $p = ½$, yields a profit of $\pi \approx 0.086$. Likewise, a firm that sets $\mu = 1$ will set a price from (9.22) of $p \approx 0.707$ and earn a margin of 0.293 on each of the 0.293 units it sells for a total profit of $\pi \approx 0.086$ again.

16  Johnson and Myatt (2006) offer a more nuanced consideration of the information provision issue. In their analysis, the firm's advertising will include little information (other than availability) when consumer tastes are relatively homogeneous, and the goal is to shift the demand curve out. However, when consumers' tastes are significantly heterogeneous, the firm will provide much more real and specific information to indicate the quality of the match to each consumer and so make it possible to charge a high price to those consumers for whom the product is a really good match.

17  When the monopolist chooses to disclose information there is an increase in price as well as now the firm will sell to those consumers who highly value the kind of product marketed by the monopolist.

18  Ellison and Ellison (2009) offer an insightful discussion of information suppression or what they call obfuscation in Internet advertising where firms, for example, may advertise a low price, but offset this with high transport costs that are not revealed until one goes to the product website.

# 9.7 REFERENCES

Anderson, S., and R. Renault. 2006. "Advertising Content." *American Economic Review* 96 (March), 93–113.

Anderson, S., and R. Renault. 2009. "Comparative Advertising: Disclosing Horizontal Match Information." *RAND Journal of Economics* 40 (Autumn), 558–81.

Caves, R. E., and D. P. Green. 1996. "Brands' Quality Levels, Prices, and Advertising Outlays: Empirical Evidence on Signals and Information Costs." *International Journal of Industrial Organization* 14 (January), 29–52.

Corts, K. 2014. "Finite Optimal Penalties for False Advertising." *The Journal of Industrial Economics* 22 (December), 661–81.

Ellison, G., and S. F. Ellison. 2009. "Search, Obfuscation, and Price Elasticities on the Internet." *Econometrica* 77 (March), 427–52.

Farrell, J. 1986. "Voluntary Disclosure: Robustness of the Unraveling Result." In *Antitrust and Regulation*, ed. R. Grieson (91–103). Lanham, MD: Lexington Books.

Johnson, J., and D. P. Myatt. 2006. "On the Simple Economics of Advertising, Marketing, and Product Design." *American Economic Review* 96 (June), 756–84.

Jovanovic, B. 1982. "Truthful Disclosure of Information." *The Bell Journal of Economics* 13 (Spring), 36–44.

Kamenica, E., and M. Gentzkow. 2011. "Bayesian Persuasion." *American Economic Review* 101 (October), 2590–2615.

Kihlstrom, R., and M. Riordan. 1984. "Advertising as a Signal." *Journal of Political Economy*, 92 (June), 427–50.

Kotowitz, Y., and G. F. Mathewson. 1984. "Advertising and Consumer Learning." In *Empirical Approaches to Consumer Protection Economics*, ed. M. Ippolito and D. T. Schefman. Washington, DC: US Government Printing Office, pp. 109–35.

Lewis, T. and D. Sappington. 1994. "Supplying Information to Facilitate Price Discrimination." *International Economic Review* 35 (May), 309–27.

Meurer, M., and D. Stahl. 1994. "Informative Advertising and Product Match." *International Journal of Industrial Organization* 12 (March), 1–19.

Milgrom, P. 1981. "Good News and Bad News: Representation Theorems and Applications." *The Bell Journal of Economics* 12 (Autumn), 380–91.

Milgrom, P., and J. Roberts. 1986. "Price and Advertising Signals of Product Quality." *Journal of Political Economy* 94 (August), 796–821.

Moorthy, S., and H. Zhao. 2000. "Advertising Spending and Perceived Quality." *Marketing Letters* 11 (August), 221–33.

Nelson, P. 1970. "Information and Consumer Behavior." *Journal of Political Economy* 78 (March/April), 311–29.

Nelson, P. 1974. "Advertising as Information." *Journal of Political Economy* 82 (July/August), 729–54.

Schmalensee, R. 1978. "A Model of Advertising and Product Quality." *Journal of Political Economy* 86 (June), 485–503.

Spence, A. M. 1973. "Job Market Signaling." *Quarterly Journal of Economics* 87 (August), 355–74.

# 10
# Networks, Platforms, and Advertising

## 10.1 INTRODUCTION

We now turn to a set of topics related to advertising in the digital age. It is an age of super connectivity in which millions of individuals can make contact with millions of others through social and business network platforms such as Facebook and LinkedIn. Consumers and businesses are also linked via banking and credit card networks. Video game players connect with rivals and friends across the globe. These and other examples illustrate major changes to economic and social relations of the last twenty years. Advertising has been part of this change. Many of the dominant platforms such as Google and Amazon earn a significant amount of revenue from advertisers trying to connect with those same millions of consumers. Any contemporary analysis of advertising must therefore address the phenomena of these networks and platforms.

Fortunately, economists have done a lot of work on networks and platforms. The study of network markets had already produced some key insights before the Internet Age. We begin this chapter by reviewing this work and its major results. We then turn to the more recent analyses of two-sided platforms, such as Google, which typically exhibit so-called indirect network effects. This foundation allows us to address the issue of advertising as a critical element and funding source for many platform firms.

## 10.2 NETWORK MARKETS

For most product markets, it is appropriate to view a consumer's utility from consumption as dependent only on how much of a good as well as complementary goods the consumer has. A consumer who brings a pizza home gets satisfaction from eating a slice regardless of whether their neighbors are having pizza, or whether half of their town is. To be sure, if everyone is buying pizza that night, the price might be driven higher, but that outcome depends on the industry supply curve. In short, a consumer's basic willingness to pay for pizza is not affected by how many others like and consume pizza in the same time interval.

The above reasoning about what a consumer's utility depends upon breaks down when we think about the utility of goods such as a phone or a fax machine. The consumption value of a phone, for example, is very much dependent on how many others have phones. It has virtually no value for a consumer if that consumer is essentially the only one with a phone. As more people acquire a phone, the individual value of owning one becomes higher and higher to any one phone holder because the number of people the consumer can reach directly as well as indirectly rises rapidly.

The phone and the fax machine are examples of direct network effects. Any one consumer's enjoyment of the product rises as the number of other consumers that join the network of users rises. Somewhat symmetrically to the way in which there is often, because of scale economies, a fall in average cost as the volume of production rises, the rise in the consumer's valuation of a good can rise as the volume of users rises. In that sense, such network effects act as a kind of scale economy on the demand side. To put it another way, the direct network effect of a phone service implies a positive feedback loop such that the more people that have the phone service, the more any one consumer is willing to pay to get such service.

There are many network effects, however, that are indirect. These typically reflect a positive feedback loop between two complementary services. Consider, for example, credit cards. A credit card provides both a means of accessing credit for consumers and a means of payment to retailers. The more retailers that accept a particular credit card, e.g., *Visa*, the more consumers want to use *Visa* cards. Likewise, the more consumers that use *Visa*, the more businesses are willing to accept it as a form of payment. Similarly, the more programs and games that run on the *Xbox* console, the more consumers will pay for an *Xbox*; while the more players there are that use *Xbox*, the more app developers want to write programs for that device.

Whether the effects are direct or indirect, network effects bring important, new strategic considerations into play. Correspondingly, outcomes in markets with network effects exhibit features that we have not fully addressed in previous chapters. As we will see, network markets can be quite unstable and "tippy," with multiple equilibria, some of which are clearly inferior to others.[1]

## 10.3  MODELS OF NETWORK MARKETS

In order to understand some of the key features of network markets, we present two models. The first is set in a monopoly market and highlights the role of the externality in consumption as a driver of the market equilibrium. The second is placed in a duopoly market and allows explicit analysis of the impact of network effects on the intensity of competition.

### 10.3.1  Monopoly Provision of a Network Service

An early but insightful analysis of network effects is Rohlfs' (1974). Rohlfs' approach is straightforward and draws attention to the main issues that arise in markets with network effects. By assuming a monopoly market, the analysis can focus on the central demand-side aspects that give rise to network effects. We present a modified version of Rohlfs' (1974) model here.

Assume that the monopolist, say a telecommunications firm, charges its customers an access fee, but does not impose a per usage charge. That is, the consumer is charged a single price $p$ for "hooking up" to the network, but each individual call on the network is free, perhaps because the marginal cost of a call is zero.[2] We also assume that there is a maximum size of the market, say one million potential customers, reflecting the maximum number $N$ of consumers who would ever willingly buy the service even if the access fee were zero. By fixing the total amount of potential customers at $N$, we can talk interchangeably about the fraction $f$ of the market served and the actual number of customers $fN$ served. That is, if the maximum size of the market is one million, we can characterize a market outcome in which 100,000 customers purchase the service either in terms of the fraction $f = 0.10$ or the number of customers $fN = 100,000$ served.

Consumers all agree that the service is more valuable the greater the fraction $f$ of the market that signs up for it. However, even if everyone acquires the service ($f = 1$), there would likely be variation in what consumers would be willing to pay for the service. Specifically, we denote the valuation of the $i$th consumer, when $f = 1$, as $v_i$. These valuations or $v_i$'s are assumed to be uniformly distributed between \$0 and \$100. For example, the 1 percent of consumers who most value the service (about 10,000 individuals in our case) would willingly pay close to \$100 for it if they knew that all other consumers would also acquire it.

Unfortunately, when the consumer signs on, they do not know the actual fraction $f$ of potential users that will sign on to the network. Instead, the consumer's willingness to pay depends on the fraction $f^e$ of users *expected* to sign up. We capture this effect by assuming that the $i$th consumer's willingness to pay for network membership is given by $f^e v_i$. Each consumer will either join the network or not depending on how the price $p$ compares with their willingness to pay $f^e v_i$. Specifically, the demand by consumer $i$ for a hookup to the service is given by:

$$q_i^D = \begin{bmatrix} 0 & \text{if } f^e v_i < p \\ 1 & \text{if } f^e v_i \geq p \end{bmatrix} \tag{10.1}$$

Equation (10.1) makes clear that consumer $i$'s actual willingness to pay for the service $f^e v_i$ increases with the fraction of potential buyers $f^e$ that are expected to buy it. This positive feedback is what leads to network externalities. For any one user, it is still their own valuation that determines whether they buy or not. However, that valuation depends positively on the number of others who are expected to buy. Equally important, no individual consumer considers the fact that joining the network will improve the usefulness of the network to all the other users due to the fact that their joining makes the network bigger.

We can use equation (10.1) to calculate the actual fraction $f$ of consumers who buy into the service at any given price $p$. The insight here is simply to recognize that in any true equilibrium, the actual fraction $f$ must equal the expected fraction $f^e$—otherwise, individuals would revise their expectations. As usual, we start by focusing on the marginal consumer denoted by the reservation valuation $\hat{v}_i$. This is the consumer who is indifferent between buying into the service network and not buying into it so that $f^e\hat{v}_i = p$, which in turn implies that $\hat{v}_i = p/f^e$. Consumers with a valuation less than $\hat{v}_i$ will not subscribe to the service. The remainder will subscribe. Since $\hat{v}_i$ is distributed uniformly between 0 and 100, the fraction of consumers with a valuation below $\hat{v}_i$ is simply $\hat{v}_i/100$. Hence, the fraction of consumers $f$ with valuations greater than or equal to $\hat{v}_i$, and who therefore acquire the service is:

$$f = (100 - \hat{v}_i) / 100 = 1 - \frac{p}{100 f^e} = 1 - \frac{p}{100 f} \tag{10.2}$$

where the last equation reflects the equilibrium condition that $f = f^e$ for this outcome to be an equilibrium.

If we now solve for $p$, we obtain the inverse demand function confronting the monopolist expressed in terms of the fraction $f$ of the maximum potential number of customers who actually buy the service in equilibrium:

$$p = 100f (1 - f) \tag{10.3}$$

The total number of customers, of course, is $q = fN = f1,000,000$ if $N = 1,000,000$. Hence, the firm's revenue (in thousands) is given by:

$$\text{Revenue} = pq = 100,000f^2(1 - f) \tag{10.4}$$

For illustrative purposes, it is convenient to imagine that the firm's costs are all in the form of design and setup costs, and that the marginal cost of servicing a customer is 0. In that case, profit maximization is the same as revenue maximization, which from equation (10.4) requires choosing $f$ to maximize (10.4) or $f = 2/3$. Substituting this result into the price equation (10.3) implies that the firm's optimal price is $22.22.

Unfortunately, the profit-maximization problem is not quite as straightforward as the foregoing might make it seem. The difficulty can be seen by looking at a graph of the price equation (10.3), which we show in Figure 10.1. For any positive price less than $25, there are *two* points, i.e., two values of $f$ that satisfy that equation. The profit-maximizing price of $22.22 is associated with two potential equilibrium outcomes.

One potential market outcome when price is set at $p = $22.22 is that $f = 2/3$, leading to a total revenue of $14,815 (again in thousands). However, as Figure 10.1 makes clear, $p = $22.22 is also consistent with $f = 1/3$ and the much lower revenue of $7,407 (in thousands). There is also a third possibility, which is that no one buys and the market collapses totally to a price of zero.[3]

These equilibria are not created equally, however. Consider the outcome at the low-level equilibrium in which $f = f^e = 1/3$ and $p = $22.22. At this point, the marginal consumer valuation is: $\hat{v}_i = p/f^e = \dfrac{\$22.22}{0.333} = \$66.67$, which is relatively high as only the top third of the population are actually buying the service. Suppose that starting from this point, there is a small decrease in the expected fraction $f^e$ to 0.30.

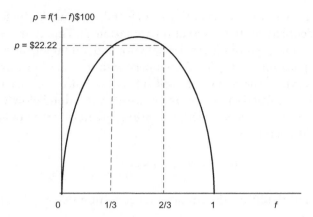

$p = f(1 - f)\$100$

$p = \$22.22$

0     1/3     2/3     1     f

*Note:* The price \$22.22 maximizes the monopolist's network revenue when 2/3 of the potential customers sign on to the network. However, the network externality indicates that a price of \$22.22 is also consistent with only 1/3 of the potential customers signing.

**Figure 10.1** Multiple equilibria for monopoly network

At this value of $f^e$, the marginal consumer is now characterized by a valuation of $\hat{v}_i = p/f^e = \dfrac{\$22.22}{0.30} = \$74$. That is, now only consumers with $v_i$ values greater than or equal to \$74 are expected to buy the product. Yet, that is just 26 percent of consumers. This fraction is not only less than the 33.33 percent buying before the shock, but even less than the 30 percent caused by the shock. Realizing this, more consumers will be expected to leave which, in turn, will raise $\hat{v}_i$ still higher, implying an even lower fraction $f$ of potential users who will use the service. Hence, even more will drop it and so on. In short, starting from $f = 1/3$, an initial small decline in $f^e$ leads to an unraveling in which both $f^e$ and $f$ continue to decline until the process reaches its logical conclusion with $f^e = f = 0$. All the firm's customers leave and the market collapses.

This, however, is not the case for the larger market equilibrium when $f^e = f = 2/3$. In this case the marginal valuation is: $\hat{v}_i = p/f^e = \dfrac{\$22.22}{0.67} = \$33.33$. A small fall in $f^e$ to say 0.64 raises $\hat{v}_i = p/f^e = \dfrac{\$33.33}{0.64} = \$34.72$. This valuation though is consistent with over 65 percent of the consumer population buying the product, which is greater than the shock leading to 64 percent. Consumers will realize that more customers should be expected to buy, and this will raise the value of the service to all such that this expectation will be realized. Again, the process will repeat itself, but this time *raising* participation until the initial equilibrium of $\hat{v}_i = p/f^e = \dfrac{\$22.22}{0.67} = \$33.33$ is restored.

If we repeat the above thought experiments for small *increases* in $f^e$, we will find that for the low-level equilibrium, with $f = f^e = 1/3$, a small rise in $f^e$ is, like a small decrease at this point, self-reinforcing such that $f^e$ and $f$ continue to rise further until the market settles at the high-level equilibrium with $f = f^e = 2/3$. However, starting from that higher equilibrium, a small rise in $f^e$ will be self-defeating in that it will set in motion forces to restore $f = f^e = 2/3$.

In sum, of the two equilibria associated with a price $p = \$22.22$, only the high-level one with $f = f^e = 2/3$ is stable in that small deviations from it trigger market forces that ultimately restore that equilibrium. In contrast, the low-level equilibrium is unstable. Any rise above $f = f^e = 1/3$ and $f$ continues to rise to the stable equilibrium. Any movement below $f = f^e = 1/3$ and the market collapses. For this reason, Rohlfs (1974) characterizes the low-level equilibrium as the "critical mass." The firm must somehow make sure that it crosses this threshold. If it does, it can reach the stable, profit-maximizing equilibrium. If it does not though, it will die.

Simple as it is, the Rohlfs (1974) model exhibits some key features that characterize network markets. First, there are often multiple equilibria and there may be no guarantee that the market will settle on the "right" or welfare-maximizing one. Second, such markets can be "tippy" in that in some cases, at least, even small shocks can lead to very dramatic changes. Third, the imperative to reach a critical mass or minimal network size can make such markets fiercely competitive. We will show this in the next section, but the essential intuition is easy to see. If firms have to reach a large critical mass just to survive, then the competition is likely to be fierce because failure means corporate death.

## 10.3.2 Price Competition in the Presence of Network Effects

To introduce competition into the market, we return to the Hotelling (1929) product differentiated model where two firms are located at either end of the one mile long Main Street and $N$ consumers are distributed uniformly between them. Firm 1 is located at the West end of town ($x = 0$) and firm 2 is located at the East end of town ($x = 1$). Each firm has a constant marginal cost of $c$. Each consumer buys at most one unit of the good either from firm A or firm B and incurs a cost of $t$ per unit of distance traveled.

A consumer incurs a round trip transport or disutilty cost of $t$ per unit of distance to buy a good that is not their preferred good. However, the utility derived from each differentiated product exhibits network effects. To capture these, we assume that a consumer's surplus depending on the consumer's location $x$ is:

$$
\begin{array}{ll}
V + ks_1^e - tx - p_1 & \text{if buys from firm 1; and} \\
V + ks_2^e - t(1 - x) - p_2 & \text{if buys from firm 2}
\end{array}
\tag{10.5}
$$

Here, $s_1^e$ and $s_2^e$ are the market shares that the typical consumer *expects* for good 1 and good 2, respectively and $k$ measures the strength of the network effect. For tractability, we assume that $k < t$. As before, an equilibrium condition is that the expected shares equal the actual shares, otherwise consumer expectations would change, and we would not be in an equilibrium. If there is a marginal consumer $x^M$ such that all to the left of $x^M$ buys from firm 1 and all to the right of $x^M$ buys from firm 2, then it must be the case that these market shares are: $s_1 = x^M$ and $s_2 = (1 - x^M)$.

We assume that consumer willingness to pay $V$ is sufficiently large so that each consumer buys from one of the two firms, i.e., the market is covered. This implies that the marginal consumer $x^M$ is that consumer who is just indifferent between the products of two firms. That is, $x^M$ must satisfy:

$$V + ks_1^e - tx^M - p_1 = V + ks_2^e - t(1 - x^M) - p_2 \qquad (10.6)$$

Recognizing that in any equilibrium $s_1 = x^M$ and $s_2 = (1 - x^M)$, we may substitute these values into equation (10.6) to solve for the equilibrium value of the marginal consumer. That is:

$$x^M = \frac{1}{2} + \frac{p_2 - p_1}{2(t - k)} \qquad (10.7)$$

As firm 1's demand is $q_1 = Nx^M \geq 0$ and firm 2's demand is $q_2 = N(1 - x^M) \geq 0$, the inverse demand equation facing each firm is for:

$$p_1 = (t - k) + p_2 - \frac{2(t - k)}{N} q_1$$
$$\qquad (10.8)$$
$$p_2 = (t - k) + p_1 - \frac{2(t - k)}{N} q_2$$

We may now apply the twice-as-steep rule to translate the inverse demand equations into marginal revenue ones. Equating these latter equations with the marginal cost $c$ of each firm then yields the best response function for each firm:

$$\text{Firm 1 best response:} \quad p_1 = \frac{c + t - k + p_2}{2} > 0$$
$$\qquad (10.9)$$
$$\text{Firm 2 best response:} \quad p_2 = \frac{c + t - k + p_1}{2} > 0$$

In a Nash equilibrium both firms are on their best response function. Solving equations (10.9) simultaneously yields equilibrium prices:

$$p_1 = p_2 = c + t - k > 0 \qquad (10.10)$$

Recall that $k$ is a network externality parameter. The larger $k$ is, the stronger are the external benefits a consumer gets from joining a network. If $k$ is zero, there are no network effects and each firm sets a price $p_1 = p_2 = c + t$. However, as $k$ rises and belonging to a large network becomes more important to consumers, firms cut their price below this level. The reason is clear. The value to a firm of gaining additional customers from one's rival now is enhanced as that makes consumers more willing to pay for the firm's service. Competition, therefore, becomes more intense and prices fall below $p_1 = p_2 = c + t$ by the amount $k$.

In sum, network markets typically have multiple equilibria that can be ranked in terms of total social welfare. Some of the equilibria are unstable, suggesting that network markets can be subject to wide swings in sales and profits. Each firm will often need to achieve some critical mass or sufficiently large customer base to insure its survival. Because a failure to achieve that critical base is corporate death, we can expect to find that firms in markets with strong network effects compete vigorously to "buy" the customers of other brands via aggressive price-cutting. This means that the price-cost margin is small. This intensifies the need to operate on a large scale to generate revenues enough to cover fixed overhead costs. A further consequence of firms needing to operate on a large scale is that network industries will tend to be quite concentrated.

## 10.4 TWO-SIDED PLATFORMS

Network effects are relevant to advertising because they are a critical feature of modern mass-media, which are the major distributers of advertising messages. Newspapers, radio, magazines, television, and many Internet services serve as media platforms that bring together two sides of a market. One side is comprised of consumers with potential buying power who are attracted to the platform because of the content it offers. The content could be news, music, sports, entertainment, or shopping information. The other side is comprised of firms that are trying to reach potential consumers about their products and will pay platform operators to reach these consumers. To analyze markets with two-sided platforms, we need to be a bit more precise about what we mean by a "platform."

Many firms bring together buyers and sellers. Indeed, this is what most retailers do. They buy a variety of products from different firms at wholesale prices and then offer these to consumers at a higher retail price. In so doing, these firms provide many services. To a varying extent, retail stores provide some assurance of the quality of the goods they sell. Many "high-end" department stores offer only high-quality products while discount stores sell a range of lower-quality goods. This allows consumers "to sort" themselves efficiently—those willing to pay a lot for a high-quality product and those who can afford less know where to go to obtain the goods that match their preferences. In addition, retailers provide other services such as clean and well-organized shopping venues.

Two-sided platform operators also bring buyers and sellers together, and typically both benefit from network effects. The more consumers that visit a platform, e.g., Google search, the more firms will want to advertise on that platform. In turn, the greater the number of sellers for which Google provides advertising raises the likelihood that any one buyer will find a match and so raises the number of consumers who want Google as their search engine. Platforms, unlike retailers, are typically characterized by network effects.

Another difference between a retailer and a platform concerns pricing. A retailer intermediates between buyers and sellers. It negotiates a wholesale price with each seller and then sets retail prices to buyers, earning revenue from the difference. The platform also brings together sellers and potential buyers. However, rather than intermediate, the platform simply makes a market. It is not involved in setting the price of any transaction that may occur between a buyer and a seller. Instead, the platform earns revenue from the fees it sets to both sides of this market, buyers and advertising firms.

### 10.4.1 A Monopoly Platform Model

To better understand two-sided platforms, we again start with a simple, stripped down model. To begin let's suppose that the platform is a print medium, such as a newspaper, and we begin with the case of a monopoly. This actually is not an unrealistic assumption. Increasingly, many cities and towns are served by just one local paper (Noam, 2009; Berry and Waldfogel, 2010).

The newspaper is a medium platform that serves two groups. One is a set of $N$ consumers who buy the paper for its news stories and other content. We assume that consumer surplus for this service is equal to $V - P_S$, where $V$ is maximum consumer surplus at a price of zero, and $P_S$ is the subscription price of the newspaper per some unit of time, e.g., daily. The total number $Q_S$ of consumers that subscribe to the paper is assumed to be a function of $V - P_S$, i.e.,

$$Q_S = N(V - P_S) \tag{10.11}$$

The other group served by the newspaper is the set of firms that pay for space in the newspaper to advertise their products. Firms that choose to advertise pay for an ad space in the paper, again for some unit of time, at a price of $P_A$. Running a daily ad in the paper leads to a sale with probability $\lambda$, and on each such sale the firm earns a price-cost margin equal to $Z$. A firm's expected gross revenue from running a daily newspaper ad is $\lambda Z Q_S = \lambda Z N(V - P_S)$. We assume that the number of firms $n$ who choose to advertise, or the quantity of daily advertisements $Q_A$, is an increasing function of the net revenue advertising generates. That is:

$$Q_A = n[\lambda Z N(V - P_S) - P_A] \tag{10.12}$$

Here, there is an indirect network effect in the demand for advertising, but not in the demand for newspapers. That is, the number of firms $n$ running advertisements does not affect consumer demand for the news service, but the number of reading subscribers $N$ does matter to firms deciding on whether to advertise or not.

In some models, notably Anderson and Coate (2005), consumers are treated as disliking advertising, and there is a negative impact on their utility and the demand for newspapers as more space is sold to advertisers. In principle, of course, reader preferences could also be favorable toward advertising, either because it provides information or more directly contributes positively toward the reader's utility. We take a neutral approach here because it simplifies the analysis. Such reader neutrality can be justified either by an assumption that annoyance with advertising is offset by the information it provides or, in the case of newspapers, by arguing that readers can easily avoid advertising just by skipping a page or part of it.

The newspaper, or media platform in this case, collects the subscription price $P_S$ from each reader and the price of advertising space $P_A$ from each advertiser. We will assume that the (constant) marginal cost of printing a paper is $c_S$ and of allocating space is $c_A$. Hence, the profit of the newspaper platform is:

$$\pi = (P_S - c_S)Q_S + (P_A - c_A)Q_A$$
$$= (P_S - c_S)N(V - P_S) + (P_A - c_A)n[\lambda ZN(V-P_S) - P_A]$$

(10.13)

The newspaper must choose both the subscription price $P_S$ and the advertising price $P_A$ to maximize the profit in (10.13). The necessary first-order conditions for profit maximization then are:

$$\frac{\partial \pi}{\partial P_S} = N(V - P_S) - (P_S - c_S)N - (P_A - c_A)\lambda ZNn = 0$$

(10.14)

$$\frac{\partial \pi}{\partial P_A} = n[\lambda ZN(V - P_S) - P_A] - (P_A - c_A)n = 0$$

A little examination reveals that the second of these two first-order conditions is really the familiar Lerner condition that the price-cost margin of advertising space be set equal to the inverse of the price elasticity of demand for advertising. That is, the newspaper will find it optimal to set the advertising price to firms such that it satisfies $\dfrac{(P_A - c_A)}{P_A} = \dfrac{1}{\varepsilon_P^A}$, where is $\varepsilon_P^A$ the absolute value of the price elasticity of advertising demand for a given readership $N$.[4] On this side of the market, the newspaper sets a price of advertising as would a conventional monopolist.

The other first-order condition, which relates to the optimal subscription price set to consumers, is, however, more complicated. Recognizing that the optimal advertising price implies $\dfrac{(P_A - c_A)}{P_A} = \dfrac{1}{\varepsilon_P^A} = \dfrac{[\lambda ZN(V - P_S) - P_A]}{P_A}$, and that $\varepsilon_P^S = \dfrac{dQ_S / Q_S}{dP_S / P_S} = \dfrac{P_S}{(V - P_S)}$, the first-order condition with respect to the subscription price can be written as:

$$P_S = c_S + \frac{P_S}{\varepsilon_P^S} - n\lambda Z \frac{P_A}{\varepsilon_P^A}$$

(10.15)

Analogous to the advertising price $P_A$ condition, the first two right-hand-side terms of equation (10.15) are simply another way to capture the Lerner condition. Ignoring the third right-hand-side term, the equation says that the monopoly newspaper's price should be set equal to marginal cost plus a margin implicitly determined by the price elasticity of subscriber demand. However, the third term enters with a negative sign implying that the newspaper will maximize its overall profit by setting a subscription price *below* that implied by the standard Lerner condition.

The reason for the above outcome is not hard to see. Advertising firms care about the number of consumers that their newspaper advertising reaches. Setting a subscription price $P_S$ below the value implied by the Lerner condition may cost the newspaper some profit in the subscriber market, but it increases advertising demand and makes greater profit possible from the advertising market. The net result is that the newspaper's profit increases overall.

The same reasoning also explains why advertisers do not receive a discount from the standard textbook monopoly price. Because consumers of newspapers are neither negatively nor positively affected by the advertising in the newspaper, getting more firms to advertise has no impact on subscriber demand. It therefore brings no external benefit (or loss) that would alter the firm's standard textbook monopoly pricing of advertising space.

Note that the discount in the price of a newspaper that newspaper subscribers enjoy depends on the effectiveness of a firm's advertising in generating sales, i.e., $\lambda$, and the operating profit margin earned on such sales, i.e., $Z$. If either of these parameters were zero, there would be no valuable network externality to increasing the number of subscribers and hence, no discount.

Conversely, the larger the external network gain from increasing its subscription base, the larger will be the discount the newspaper platform finds optimal to offer subscribers. In fact, it is possible that the newspaper will set a subscription price below the publication cost $c_S$ and, as happens with many local newspapers, even set $P_S$ equal to zero. In such cases, the newspaper is free to subscribers and financed entirely by advertising revenue.

While the above insights have been generated by a simple model of a two-sided platform, they nonetheless are general. For instance, even if we had assumed that subscribers benefit from receiving more advertising, they would still receive a larger discount relative to the standard monopoly price so long as the external gain to subscribers from increasing the number of advertisements is less than the gain that advertising firms enjoy as the number of subscribers rises. In general, any for-profit, two-sided platform will offer the steepest discount or subsidy to that side of the market that confers the greatest external benefit to the other side.

Whatever the discount offered to customers on either side of its platform, it is important to recognize that this is not a case of price discrimination based on the different demand elasticities. In the simple model used here, for instance, subscribers would receive a discount while advertisers would not even if both had the same price elasticity of demand. Instead, the discount reflects the optimum *price structure* needed to maximize profit across two, interrelated markets.

## 10.4.2 Platform Competition

The platform model analyzed in the previous section was a monopoly newspaper. While this is not an unrealistic assumption in many newspaper markets and while the model yields valuable insights, the question of the impact of competition remains. To explore this issue, we merge the model in the above section with a version of the Hotelling model like that in section 10.3.2.

We assume that there are $N$ newspaper subscribers distributed uniformly along a product differentiated line of unit length. Newspaper or platform 1 is located at the left-hand side of the line and newspaper or platform 2 is located at the right-hand side of the line. The $N$ potential subscribers incur a disutility cost $t^S$ per unit of distance "travelled" in product space to subscribe to a specific platform or newspaper. The assumption that subscribers choose only one newspaper or, more generally, one platform, is known as the "single-homing" assumption.

There are also $n$ potential advertising firms that also single-home and therefore, must choose one of the two newspapers (if any) for their platform for ads. We again assume that the firms' preferences for newspapers platforms are distributed uniformly along the same product space as consumers, i.e., the unit line. Analogous to subscribers of newspapers, each firm who advertises also incurs a cost $t^A$ per unit of distance between the firm's location and the location of the newspaper in which the firm advertises.

Define the location of each potential subscriber as $x_i$ and the location of each potential advertiser as $y_i$, with $0 \leq x_i \leq 1$ and $0 \leq y_i \leq 1$. Letting the subscription prices be $P_1^S$ and $P_2^S$, and the advertising prices be $P_1^A$ and $P_2^A$, the consumer surplus realized by any consumer $x_i$ who subscribes to a newspaper is:

$$
\begin{aligned}
&V^S - P_1^S - t^S x_i && \text{if subscribing to newspaper 1} \\
&V^S - P_2^S - t^S(1 - x_i) && \text{if subscribing to newspaper 2}
\end{aligned}
$$
(10.16)

Similarly, the surplus realized by any advertiser $y_i$ who advertises in a newspaper is:

$$
\begin{aligned}
&\lambda Z S_1 - P_1^A - t^A y_i && \text{if advertising in newspaper 1} \\
&\lambda Z S_2 - P_2^A - t^A(1 - y_i) && \text{if advertising in newspaper 2}
\end{aligned}
$$
(10.17)

Here, $S_1$ and $S_2$ are the number of subscribers to newspapers 1 and 2, respectively. Hence, $\dfrac{S_1}{N}$ is the share of potential subscribers that sign on with newspaper 1, and $\dfrac{S_2}{N}$ is the share of potential subscribers signing on with newspaper 2. As before, $\lambda$ is the probability per subscriber that an advertisement generates a sale and $Z$ is the operating profit earned on such a sale. The equations in (10.17) reflect the fact that advertisers in any newspaper earn more sales the larger is that paper's subscription base. Consumers, on the other hand, are again neutral about advertising.

We assume that $V^S$ is sufficiently high such that all subscribers find a news service sufficiently valuable and buy a subscription. Similarly, $\lambda Z$ is sufficiently high that firms contract to place ads in either one paper or the other. Thus, all $N$ subscribers buy a newspaper and all $n$ firms advertise.

Given the subscription price and advertising prices $P_i^S$ and $P_i^A$, set by newspaper $i$, where $i = 1, 2$, we may define a marginal subscriber $\hat{x}$ indifferent between reading newspaper 1 and newspaper 2, and a marginal advertiser $\hat{z}$ indifferent between advertising in either paper. Hence:

$$
V^S - P_1^S - t^S \hat{x} = V^S - P_2^S - t^S(1 - \hat{x})
$$

and
(10.18)

$$\lambda Z \hat{x} N - P_1^A - t^A \hat{y} = \lambda Z(1 - \hat{x})N - P_2^A - t^A(1 - \hat{y})$$

Here, we have made use of the fact that $\hat{x} = \dfrac{S_1}{N}$ implying that $\dfrac{S_2}{N} = 1 - \dfrac{S_1}{N} = 1 - \hat{x}$. In turn, equations (10.18) imply:

$$\hat{x} = \frac{1}{2} + \frac{P_2^S - P_1^S}{2t^S}$$

$$\hat{y} = \frac{1}{2} + \frac{P_2^A - P_1^A}{2t^A} + \frac{\lambda ZN(2\hat{x} - 1)}{2t^A} \qquad (10.19)$$

Substituting for $\hat{x}$ then implies that $\hat{y} = \dfrac{1}{2} + \dfrac{P_2^A - P_1^A}{2t^A} + \dfrac{\lambda Z(P_2^S - P_1^S)N}{2t^A t^S}$.

Recall that there are $n$ firms that advertise. From (10.19), newspaper 1 has subscriber demand $\hat{x}N$ and advertising demand $\hat{y}n$, while platform 2 has subscriber demand $(1 - \hat{x})N$ and advertising demand $(1 - \hat{y})n$, respectively. We assume that the cost of printing the paper is $c^S$, while the cost of running an ad is $c^A$, and that these are the same for either newspaper. Profit for newspaper 1 $\pi_1$ then is:

$$\pi_1 = (P_1^S - c^S)\left(\frac{1}{2} + \frac{P_2^S - P_1^S}{2t^S}\right)N + (P_1^A - c^A)\left(\frac{1}{2} + \frac{P_2^A - P_1^A}{2t^A} + \frac{\lambda Z(P_2^S - P_1^S)}{2t^A t^S}N\right)n \quad (10.20)$$

The necessary first-order conditions for profit maximization then are:

$$\frac{\partial \pi_1}{\partial P_1^S} = \left(\frac{1}{2} + \frac{P_2^S - P_1^S}{2t^S}\right)N - \frac{(P_1^S - c^S)}{2t^S}N - (P_1^A - c^A)\frac{\lambda Z}{2t^A t^S}Nn = 0$$

and $\qquad (10.21)$

$$\frac{\partial \pi_1}{\partial P_1^A} = \left(\frac{1}{2} + \frac{P_2^A - P_1^A}{2t^A} + \frac{\lambda Z(P_2^S - P_1^S)N}{2t^A t^S}\right)n - \frac{(P_1^A - c^A)}{2t^A}n = 0$$

We could derive similar profit first-order conditions for firm 2 and then derive the Nash equilibrium set of prices for this duopoly game. A convenient short-cut in a symmetric game, i.e., one in which the newspapers are identical in terms of demand and cost structure, is to make use of the fact that in equilibrium they will behave identically and so $P_1^S = P_2^S = P^S$ and $P_1^A = P_2^A = P^A$. This allows us to simplify the equations in (10.21). Substituting first $P_1^S = P_2^S = P^S$ and $P_1^A = P_2^A = P^A$ into the equation $\dfrac{\partial \pi_1}{\partial P_1^A} = 0$, we find:

$$P^A = c^A + t^A \qquad (10.22a)$$

And substituting (10.22a) $P_1^S = P_2^S = P^S$ and $P_1^A = P_2^A = P^A$ into the equation for $\dfrac{\partial \pi_1}{\partial P_1^S} = 0$, we find:

$$P_1^S = P_2^S = c^S + t^S - \lambda Zn \qquad (10.22b)$$

Recall that in the standard Hotelling (1929) model[5] the equilibrium prices without the indirect network effect would be $P_1^A = P_2^A = c^A + t^A$, and $P_1^S = P_2^S = c^S + t^S$. We can see that a network effect on the demand of advertisers, arising from the number of subscribers, leads to a price discount to subscribers, (10.22b). Because there is no network effect in reverse, i.e., subscribers do not care about the number of firms that advertise, the price of advertising space is the same as in the standard model, (10.22a). It is their subscription that provides the external benefit to advertisers.

In this duopoly model, all consumers are served and so a subscription price cut by one newspaper does not expand the total readership, but simply steals subscribers from the rival. Because of this competitive rivalry for subscribers, in order to attract advertisers there is still a discount offered to subscribers.[6]

We assume that there are disutility costs, $t^S$ and $t^A$ to subscribers and advertisers, respectively, when they subscribe or advertise in a paper whose differentiated content is not their preferred one. In this light, it is interesting to consider what happens if subscribers still have strong "locational" preferences over which newspaper they buy, but advertisers have no such preferences and care only about total subscriptions. That is, suppose that $t^A = 0$. In that case, a symmetric duopoly solution does not exist. One firm or the other will cut subscription prices sufficiently low that it gains the entire advertising market as a monopoly.[7] As we indicated earlier, network markets have a "winner-take-all" feature that makes them somewhat unstable.

Another point to make arises in connection with our assumption that both subscribers and advertisers "single-home." That is, consumers subscribe to one newspaper and firms advertise in only one newspaper. While single-homing may characterize newspaper subscribers, advertisers are more likely to run promotions in more than one newspaper. In this case, a "competitive bottleneck" can emerge. In our duopoly market, competition for subscribers results in consumers being evenly divided between newspaper 1 and newspaper 2. From the viewpoint of advertisers then, each newspaper has a monopoly over half of the subscription market. If advertisers run a promotion in just one newspaper, then each newspaper has to compete to become the single home of each advertising firm. If, on the other hand, advertisers multi-home and run ads in both newspapers, the incentive to compete to win their exclusive business is removed. This puts advertisers at a disadvantage as each newspaper can now act as a monopolist in terms of granting advertisers access to that paper's half of the subscribing market. This outcome is known as a "competitive bottleneck" in that advertisers essentially face monopoly pricing to place ads to either group of subscribers even though the platform market is not monopolized.[8]

## 10.5 SOME WELFARE ISSUES OF ADVERTISING AND PLATFORMS

Network effects and two-sided media platforms are central parts of the environment in which most advertising takes place. Advertising requires communication and communication requires a medium. The media available—newspaper and magazine print, radio and television airwaves, Internet search engines and social network sites—all operate as two-sided platforms with notable network externalities. Recognition of this feature and an understanding of how the two sides of a platform interact, leads naturally to some questions related to advertising.

Many of the welfare questions of advertising revenue in platform markets with single-homing and strong network effects raise issues of antitrust policy. We defer the bulk of this discussion to Chapter 12. Here, we discuss three general welfare concerns that are not easily addressed by antitrust policy per se.

## 10.5.1 Advertising Levels

One welfare issue is the overall level of advertising. Does the fact that advertisers reach their audience through a platform medium imply an advertising volume above or below the optimal level? If we assume that subscribers to or users of a platform are indifferent about the amount of advertising, then the level of advertising that will be offered is generally *below* the optimal level, particularly when a competitive bottleneck emerges.[9] The intuitive reason why is that the platform fee to advertisers is too high due to the imperfect competition in the platform market.

There are, however, qualifications. For example, in the Hotelling model discussed above, a firm either advertises or not and, if it does, pays a price or fee to advertise. There is no choice over the number of ads or, for TV or radio, the number of advertising minutes. If we allow the volume of advertising to vary, alternative pricing of advertising becomes possible. For example, we could imagine the platform charging a two-part price comprised of a lump-sum initial fee followed by a low price per advertising page or advertising minute.[10] This would lead to more advertising.

Somewhat conversely, some media platforms such as television and radio may exhibit a congestion externality. For example, suppose that viewers can only absorb a given number of advertisements per unit of time. If the number of ads exceeds that limit, each ad uses up some of the total time that could have been available to other ads. However, no firm that advertises takes this external effect into account. In turn, the fact that no advertiser considers the cost that it imposes on other advertisers leads each to underestimate the true cost of advertising and to advertise excessively. The problem is especially pronounced in all-advertising-financed media platforms where consumers watch or listen without making any dollar payment.[11] In addition, the use of ad-skipping devices such as TiVo suggests that advertising has a negative effect on consumer utility. In this case, the possibility of excessive advertising is even stronger.

It is also important to note that if subscribers regard advertising as a nuisance then more competition by way of more platforms should lead to less advertising per consumer. The reason is that when subscribers dislike advertising the number of ads they receive is effectively the "price" they pay for access to the platform. More platforms lead to more competition and a lower "price" to subscribers. In turn, this implies that as the number of platforms rises, advertisers now reach fewer customers. In other words, increased platform competition can lead to *higher* prices for advertising firms.

Whether or not this prediction holds in real market settings,[12] calling it to attention can remind us that we cannot simply analyze two-sided platform competition from the view of one side of the market alone. Again, platforms do not simply set a price to each side they serve. Instead, platforms choose a *price structure* across both sides with the aim of maximizing profit.

## 10.5.2 Platform Content Variety and Quality

Other welfare issues relate to the diversity of the content offered on media platforms. Newspapers, radio, and television do more than simply serve as a forum where subscribers and advertisers meet. They also provide news, information, and/or entertainment content. Important questions concern the nature of the content that the platform market will support. Will it be diverse? Will it be of high or low quality?

If the network effects on a platform are sufficiently strong and/or if the locational preferences of the two groups served by the platform are sufficiently weak, only one platform is likely sustainable in equilibrium. That platform will then have exclusive power to choose the platform's content. Such a monopoly suggests that the diversity of content, be it on a print, radio, or television platform, will be limited.

Even with two or more competing platforms, the competition for subscribers can lead to duplication and limited variety, as Steiner (1952) argued many years ago. Consider two television stations that are entirely advertising-financed, i.e., viewers watch for free. The fact that each depends on advertisers to finance their programming means that each will strive to attract the largest possible audience they can. Suppose then that 80 percent of the viewers prefer sitcoms and 20 percent prefer news documentaries. In equilibrium, both stations will choose to air sitcoms.

The heuristic argument was shown to hold in Gabszewicz et al. (2002). Their model suggests that in "all-advertising-financed media" platforms, often found in radio, television, and some print media, the platforms tend to duplicate their content. However, once subscribers—listeners, viewers, or readers—can be charged a positive price, the platforms will have a greater incentive to differentiate their content. The intuition is clear. Once platforms compete for subscribers with positive subscription prices, they have an incentive to soften the intensity of that price competition by differentiating their products. To put it somewhat differently, once subscribers become an important source of revenue, their content preferences, and not just those of advertisers, become important to the platform operator, as well.

As far as the quality of the content offered on a media platform is concerned, it is more difficult to reach any general conclusions, in part, because program quality is difficult to measure. However, one conclusion holds when there is some consensus on the measure of quality. This is that the market will provide more high-quality programming the less it relies on all-advertising-financed platforms. The underlying intuition is again simple. When a medium is entirely financed by advertising, the platform will typically maximize revenue by maximizing the number of viewers or listeners. This, in turn, induces the platforms to select content that has a "lowest common denominator" or the widest appeal.[13]

### 10.5.3 Advertising Finance and News Bias

The first amendment made to the US Constitution forbade any legislation restricting the freedom of the press. This reflected the broader view that free speech and the free exchange of ideas were fundamental preconditions for having a well-informed public, and hence, for the success of a self-governing democratic republic. In the US, and to a large extent in other Western-style democracies, two-sided platforms—newspapers, television, radio, and increasingly, Internet sites such as Facebook—serve as the locus of access for individuals interested in the news and information. A central question that has emerged in recent years is how well a market-based system will perform in providing what is essentially a public good, news and information. Specifically, there has been growing concern that platform-based, mostly advertising-financed news will exhibit a bias in providing this public good.[14]

At the most basic level, the source of some bias is easy to see. If just a few advertisers, e.g., *Coca-Cola*, are the major source of a platform's advertising finance, then the platform will be reluctant to release news reports critical of that firm. Yet while plausible, this argument is limited in that it is rooted in the idea that a platform faces monopoly power on the advertising side. It is more likely, however, that there are many firms (including e.g., *Pepsi-Cola*) that wish to advertise. The more interesting question is whether and how media platforms will exhibit a bias when there are several firms competing for advertising on the platform.

Economists have now made important progress in understanding how mostly advertising-financed platforms can yield biased reporting in the news. An early contribution to how this might come about is Strömberg (2004). In that analysis, political parties compete by committing to different social policies, each of which yields benefits to specific societal groups. In turn, the news media covering these political differences effectively frame the associated policy debate between candidates and parties. However, because the media platforms are predominantly advertising-financed, they will primarily focus their coverage on those policies that affect large groups and/or groups with some income, as these are the characteristics of the viewing population that advertisers want to reach. In Strömberg (2004), this outcome suggests that there will likely be little media coverage of, say, issues affecting the poor. Anticipating this coverage, politicians will have little incentive to commit to policies on poverty precisely because these will get little coverage, and therefore have little impact on an election. Hence, the press bias in coverage can result in an important bias in policy.

An alternative but also insightful approach to news bias is offered by Gal-Or et al. (2012). Their analysis builds on our earlier discussion of single- versus multi-homing. In their view, advertisers are heterogeneous in terms of their product's appeal and this heterogeneity maps into a similar diversity among consumers. For example, solar panel producers are likely to be of interest to environmentally conscious consumers while fossil fuel firms are likely to generate more interest in consumers who drive pick-up trucks and other heavy users of gasoline.

As Gal-Or et al. (2012) note, news media that compete for subscribers, in part by the subscription price, have an incentive to differentiate their content by catering to specific groups. In terms of the example above, we might have news platform 1 that promotes advertisers with green policies and another news platform 2 that tends to have advertising that plays down the issue of climate change. If we assume that subscribers single-home and choose one of the two news platforms that best meets their interests, then environmentally concerned subscribers will sign on with platform 1 while car and truck fans will subscribe to platform 2.

Of course, advertising firms do face a tradeoff between multi-homing, i.e., advertising on more than one platform and reaching a large audience, or single-homing and reaching an audience whose tastes match better with the features of the advertiser's product. Yet if the heterogeneity among advertisers is relatively strong, the latter strategy will dominate, and advertisers will single-home. As a result, the news platforms will have an even greater incentive to accentuate their bias to extract more funding from their advertisers. In turn, this will lead each platform to focus more on providing news and content that matches with its subscribers' preferences. The market outcome in the Gal-Or et al. (2012) model will be one in which the news platforms are each biased in terms of the issues they cover and in which the subscription base of each platform has a relatively narrow and strongly opinionated view of the issues.[15]

Any discussion of media bias must also recognize that *both* the nature of any such bias *and* the source of the bias matter—a point emphasized by Gentzkow et al. (2016). Some biased reporting, for example, reflects deliberate distortion or filtering of information. Suppose there is an event for which there are $M$ possible outcomes, each outcome denoted by $x_i$. Assume that for each event $x_i$ there is an accurate news report $n_i$. Deliberately distorted reporting would report $n_j$ rather than the correct $n_i$ with the direction of distortion depending on the objective of the reporter.

Alternatively, the bias may instead reflect filtering. Suppose for example, that the $x_i$ possible outcomes refer to "points" scored by the Republican candidate in a US presidential debate, and the points are distributed along an interval of say 1 to 100. In reporting the outcome, the news platform reports simply whether the Republican or Democratic candidate won—this is a (1,0) binary description. A neutral observer might use a cutoff of $x_i = 50$ to decide the winner. However, a conservative news station might use a low threshold of $x_i = 30$ (out of 100) to declare the Republican the winner. A liberal news station might instead use a threshold of $x_i = 70$. The distortion or bias in this case "coarsens" the reporting to be a (1,0) binary description rather than reporting a continuous score $x_i$ along with a difference in how the information is filtered to announce whether the Republican ($n_i = 1$) or the Democrat ($n_i = 0$) won.

Gentzkow et al. (2016) also distinguish between supplier-based sources of bias and demand-based sources. The former would include situations in which the owner of a media platform, e.g., Rupert Murdoch, is not neutral and cares about policy outcomes as well as profits. In that case, the owner has a direct incentive to bias the reporting. It follows that distortive reporting is more likely when there are supplier-based sources of bias. Both distorted and filtered bias can be present then even when consumers have no party preferences and care only about the accuracy of the reporting. However, if consumers are neutral, bias in news will be reduced by increased competition as news platforms try to compete for the mass of neutral subscribers.

In contrast, demand-based bias is a market outcome that emerges in response to voter preferences. Consider our debate example once more. Suen (2004) shows that the biased filtering, as described above, will be reinforced by subscribers who have beliefs about whether a Republican or Democrat is the preferred candidate. A Republican voter, for instance, will have little reason to listen to a Democrat-leaning news service as this service will likely declare the Democrat as the debate winner—a report that the Republican voter will simply discount knowing that platform's bias. Even in the rare circumstance that $x_i > 70$, and the Democrat-leaning news service does in fact report that the Republican won the debate, it only serves to confirm what the Republican voter already believed. So, there is little for a Republican to gain from subscribing to a Democrat-leaning service.

In contrast, such a voter can gain real news from a like-minded, Republican news platform because this service will report that a Democrat won the debate only when the news platform has a very strong signal ($x_i < 30$) that this is the case. However, it is *only* such a strong signal that can induce the Republican voter to revise their prior views on the preferred candidate.[16] The result is that Republican-leaning voters stick to Republican-leaning news services and Democrat-leaning voters stick to Democrat-leaning ones.

In short, it is possible to demonstrate that a market made up of mainly advertising-financed news platforms can lead to a market outcome in which the news platforms exhibit significant biases. These can occur for a variety of reasons. One is when the owners of news media platforms have an objective other than profit maximization and are prepared to pursue it. However, it can also occur as a result of the interaction of consumer preferences and the needs of advertising-financed platforms to attract audiences of interest to the advertiser, e.g., consumers with higher incomes. The reality that different news media may well be biased (in either direction) is a painful but important fact to recognize.

### 10.5.4 Consumer Data, Targeted Advertising, and Price Discrimination

Two-sided platforms may be able to collect information about consumer preferences that is valuable in and of itself. This is particularly true in the current era of digitalized commerce where data on consumer tastes is easy to record and store, e.g., cookies. In turn, the vast volume of "big data" collected on Internet platforms can be shared or sold to data brokers such as Acxiom or Transfax. One main concern here is the loss of "privacy" as detailed information on a consumer's location, age, gender, and buying habits are collected in the public space of the Internet.[17] Another concern is with how the availability and growth of data affects advertising and, in turn, how the advertising strategies that emerge in the era of e-commerce affect market outcomes.

A major innovation resulting from the emergence of "big data" has been the rise of "targeted advertising." Targeted advertising refers to advertising strategies that are differentiated by consumer type. Some consumers receive one kind of ad from the firm, while other consumers receive a different kind of ad. Internet search engines are where targeted advertising is the norm. A consumer makes a search query and the search engine responds with a list of "sponsored links," targeted to that consumer, followed by a list of "organic links." The price the consumer or user pays for searching is zero, i.e., the user can search for free. For a sponsored or advertised link, the advertiser is charged only when the user or potential consumer clicks on that sponsored link. In that case, the advertiser pays the search engine a fee.

We will investigate in the next chapter how the fee paid by the advertiser is determined by an auction, and to enter the auction each advertiser submits a bid and an advertisement containing keywords. At this juncture, the point is simply to recognize that the keywords chosen by the consumer, enable firms to better target or fashion their ads to her more precisely than is possible in general access media such as radio, television, and daily newspapers.

To be sure, search engines are not the only way that firms can target their advertising. One alternative is to advertise in particular "locations," e.g., sporting goods firms can advertise heavily in *Sports Illustrated*. Similarly, it is not uncommon now for consumers to leave either a street or an email address when purchasing an item. This tracking can similarly permit firms to send specific promotional material directly to particular customers.

Nevertheless, the rise of the Internet has greatly enhanced the ability of firms to engage in targeted advertising. What is the impact of such targeting? Two quick advantages are clear. First, targeting is likely to lead to better matches between products and consumers. To the extent that advertising is costly, targeting is a more efficient matching mechanism in that it reduces the waste of a firm sending ads to consumers who are not really interested in its product (see Athey and Gans, 2010).

Second, the ability to target advertising can help small niche firms relative to larger, less specialized firms. When advertising is restricted to broad-based media outlets, large firms selling standardized products with wide appeal will tend to dominate as these are the firms for which advertising on these platforms is worthwhile. However, once targeting becomes feasible and media platforms can unbundle or sort potential consumers into narrower group-based preferences, niche firms can find a group for which advertising is worthwhile (Bergemann and Bonatti, 2011).

The ultimate impact of targeted advertising on the prices and profits of firms practicing targeted advertising is complicated. On the one hand, targeting generally leads to more efficient searches because consumers can be confident that if they do not purchase from the first advertised site visited, the next advertised site is likely a very good substitute. This, in turn, intensifies price competition among those firms targeting their advertising to this group, leading to lower markups to the benefit of consumers. On the other hand, very specific targeting can permit firms to identify consumers with very specific and hence inelastic demands, and this facilitates higher markups.[18]

Any consideration of targeted advertising in the era of "big data" would not be complete without discussing price discrimination—the practice of charging different customers a different price for the same product. Such discrimination is frequently observed in everyday transactions. Tickets to a matinee performance are usually cheaper than tickets for the same film shown in the evening. Senior citizen discounts are a common type of price discrimination based on age. Those who order a bottle of wine at a restaurant pay less per ounce than those who order by the glass. Air travelers booking in advance and staying over a Saturday night typically get a lower air fare than their (usually business) counterparts who fly mid-week and return home quickly.

To understand the incentive to price differentially to consumers, consider a simple example of a small land-owner who has the only freshwater well for several miles from which water can be pumped at essentially zero cost. We will assume that there are three other farms nearby and each of them would like to buy the well water. One of these farms is willing to pay $50 for a weekly water allotment, one is willing to pay $30, and one is willing to pay $15. If the well owner charges the same or *uniform* price to each nearby farm, it is easy to see that the best bet is to set a price of $30. Two of the three farms will then each pay this amount for a total weekly revenue and profit equal to $60.

The uniform-pricing outcome means that the farmer willing to pay $50 only pays $30 for water and so gets a $20 break, while the third farmer willing to pay $15, which is above the cost, gets no water at all. What stops the well owner from lowering the price to $15 to win the patronage of this third farmer is the loss this implies on each of the other two sales, currently bringing in $30 each.

Ideally, the well owner would like to sell water at a weekly price of $50 to the one farmer willing to pay that amount; an additional water allotment at $30 to that farmer with the next-highest valuation; and then charge $15 for supplying water to the third. That is, the well owner would do much better by not selling at a uniform price and instead discriminating across farmers and charging each a different price for water. This can look like "price gouging." However, before condemning such "gouging," we should point out two important aspects of such price discrimination when it can indeed be implemented. First, while the farmer willing to pay $50 is definitely worse off, the farm's loss ($20) is completely offset by the well owner's gain. Hence, this is not a loss from the viewpoint of the total surplus. It is simply a transfer of $20 from buyer to seller. Second, price discrimination would also enable *more* water to be sold as now the third farmer purchases well water who before was unable to buy any. Indeed, this sale creates another $15 of surplus. Price discrimination then may not only be profitable, but also welfare-improving from a total surplus perspective.

Of course, the total surplus—consumer surplus plus producer surplus—may not be the primary concern. In the example above, price discrimination reduces consumer surplus overall, but increases producer surplus by more than this loss. If consumer surplus is the primary policy goal, price discrimination is not necessarily beneficial. Moreover, in some cases the fall in consumer surplus can outweigh any gain in producer surplus so the total surplus may fall as well.[19]

Two conditions must be met for any firm that wishes to price discriminate. First, it must have information about who is who on the demand curve. Which customers are willing to pay a high price, and which are willing only to pay a low price? Second, the firm must be able to prevent buyers from arbitraging such that one who buys at a low price cannot resell to another who would have bought from the firm at a high price.[20]

The potential role of "big data" in facilitating price discrimination should now be clear. It enables firms to gain more information about each individual consumer's demand. Individual consumer information that is now available typically includes age, gender, residential location, prior purchases, search history, credit record, and possibly much more. Yet while firms may have such information across many potential customers, consumers rarely do. This makes it difficult for consumers to arbitrage. Thus, the requirements for successful price discrimination are much more likely to be met in the era of big data.

Implementing discriminatory pricing will typically require targeted advertising. That is, putting a price-discrimination strategy into action, especially in cyber space, will usually require commercial ads that quote different price and/or product offerings to different consumers. There is now substantial empirical evidence of such targeting and the resultant price discrimination, e.g., Valentino-DeVries et al. (2012) and Mikians et al. (2013). Again, however, we note that the impact of discriminatory prices on firms and consumers is complicated. Producers are hurt, and consumers are helped when targeted advertising intensifies price competition often because competition between rivals in discriminatory prices is fiercer (Thisse and Vives, 1988).[21] However, not all consumers will gain from the more intense competition. Some may end up paying more and others less depending on the structure of demand (see Taylor and Wagman, 2014).

## 10.6 SUMMARY

Advertising requires a media platform whether it is print, radio, television, or the web. In turn, these media platforms serve two markets. On one side, they sell space or time to advertisers. On the other, they produce or sell content to consumers that attracts them to the platform. These are the consumers whom the advertisers wish to reach.

Two-sided media platforms generally benefit from indirect network effects. The more consumers subscribe to the platform's content, the larger the audience that advertisers can reach and the more they want to advertise on that platform. It is also possible that the greater number of firms advertising on the platform, say in a fashion magazine, the more consumers may wish to subscribe to the content of the platform.

Markets for which there are important network effects tend to be concentrated markets. The advantages to having a large network often leads to the survival of only a few firms. For example, both the credit card and mobile phone industries, for which there are large network effects, are dominated by just three or four firms. Network competition can be particularly fierce given that only a few firms ultimately make it and there may be a non-trivial element of luck in determining those that do.

The operator of a two-sided platform maximizes profit by choosing a *price structure* across both sides of its platforms. Credit card companies must set fees to both the consumers using their cards and the merchants accepting them. Likewise, newspapers and other media platforms need to set a fee structure comprised of the fee charged to subscribers and the fee charged to advertisers. A useful rule of thumb is that the platform will offer the largest discount to that side of its operations where network effects are most important.

The fact that so much advertising is carried out by two-sided media platforms raises a number of important questions. One is whether such media platforms make it more or less likely that the overall level of advertising will be the socially optimal one. The answer to this question depends on the nature of platform financing and competition, the side of the market with the greatest network effects, and whether consumers regard advertisements as a benefit, a nuisance, or are simply indifferent to them.

Another set of issues stems from the fact that the content that many platforms sell to their subscribers is public news and information. These are public goods and it is natural to ask whether the platforms will provide information accurately or incorporate a bias. In general, the incentive to differentiate content, along with the need to "coarsen" their reporting so that it transmits new information in a less detailed way, suggests that different news media will report events with different biases. Further, news events with little popular appeal will receive little press coverage and, therefore, little attention from policy-makers. In turn, that lack of policy attention will reinforce the bias of the news media against covering such events.

Finally, the rise of digital platforms built on keyword searches such as Google and Amazon and, more generally, the access to extensive consumer data that these and other firms have as the result of conducting business on the Internet raises the possibility that advertising may be directed to very specific consumers rather than presented to a very large audience as in the case of television prior to the rise of cable systems. It seems clear that the ability to target ads yields better matches between consumers and producers. Targeted advertising may also intensify price competition among producers. However, targeted advertising may also facilitate price discrimination and the welfare effects of this are complicated.

Beyond the implications of platform markets for advertising levels, content bias, and price discrimination, there is also the question of how two-sided media platforms compete and what this competition implies for the infrastructure of the advertising market itself. The clear network effects that media platforms, especially digital ones, exhibit force one to recognize that between-platform competition may yield anomalous outcomes. The "tippiness" and "winner-take-all" quality of network markets suggests that in the end, just one or two media platforms will survive and dominate the market, e.g., Google or Facebook. The potential for such dominant firms then to exercise and possibly abuse their resultant monopoly power also raises important antitrust questions connected to advertising. We look to address these issues more fully in Chapter 12.

## NOTES

1   For a formal but very readable introduction to network externalities, see Economides (1996).

2   Note that this pricing policy is essentially that of a two-part tariff as described in Chapter 6.

3   Though not shown in Figure 10.1, zero consumer demand is consistent as a part of an equilibrium with any non-negative price.

4   $\varepsilon_P^A = \dfrac{dQ_A / Q_A}{dP_A / P_A} = \dfrac{P_A}{[\lambda ZN(V - P_S) - P_A]}$.

5   Refer to Chapter 5.

6   To see this, suppose that there is only one newspaper serving the market and assume as well that consumer willingness to pay for a newspaper is sufficiently high relative to cost. Then the monopolist would serve the entire market regardless of the network effect. In this case, there would be no discount offered to subscribers. The equation in (10.22b) does look similar to the one we derived for the monopoly case in section 10.4.1, i.e., equation (10.15), but the difference is that the monopolist in that case does not serve the entire market and so discounting the price to subscribers increases the number of subscribers and allows the monopolist to charge more for advertising.

7   See, e.g., Armstrong (2006).

8   Gabszewicz et al. (2002) seem to be the first to have discovered this result. See also, however, Anderson and Coate (2005), and Armstrong (2006).

9   One must be careful here. In the duopoly model presented, the assumption that the market is fully covered implies that the size of the market is fixed. Hence, price changes cause transfers of surplus rather than changes in the total surplus.

10   Under two-part pricing the platform sets a lump-sum access fee and then a separate fee per transaction. The platform could set these on both sides of the platform. For example, an online newspaper could charge subscribers a fixed fee for general access but add on a separate charge each time the user views a specific key section, such as an editorial page or a crossword page. At the same time, the newspaper could also charge advertisers an up-front fee to do any advertising and then an additional fee dependent on the size or number of ads. This results in a platform having four price parameters to set, which permits a good deal of freedom. Interested readers should refer to Armstrong (2006).

11   See Anderson et al. (2011).

12   See, e.g., Mooney (2010), Sweeting (2010), and Jeziorski (2014).

13   See, e.g., Armstrong (2005).

14   A recent survey by the Pew Research Center found that only 47 percent of US residents felt that the news media reported political issues fairly (Mitchell et al., 2018).

15   If the heterogeneity among advertisers is not too large, advertisers will instead choose to multi-home and focus on pursuing large audiences. This, in turn, will lead the news platforms to seek a similarly broad appeal inducing each to pursue more centrist reporting.

16   See Suen (2004) for a formal presentation of this argument.

17   See Evans (2009) and Acquisti et al. (2016) for a discussion of these issues. However, see Athey et al. (2017) for evidence that consumers may put very little value on protecting their private information.

18   See de Cornière (2016). His analysis also notes that the common practice in which the advertising firm pays the platform a fee per click through effectively turns that fee into a marginal cost that, in turn, also raises the market price.

19 A rough rule of thumb is that the total surplus will decline if the total quantity declines. See, e.g., Schmalensee (1981).

20 See Lane et al. (2014) for documentation of the large market for privacy information. See also Taylor (2004).

21 Under uniform pricing, a firm can only offer a price reduction to a rival's customers by extending that price reduction to all the firm's current customers. When prices are discriminatory, price cuts may be more selective. So, there is less of a disincentive to making them.

# 10.7 REFERENCES

Acquisti, A., C. Taylor, and L. Wagman. 2016. "The Economics of Privacy." *Journal of Economic Literature* 54 (June), 442–92.

Anderson, S., and S. Coate. 2005. "Market Provision of Broadcasting: A Welfare Analysis." *Review of Economic Studies* 72 (October), 947–72.

Anderson, S., O. Foros, H. J. Kind, and M. Peitz. 2011. "Media Market Concentration, Advertising Levels, and Ad Prices." CDSifo Working Paper No. 3677.

Armstrong, M. 2005. "Public Service Broadcasting." *Fiscal Studies* 26 (September), 281–99.

Armstrong, M. 2006. "Competition in Two-Sided Markets." *RAND Journal of Economics* 37 (Autumn), 668–91.

Athey, S., C. Catalini, and C. Tucker. 2017. "The Digital Privacy Paradox: Small Money, Small Costs, Small Talk." NBER Working Paper 23488.

Athey, S., and J. Gans. 2010. "The Impact of Targeting Technology on Advertising Markets and Competition." *American Economic Review* 100 (May), 608–13.

Bergemann, D., and A. Bonatti. 2011. "Targeting in Advertising Markets: Implications for Offline Versus Online Media." *RAND Journal of Economics* 42 (Fall), 417–43.

Berry, S., and J. Waldfogel. 2010. "Product Quality and Market Size." *Journal of Industrial Economics* 58 (March), 1–31.

de Cornière, A. 2016. "Search Advertising." *American Economic Journal: Microeconomics* 8 (August), 156–88.

Economides, N. 1996. "The Economics of Networks." *International Journal of Industrial Organization* 14 (October), 673–99.

Evans, D. 2009. "The Online Advertising Industry: Economics, Evolution, and Privacy." *Journal of Economic Perspectives* 23 (Summer), 37–60.

Gabszewicz, J.-J., D. Laussel, and N. Sonnac. 2002. "Press Advertising and the Political Differentiation of Newspapers." *Journal of Public Economic Theory* 4 (July), 317–34.

Gal-Or, E., T. Geylani, and T. P. Yildirim. 2012. "The Impact of Advertising on Media Bias." *Journal of Marketing Research* 49 (February), 92–99.

Gentzkow, M., J. Shapiro, and D. Stone (2016). "Media Bias in the Marketplace: Theory." In *Handbook of Media Economics, Volume 1B*, ed. S. Anderson, J. Waldfogel, and D. Strömberg (623–46). Amsterdam: Elsevier.

Hotelling, H. 1929. "Stability in Competition." *Economic Journal* 39 (March), 41–57.

Jeziorski, P. 2014. "Effects of Mergers in Two-Sided Markets: The U.S. Radio Industry." *American Economic Journal: Microeconomics* 6 (November), 36–73.

Lane, J., V. Stodden, S. Bender, and H. Nissenbaum. 2014. *Privacy, Big Data, and the Public Good: Frameworks for Engagement*. Cambridge: Cambridge University Press.

Mikians, J., L. Gyarmati, V. Erramilli, and N. Laoutaris. 2013. "Crowd-Assisted Search for Price Discrimination in E-Commerce: First Results." In *Proceedings of the 9th ACM Conference on Emerging Networking Experiments and Technologies*, 1–6.

Mitchell, A., K. Simmons, K. Matsa, and L. Silver. 2018. "Publics Globally Want Unbiased News Coverage, but Are Divided on Whether Their News Media Deliver." Pew Research Center (January). https://www.pewresearch.org/global/2018/01/11/publics-globally-want-unbiased-news-coverage-but-are-divided-on-whether-their-news-media-deliver/ (accessed 19 January, 2020).

Mooney, C. T. 2010. "A Two-Sided Market Analysis of Radio Ownership Caps." Working Paper, Economics Department, University of Oklahoma.

Noam, E. 2009. *Media Ownership and Concentration in America*. Oxford: Oxford University Press.

Rohlfs, J. 1974. "A Theory of Interdependent Demand for a Communications Service." *The Bell Journal of Economics* 5 (Spring), 16–37.

Schmalensee, R. 1981. "Output and Welfare Implications of Monopolistic, Third-Degree Price Discrimination." *American Economic Review* 71 (March), 242–47.

Steiner, P. O. 1952. "Program Patterns and Preferences, and the Workability of Competition in Radio Broadcasting." *Quarterly Journal of Economics* 66 (May), 194–223.

Strömberg, D. 2004. "Mass Media Competition, Political Competition, and Public Policy." *The Review of Economics and Statistics* 71 (January), 265–84.

Suen, W. 2004. "The Self-Perpetuation of Biased Beliefs." *The Economic Journal* 114 (April), 377–96.

Sweeting, A. 2010. "The Effects of Horizontal Mergers on Product Positioning: Evidence from the Music Radio Industry." *RAND Journal of Economics* 41 (Summer), 372–97.

Taylor, C. 2004. "Consumer Privacy and the Market for Customer Information." *RAND Journal of Economics* 35 (Winter), 631–50.

Taylor, C., and L. Wagman. 2014. "Consumer Privacy in Oligopolistic Markets: Winners, Losers, and Welfare." *International Journal of Industrial Organization* 34 (May), 80–84.

Thisse, J.-F., and X. Vives. 1988. "On the Strategic Choice of Spatial Price Policy." *American Economic Review* 78 (March), 122–37.

Valentino-DeVries, J., J. Singer-Vine, and A. Soltani. 2012. "Websites Vary Prices, Deals Based on Users' Information." *Wall Street Journal*, December 24, p. 1.

# 11
# Platforms Advertising: Pricing and Profitability

## 11.1 INTRODUCTION

Advertising needs a medium, and that medium is typically a two-sided platform such as a television or radio station, newspaper, search engine, or website. This, of course, is costly. Media platforms charge for advertising space in print or digital media and for airtime on radio or TV. In some cases, the media platform sets a fixed fee for the space or time slot, but often platform pricing for advertising is more complicated. In this chapter, we investigate how the price for advertising space is determined. That is, we examine the "nuts-and-bolts" of the pricing of advertising slots on media platforms.

Expenditure on advertising across the various media platforms is large—over $240 billion in 2019 for the US and roughly $600 billion worldwide. Equally important as the volume of advertising expenditure is its distribution across different media platforms. Figure 11.1 shows this distribution for 2019. It is important to note that digital advertising now accounts for more than half of all advertising expenditures in the US and this has been the case since 2016. However, the rest of the world has also experienced a growing movement of advertising expenditures away from traditional media platforms and toward the Internet.[1]

Media platforms can sell on the two sides of their market: the viewers or users on one side and advertisers on the other side. It is the interaction of users on one side and the interaction across the two sides that generates network effects. The profit-maximizing platform will recognize that its method for allocating slots to advertisers has implications for the volume and quality of advertising. In turn, that advertising experience will affect the number and kind of consumers or users that the platform attracts, which then feeds back to advertisers' demand for advertising slots.

In the case of traditional media platforms, such as radio and television, advertising minutes compete directly with airtime of a station's programming content. In such cases, the platform will likely find it necessary to limit advertising time—perhaps by raising the price. Digital advertising is different in this regard. Generally, digital advertising can be broken down into two different categories: search advertising, e.g., keyword purchases on a search engine, and display advertising, e.g., banners and videos. The easily expandable quality of cyber space creates a different type of "space" from the finite number of minutes or pages of space available on a traditional media platform.

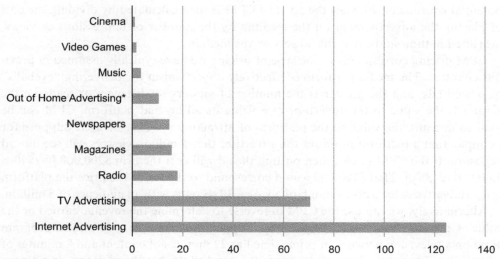

*Note:* *Includes any visual advertising media found outside the home, e.g., billboards.

*Source:* IAB Internet Advertising Revenue Report: https://www.iab.com/wp-content/uploads/2020/05/FY19-IAB-Internet-Ad-Revenue-Report_Final.pdf.

**Figure 11.1** US 2019 advertising revenues by media platform ($ billion)

Even on digital platforms, however, there is still the risk of congestion, i.e., that landing page space may have so many ads that consumers cannot easily focus on any single one or the platform's content.

The pricing mechanisms that have been developed for advertising on digital platforms differ notably from those adopted by the traditional platforms. We examine the pricing of advertising space on first traditional and then digital media platforms in the next two sections. We focus on the pricing mechanisms used by Google and Facebook in section 11.4. Given the advertising revenue that these platforms earn, and hence the advertising expenditure that firms incur on them, a natural question to ask is whether such advertising expenditures are worthwhile. Accordingly, we turn in section 11.5 to a consideration of the effectiveness of digital advertising and whether the implied return on this investment justifies its cost. Section 11.6 provides a summary of the chapter's main results.

## 11.2 TRADITIONAL MEDIA PRICING: COST PER MILLE

The most popular method for pricing advertising on traditional media platforms employs a measure known as Cost per Mille or CPM. Here, "mille" refers to the number of impressions or views, measured in thousands, that an ad posted on that platform is expected to receive. The CPM combines two pieces of data relevant to an advertiser. The first is the price set by the platform for placing the ad and the second is how many potential consumers will view the ad. The CPM is then calculated by dividing the cost of placing the advertisement on the medium by the number of impressions or views, measured in thousands, that the ad gets on the medium.

CPM pricing corresponds to the type of pricing we have typically assumed in previous chapters. The media platform is effectively a mechanism for delivering "eyeballs" to posted ads, and the greater is the number of viewers (or listeners or readers), the greater is the value to the advertiser of posting its ad on that platform. CPM can be used to measure the value to the platform of attracting a viewer or user. Suppose for example, that a platform promises the advertiser that 5 million viewers will see one ad exposure. If the CPM is $40, then posting the ad will cost the firm $200,000 [= ($40 × 5,000,000)/1,000]. That $200,000 would correspond to the fee or the price the platform sets to advertisers for a given standard ad, e.g., 30 seconds with an audience of 5 million.

Alternatively, we can use the CPM in reverse to determine the revenue earned or the value of any one consumer to the platform. Suppose, for example, a 30-minute program aired on a television network at prime time has 22 minutes of content and 8 minutes of advertising. There are, therefore, sixteen 30-second spots that the platform or network can sell to potential advertisers. Suppose that the CPM for one 30 second ad spot is $25. That means an advertiser is willing to pay the platform $0.025 for each viewer of the 30 seconds of advertising. The network or platform earns in ad revenue from each viewer of the 30-minute program 16 × $.025 = $0.40. That's roughly how much each viewer of a program is worth to the platform that airs the program.

Different media have different CPMs with the differences arising from both the composition of the viewing audiences and the ability of the medium to engage ad viewers. Largely because television offers an immediate experience that is both visual and audible, the CPM for advertising on a television network is typically more expensive than that for radio or print media. Depending on the audience, the CPM on television can range from $5 for a 30-second spot on a local network outside of prime time to $36 for a 30-second ad airing in prime time on a major network.[2] The CPM for an outdoor billboard, on the other hand is roughly $5. Alternatively, a freeway billboard that gets 400,000 views per period will be priced at $2,000 per period, whereas a billboard on a country road with only 30,000 views per period will be priced at $600 per period.[3]

There is a good bit of variation in CPMs even within the same medium. This variation is largely due to variation in the size and composition of the viewing audience of a program or content on the platform. A network needs to know how many viewers are watching a show as well as the mix of demographic groups in that total. A magazine or newspaper publisher needs to have some idea of how many subscribers it has, as well as the breakdown of that readership by age, race, gender, location, and income, in determining the CPM that it will charge advertisers. The CPM rate will also depend upon the size of the printed ad space, whether it is in color or in black and white, and its location in the magazine.

Nielsen Media Research emerged by the mid-twentieth century as the dominant firm providing TV and radio networks with measures of the size and composition of the audience for particular magazines, or particular TV shows and specific time slots.[4]

Nielsen started radio ratings in the 1940s, and expanded to television ratings in the 1950s. Originally data on radio listeners and then TV viewers were collected using diaries in which households recorded their listening and viewing habits. Nielsen targeted various demographics to measure their viewing habits by program, network, and time of day. Later metering boxes attached to the televisions of recruited households were used to transmit information about viewing habits over the telephone system on a minute-to-minute basis. The television program that has achieved the highest Nielsen rating over the past decade is NBC's *Sunday Night Football*, which averages around 21 million viewers.

Now in the twenty-first century, Nielsen has expanded its measurement tools into digital and streaming platforms. Internet streaming and television viewing is a rapidly growing market. Platforms such as iTunes, Hulu, and YouTube as well as TV networks' websites provide full-length web-based programming that is either subscription-based or ad-supported. These platforms can measure the popularity of a program, but TV networks, on the other hand, face the challenge in identifying overlap between traditional television viewers and live stream viewers of its program. Nielsen is expanding its market research offerings to meet this challenge and to track viewers over multiple digital platforms.[5]

It is important to understand that the composition of audience or subscription base is critical as this permits the advertising firm to know where and how to direct its advertising efforts. For example, pet supply firms primarily sell to pet owners. Hence, it is natural that such firms advertise heavily in programs or magazines or websites that are popular with pet owners. In contrast, prime time television programs often appeal to a wide variety of viewers who differ by gender, age, race, location, hobbies, interests, and so on, and so we should expect the advertising on such programs to be for products or services that have broader appeal.

## 11.3 DIGITAL ADVERTISING: FROM COST PER MILLE TO COST PER CLICK

Advertising on digital platforms, which started in the 1990s, began with display ads that were priced on the CPM model of traditional media platforms. Like print or TV, the number of impressions or views on a digital platform was calculated to be the number of users who viewed the ad on the platform. CPM is still used today on many digital platforms. In 2018 the average CPM over the entire Google network was roughly $2.80,[6] whereas the typical CPM on Facebook Ads is around $10, but closer to $5 on Instagram.[7]

However, digital platforms differ from traditional media platforms in that they have an explicit capability to allow the user to interact actively with the medium. The interactive capability of a digital platform soon led to a different way of price advertising, and that way has now come to dominate the pricing of advertising on digital media platforms. This way of pricing is called Cost per Click or CPC. It began in 1996 when

Procter & Gamble and Yahoo! entered a contract by which Procter & Gamble agreed to pay for its advertising on Yahoo! only when a user on Yahoo! interacted or "clicked" on its ad.

Interestingly, the pioneering of CPC evolved early on while use of the Internet was growing exponentially. In particular, the late 1990s witnessed an explosion in the number of company web pages. Web users increasingly found it difficult to navigate the thousands of web pages without the aid of a search engine such as Yahoo! It was search engine platforms that adopted the CPC pricing model, and in many fundamental ways, it is the search engine Google that transformed advertising in the digital age. We explore more deeply how Google prices ad space in the next section.

A digital platform user who interacts or clicks on an ad reveals their interest in the ad. The click is how the digital platform can measure that the ad was viewed by the user. Digital platforms, unlike traditional ones, can therefore obtain better measures of user engagement, and this is a key difference. It is not technically feasible to measure whether an ad was viewed or heard on radio, or on TV or in print. A TV viewer might leave the room during a commercial or a newspaper reader might not even open the page with the ad. A traditional media platform's estimate of its viewing audience, say the magazine's readership, is therefore less accurate in pricing its ad space because it cannot guarantee the ad will reach the user of the platform. Nor can it be sure that the ad will make an impression on all who see it. In contrast, the web browser who clicks on a link directing the user to a firm's website has shown a clear interest in the firm's products.

Data on clicks is extremely useful to the platform in assessing the value of an advertiser on the one side to the potential user on the other. Perhaps more importantly this interactive feature of a digital platform is highly valued by the advertiser. The platform can learn a great deal about the preferences of a user from their pattern of "clicks," and with this information it can help the advertiser target its ads to potential consumers more effectively. Moreover, the use of cookies and other identification techniques also permit the platform and advertiser to know something of the history of the consumer's searches. As we will see, this cache of information has been an important part of Google's rise as the dominant search engine.

Digital advertising is not completely without a downside. There can be so many ads on a site that any one ad struggles to win the consumer's undivided attention. With television and radio platforms, different ads are less likely to be competing at the same time for the viewer's eyeballs. Yet, while it is difficult to target advertising on such platforms, these platforms can still offer an advantage over digital ones, particularly when the goal is to reach a wide pool of consumers in each region.

Reaching a large swath of consumers may be particularly critical for a new product or service. The major advertising objective for a new product is to inform many consumers about the product, its functions and availability. In this context, a digital ad campaign may be less effective as potential consumers are not likely to click on an ad for a product and/or a brand that they know nothing about.

## 11.4 DETERMINING THE CPC IN AN AUCTION

In Chapter 10 we used a simple advertising model in which a platform had a standard size or time duration for an "ad" that would run over some standard space of time. The platform set a price per ad with a view toward maximizing its profit considering the network effects that might exist on either or both sides of its market. The usefulness of this approach is demonstrated by the many insights that it provides about the behavior of the media platform, its viewers and its advertisers. However, in the real digital world, the pricing of ad space on digital platforms is different. Specifically, CPC pricing is based on the outcome of an auction.

Google was a pioneer in the use of auctions in CPC pricing for search advertising through its Ad Words exchange developed in 2002. To see how Ad Words works, suppose you are searching for London accommodation during the Labor Day weekend, and you type the words "London hotel" into a Google search. In a split second several things happen simultaneously and very quickly. Google Ad Words will list the keywords "hotel in London" on its exchange. Hotel chains and independent hotels in the London area will place bids quoting the CPC rate they are willing to pay to be listed in the sponsored search results that will appear to you. Again, all this is done in milliseconds. Google runs an auction and the advertisers with the top three, *quality-adjusted* bids will have their ads loaded on the page ranked from top to bottom before you notice that anything has happened. Google runs literally millions of such auctions each second.

We highlight the term "*quality-adjusted*" bids. Google does not simply rank the bids in terms of those advertisers bidding highest, the next highest, and so on. Instead, Google "adjusts" the bids to determine an ad ranking that Google believes will satisfy both the needs of the advertisers to reach consumers and the needs of consumers to have a good search experience. Satisfying both sides of its search engine market is the key to maximizing its profit. To understand how Google does this adjustment, and more generally how Ad Words works, it is helpful first to have some understanding of basic auction theory.

### 11.4.1 Google and Auctions

A common kind of auction is known as a first-price sealed bid auction. Bidders put their bids for the item being auctioned off in a sealed envelope and the auctioneer opens them up and awards the item to the highest bidder; collecting the amount the highest bidder bid for the item. The defining characteristic of a first-price auction is that the winner of the auction pays the price that they bid.

In a first-price auction, however, bidders have an incentive to bid less than how much they really value the item being auctioned, but at the same time bid enough so that they can expect to win. The bidder's incentive in a first-price bid auction is to win the auction and pay something less than their maximum willingness to pay or the true value to them of the auctioned off item. If a search engine uses a first-price auction to allocate a sponsored link on its results page, the auction will likely lead to unstable bidding strategies among the advertisers bidding for the link. It also means that the revenue earned by the search engine may be less than what it could have been had the highest bidder revealed and paid their true willingness to pay.

A different kind of auction is known as a second-price sealed bid auction or Vickrey auction.[8] Again, the bidder with the highest bid wins the auction, but in this case the bidder pays a price equal to the *second*-highest bid price. In a second-price auction, bidders *do* have an incentive to reveal their maximum willingness to pay when they bid for the item. There is now no benefit to bidding less because doing so only affects your chance of winning the auction, and *not* the amount paid.

To see this point more clearly, suppose that the maximum value you place on an item is $100, so that if you win the auction your net gain is $100 less the price you pay. Suppose you bid more than $100. Doing this will improve your chance of winning the auction, but if the second-highest bidder also bids a little more than $100, you incur a loss because you will pay more for the item than it is worth to you! If you bid more than $100 and the second-highest bidder bids less than $100 you do not improve your chances of winning, as a bid of $100 would have won the auction. If you bid less than $100, you reduce the chance of winning but not the price you pay for the item. It follows that your best strategy is simply to bid $100, your true value of the auctioned item.

It is possible that a first-price, sealed bid auction could yield a similar result. If, for instance, we assume that all bidders understand the distribution of individual values, each can shade their bid below their own value to their estimate of the next-highest amount. That's a strong assumption, however. If bidders instead differ in their view on how values are distributed, the optimal bidding strategy becomes complicated and changeable. Hence, the first-price sealed bid auction can easily lead to unstable bidding strategies, whereas a second-price auction will incentivize advertisers to bid their true value for the space being auctioned off. Early on in its development of an online advertising system, Ad Words, Google adopted a second-price auction, largely because in a second-price sealed auction, bidding one's true value is an optimal strategy.

Returning to our example of searching for "London hotels" suppose that Google will display three sponsored hotel links in response to the search inquiry and that there are four hotels bidding for these keywords. Their bids per click are $0.20, $0.15, $0.12, and $0.10, and these bids reflect each hotel's respective value of winning the desired sponsored link. In a simple second-price auction, the highest bidder would win the top spot but pay for a click on that link, i.e., CPC, a bid that was made by the second-highest bidder, namely, $0.15. Likewise, the second-highest bidder would win the second slot but pay for a click the bid amount of the third-highest bidder, $0.12. Finally, the third-highest bidder would win the third slot but pay the amount of $0.10 for a click on its link. The fourth-highest bidder would not be listed in the sponsored ads that top the search query response.

The fourth-highest bidder does not win a sponsored link slot. To win one would have required that the bid submitted be more than $0.10, which is more than the value the bidder put on the sponsored link. Being outbid makes the bidder no worse off. Indeed, the fourth-highest bidder would be worse off if the bidder had "won" a slot by paying more than $0.10.

Alternatively, suppose the top-valuation bidder submitted a bid below the true valuation of $0.20 per click, e.g., imagine that the bidder instead submitted a value of $0.16. The bidder in this example still wins and still pays $0.15 per click. However, if the valuation of the second-highest bidder had instead been $0.18 per click, then bidding a $0.16 value would have lost the high valuation bidder the top link and the chance to enjoy a $0.02 gain in the value of click over what the bidder pays per click. More generally, any bidder who bids less than the true valuation in the second-price auction does not lower the price paid if the bidder does win and runs the risk of being outbid and losing the chance for pure gain.[9] In a second-price sealed auction, bidding one's true value is an optimal strategy.[10]

Google adopts the second-price auction with the added twist of *quality adjustment*. Google wants to post advertisers' ads that are relevant to the user's search query. Just because an advertiser bids a high amount to show its ad does not mean that their ad will be relevant or useful to the searcher. To ensure relevancy in the auction, Google does not rank, as we did in the above example, the advertisers solely by the bids they submit. The ranking of advertisers in an Ad Words auction is determined by the advertiser's bid and by a measure of the *quality* of the advertiser's ad.

How quality is measured is Google's "secret sauce" and depends on such factors as the relevancy of the ad to the user's search query, the quality of the landing page that the user goes to when the user clicks, and the expected clickthrough rate (CTR) of the ad. CTR measures the percentage of viewers who saw the ad and clicked on it; i.e., CTR = (Total Clicks on Ad)/(Total Number of Views). Google earns revenue when the user clicks on a sponsored link. Ads for sites with high-expected CTRs are likely sites to which users have often gone before. Google as a search engine has a vast amount of search data to estimate expected CTR. The high bid of $0.20 in our example above will not bring in revenue if the user is not likely to click on that ad.

It is Google's measure of "*quality*" times the advertiser's bid that determines the Ad Rank, or where the ad is shown on the page or whether the ad is shown at all. An advertiser with a relatively low bid for a click can have a higher Ad Rank and beat out a competing advertiser with a higher bid if that advertiser has a higher measure of *quality*. In addition, the advertiser who won the space in the auction does not pay as CPC what the advertiser bid in the auction. The advertiser pays a CPC that is just enough to beat the Ad Rank of the advertiser that is just below it in the ranking.

Our numerical example can be used to illustrate Google's Ad Rank in a search. The first column of Table 11.1 identifies each bidder. The next two columns show the amount submitted by each bidder and the *ad quality* score that Google assigns to each bidder. The product of these two values then determines the "adjusted" bid shown in the fourth column of the table.

The adjusted bid is what determines the bidder's Ad Rank. As illustrated, Bidder B has a high-quality score of 9. Bidder B wins the highest rank even though the amount bid of $0.15 was less than the $0.20 bid by Bidder A. Bidder A has a quality of score of only 6.

**Table 11.1** Google auction, Ad Rank, and CPC

| Bidder ID | Amount Bid | Quality Score | Adjusted Bid | Ad Rank | CPC |
|-----------|-----------|---------------|--------------|---------|-----|
| A | $0.20 | 6 | $1.20 | 2 | $0.1167 |
| B | $0.15 | 9 | $1.35 | 1 | $0.1333 |
| C | $0.12 | 5 | $0.60 | 4 | — |
| D | $0.10 | 7 | $0.70 | 3 | $0.0857 |

Somewhat similarly, Bidder D is now ranked higher that Bidder C, even though the bid of $0.10 was less than the bid of $0.12 submitted by Bidder C who is now out of the running.

The fifth column of Table 11.1 illustrates the way CPC is determined. The CPC charged to the top-ranked bidder, Bidder B, is the amount just needed to match the adjusted bid value of the second-ranked bidder, Bidder A, and maintain B's top ranking. Given its quality score of 9, Bidder B would need to pay a CPC price of $0.1333 to match the adjusted bid of Bidder A as $9 \times \$0.13333 = \$1.20$. Similarly, given its quality score of 6, Bidder A would have to pay a CPC of $0.1167 to match the adjusted bid of Bidder D, which is $0.70. For bidder D, the CPC rate of $0.0857 is the amount needed to match the adjusted bid of $0.60 submitted by Bidder C.

## 11.4.2 Facebook and the Vickery-Clarke-Groves Pricing Mechanism

Keyword advertising on Google's search engine is an important component of digital advertising. Search advertising accounts for roughly 45 percent of all US digital advertising expenditure, and Google is the dominant player in this market. Recent estimates indicate that Google has an 86 percent market share, leaving others such as Yahoo! and Bing far behind.[11]

Search advertising is, however, not the only form of digital advertising. Facebook for example is not a search engine and yet as a two-sided platform it earns sizable revenue from advertising. Similarly, YouTube, the *New York Times* web page, and Yelp are also two-sided platforms that earn revenue from advertising. On these platforms, advertisers bid for advertising displays, including banners and videos. Display advertising accounts for another 40 percent of digital advertising expenditure. We focus here on how Facebook allocates space on its platform to display advertising.

Facebook is primarily a social network. Its business model is based on advertising revenue because as a two-sided platform it can bring advertisers into contact with potential customers. Unlike a Google user who is searching for information, a Facebook user may be on the platform to see friends' vacation pictures. Whereas Google can allocate space to advertisers that are relevant to the user's search for information, Facebook risks allocating space to an advertiser away from some alternative use that is more highly valued by the user.

One way for Facebook to price the space being allocated to advertising is to determine how much value is being displaced from not allocating that space to its alternative uses. Alternatively, how would that space be valued if the advertiser did not participate in the bidding for the space? That value could be the value of lost clicks and lost sales, or lost likes and lost utility that other users incurred because the space was not allocated to them. An allocation that reflects the opportunity cost of not making that allocation is the basis for the Vickery-Clarke-Groves (VCG) mechanism, and it is used by Facebook in the design of its ad auctions.

To illustrate how a VCG auction works, we return to our numerical example above. Suppose again that there are four bidders—A, B, C, and D—each valuing a click or interaction with their Facebook post of $0.20, $0.15, $0.12, and $0.10, respectively. In this example, they are not bidding for a sponsored link, but say for one of two display ads on a Facebook Newsfeed, each of which will run for, say, one week. Over this time, each display is expected to generate 1000 clickthroughs. Hence, the value of a Facebook weekly display to the four bidders would be $200, $150, $120, and $100, respectively.

Facebook wants to allocate that space to the most valuable use and wants the four bidders to submit truthful valuations of their post. In an auction that is designed to reveal truthful bidding, the two display ads will go to Bidders A and B. How can Facebook design an auction so that bids will be truthful, or alternatively, what price should winners pay for the displays to ensure truthful bidding? If the two bidders with the two highest valuations, Bidder A and B, are the auction winners, we know that Bidder A gets a display valued at $200 per week and Bidder B gets one valued at $150 per week. Neither Bidders C nor D get a display.

In this setting, the VCG mechanism starts by asking, "How would matters be different for Bidders B, C, and D if Bidder A had been excluded and the two displays awarded to the remaining top two bidders?" In that case, Bidder B would now be the highest bidder and again, obtain a display valued at $150. However, with A gone, Bidder C now becomes the second-highest bidder and so wins the second display, which is valued at $120. Bidder D of course still gets nothing. So, in this case, the total value obtained by Bidders B, C, and D is $150 + $120 + $0 = $270. Considering these results, the VCG mechanism says that the net "cost" to all the *other* bidders (B, C, and D combined) that A's participation imposes is: $270 – $150 = $120.

Now consider the same exercise with Bidder B. With B participating in the auction, both Bidder B and Bidder A win, while Bidders C and D get nothing. Hence, the total value received by all the bidders *except B* is: $200 + $0 + $0 = $200. If, however, Bidder B is excluded from the bidding, then the top two valuations are those of Bidders A and C, namely, $200 + $120, respectively. As Bidder D would again get nothing, the total value received by all the bidders other than B in this case is: $200 + $120 + $0 = $320. Hence, the VCG mechanism calculates that the "cost" that B's participation imposes on the other three bidders is: $320 – $200 = $120—the same as for Bidder A.

The value of $120 is of course not arbitrary. It is in fact the maximum value that Bidder C would be willing to pay for the display ad. If Facebook ran an ascending or English auction where the price of a display ad continued to rise until just two bidders were left, the auction-clearing price would in fact be $120. Once the price hits that level (or just a bit higher), both Bidders C and D would drop out leaving Bidders A and B to claim the two displays.

Facebook's VCG auction follows the above logic. In our example, Facebook would invite sealed bids from all four bidders with the two winning bidders paying a price equal to the third-highest bid, namely, $120. There is a clear similarity then to the second-price auction described earlier. Moreover, the intuition as to why each bidder will bid their true value is again the same. No bidder has an incentive to bid above their valuation as this does not enhance the chance for a net gain.

For Bidders A and B, submitting bids above $200 or $150, respectively, does nothing to improve their chance of winning a display. Similarly, if Bidder C bid say, $160, then Bidder C would win a display but, in this case, Bidder B's bid of $150 would be the third-highest bid and hence the price that the VCG auction would charge. In that case, Bidder C would end up paying $150 for a display that Bidder C values at only $120. Likewise, there is no gain from bidding below one's valuation because again, the "price" a bidder pays is not based on the bidder's submitted bid, but on the bids submitted (valuations revealed) by other bidders.

This VCG outcome is quite general. If $K$ displays were up for auction, the VCG approach would award the $K$ displays to the $K$ highest bidders and charge each of them the $K+1$th highest bid. With bidders bidding their true values, this ensures that the $K$ displays will be awarded to the advertisers with the $K$ highest display valuations. Of course, with each bidder submitting a single bid, the auction process is much faster than an ascending (English) auction.

Whereas Google dominates in search advertising, Facebook has considerable market power in display advertising, e.g., videos, banners, or sponsored pages, accounting for roughly 50 percent of the display market. This is four times larger than Google's share of display advertising.[12] Obviously, large as they are, Google and Facebook are not the only digital advertising platforms. There are a number of ad exchanges (some of which are operated by Google) that intermediate between advertisers and other platforms such as, say, an online newspaper site with a pool of ad spaces to sell to those advertisers.[13] Here, as in the stock exchanges, the winning bidder pays the amount bid, i.e., these ad exchanges generally run first-price auctions.[14]

Google uses second-price auctions for the ad space on platforms where it controls the end-to-end buying transaction, such as on YouTube, and Google Search. However, Google offers other services in the digital advertising industry, including an ad exchange platform that also uses auctions. An ad exchange platform enables advertisers and digital publishers to buy and sell advertising space across multiple digital sites. It is like a big pool of ad spaces that digital publishers hope advertisers will buy. Advertisers decide which spaces or impressions they would like to purchase or bid on and their bids vary depending on time of day, platform, device, or targeted audience.[15] The winning bids are determined on Google's ad exchange network in an auction, but in this case a first-price auction.[16]

Why are auctions—in a variety of formats—the predominant way of pricing advertising on the Internet? The primary reason is targeting. The impact and therefore the value of advertising depends on the key features that identify the product. Internet searching focused on keywords makes it possible to commoditize those words. Instead of charging for space in a newspaper or a time slot on a television network, the Internet makes it possible to charge for those keywords directly and auctions are a very efficient way to determine the optimal price for those keywords.[17]

# 11.5  MEASURING THE RETURN TO DIGITAL ADVERTISING

Because millions of ad impressions are traded through exchanges, shown in displays, and turned up in sponsored links, measuring the return to digital advertising can be particularly vexing. The precise targeting of digital ads via keywords and the ability to track users' web history via "cookies" holds the hope that such advertising will be more effective than the broad-based advertising common to, say, radio and television. Whether that hope is realized or not remains, however, an open question. In this section, we look at recent efforts to provide an answer.

Before we begin, it is worth reviewing some of the problems that plague the effort to isolate the impact of advertising on sales. Seasonal effects are likely to be important. In addition, the impact of advertising will likely depend on the reputation of the firm, e.g., whether it is a well-known established firm or an upstart entrant trying to become better known. It may also depend on the type of product, e.g., products that are technologically complex versus those that are standardized and well understood. The type of consumer that sees the ad, e.g., a first-time user of a product or one with a long history of use, may also be important. The extensive data that is generated by each consumer's online activity may be used to help address these difficulties. Whether or not that is enough to allow us to measure the impact of Internet advertising on consumer behavior is another question.

## 11.5.1  The Effectiveness of Internet Marketing—the eBay Study

Internet advertising includes sponsored search links and banner or video display. The first, as we have discussed, is when firms pay or bid to be listed on, say, Google's sponsored links list. This is referred to as search engine marketing (SEM). It comprises a significant share of Internet advertising expenditure and is the major source of Google's revenue. To date, one of the most provocative and possibly most compelling investigations of such SEM advertising is the study on eBay advertising by Blake et al. (2015). They use a random control trial to estimate eBay's return on investment (ROI) in bidding for sponsored links on search engines such as Google and Microsoft's Bing. As a preview, they show that the data collected could be presented in ways that suggest ROI values that range from –63 percent to +4,173 percent. That's an enormous range, of course. What accounts for this vast variation?

A large part of the variation comes from the failure to recognize the endogeneity of advertising expenditures. In fact, the wide range of *positive* estimates for *eBay's*

ROI for advertising expenditures are estimates obtained by Blake et al. (2015) when they do *not* control for endogeneity. In contrast, they find negative estimates for ROI when they address the endogeneity issues that arise in keyword advertising expenditure.

Endogeneity leads to biases in the ordinary least squares (OLS) estimates of the effect of keyword advertising on a dependent variable such as sales. For example, if we denote by $Sales_{it}$ the logarithm of eBay's online sales in market $i$ at time $t$, and by $AS_{it}$ the logarithm of its search engine advertising spending in that same market $i$ at time $t$, then the hypothesis that advertising spending causes more sales may be represented by a simple regression:

$$Sales_{it} = \beta_0 + \beta_1 AS_{it} + \varepsilon_{it} \qquad (11.1)$$

Here, $\varepsilon_{it}$ is a residual term meant to capture all other random shocks in market $i$ at time $t$, that are *independent* of the level of advertising spending $AS_{it}$.

However, the independence of $AS_{it}$ and $\varepsilon_{it}$ is exactly what the endogeneity of $AS_{it}$ calls into question. Broadly speaking, it is quite probable that a random shock that leads consumers in the market $i$ at time $t$ to want to buy more products will also lead eBay to want to spend more on advertising to exploit that opportunity. Indeed, in the case of paid keyword links, this connection is almost automatic. That is, a positive shock or value of $\varepsilon_{it}$ that causes consumers to buy more, and hence, for eBay to enjoy greater sales, will also cause consumers to click more frequently on eBay's paid links which will automatically lead to more advertising spending. There will then be a strong positive relation between advertising spending and sales, but that link will reflect a causality running from sales to advertising expenditure, or from $Sales_{it}$ to $AS_{it}$—and not one that measures the causal effect that advertising expenditure has on sales.

What we want on the right-hand side of equation (11.1) is a measure of advertising spending that is *exogenous*, i.e., that reflects only the explicit decision of the firm to do more such spending—not the spending induced by other shocks. For natural scientists, e.g., a biologist working in a lab, such endogeneity is typically not an issue. As the biologist completely controls the administration of any treatment, e.g., the amount of an antibiotic injected into a Petri dish culture, it is fairly straightforward to identify the effects of the antibiotic on that culture. Analogously, economists would also like to conduct controlled experiments. Sometimes, this is possible.

However, given that the observational data with which economists work typically comes from uncontrolled market interactions, they must often resort to a non-experimental strategy. In practice, this means trying to filter out all the relevant factors that affect a particular outcome, e.g., sales other than the treatment, e.g., the level of advertising, so that any remaining change in sales can reasonably be ascribed to the change in advertising. This is essentially the approach taken in a difference-in-difference regression. Alternatively, one can try to identify and separate out the endogenous part of advertising $(AS_{it})$—so that what remains on the right-hand side of equation (11.1) is a measure of advertising spending that truly is independent of the shock term $\varepsilon_{it}$. This is essentially the approach taken in an instrumental variables or two-stage least squares procedure.[18]

Blake et al. (2015) use a variety of techniques to identify the effect of eBay's SEM on its sales. Their starting point is the recognition that Internet users have alternative ways to get to eBay and shop beside clicking on the paid search links in response to a keyword inquiry. Some consumers may go directly to the firm's website, especially if they've used it before without such searching. Those using a search engine can skip the paid links and scroll down to what are known as organic or natural links, i.e., those that are not paid for but are simply listed by the search engine as the most relevant linked results to the search inquiry. If these alternatives are easy for consumers to use, the need for a firm to bid and pay a CPC for sponsored keyword searches becomes questionable.

To consider whether the alternatives to paid search links can substitute effectively for sponsored links, the authors first considered what are known as branded search keywords. Macy's or L. L. Bean or Starbucks are branded keywords. If a user's search inquiry includes a brand name, say L. L. Bean, a search engine such as Google will list first a sponsored link to L. L. Bean's site, provided of course that L. L. Bean bid on the keywords "L. L. Bean." L. L. Bean will pay the CPC to Google if the user then clicks on that link. However, just a bit below the sponsored link is the link to L. L. Bean's website that comes up first in the organic search results. In this case, we wonder if a retailer such as L. L. Bean would lose much traffic if it stopped bidding on branded search advertising and relied on consumers clicking on the organic search results.

To test their hypothesis, Blake et al. (2015) worked with eBay to conduct some simple experiments. The results of the first experiment are illustrated in Figure 11.2. In this experiment, eBay stopped running any branded search ads on Google during the month of July 2012. During this time, any user who wanted to visit eBay to purchase, say, a pair of hiking boots, or a bicycle, or any other item, would only be able to get to eBay using Google by clicking on the organic link. The results are striking.

As Figure 11.2 shows, clicks to eBay's site from Google paid sponsored links—indicated by the solid black line trajectory—fell to zero during the month of July 2012. That was of course the result of eBay not running such ads during this time. Yet during that same month, clicks from organic links to eBay's site rose by an almost exactly offsetting amount. Indeed, statistical analysis indicates that eBay lost only about 3 percent of the clickthroughs that it would have received had it continued to pay for and run branded search ads.

The authors and eBay conducted a similar experiment on branded search with the Bing search engine. The results were essentially the same. The implied conclusion from both experiments is that if consumers really want to get to the site of eBay, or L. L. Bean, or any other well-known retailer, they can easily find a way to get to there without the use of branded search ads. In other words, it seems a waste for such firms to spend money (pay Google or Bing) to bid for their brand as a keyword.

Apart from the fact that eBay and other firms were paying millions of dollars to search engines for branded search links, it may not be totally surprising that paying

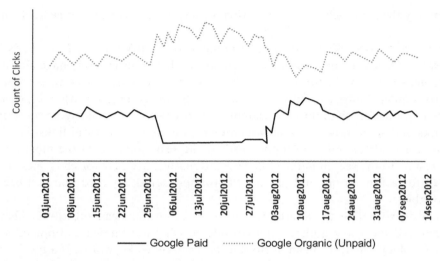

**Figure 11.2** Paid versus organic branded search

for brand name keywords does not lead to more clickthroughs to a firm's web page. Especially for a well-known brand such as eBay, it seems quite plausible that consumers can navigate to those web pages if they really want to do so without such branded search advertising. A more fundamental question regards the value of *non*-brand keyword advertising. For example, what is the ROI for, say, L. L. Bean simply bidding for the keywords, "hiking boots."

To understand the value of non-branded keyword advertising, Blake et al. (2015) continued to work with eBay to conduct a more complex randomized controlled experiment based on the 210 distinct market areas (DMA) that the Nielsen rating company uses. This is useful because Google's geographic tech capability enables any search inquiry to be identified in terms of the DMA from which it originated. As a result, the authors were able to compute the total purchases made by any user in any DMA within 24 hours of that user's clicking through to eBay's website after a non-branded keyword search. In turn, this permitted a calculation of the total sales generated in any DMA over a specified time interval by non-branded keyword search advertising.

Armed with these data capabilities, the experiment conducted was then relatively straightforward. A test period was defined during which eBay turned off (did not buy) any non-brand keywords in 68 of the 210 DMAs. The test of the effectiveness of such search engine marketing then becomes whether the total sales were different in the 68 DMAs without any search advertising from those in the other 142 control DMAs where such non-branded search continued.

To answer this question Blake et al. (2015) run a simple difference-in-difference regression of the form shown below:

$$Sales_{it} = \beta_{0i} + \beta_1 Test_t + \beta_2 Group_i + \beta_3 TestGroup_{it} + \varepsilon_{it} \qquad (11.2)$$

Here, $Sales_{it}$ is, as before, the log of total attributed sales in DMA $i$ at time $t$. The constant $\beta_{0i}$ stands in for a fixed effect term for each DMA meant to account for any inherent differences between the 210 test areas. $Test_t$ is a 1,0 dummy variable equal to 1 if the time corresponds to the period when the experiment was being conducted and 0 otherwise. $Group_i$ is a 1,0 dummy equal to 1 if the DMA was in the control group that kept search keyword spending on during the test period, and 0 if it were in the group of 68 DMAs that did not. Finally, $TestGroup_{it}$ is a dummy variable equal to 1 if both $Test_t$ and $Group_i$ are equal to 1, and 0 otherwise. It is this variable that separately identifies those DMAs that continued their non-branded search spending during the time of the experiment. Hence, it is the estimate of this variable's coefficient $\beta_3$ (the difference-in-difference estimator) that will indicate the impact of non-brand search advertising on sales. If it is strongly and significantly positive, then such advertising is effective. If it is not significantly different from zero, however, then the evidence suggests that eBay gained no extra sales in DMAs in which search advertising was continued relative to those DMAs in which it was not.

Blake et al. (2015) run several different versions of the regression described in equation (11.2). The estimates for $\beta_3$ are consistent across each of these regressions and they average roughly about 0.006. That is, DMAs that kept investing in search advertising enjoyed a very small sales increase of about six-tenths of 1 percent over DMAs that suspended such advertising. This estimate is not only small, it is also never statistically significant. It is therefore very difficult to reject the hypothesis that keyword search spending generated *no* additional sales.

However, when the authors ignore any endogeneity and simply regress the log of generated sales in DMA $i$ at time $t$ on the log of the paid search advertising expenditures in that time and region $AS_{it}$ (effectively ignoring the endogeneity issue), the estimate of the effect is markedly different. They find that a 10 percent increase in search advertising expenditures raises sales by as much as 9 percent, implying a very large and positive ROI. This difference suggests that the endogeneity of the amount of non-brand search spending in DMA $i$ at time $t$ or $AS_{it}$, the right-hand variable, is a real problem.

The final step in the Blake et al. (2015) analysis is to extend the analysis to investigate the endogeneity issue quite explicitly. Again, a standard way to deal with an endogenous right-hand-side variable is to generate a substitute exogenous variable or instrument to use for that variable in a two-stage least squares or instrumental variables approach. To generate an exogenous measure of such ad spending, Blake et al. (2015) regress that variable on the same set of right-hand dummies used in the difference-in-difference estimation. This set includes the 1,0 dummy test variables that control for group, region, and experimental differences in making non-branded search expenses. The predicted value they generate or $\widehat{AS}_{it}$ ought to be reasonably representative of the exogenous component of such expenditures—the amount that would be spent in the absence of shocks that move sales and advertising spending together.

When the authors use an endogeneity-corrected measure of advertising expenditure, $\widehat{AS}_{it}$ on the right-hand side, the effect of non-brand search advertising on sales vanishes. As a result, the estimated ROI turns sharply negative ranging from –22 to –63 percent.

All together then, the Blake et al. (2015) results imply that paying for keyword links—whether for branded search terms or non-branded ones—is not a good investment.

The richness of the data set used in Blake et al. (2015) also allows the response of individual consumers to having access to paid search links for eBay to be identified. Here they find that while there are few positive effects of SEM efforts overall, such advertising does seem to induce more sales from "new" consumers who had not purchased from the eBay site in the previous year. However, this effect decreases rapidly to zero once a user has made three purchases over the last 365 days. This suggests that non-branded search advertising is largely informative as it appears to have little impact on consumers who know eBay from previous purchase experiences.

## 11.5.2 The Effectiveness of Internet Marketing—Other Studies

While compelling, the Blake et al. (2015) study is not the only study of the impact of Internet advertising. By contrast Lewis and Reiley (2014) present experimental evidence that online advertising is effective. In their experiment, large block ads or display ads for a nation-wide retailer appeared on various Yahoo! sites such as mail.yahoo.com, groups.yahoo.com, and maps.yahoo.com over a two-week period in 2007. Of nearly 1.6 million Yahoo! users, 1.3 million were possibly exposed to those ads and roughly 300,000 were not. Both groups saw ads by retailers other than the one selected for the field experiment. Subsequently, an independent third-party used retailer data to match exposure to the retailer ads to actual sales by individuals.

The Lewis and Reiley (2014) experiment finds that the online advertising *does* work. Specifically, Lewis and Reiley (2014) found that, controlling for which individuals in the large group of 1.3 million users actually saw the ads (based on their observed Internet histories), the effect of seeing the retailer ads was to raise sales and profits significantly, with a very positive ROI. Perhaps more interesting, however, is the fact that 90 percent of the rise in the retailer's sales that the online ads appear to have generated were not online sales, but purchases made in the retailer's brick-and-mortar locations. Indeed, 78 percent of the sales increase in such in-store locations came from consumers who, though they had seen the online ad, never clicked on it.

Somewhat relatedly, Goldfarb and Tucker (2011) use a large field experiment examining the impact of banner ads. In this experiment, a firm runs an ad campaign in which a banner ad is placed on a website that is randomly shown to some consumers, but not others. This was done for an average sample of 850 consumers over nearly 2,900 separate campaigns, thereby generating over 2.4 million observations. Immediately after browsing the website, consumers were invited to take a survey that, in addition to information such as the user's gender, age, and income, also included a question on how likely it was that the consumer would now buy the advertised product. They converted this to a 1,0 variable equal to 1 if the consumer answered this question with the highest possible probability of "very likely to make a purchase" and 0 for all other responses.

Goldfarb and Tucker (2011) found that viewing a banner display generally raised the consumer's self-reported probability of buying by a small but significant amount of just under 0.5 percent. Interestingly, this effect was stronger if the ad was located on a website that was complementary to the advertiser's product or service (e.g., a cruise ship banner ad on a travel website). The effect was also somewhat larger if the banner was more visible (e.g., occupies the full computer screen or automatically plays audio and video). However, when *both* characteristics were present, their combined effect on the user's intent to purchase was negative.

Of course, a consumer indicating "very likely to make a purchase" is far from a guarantee to purchase. Goldfarb and Tucker (2011) therefore cannot provide direct evidence on the value of such banner ads. However, given rough estimates on the cost of banner advertising, the authors conclude that such advertising is worthwhile if raising the reported intent to purchase to the "very likely" category is worth at least $0.42 to the advertiser.

A very similar experiment was conducted by Dai et al. (2018) using the Yelp website. Among other services, Yelp offers businesses a standardized advertising package at a fixed monthly fee. In return for this charge, a business will be listed first in search inquiries enough times to receive a specified minimum number of ad views and page visits that month. The authors then arrange for this package to be given to about one half of 18,295 restaurants chosen randomly and divided into four subcategories of: (1) those that use the Yelp Reservation app; (2) those that use the Open Table reservation app; (3) those that use the Yelp delivery service; and (4) all others. They then track the response of over 200,000 Yelp users making restaurant inquiries during the three-month period of the trial. Differentiating between those users who see the ad and those who do not allows the authors to infer the impact of the advertising display.

Like Goldfarb and Tucker (2011), Dai et al. (2018) cannot directly observe induced sales. However, they can observe other indicators of interest such as asking for map directions or later leaving a restaurant review. Assuming what they regard as a conventional conversion from clicks on these kinds of sites to actual sales, their overall finding of these is that the ROI of advertising on a Yelp site is at least 100 percent.

Two features of the foregoing studies and many other investigations of Internet advertising stand out. One of these is that the advent of the Internet has made it possible for firms, as well as researchers, to gather vast amounts of information. As a result, the sample sizes are huge—running from hundreds of thousands to a million or more observations. This is definitely the era of "big data."

The second feature is that the empirical findings are decidedly mixed. This is perhaps not surprising. To begin with, the impact of online advertising for a well-known company such as eBay may not be very large. Yet it may be quite important for a small or new company trying to make consumers aware of its existence. Hence, any measured effect of advertising will need to take account of the type of firm doing the advertising.

Additional care must be taken in evaluating consumer responses to ads. There is something of a leap of faith in asserting that because a consumer saw an ad and then made a purchase, it was viewing the ad that led to the purchase. Remember, ads are typically targeted to specific groups. An ad for a mortgage company will, for instance, be aimed at consumers who are looking for a mortgage and, therefore, have the intent to buy. It can, consequently, be quite difficult *ex post* to determine how much of the consumer's decision to sign with a specific lender was due to viewing that firm's ad. Presumably, the consumer was going to borrow from someone. Similarly, in the case of restaurants, it may be that a Yelp user decides to patronize an Italian restaurant after viewing an ad for a French one and discovering that they did not like what the local French bistro had to offer, i.e., the platform user may choose to buy from a firm from which the platform user *never* saw an ad.

On the other hand, as Lewis and Reiley (2014) show, Internet advertising could also lead to sales at a firm's brick-and-mortar store. In that case, a measure of advertising's cost effectiveness that simply looks at online sales will understate its favorable effect. Somewhat contrarily, some consumers browse the web much more than others and, accordingly, visit more web pages and make more online purchases. Analyzing the effect of an Internet ad campaign on consumers will, in this case, need to take account of what kind of consumers comprise the sample, as again the heavy-browsing consumers are more likely to buy in the first place.

To put it somewhat differently, even after efforts are made to address selection and endogeneity issues, empirical studies that measure the impact of Internet advertising (or advertising in general) on web page visits, stated likelihood of purchase, or even sales are still at least one step short of a direct measure of the advertising ROI. In turn, back-of-the-envelope calculations of the ROI that are based on the above estimates quickly compound the estimates' standard errors so that the ROI calculation is subject to a very wide confidence interval. In a study based on 25 large, randomized control trials, Lewis and Rao (2015) find that a 95 percent confidence interval for the ROI was over 100 percentage points wide, making it very difficult to make judgments about the profitability of the examined ad campaigns. For nine of the 25 field experiments, the authors could not rule out that the advertising had no effect, implying an ROI of –100 percent. Only three of the 25 studies could distinguish between a zero percent ROI and one of 50 percent given the standard errors of the estimates. In other words, less than one-eighth of the studies could distinguish between a clear losing campaign and a wildly successful one.[19] The variety of findings in this and the other studies just discussed confirms the fact that measuring the effectiveness of advertising is a difficult task.

## 11.6 SUMMARY

Advertising on Internet platforms such as Google, Facebook, Yelp, newspaper web pages, and so on, now accounts for 50 percent or more of annual US advertising expenditures. In this chapter, we have focused on two of the many questions that this development raises. First, how do platforms set the price for digital advertising space? Second, how effective is the digital advertising that firms buy at these prices?

Unlike older media such as newsprint, television, and radio in which the price charged to advertisers is set as a cost-per-thousand viewers (CPM), digital advertising prices are very often set on a cost-per-click basis (CPC). That is, the advertising firm only pays the platform when a user clicks on the firm's sponsored link or display ad. This practice points to one of the great advantages of Internet platforms, namely, their inherent ability to observe and track a consumer's engagement with the advertising.

With the Internet, it is much less necessary for advertising firms to seek out specialized platforms such as *Car and Driver* or *Brides* magazines in order to reach a specific audience. Such targeting can instead be achieved simply by focusing on specialized keywords, such as automotive or bridal gowns. Not only can Internet platforms judge a user's engagement with an ad by observing whether they click on the link, they can also build up a rich data set by tracking the click histories for both users and links. This, in turn, permits these platforms to target ads even more precisely as these data accumulate.

For many platforms, whether the pricing is a CPC rate or just the purchase of a display banner, the digital advertising space is sold via automated auctions. For instance, every Google search inquiry effectively initiates a behind-the-scenes and almost instantaneous auction in which firms bid on the search keywords to be among those listed prominently in response to the user's inquiry. The auction design used is a variant of what is known as a second-price or Vickrey auction. In such auctions, winning bidders are not charged what they bid, but only a price equal to the bid of the next-highest bidder. Such auctions are efficient in that they encourage bidders to bid an amount equal to his or her true valuation of the digital space. This tends to maximize the platform's revenue. Moreover, the use of computerized algorithms permits such cyber auctions to happen very quickly so that the price of advertising can respond to market changes almost continuously.

Despite the large and increasing volume of Internet advertising, its economic value remains in question. A highly provocative but very careful study by Blake et al. (2015) found that eBay's investment in search engine marketing on Google had a large negative return. Other studies such as Goldfarb and Tucker (2011) and Dai et al. (2018) find more positive returns to some forms of Internet advertising. A common finding among all these studies is that to the extent it works, digital advertising is most effective in generating sales from new consumers and for new firms. This finding suggests that such advertising largely works by providing information to the consumer.

One problem with studies on the profitability of Internet advertising lies in the fact that there is not a precise causal link from a paid-for click to an actual sale. Specifically, the fact that a user clicked on a firm's paid link and then made a purchase does not necessarily mean that the link led to the purchase. The consumer may have been intent on making the purchase in any case. Conversely, just viewing an Internet ad may lead some consumers to make a purchase without clicking on a link and instead going to a firm's brick-and-mortar store.

Such problems in fact plague studies of advertising's cost effectiveness. The opportunities for random control trials using very large data sets that Internet platforms make offer us some hope that, in time, economists may in fact be able to better determine the true return on an advertising investment.

## NOTES

1 Digital ad sales in 2016 totaled $70 billion compared to $67 billion for national and local TV. https://adage.com/article/advertising/magna-u-s-digital-ad-sales-top-tv-time-2016/308468; https://www.emarketer.com/Article/Worldwide-Ad-Spending-Growth-Revised-Downward/1013858 (accessed 29 March, 2020; 30 April, 2020).

2 https://liftintent.com/blog/how-much-does-local-tv-advertising-cost/ (accessed 27 May, 2021).

3 https://www.pjsolomon.com/wp-content/uploads/2018/11/April-2018-PJ-SOLOMON-Media-Monthly-Newsletter_F.pdf (accessed 27 May, 2021).

4 See https://en.wikipedia.org/wiki/Nielsen_ratings (accessed 19 July, 2020).

5 https://www.nielsen.com/us/en/solutions/capabilities/digital-content-ratings/ (accessed 11 June, 2020).

6 https://smallbusiness.chron.com/typical-cpm-74763.html (accessed 15 April, 2020).

7 https://www.wordstream.com/blog/ws/2017/06/05/instagram-ads-cost (accessed 17 May, 2020).

8 William Vickrey is generally regarded as the intellectual father of modern auction theory owing to his classic paper that was the first to analyze the equilibrium outcomes for many kinds of auctions. See Vickrey (1961).

9 Note that when just one item is up for bid, if all bidders follow the strategy of bidding one's true value, the outcome will be exactly the same as an ascending or English auction where bidding starts at some value then rises as new, higher bids are called out until it reaches a price at which all but one bidder has dropped out. In such an auction, that will happen once the price reaches the value of the second-highest bidder (plus ε) in which case the highest value bidder pays a price asymptotically equal to the value of the second-highest bidder.

10 In actuality, the optimal bidding strategy in the Google auction is a bit more complicated even apart from Google's "quality adjustment." This is because advertisers may be reasonably happy with, say, a second place (or even a third) ad ranking. That is, there is still a net gain possible even if one does not finish first in the ranking.

11 https://www.statista.com/statistics/216573/worldwide-market-share-of-search-engines/#:~:text=Ever%20since%20the%20introduction%20of,revenues%20are%20generated%20through%20advertising.

12 https://promarket.org/2020/02/24/how-google-and-facebook-made-digital-advertising-markets-increasingly-opaque-to-protect-their-dominance/.

13 https://digiday.com/media/what-is-an-ad-exchange/.

14 https://marketingland.com/google-shares-details-on-how-first-price-auctions-in-google-ad-manager-will-work-260830.

15 https://digiday.com/media/what-is-an-ad-exchange/.

16 https://marketingland.com/google-shares-details-on-how-first-price-auctions-in-google-ad-manager-will-work-260830.

17 The insight of using auctions to price keyword search appears to have been first recognized by the early search engine, GoTo.com. That firm was eventually acquired by Yahoo! after first changing its name to Overture.

18 We discussed both the difference-in-difference approach and instrumental variables regression in Chapter 7.

19 See also Lewis et al. (2015).

# 11.7 REFERENCES

Blake, T., C. Nosko, and S. Tadelis. 2015. "Consumer Heterogeneity and Paid Search Effectiveness: A Large-Scale Field Experiment." *Econometrica* 83 (January), 155–74.

Dai, W., H. Kim, and M. Luca. 2018. "Effectiveness of Paid Search Advertising: Experimental Evidence." Working Paper, Krannert School of Management, Purdue University.

Goldfarb, A., and C. Tucker. 2011. "Online Display Advertising: Targeting and Obtrusiveness." *Management Science* 30 (May–June), 389–404.

Lewis, R., and J. Rao. 2015. "The Unfavorable Economics of Measuring the Returns to Advertising." *Quarterly Journal of Economics* 130 (November), 1941–73.

Lewis, R., J. Rao, and D. H. Reiley. 2015. "Measuring the Effects of Advertising: The Digital Frontier." In *The Economic Analysis of the Digital Economy*, ed. A. Goldfarb, S. M. Greenstein, and C. E. Tucker (191–218). Chicago: University of Chicago Press.

Lewis, R., and D. H. Reiley. 2014. "Online Ads and Offline Sales: Measuring the Effect of Retail Advertising via a Controlled Experiment on Yahoo!" *Quantitative Marketing and Economics* 12 (September), 235–66.

Vickrey, W. 1961. "Counterspeculation, Auctions, and Competitive Sealed Tenders." *Journal of Finance* 16 (March), 8–37.

# 12
# Platforms, Advertising, and Competition Policy

## 12.1 INTRODUCTION

In this final chapter, we address some of the issues for competition policy that advertising presents in the digital age. Concern regarding the impact of advertising on price competition, product variety, and innovation has a long history in economics. We now consider some of these issues in a context that explicitly recognizes that advertising is generally transmitted via a two-sided platform and in which, increasingly, that platform is a digital one. This introduces some new considerations given that these platforms not only earn much or most of their revenues from advertising, but the platforms also engage in advertising themselves. Any investigation into the antitrust issues regarding modern advertising must involve an analysis of the competitive issues attending to platforms themselves.

As discussed in Chapter 10, two-sided platforms benefit from important but indirect network effects. In the case of advertising, firms on one side of the platform benefit from having lots of consumers on the other side viewing their ads. Similarly, consumers will benefit more from using a platform, e.g., a search engine, the greater the number of firms that the platform enables them to "visit." There is a cross-side externality in that the attractiveness of the platform to one side depends *positively* on the number of users on the other side. However, what we did not discuss in Chapter 10 is that there can also be a *negative* externality for users on the same side of the platform, specifically, the firms who advertise. As more firms crowd into the advertising side, competition between firms selling similar products intensifies. This, in turn, reduces the profitability of platform participation to any one firm. We may classify this last, within-group effect, as competition *within* a platform.

We also need to extend our consideration of competition between different platforms, e.g., different search engines, initiated in Chapter 10. The presence of strong network effects and substantial scale economies implies that only a few large platforms will ultimately survive. This is particularly true in the digital age. This "be-large-or-perish" pressure can intensify inter-platform competition in a way that makes it very difficult to distinguish predatory actions from legitimate price-cutting and other competitive strategies. Moreover, once one or a few dominant platforms emerge, any new entrant faces a very difficult challenge. It will not be enough to enter with a better product or a lower price. The network and scale effects mean that the new entrant must also persuade a large number of customers of the incumbent platform(s) to switch simultaneously to its platform so as to exploit the same scale and network effects. In this setting, it may be relatively easy for an incumbent to exploit its market power and maintain its dominant position.

The nature and outcome of competition *between* platforms will also interact with competition *within* a platform. Competition between airlines, for example, may likely be affected by competition between ticket price search engines. Both within-platform and between-platform competition can influence the competitive role of advertising on digital two-sided platforms.

In this chapter, we begin with an examination of a within-platform competition and consider the case of a monopoly platform. Then we consider whether between-platform competition might alter these results. Next, we turn to other issues regarding competition policy in the digital age. These include the potential for dominant platforms to leverage their power into additional markets and the competitive impact of the vast amounts of consumer data that both advertisers and platforms acquire and how this "big data" affects market competition as well.

## 12.2 WITHIN-PLATFORM COMPETITION

Consider first a monopoly platform. In the case of search engines, this is not such a far-fetched assumption as Google accounts for close to 90 percent of global searches and close to three-fourths of the online advertising market.[1] For other two-sided platforms such as media (print or digital), monopoly power is much less prevalent. However, many of the insights from the monopoly case appear to remain valid.

As in Chapter 10, we suppose that the platform is an intermediary selling advertising space or time to firms on one side and selling content and access to those ads to consumers on the other side. Within any given product category, firms will compete to be "found" by consumers who are searching within a category relevant to what the firms offer. We will assume that if firms want to compete in any such relevant product market, they must pay a fee to a platform to ensure that their advertisement is seen or heard.

### 12.2.1 Within-Platform Competition and Product Differentiation on a Monopoly Platform

To analyze advertising competition across firms, we adopt a model from Belleflamme and Peitz (2019) that can shed light on the complicated issues of two-sided platforms. Suppose that there are $N$ symmetric firms that compete for consumers by selling differentiated products. There are $M$ identical potential consumers for their goods. Each consumer has an inverse demand for each product $i$ given by:

$$p_i = 1 - q_i - \beta Q_{-i} \qquad (12.1)$$

Here, $p_i$ is the price of firm $i$'s good, $q_i$ is firm $i$'s output, and $Q_{-i}$ is the output of all the other $N$–1 firms. The parameter $\beta$, where $0 < \beta < 1$, is an inverse measure of product differentiation. Larger values of $\beta$ indicate that greater combined output $Q_{-i}$ (and hence lower prices) across all a firm's rivals exerts more downward pressure on firm $i$'s price and profit. Conversely, when $\beta = 0$, each firm $i$ is a monopoly facing no rival substitute products.

Firms compete in their output choices. That is, each firm chooses a quantity $q_i$ and all their choices $q_1, q_2, \dots q_N$ determine the equilibrium price $p_i$ for each product. We also assume for simplicity that each firm has a constant marginal cost, set equal to 0, and a fixed cost of advertising $F_A$. From Belleflamme and Peitz (2019) we can show that under perfect information the equilibrium price, output, and profit levels for each firm $i$ are:

$$p_i = \frac{1}{(2 + \beta(N - 1))} \tag{12.2a}$$

$$q_i = M \frac{1}{(2 + \beta(N - 1))} \tag{12.2b}$$

$$\pi_i = M \frac{1}{(2 + \beta(N - 1))^2} - F_A \tag{12.2c}$$

Similarly, we can show that consumer surplus $CS$ for each consumer $h$ on the platform is given by:

$$CS = N \frac{(1 + \beta(N - 1))}{2(2 + \beta(N - 1))^2} \tag{12.3}$$

Observe that an increase in the parameter $\beta$ means that the goods become more substitutable in consumption. In this case, the consumer buys less of each good and consumer surplus is lower. This is so even though prices of goods are lower when $\beta$ increases. The reason is that consumers have a taste for variety and their welfare is higher when there is increased product variety available on the platform.

The platform is a monopoly. It brings firms and consumers together for possible transactions. The platform does this because in the absence of a platform the $N$ firms and $M$ consumers cannot find each other. The fixed fee $F_A$ is what the platform charges firms to place ads, or have its ads "found," on the platform. If we assume that such advertising expenditure generates a sales transaction with probability $\lambda$, we may rewrite equations (12.2c) and (12.3) as:

$$\pi = \lambda M \frac{1}{(2 + \beta(N - 1))^2} - F_A \tag{12.4}$$

$$CS = \lambda N \frac{(1 + \beta(N - 1))}{2(2 + \beta(N - 1))^2} \tag{12.5}$$

Equation (12.4) may be used to determine the equilibrium number of firms $N$ buying an advertising slot on the platform under the assumption that firms will compete on the platform until $\pi_i = 0$.[2] The zero-profit condition can be used to define the number of sellers on the platform $N$ as a function of the parameters: the probability of a transaction $\lambda$, a measure of product differentiation $\beta$, the fee for advertising $F_A$, and the equilibrium number of consumers $M$. We write this function as $N = N(\lambda, \beta, F_A, M)$, where $\dfrac{\partial N}{\partial \lambda} > 0$; $\dfrac{\partial N}{\partial \beta} < 0$; $\dfrac{\partial N}{\partial F_A} < 0$ and $\dfrac{\partial N}{\partial M} > 0$.

The intuition behind these effects is straightforward. An increase in the advertising fee $F_A$ reduces the profitability of finding consumers and reduces the number of firms competing, whereas an increase in the effectiveness of advertising $\lambda$ has the opposite effect. By contrast, a rise in $\beta$ implies tougher competition and hence, a lower price-cost margin. As a result, the number of firms advertising on the platform declines. That $\dfrac{\partial N}{\partial M} > 0$ reflects the indirect network effects of a two-sided platform. More firms can successfully compete and pay for advertising when the market has a larger number of potential consumers on the platform.

Turning to consumers who use the platform to search, we assume that there is some activity, other than being on the platform, that gives a consumer $h$ utility $\bar{u}_h$. Only consumers for whom $CS - \bar{u}_h > 0$ will go onto the platform. The greater is $CS$, the greater is the number of consumers $M$ using the platform. There is again a relationship between the parameters affecting consumer surplus and the number of consumers on the platform, which we describe by: $M = M(\lambda, \beta, N)$ where $\dfrac{\partial M}{\partial \lambda} > 0$; $\dfrac{\partial M}{\partial \beta} < 0$ and $\dfrac{\partial M}{\partial N} > 0$.[3]

$\dfrac{\partial M}{\partial \lambda} > 0$ says that as the effectiveness of advertising increases there are more trades and more surplus realized, increasing the number of consumers on the platform. An increase in the parameter $\beta$ means that goods are more homogeneous, and this leads to lower consumer surplus and hence fewer consumers $M$ will participate in the market. The positive value for $\dfrac{\partial M}{\partial N}$ reflects the indirect network effect that consumers gain from having more firms advertising their products on the platform.

We assume that the platform raises revenue from only one side of the platform, namely, from the firms who wish to advertise. Potential consumers on the other side use the platform for free. The platform's revenue is:

$$R_A = F_A N(\lambda, \beta, F_A, M) \qquad (12.6)$$

If the cost of operating the two-sided platform is largely fixed, the platform's goal of maximizing profit will lead the platform to set its fee $F_A$ to maximize advertising revenue $R_A$. The setting is then like the standard monopoly problem that while a higher fee $F_A$ raises revenue for a given number of firms $N$, that number of firms participating on the platform falls as $F_A$ rises. The optimal value of $F_A$ just balances these two opposing forces at the margin.

The platform's choice of $F_A$ determines the number of firms $N$ competing. When the platform increases the cost of advertising, fewer firms can compete profitability. Those fewer remaining firms compete less intensely, earning a higher price-cost margin, but paying more in advertising expense.

The case is heuristically illustrated in Figure 12.1.[4] Here, the $MM$ curve shows the number of consumers $M = M(\lambda, \beta, F_A, N)$ on one side of the platform as an increasing function of the number of firms $N$, on the other side, holding the key parameters $\lambda$, $\beta$, and $F_A$ constant. Similarly, the $NN$ curve shows the number of firms $N = N(\lambda, \beta, F_A, M)$ as an increasing function of the number of consumers $M$, again given values for $\lambda$, $\beta$, and $F_A$.

A rise in $F_A$ shifts the $NN$ curve to the left, i.e., $N'N'$, reducing the equilibrium number of firms given the initial number of consumers $M$. However, fewer consumers now participate in the market given that the number of firms has dropped. In turn, this reduces the number of potential consumers, which further causes the number of competing firms to fall, leading to a new equilibrium where the $MM$ curve intersects the $N'N'$ curve. Ultimately, the number of firms falls from $N^e$ to $N'^e$.

Moving from an equilibrium with $N^e$ competing firms to one with $N'^e$ firms leads to a loss in consumer surplus because of the decline in competition. Because the platform does not charge consumers to use its services, its only revenue comes as the advertising fee $F_A$ that it charges to firms. The platform will, therefore, tend to ignore the effects of its decision on consumer surplus and instead be concerned with how its choice of $F_A$ affects firms' profitability and, by extension, their willingness to pay the advertising fee. As Nocke et al. (2007) point out, this means that the monopoly platform will tend to set a fee $F_A$ too high relative to the social optimum.

For a given degree of product differentiation, $\beta$, among the sellers, the two-sided platform may have an interest in limiting the firms who advertise on its platform. The platform gains from having a greater number of firms $N$ that are willing to pay for advertising space. However, as $N$ grows the competition among these firms intensifies and their price-cost margin declines, which means that the fee $F_A$ that they can afford to

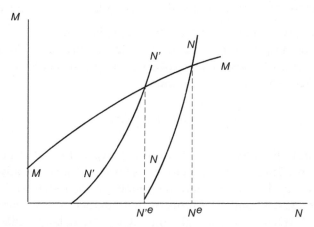

*Note:* A rise in the price charged to advertising $F_A$, reduces the number of firms advertising for any given number of consumers. The $NN$ curve shifts in to $N'N'$.

**Figure 12.1** Monopoly platform fee and within-platform competition

pay also declines. The tradeoff facing the monopoly platform is that an increase in the number of firms competing lowers each firm's ability to pay for advertising space on the platform.

What happens when the degree of product differentiation perceived by consumers changes? Specifically, suppose that the parameter $\beta$ decreases, products appear less substitutable or alternatively, consumers see more variety on the platform. This is illustrated in Figure 12.2 where again the $MM$ curve describes how the number of firms, on one side, affects the number of consumers on the other, and the $NN$ curve shows how the number of consumers, on one side, affects the number of firms on the other side. These curves are drawn for given $\lambda$, $\beta$, and $F_A$ and the initial equilibrium lies at the intersection of the two curves with $M^e$ consumers and $N^e$ firms.

When the parameter $\beta$ falls, competition among firms is softer and each firm's price-cost margin increases and so does profitability. Assuming no change in the advertising fee $F_A$, more firms will find it profitable to pay for being "found" on the platform. The $NN$ curve will shift outward to $N'N'$. In addition, the decrease in $\beta$ increases consumer surplus and so the $MM$ curve will shift upward to $M'M'$. The new equilibrium lies at the intersection of the $M'M'$ and $N'N'$ curves. As drawn, this new equilibrium features an increase in the number of competing firms and the number of participating consumers well.[5]

The decrease in $\beta$ and softening of competition among advertising firms is good news for the intermediary platform. The platform earns more revenue even if it

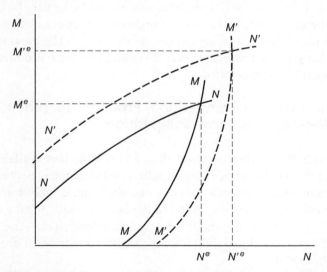

*Note:* An increase in the extent of product differentiation softens competition so that each firm earns greater profit. Hence, more firms find it profitable to pay the advertising fee $F_A$ and the $NN$ curve shifts upward to $N'N'$. In addition, the greater variety of goods induces more consumers to use the platform, shifting $MM$ to $M'M'$. There are both more firms and more consumers in the new equilibrium $N'^eM'^e$ than in the initial equilibrium $N'M'$.

**Figure 12.2 Product differentiation and within-platform competition**

keeps its fee $F_A$ unchanged. However, the platform could potentially increase revenue by increasing $F_A$, which would cause the $N'N'$ to shift downward, but not the $M'M'$ curve, leading to an equilibrium outcome that could be more profitable for the platform.

This result suggests that the platform may then have an incentive to design its search process in such a way that the products of those firms advertising are *not* perceived by consumers as close substitutes. This is an interesting potential antitrust issue in so far as platform design can affect whether consumers transact and with which firms. Transactions that occur under one design may not occur in a different one. A recent *Wall Street Journal* article did in fact find that Google's search algorithms exhibit a bias in favor of large, prominent firms.[6] This finding is not inconsistent with our simple model in so far as the model does suggest that the platform has an interest in softening competition among the firms that advertise on its platform.

However, there are at least two issues that we must consider before concluding that media platforms will limit within-platform competition. First, we have not yet investigated how competition between platforms, e.g., search engines, could affect the within-platform competition. We defer that issue to the next section.

Second, consumers' desire for variety suggests caution in concluding that softening competition among advertisers hurts consumer welfare. It is true that increased product differentiation generally softens competition and leads to higher prices, which is bad news for consumers. However, as we noted in our earlier analysis, if the preference for variety outweighs this "bad news," consumer surplus can be higher. To be sure, this will not always be the case. The "bad news" of higher prices could outweigh the effect of more variety on the platform, leaving consumers worse off.[7] The point is that any competition policy analysis must recognize that the relation between product differentiation and consumer welfare is complicated.

### 12.2.2 Within-Platform Competition, Product Differentiation, and Between-Platform Competition

We now ask what happens when a second alternative platform is available to sellers and buyers. This means there is competition for sellers and consumers between platforms as well as competition among sellers within any one platform. Conclusions are difficult to reach because much depends on the nature of the user's demand for the services of platforms. Whether participants, buyers or sellers, multi-home, that is, use both platforms also matters. However, a little careful thinking can yield a number of broad insights. We briefly discuss those here.

One way to extend the model in section 12.2.1 is to assume two, differentiated platforms, e.g., two news providers, *New York Times* and *USA Today*, that compete in prices for consumers on one side and for advertising firms on the other side. We assume that consumers and advertising firms single-home, that is, each consumer and each advertiser subscribe to, or join at most one news platform. Like a monopoly model, each platform sets a price on each side that is marked up above its marginal cost of serving a participant on that side. The markups on each side are related to the demand elasticity of the participants on that side of the platform.

If every potential consumer subscribes to one or the other of the two platforms and if every potential advertiser does the same, or if the market is fully covered, the measures of demand elasticity will be a function of the degree of product differentiation that consumers and advertisers perceive between the two platforms. Suppose with respect to the product differentiated services that each provides, the two platforms are symmetric and have identical costs. If we denote by $c_u$ and $c_A$ the marginal cost for serving users on one side and advertisers on the other, then the fees charged by the two symmetric platforms to consumers and advertisers would be the same in equilibrium. In the absence of any network effects on the platform the equilibrium fees are:

$$F_u = c_u + \tau_u$$
$$F_A = c_A + \tau_A$$

(12.7)

where $\tau_u$ and $\tau_A$ are the respective markups to consumers and advertisers and reflect the degree to which each platform's services are differentiated in the eyes of consumers and advertisers.

Now let's consider what happens when we introduce network effects across the sides and within each side of a platform. Network effects will affect the markups $\tau_u$ and $\tau_A$ because of the impact of those network effects *at the margin*. Let $\Delta v_u^u$ denote the change in value to current users on the consumer side of the platform, if one more user subscribes to the platform. Let $\Delta \theta_u^A$ denote the change in profit to current advertisers on the other side of the platform if one more user subscribes. Typically, the value to advertisers $\Delta \theta_u^A$ of one more user is greater than the value to consumers $\Delta v_u^u$. The effect of $\Delta v_u^u$ on the markup to users is likely positive, reflecting the value to users of having more of them on the same platform, whereas, $\Delta \theta_u^A$ may have a negative effect on the markup to users, reflecting the platform's incentive to attract more users and capture the increased value to advertisers in the fee set on the advertising side of the platform.

Similarly, let $\Delta v_A^u$ denote the change in value to current users on the consumer side of the platform, if one more advertiser subscribes to the platform and $\Delta \theta_A^A$ the change in profit of current advertisers on the platform if one more advertiser joins the platform.

These network effects[8] affect the fee set on each side of the platform. Accordingly, we write:

$$F_u = c_u + \tau_u + h(\Delta v_u^u, \Delta v_A^u, \Delta \theta_u^A, \Delta \theta_A^A)$$
$$F_A = c_A + \tau_A + g(\Delta v_u^u, \Delta v_A^u, \Delta \theta_u^A, \Delta \theta_A^A)$$

(12.8)

Network effects also affect the setting of fees for a monopolist. However, in a duopoly market with two platforms, we conjecture that the fees $F_u$ and $F_A$ will be less than the analogous fees charged in the monopoly case. That is because the competition between the platforms will likely increase the elasticity of demand each platform faces and, therefore, tend to lower the markups $\tau_u$ and $\tau_A$ that each would charge independent of network effects.

However, because of network effects, lower fees under duopolies may not always be the case. For instance, it may turn out that the fee $F_u$ to the user side of the platform hits the zero floor in both the monopoly and duopoly markets. This is the case for search engines, which are free platforms for users. In that case, competition between platforms does not lower the subscription fees users or consumers are charged.

Now consider the effect of adding one more advertiser to the platform. Because more advertising leads to more competition among the sellers on a platform, the effect $\Delta\theta_A^A$ on other sellers of adding one more firm running ads on a platform is likely negative. The effect $\Delta v_A^u$ on consumers from having one additional firm advertise is likely smaller. Adding one more advertiser at the margin will tend to put upward pressure on the advertising fee $F_A$ as the platform tries to internalize this externality.

In a duopoly with single-homing, each platform serves a smaller number of advertising firms than does the monopoly platform. This, coupled with the likelihood that the function $g(\cdot)$ is subject to diminishing returns in the number of advertisers, suggests that the *marginal* impact of an additional advertising firm is likely to be greater (in absolute magnitude) in the duopoly case than in the monopoly case. As a result, the upward pressure on the advertising fee $F_A$ from the within-group will be larger when there is between-platform competition than when there is only one monopoly platform. In our heuristic example, increasing inter-platform competition could leave the subscription fees to consumers unchanged (at $F_u = 0$) and raise the fee $F_A$ charged to advertisers.

It is possible then that moving from a monopoly to a more competitive platform market does not necessarily benefit the users of those platforms by way of lower prices. This is not to say that between-platform competition *will not* lower users' fees, only that it may not do so. Again, the overall effect depends on the balance between the direct effect of such competition for a given degree of *within-platform* competition, and the secondary but important impact of how that *within-platform* competition changes once competition between platforms is introduced. The outcome will depend on the nature of the platform market.

To be sure, the services of a platform are often more than simply providing a site where consumers and advertising firms can meet. This is true even for a search platform that connects users to firms. The platform can also provide other benefits such as quality control that leads to better matches and to product innovation that can improve the user experience on the platform. Between-platform competition may increase these services and benefit users even when the competition does not lead to lower user fees.

For example, many product markets are characterized by asymmetric information in which the seller typically knows more about its goods or services than does the buyer. By selecting which ads or goods they offer, a platform can provide a screening service for consumers ensuring that the ads that they see are for products that meet some minimum quality standard. By providing this service, a platform attracts more consumers, which, in turn, makes it more appealing to advertising firms. Such screening services may be intensified by between-platform competition. In this case, both users or consumers and advertising firms can gain even when the fees paid to the platform rise. In this regard, policies should be designed to promote or at least not suppress such competition. As with our earlier discussion, the point again is that competition policy must again tread carefully here. The full effect of between-platform competition, like the full effect of within-platform competition, is complicated.

## 12.3 THE DIGITAL ADVERTISING MARKET—BASIC STRUCTURE

Traditionally the focus of advertising in economics has been the impact of advertising on market competition between sellers. In today's digital world where two-sided platforms, such as Google, Facebook, and Amazon are dominant firms sustained largely by a digital advertising ecosystem, it is timely to consider whether the digital advertising ecosystem itself raises issues relevant to competition policy.

Digital advertising is mediated via online platforms that today account for more than half of all media advertising expenditure worldwide. Within the US, this market is dominated by Google, Facebook, and Amazon, whose respective shares of US digital advertising expenditures in 2019 were 39.7 percent, 19.6 percent, and 8.1 percent. Taken together then, these three platforms account for roughly two-thirds of all US online advertising expenditures.[9] Again, this concentration should not be surprising given the substantial network effects and scale economies that characterize these digital platforms.

This tendency toward a highly concentrated market is made even stronger by economies of scope, by which we mean cost advantages that are conferred to a firm that produces goods jointly rather than separately. That is, economies of scope exist when it is less costly for one firm to produce two different goods than it is for each of two firms to produce them individually. Digital data can play a key role in economies of scope. A search engine fielding lots of queries about hotels, restaurants, retail outlets, and health services in different locations can gather that data and having the data makes it easy or more efficient for the search engine to offer a mapping application as well.

We should not be surprised therefore that digital advertising platforms tend to be concentrated. However, the size and scope of these three big tech firms—all three among the five most valuable US corporations—grants them considerable market power. This, in turn, raises important issues for competition policy. Before turning to those issues, it is useful to have a basic understanding of how digital or programmatic advertising works in the marketplace. This is described in Figure 12.3. There are five main parts, starting with the supply of space for digital advertising to advertisers' demand for that space.

The supply side consists of the websites or platforms with an inventory of available advertising space that they wish to sell. These can include search engines, media sites, comparison-shopping sites, and similar digital firms. They are often referred to collectively as publishers. Analogously, the demand side includes advertisers, such as retailers and manufacturers, that wish to buy advertising space. The supply and demand are cleared at prices via electronic exchanges that are not unlike the major stock exchanges. As described in Chapter 11, these exchanges conduct millions of trades every minute of the day.

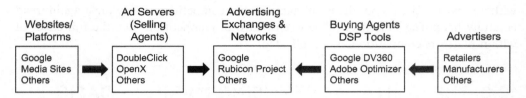

**Figure 12.3** The structure of the market for programmatic advertising

There is a further similarity between markets for digital advertising and financial markets. Much as a buyer or a seller needs a registered trader or broker to sell and buy financial assets, publishers and advertisers each need an "agent" to connect to the exchanges. In this case, the agents are software tools that interact with the exchange to offer sale or purchase of the advertising "space." The tools used by publishers are generally called ad servers. The tools used by firms buying advertising are generally referred to as Demand Side Platforms (DSPs).[10]

As the diagram makes clear, one firm can be involved in many parts of this programmatic trading. Google is a case in point. It clearly has advertising space to sell both on its own platform and on its major subsidiary, YouTube. However, Google also operates the largest of the digital advertising exchanges and networks. In addition, Google's DoubleClick ad server is one of the most widely used selling tools and its DV360 program is one of the most widely used DSPs. Google also has its own goods to sell in the market such as its Android-based phones and its Nest thermostat products.

Google is not the only company playing multiple roles in this advertising market. Facebook sells advertising space and operates a major ad server, a major DSP buying tool, and its own ad network. Amazon does the same. Like Google, Amazon also has its own products to sell under such brand names as Amazon Basics, Lark and Ro, and North Eleven. To understand the potential advantages or drawbacks of linking these different activities via one company it is helpful to understand the mechanics of advertising in this digital ecosystem.

As soon as a user visits a web page, such as a newspaper or other site, the ad server used by that publisher goes to work identifying the user, as much as possible, based on the ad server's accumulated data. Subsequently, the ad server submits that information along with its available ad space to one or more exchanges. In turn, the exchanges then contact the DSPs of the advertisers connected to those exchanges asking them to submit bids for the available space to be viewed by that user. There is then an instantaneous auction with the bids reported to the ad server and the ad server choosing the winning bid(s). Because every part of this process is run by an algorithm and operates in digital space, the whole process can take less than 0.5 seconds.

The advantages of being involved in multiple stages of this ecosystem—especially those that come from jointly operating an ad server, ad exchange, and DSP buying tool—should be clear. It permits offering advertisers a seamless link to those publishers with relevant advertising space to sell. Moreover, it does so quickly and efficiently.

## 12.4 COMPETITION POLICY ISSUES IN DIGITAL PLATFORM MARKETS

The nature of the digital advertising ecosystem is such that platforms can exploit important economies of scope by being active in the different segments. Moreover, this is another case in which scale and network effects combine to create a further tendency toward a highly concentrated market for digital advertising. However, the fact that only a few advertising platforms integrated with ad servers, exchanges, and DSPs may ultimately survive does not *a priori* imply a lack of competitive pressure. Competition can be intense even when there are as few as two firms in the market, as the periodic price wars between Boeing and Airbus demonstrate. Additional competitive pressure can also come from new entrants who can challenge and replace established incumbents.

The entry of new firms that causes the displacement of old incumbents means a concentrated market can remain even as the names of the dominant firms change. Google overtook and eventually displaced Yahoo! Similarly, Facebook started well behind MySpace, but eventually became the dominant social network. Amazon successfully surpassed eBay as the leading online retailer. This anecdotal history suggests that competitive pressures are there even when the number of active firms at any one time is few.

At the same time, however, there is reason for concern regarding the market power of the three major advertising platforms. The observation that Google and Facebook could overtake incumbent rivals may be due to the market being in a formative evolutionary stage, one before the results of the "winner-take-most" competition were known. Now, the market for these digital platforms has matured and the winning survivors have emerged. Successful new entry may have become less feasible.

Moreover, the fact that only a few dominant platforms have survived has implications beyond how the platforms compete among themselves for advertising dollars. Their dominance affects their role as platforms mediating transaction between the two sides. For example, Google acts, via its ad server, on behalf of a publisher website, but Google also competes with that publisher with a website of its own that attracts advertising. Similar conflicts arise because Google markets its own products, such as Nest, and they compete with products of other firms that reach the advertising market via Google's DSP.

Competition policy with respect to the advertising platforms must once more be cautious. It must try to preserve competitive pressures and encourage innovation, but also recognize that the forces of network, scale, and scope economies underlie a concentrated market structure. Policies should be designed to ensure competition within the platforms by making sure that all advertisers are able to compete for consumers, without biasing transactions in favor of some advertisers. Policy-makers must at the same time avoid falling inadvertently into the trap of protecting inefficient competitors simply because they are "small." In what follows, we discuss the major practices of the dominant platforms that have generated the most policy concern.

### 12.4.1 Self-Preferencing, Leveraging Market Power, and Other Competitive Issues

Important economies of scope make it natural that advertising platforms will find it profitable to engage in several related activities within the advertising ecosystem. Google is well positioned in this system to operate an ad server, an ad exchange, and a DSP buying tool. Yet it is possible that Google's extension into these related activities, and especially its rapid rise to dominance there, reflects more than economies of scope. It may reflect the fact that Google can exploit advantages that enable it to extend its market power and beat out potential competitors also operating in the advertising ecosystem. For example, in soliciting bids from different DSPs, Google's exchange may send better information about the space available to its own buying tool. Similarly, Google's ad server and buying tool can favor routing solicitations and bids through Google's exchange. Srinivasan (2020) notes that the nature of this self-preference need not be large to have an impact. Even providing the same information to, say, all DSPs but with a slight speed advantage—measured in milliseconds—can be enough to slant the results significantly given the short time in which these transactions are consummated. In other words, Google may leverage its overall market power in one sector, e.g., search, into winning a dominant position in related markets.

Yet while the conflicts described above are important, the most publicly discussed cases of self-preferencing to leverage market power have been those in which the dominant platform also competes with other publishers that the platform hosts. Again, Google is a case in point.

Google's search process typically generates three sets of responses to a user's search query. One of these is the set of organic links ranked by the Google algorithm in terms of their match with that user's query. Advertisers do not pay to show up on these links nor do they pay if a user clicks on one of the links.[11] Appearing above the organic links, however, is a set of sponsored links for which the advertisers pay if a user clicks on a link. As discussed in Chapter 11, the pay per click fee is determined by an auction in dollar bids, adjusted for quality as measured by Google itself. Finally, Google also typically presents to the user a box filled with specialized display ads, that also generate click-based revenues for Google, and which are usually placed in a prominent position on the search results page. That box contains links not only to specific firm sites that have again made a payment, but also to Google's own comparison-shopping sites, such as Google Shopping or Google Flights.

For example, a search for lawnmowers will likely show a box at the top of the page presenting several (local and online) retailers selling lawnmowers of various sorts and the prices they are asking. Clicking on the link at the top of the box, e.g., "See Lawn Mowers", or on the "View All" link that appears at the end of the carousel display, will take the user to Google's own comparison-shopping site. Similarly, a query about Boston-to-Dallas flights will feature a boxed list of different airlines offering service between the two cities, with some additional information on the fare, whether it is a direct flight or one with connections, and an estimation of the time required to complete the trip. If the user then clicks on "Show Flights" in order to get more information, they will be taken to Google Flights.

Other comparison-shopping sites such as Foundem (in the UK), Yelp!, and TripAdvisor compete directly with Google's comparison-shopping sites. Many of these sites have filed complaints with antitrust authorities in both the US and Europe charging that Google abuses its dominant position in search to steer consumers to its own specialized search sites at the expense of specialized search rivals and does so even when the other sites may be better matched to the user. There is indeed some evidence of such bias.

For example, Google reworked its algorithm for ranking sites listed in generic searches in 2011, not long before Google Shopping switched to a "pay-to-play" model in which sellers must pay to be listed on that service. The visibility of alternative or rival comparison-shopping sites appears to have fallen dramatically as their rank in generic search results declined.[12] More recently, studies sponsored by the *Wall Street Journal* have also uncovered biases in favor of Google sites such as YouTube.[13]

To the extent that Google search procedures direct search traffic to Google's comparison-shopping sites and diminish the volume of such traffic at competing sites, it clearly hurts Google competitors. The more traffic such a website has, the more merchants are willing to provide product and service information to the site, enhancing its usefulness to potential consumers. Further, more traffic allows a shopping site to learn precisely what consumers value, which in turn permits the site to improve its service. Finally, sites that include customer product reviews are more credible the larger the sample of consumers providing those reviews.

However, the fact that Google has introduced its own comparison-shopping site does not necessarily imply that the impact on rival comparison sites is an abuse of Google's market power in search. The antitrust laws are meant to protect competition *not* competitors. Google has defended its actions as legitimate ways to improve its primary function as a search engine and benefit its users. Google has made the argument that the prominent boxed display of links in the search response is there to provide links that are directly related to the user's search, e.g., local and online lawnmower sellers. The box enables a user interested in buying a new lawnmower to get more quickly or more efficiently to the site of a merchant from whom they can readily purchase one with just a single click. If Google captures more user traffic because of improved service rather than due to a self-preferencing bias, its actions are much more legitimate.

The debate over whether Google's search engine procedures unfairly privilege its own sites over those of rivals is not an "open and shut" case. The complexity of the debate was made clear by the wide difference between the response of the American and European antitrust authorities to the charges of Google's search bias. In 2013, the US Federal Trade Commission (unanimously) declined to pursue antitrust charges against Google finding that Google primarily changed its search procedures "to improve the quality of its search results, and that any negative impact on actual or potential competitors was incidental."[14] In contrast, the European Commission found in 2017 that Google *was* guilty of biasing its search procedures in a way that abused its monopoly power, ordered it to change those procedures, and fined the company €2.4 billion ($2.7 billion).[15]

Similar accusations of self-interested and unfair bias have been made against Amazon. Any product search on Amazon will lead the user to pages of product listings. While consumers can in principle search through all of these, casual observation suggests that few consumers extend their search beyond the first page and many do not even look beyond the top half of that page. Hence, being listed high on that first page can be critical to making an actual sale.

Amazon provides not only a search platform for sellers to reach consumers, but Amazon itself is a seller. The company offers thousands of its own, private label goods ranging from batteries and paper towels to women's dresses and men's shirts. Mattioli (2019) presents evidence that Amazon's search algorithm has been preferencing its own products in consumer searches, giving them prominent and expansive visibility on the first page of results.

One feature that makes this bias charge against Amazon particularly worrisome is the nature of Amazon's standard agreement with a third-party seller. Apart from legally protected trademarks and copyrights, that agreement gives Amazon very broad rights to the seller's materials. Amazon can review the various features of a seller's product listing that lead its algorithm to give that seller prominence in the search results and use this information to incorporate those features into its own product listing. Alternatively, Amazon can adjust its algorithm to prioritize the features of the Amazon product. In either case, Amazon can, similar to Google, claim that its algorithm is designed to optimize the consumer's experience on its platform and the fact that the search process increasingly lists Amazon's products highly is just an inadvertent by-product of this neutral goal.[16]

## 12.4.2 Foreclosure, Tying, and MFN Clauses

Partly because of big tech's merger acquisitions, e.g., Facebook's purchase of Instagram, and partly because of their product extensions, e.g., Google's launch of Google Shopping, the major advertising platforms today compete with other sellers using their platform services to reach users or consumers with similar services and products. This has led to a fear that the major platforms will bias or self-preference consumers to choose their platform's version of the product or service over the similar services that rivals offer. In addition to the charges of biases in search algorithms that have been made against Google, there are other platform practices that raise issues for antitrust policy. One potentially anti-competitive practice is foreclosure by which a platform may prohibit a rival from using some, or all, of its services.

For example, Twitter launched a video-sharing app called Vine in early 2013. Facebook quickly responded by blocking Vine users from interacting with any of their Facebook data. This prevented Vine users from sharing Vine videos with Facebook friends and from inviting their Facebook friends to join Vine. To many observers, Facebook's decision was clearly based on its fear that Vine posed a direct threat to its central social network and messaging services. This view received some confirmation from the release of internal Facebook emails reviewed in the British Parliament's Digital, Culture, Media and Sport Committee (Hamilton, 2018).[17]

Somewhat related to foreclosure is the practice of tying, in which a firm makes the purchase of one of its services contingent on the consumer purchasing not only that good, but also an additional good produced by the firm.[18] For example, when Google attempted to create its own social network, Google+, it required users of its YouTube service to create Google+ accounts if they wanted to comment on any YouTube videos. Similarly, Google required equipment manufacturers using its Android system to pre-install both its search application and its web browser Chrome, as a condition for gaining access to its app store (Google Play). Here again, many analysts view these actions as Google's attempt to leverage its dominant search engine position into a major presence in these other markets as well as to limit the ability of other search engines to attract users. In fact, the European Commission found Google guilty of abusing its dominant search position via these tying arrangements and fined the company €4.34 billion ($5 billion at the time) in July 2018.[19]

Most-Favored-Nation (MFN) restrictions, sometimes called parity clauses, are a third practice that has raised antitrust issues regarding the large advertising platforms. These are contractual clauses that forbid one of the parties from selling its services for a lower price than agreed to with the other party. For example, until recently, third-party sellers using Amazon's platform were contractually prohibited from selling their products for a lower price anywhere else, including their own home websites. Similarly, many price-comparison websites (PCWs) require participating sellers to agree that they will not offer their services at a lower price than shown on the PCW.

There is an economic rationale for these MFN agreements. The host site such as Amazon, or a PCW, has an investment in creating a site that provides a great deal of useful information and related services to consumers. These services of course benefit the third-party sellers listed on that site. However, if these third-party sellers are then free to offer a lower price to consumers, they may "free ride" on Amazon—using it to attract consumers, but then luring those consumers to its own site with a lower price on which it does not have to pay any commission or clickthrough fee to the host site. If widespread, such free-riding will cause the host site to lose money on its investment.[20]

However, MFNs can also facilitate anti-competitive practices. In an oligopoly setting, in which a few large firms compete, it may assist collusion. If the firms have agreed (either explicitly or tacitly) to a particular price, the MFN acts as a deterrent to any one firm cutting its price selectively to any customer, as it would then have to lower its price to others as well.

In addition, an MFN can make entry and growth difficult for alternative platforms. Suppose, for example, that a third-party seller that currently sells through Amazon is considering selling on a new platform that hopes to rival Amazon. Because the new rival platform does not have many sellers yet, i.e., because it has a small network, the third-party seller may decide that few potential buyers will search that site for products. Hence, if the third-party seller wishes to consummate any sales there, the seller may well have to do so at a lower price. Yet if it is restrained by an Amazon MFN agreement, then offering a lower price will require it to leave Amazon altogether. This, of course, acts as a major deterrent to the third-party seller to join the new platform. As all third-party sellers are likely to feel the same, the new platform will have trouble reaching its critical mass.

All of the foregoing serves to make one central point. Designing and implementing competition policies in platform markets is tricky. Recognizing that fact, however, should not induce policy paralysis. At present, the starting point must include the recognition that Google, Facebook, and Amazon have significant market power. In this light, it is reasonable to investigate and assess these companies' strategies somewhat differently than would be the case when these same strategies are employed by more competitive firms, or ones with less market power.

### 12.4.3 Switching Costs and Personal Data

Viewing a platform market from the user side raises further antitrust issues. Consider, for instance, a Facebook user, thinking about joining an alternative social network. Clearly, the user will want to continue linking with Facebook friends. This will require that they transfer their own identity information, friends' contact lists, and other data. To some extent, existing platforms do permit such portability. For example, Google Takeout allows users to download their search history, post YouTube videos, and other items. Facebook has recently made it much easier to transfer photos and videos to other sites. However, connecting with old Facebook friends via the new network is not possible unless these friends join it as well. This creates a "switching cost" that locks Facebook users in such that it is difficult for rival social networks to compete for those users. Hence, policies that incentivize (require?) platforms to give users extensive data portability may play a pro-competitive role.

In this connection, it is important to understand that while users of platforms such as Facebook do not pay any fees to use the platform, they nonetheless transfer something of value to the platforms, namely, data. Moreover, these data include many dimensions of information that the user does not see. The user's activity itself in terms of browsing, searching, posting, creating a network of friends, making purchases and so forth all generate data of value to the platform, particularly for advertising. Among other things, a platform can use these data to improve its search algorithms, to target advertisements more precisely, and to discover which items are "hot" and what features account for this. Much of this data is kept by the platform even if a user switches to another social network or adopts a different default search engine. Inability to access that data creates a further disadvantage for rivals. A further policy question that then emerges is whether platforms should be required to share their data.

## 12.4.4 Mergers

In standard economics it is the entry of new firms, possibly with better products, that is the market's correction to monopoly power. Typically, such entry leads to lower prices for consumers. Perhaps more importantly, the new products that the entrants bring to a market increase the pressure for the existing market incumbents to innovate.

However, the potential threat that upstart, new entrant firms present can be blunted by buying them out. As Kwoka (2020) notes, the large platforms such as Google and Facebook, have acquired hundreds of firms over the past 15 years. These have included several high-tech firms that could have potentially competed with either the platforms themselves or with the applications that those platforms host. Perhaps Instagram and WhatsApp could both have evolved into alternative social networks rivaling Facebook. Instead Facebook acquired both.[21] Somewhat similarly, Google's acquisition of Waze reflects the purchase of an application that is a clear alternative to Google Maps.

The competitive impact of purchasing a potential rival is complicated. On the one hand, the acquisition transforms that threatened rival into an in-house ally. On the other, if incumbents are prepared to buy out a potential rival every time one appears, they will soon see a steady stream of would-be entrants hoping to be bought off. Indeed, it is well known that the hope of many startup firms is to be bought out, often by one of the big tech firms.[22]

At the same time, there is a widespread view among economists that merger policy in general has been too lenient and needs to be tightened, particularly with respect to the digital tech firms.[23] To a large extent, this view rests on the role of competition in spurring innovation. There is now a good deal of evidence, e.g., Aghion et al. (2009), Bloom et al. (2016), Federico et al. (2020), that rival entry promotes innovative activity, especially in technologically advanced sectors. The role of innovation in the platform markets is particularly critical because, as we have seen, the dollar (but not the data) price charged for at least one side of the market, usually the user side, is often zero. Hence, on the face of it, any official challenge to such a merger faces difficulty if based on the price-rising effects of increased market power.

## 12.5 DIGITAL PLATFORMS AND COMPETITION POLICY—RECENT PROPOSALS

The five largest US firms, in terms of capitalized value, are now the five "big tech" firms: Apple, Google, Microsoft, Amazon, and Facebook. The size of these firms combined with the understanding that their market preeminence is rooted in the network, scale, and scope economies of the information age has generated much public concern. Not surprisingly, several governments in OECD countries as well as research institutions have generated lengthy reports with proposals for how competition policy may best deal with the new dominant firms of the digital age.[24]

Regarding the use of price parity or MFN clauses and tying arrangements, there is an emerging consensus that these should be of limited legality, especially when imposed by a dominant firm such as Google or Facebook. For example, Crémer et al. (2019) argue that MFNs should be prohibited when applied broadly to restrict price cuts on any other site. However, they might be legitimate if written to allow a firm to offer a lower price on its own website, but not on other platforms. Both Furman et al. (2019) and Scott Morton et al. (2019) explicitly recognize the possible anti-competitive harm from tying and MFN clauses, and urge that these activities be restricted much more severely than current practice dictates.

There is also wide agreement that merger policy needs to become much more restrictive, especially in the tech sector. Scott Morton et al. (2019) argue that the usual burden of proof requires the government's challenge to a merger to show that the merger significantly harms competition and this burden of proof should be reversed for tech firms. In other words, mergers among tech firms will generally be blocked unless the merging parties can show that the merger benefits competition. Somewhat similarly, Bryan and Hovenkamp (2020) propose that any dominant firm be substantially restricted from acquiring startups. Others call for a more modest but still a significant degree of tightening in merger policy. Specifically, they advocate that the legal evaluation of mergers in the tech sector must give much more weight to the impact of the merger on innovation and potential competition.[25]

There is also an emerging consensus that data portability of some degree be mandatory. Zingales and Rolnik (2017), for example, propose that platform users be given property rights to all the digital connections that they create. Under this proposal, for example, a Facebook user could switch to a rival and reroute all their friends' messages through this new rival. Gans et al. (2001) and Gans (2018) call for an even broader right that would allow a user to transfer their complete digital identity and enjoy interoperability between platforms.

Support for this idea may also be found in Scott Morton et al. (2019) who call not only for data portability, but also for requiring dominant tech platforms to make their operations fully interoperable with others. This would mimic the way that the telephone companies were earlier required to make their systems fully interoperative so that users on one system could easily connect with users on another. Crémer et al. (2019) echo this proposal, as well.[26]

A common theme among competition policy-makers is that digital platforms are a somewhat new and special sector. Embedded in this theme is the recognition that the issues have a strong technical component and that the economic implications can be tricky, as we have repeatedly noted. This is true even with regard to the proposals just discussed. For example, while price parity or MFN clauses may restrict competition, they may also encourage service-enhancing investments in a platform. Conversely, requiring or permitting companies to share data may reduce user switching costs and ease entry. Yet this may also facilitate collusive practices and risk violation of user privacy.[27] Finally, evaluating the competitive impact of mergers is difficult under any circumstances.

For all these reasons, several analysts have called for new government agencies that would specialize in analyzing competition policy in the tech sector. Scott Morton et al. (2019) argue for new specialized competition courts along with the creation of a special Digital Authority overseeing all aspects of digital platforms. Furman et al. (2019) call for the creation of a special Digital Markets Unit that would establish and enforce a code of competitive conduct for digital platforms as well as establish rules promoting data portability and systems interoperability with care for any possible anti-competitive effects such information sharing may have.

The most dramatic policy proposals reflect attempts to address the potential conflicts of interest and self-preferencing practices that can arise when a platform is involved in many different complementary activities as Google, Facebook, and Amazon undoubtedly are. Srinivasan (2020), for example, calls for strict rules to separate the platforms from the advertising exchanges and tools that they also operate. Such rules could, for example, require Google to route the auctioning of its search and YouTube ad space out to rival exchanges as well as its own, and further require that solicitations from its own ad exchange go to DSP buying tools other than its own.

These proposals are not without precedent. Financial markets are governed by many rules that require strict separation of any firm's exchange, broker, and dealer divisions. There have also been requirements that access to a technology be shared in an unbiased manner. For instance, in the 1970s a few individual airlines initiated the use of computerized reservations system (CRS) technology for use by travel agents. While other airlines' flights would be listed on such systems, the Department of Transportation (DOT) found that there was widespread bias in the way the systems operated. In particular, a typical travel agent was led to steer passengers to the flights of the airline that owned the CRS that the agency used and not necessarily to the best deal. Ultimately, the DOT imposed rules requiring that display screens show flight options without bias and that the CRS charge the same booking fee to each airline it listed.

Some policy-makers would go even further and require "big tech" platforms to divest these complementary activities. US Senator Elizabeth Warren, for instance, has explicitly proposed that firms with annual global revenue over $25 billion and that operate a public exchange or marketplace for connecting third-party buyers and sellers be declared "platform utilities."[28] As such, these utilities would be prohibited from owning any of the participants on the platform. Under this proposal, Google would, as a search platform, be prohibited from running Google Shopping or Google Flights on its own search platform. Likewise, Amazon could no longer sell clothes or jewelry via Lark and Ro or North Eleven. Srinivasan (2020) also raises this as a possible policy response if the guardrails that she advocates in separating a platform's related activities are not sufficiently strong.

In evaluating these proposals, it is again worth emphasizing at the outset that two-sided platform markets are complex. That complexity is partly due to the interaction between the competition among platforms for buyers and sellers, and the competition among sellers within platforms. Both kinds of competition are affected by the extent of multi-homing, and a host of other specific factors that vary from case to case.

The complexity of competition policy for two-sided markets also arises because the platform's price and non-price strategies must be evaluated from the perspective of *both* sides of the platform and not just one side. The complication of analyzing competition on both sides was made clear in the *American Express* case recently decided by the US Supreme Court. Credit cards, like American Express, are two-sided platforms facilitating transactions between potential consumers on the one side and retailers on the other side. The issue in the case was the "anti-steering" clause that American Express included in their contracts with retailers forbidding these merchants to steer customers to using other credit cards or debit cards on which the retailers paid a lower commission (Visa and MasterCard have similar contractual arrangements). The Department of Justice and many states sued, claiming that this contractual clause essentially amounted to the suppression of price competition across these platforms, and therefore violated the antitrust laws prohibiting price-fixing.

The Supreme Court rejected this claim and held in favor of American Express explicitly because of the two-sided nature of the credit card business. In the Court's view, demonstrating competitive harm required showing not just that the American Express policy resulted in higher fees to merchants, but also that these fees were not a necessary part of attracting and possibly subsidizing credit card users and/or offering them better services [*Ohio, et al. v. American Express Company*, 585 U.S. ____ (2018)].

The complexities of two-sided platforms increase when they operate in digital markets owing to the underlying technical issues that digital commerce presents. This strongly suggests that simple, broad proposals such as Senator Warren's are not likely to work. Similar to more traditional markets such as camera companies where it was "natural" for them to produce their own film and operate stores and repair services, it may well be natural for platforms to connect a number of complementary activities to provide customers on both sides with a positive experience. Calls to "break up" the platforms often do not appear to recognize this complexity. Taken literally, for example, Senator Warren's proposal could force Microsoft to divest its Xbox store.

At the same time, the complexities of digital two-sided platform markets, including technical ones, suggest that new specialized courts and/or other government institutions may be required to oversee competition policy in this area. While there is always a risk that such public institutions could ultimately be "captured" by private interests, that risk is outweighed by the need to develop expertise required for sound policy-making regarding these issues. The very large size and preeminence of the "big tech" firms only strengthen this need.

## 12.6 SUMMARY

More than half of US advertising expenditure is now directed through the digital marketplace. Because of strong network effects, and significant scale and scope economies, the bulk of this expenditure passes through just three large two-sided platforms: Google, Facebook, and Amazon. Analyzing the implications of this transformation is challenging because of the complications that attend competition between and within such platforms.

What is clear is that the rise of the digital advertising platforms has major implications for advertising itself. These platforms permit firms to target their advertising more precisely, which may intensify competitive pressures in the product markets. At the same time, the pricing structure that two-sided advertising platforms find profitable is one that is free to users, requiring a higher fee to advertising firms.

The fact that the digital advertising platforms are so large and enjoy substantial market power further suggests that the price of advertising could be too high and, possibly, that such platforms will favor advertising firms that themselves have a high markup from which the platforms can extract more revenue. Both of these factors work to limit advertising and competitive pressure in the product market. However, such analysis is complicated by the interaction of between-platform competition and within-platform competition which, in turn, reflects the nature of cross-group and within-group network effects.

Along with Apple and Microsoft, the three major advertising platforms—Google, Facebook, and Amazon—are the five most valuable private firms in the world. Collectively, these five are often referred to as "big tech." Their dramatic growth and visible market power has led to much public discussion of the role of competition policy in the case of digital, two-sided platform markets. Some consensus appears to be emerging from that discussion. One point of consensus is that merger policy needs to be more restrictive for such dominant firms and to place more weight on the proposed merger's impact on innovation and potential competition. Another point is that data portability and system interoperability should be required so that new rivals can compete more effectively against the networks of the incumbents. Implementation of these and other policy proposals may well require the creation of special courts or agencies.

Whatever public policies are adopted, it is clear that the infrastructure of advertising has changed dramatically. For marketing professionals, this will require new thinking about both the design and expense of advertising programs. For economists and policy analysts, it will require further research regarding such topics as the informative versus persuasive role of advertising in the digital domain, the competitive implications of targeted advertising, and how these effects may be altered by behavioral findings such as the observation noted by Scott Morton et al. (2019) that search engine users rarely look past the first few links that a query yields. In short, there is a good deal of work still to be done.

## NOTES

1 See CNBC, October 15, 2019, http://www.cnbc.com/2019/1015/Amazon-is-eating-into-Googles-domi nance-in-search-ads.html (accessed 10 January, 2020).

2 We assume that $\sqrt{\dfrac{\lambda M}{F_A}} > 2$.

3   From (12.5) $\dfrac{\partial CS}{\partial N} = \dfrac{\lambda\beta(2N-1)+1}{2\left(2+\beta(N-1)\right)^{2}} > 0$, and so more consumers will have $CS - \bar{u}_{h} > 0$ and use the platform.

4   We say heuristically because the curves shown are illustrative and not precise mappings of explicit functions.

5   Of course, the platform could raise the fee $F_{A}$, limiting the increase in $N$.

6   Grind et al. (2019).

7   For a recent discussion of these issues, see Belleflamme and Peitz (2019). See also, Hagiu (2009), Goos et al. (2013), and Lin et al. (2016).

8   The functions $h(\cdot)$ and $g(\cdot)$ could be negative, depending on the overall impact of the network effects.

9   https://www.smallbizgenius.net/by-the-numbers/advertising-statistics/#gref and https://www.emarketer.com/content/amazon-advertising-2019 (accessed 1 February, 2021 and 4 April, 2020).

10  Ad networks are like ad exchanges in connecting buyers and sellers, but do so more as a go-between rather than as an impersonal market exchange.

11  The algorithm is formally called PageRank.

12  The firm Sistrix is a web analytics firm that has developed a visibility index for websites based on a measure of how frequently a search inquiry triggers the site to be listed in the results and the ranking of that listing.

13  See Grind et al. (2019) and Schechner et al. (2020). Similar charges have been made that Apple favors its own apps in its app store site. See Nicas and Collins (2019).

14  https://www.ftc.gov/public-statements/2013/01/statement-federal-trade-commission-regarding-googles-search-practices (accessed 27 May, 2021).

15  https://ec.europa.eu/competition/antitrust/cases/dec_docs/39740/39740_14996_3.pdf (accessed 21 July, 2020).

16  See Fussell (2019).

17  More recently, Epic, maker of the world's most popular video game, *Fortnite*, decided to offer its games directly to the public on its own site rather than through the app stores run by Apple and Google. Both giant platforms foreclosed their app stores to *Fortnite* immediately.

18  Tying is also closely related to bundling. The difference is that tying does not specify the proportions in which the tied products are consumed whereas bundling does. For instance, the buyer of a Hewlett-Packard (HP) printer may need to use HP ink cartridges but can use any quantity of them depending on the quantity of printing she does. In contrast, cruise ship travelers may find that they can only purchase a room-and-board option that specifies a fixed number of meals with their cabin.

19  European Commission (2018).

20  The MFN terminology is taken from trade policy literature where countries signing on to a multilateral trade agreement promise to extend any tariff reduction made to one country to all others. In other words, every nation gets the most-favored trade opportunities. Within individual markets, a further benefit of MFNs is that they may also lower transaction costs, as any buyer knows they are getting the seller's best price. See Baker and Chevalier (2013) and Ezrachi (2015) for a more complete discussion of MFN clauses and their effects.

21  Kosman (2019) presents evidence that Facebook understood the potential threat from Instagram and bought it out for that very reason. Similar evidence from documents released by the United Kingdom's Digital, Culture, Media and Sports (DCMS) parliamentary committee reveals internal emails and papers documenting that Facebook had been tracking WhatsApp and its growing popularity for months and

that it was overtaking Facebook Messenger in a number of areas prior to Facebook's acquisition of the firm for a whopping $19 billion in February 2014. See Warzel and Mac (2018).

22  Sokol (2019) argues that such buyout mergers are a standard part of the business plan for startup entrepreneurs.

23  See, e.g., Moss (2019), Shapiro (2019), Kwoka (2020) and Scott Morton et al. (2019).

24  See, e.g., Scott Morton et al. (2019), Crémer et al. (2019), Furman et al. (2019), and Robertson (2020).

25  In addition to Scott Morton et al. (2019), Furman et al. (2019), and Crémer et al. (2019), see also Shapiro (2019), Federico et al. (2020), and Kwoka (2020).

26  Note that both requirements for data portability and prohibitions of mergers with potential entrants may make the emergence of new rival platforms more likely if still improbable. This could, perhaps, mitigate any self-preferencing. For example, if two search engines compete, both may be incentivized to offer high-quality matches in response to users' search queries instead of favoring their own products in search results. See Eliaz and Spiegler (2011).

27  However, see Athey et al. (2017) for evidence that consumers may place a low value on privacy.

28  See Herndon (2019).

# 12.7 REFERENCES

Aghion, P., R. Blundell, R. Griffith, P. Howitt, and S. Prantl. 2009. "The Effects of Entry on Incumbent Innovation and Productivity." *Review of Economics and Statistics* 91 (February), 20–32.

Athey, S., C. Catalini, and C. Tucker. 2017. "The Digital Privacy Paradox: Small Money, Small Costs, Small Talk." NBER Working Paper 23488.

Baker, J., and J. Chevalier. 2013. "The Competitive Consequences of Most-Favored-Nations Provisions." *Antitrust Magazine* 27 (Spring), 7–14.

Belleflamme, P., and M. Peitz. 2019. "Managing Competition on a Two-Sided Platform." *Journal of Economics and Management Strategy* 28 (Spring), 5–22.

Bloom, N., M. Draca, and J. Van Reenen. 2016. "Trade Induced Technical Change? The Impact of Chinese Imports on Innovation, IT, and Productivity." *Review of Economic Studies* 83 (January), 87–117.

Bryan, K., and E. Hovenkamp. 2020. "Antitrust Limits on Startup Acquisitions." *Review of Industrial Organization* 56, 615–36.

Crémer, J., Y.-A de Montjoye, and H. Schweitzer. 2019. "Competition Policy for the Digital Era: Final Report." *European Commission*. https://ec.europa.eu/competition/publications/reports/kd0419345enn.pdf (accessed 21 July, 2020).

Eliaz, K., and N. Spiegler. 2011. "A Simple Model of Search Engine Pricing." *The Economic Journal* 121 (November), F329–F339.

European Commission. 2018. "Antitrust: Commission Fines Google €4.34 Billion for Illegal Practices Regarding Android Mobile Devices to Strengthen Dominance of Google's Search Engine." https://ec.eu ropa.eu/commission/presscorner/detail/en/IP_18_4581 (accessed 21 July, 2020).

Ezrachi, A. 2015. "The Competitive Effects of Parity Clauses on Online Commerce." *European Competition Journal* 11 (March), 488–519.

Federico, E., F. Scott Morton, and C. Shapiro. 2020. "Antitrust and Innovation: Welcoming and Protecting Disruption." *Innovation Policy and the Economy* 20, 125–90.

Furman, J., D. Coyle, A. Fletcher, D. McAuley, and P. Marsden. 2019. "Unlocking Digital Competition: Report of the Digital Competition Expert Panel." https://www.gov.uk/government/publications/unlock ing-digital-competition-report-of-the-digital-competition-expert-panel (accessed 5 April, 2020).

Fussell, S. 2019. "Algorithms Are People." *The Atlantic*, September 18. https://www.theatlantic.com/technol ogy/archive/2019/09/is-*Amazon*s-search-algorithm-biased-its-hard-to-prove/598264/ (accessed 20 March, 2020).

Gans, J. 2018. "Enhancing Competition with Data and Identity Portability." Hamilton Project, Washington, DC: Brookings Institution.

Gans, J., S. Stephens, and G. Woodbridge. 2001. "Numbers to the People: Regulation, Ownership, and Local Number Portability." *Information Economics and Policy* 13 (June), 167–80.

Goos, M., P. Van Cayseele, and B. Willekens. 2013. "Platform Pricing in Matching Markets." *Review of Network Economics* 12 (December), 437–57.

Grind, K., S. Schechner, R. McMillan, and J. West. 2019. "How Google Interferes With Its Search Algorithms and Changes Your Results." *Wall Street Journal*, June 15, p. A1.

Hagiu, A. 2009. "Two-Sided Platforms: Product Variety and Pricing Structures." *Journal of Economics and Management Strategy* 18 (Winter), 1011–43.

Hamilton, I. 2018. "Emails Show Mark Zuckerberg Personally Approved Facebook's Decision to Cut Off Vine's Access to Data." https://www.businessinsider.nl/facebook-documents-mark-zuckerberg-restrict ed-vine-data-access-2018-12/ (accessed 27 May, 2021).

Herndon, A. 2019. "Elizabeth Warren Proposes Breaking Up Tech Giants Like Amazon and Facebook." *New York Times*, March 9, p. A15.

Kosman, J. 2019. "Facebook Boasted of Buying Instagram to Kill the Competition." *New York Post*, February 26. https://nypost.com/2019/08/01/ftc-probing-Facebook-for-snapping-up-instagram-others-to-squash-rivals/ (accessed 28 March, 2019).

Kwoka, J. 2020. *Controlling Mergers and Market Power: A Program for Reviving Antitrust in America*. Boston: Competition Policy International.

Lin, M., R. Wu, and W. Zhou. 2016. "Two-Sided Pricing and Endogenous Network Effects." Working Paper. https://ssrn.com/abstract=2426033 (accessed 27 February, 2020).

Mattioli, D. 2019. "Amazon Changed Search Algorithm in Ways That Boost Its Own Products." *Wall Street Journal*, September 16. https://www.wsj.com/articles/amazon-changed-search-algorithm-in-ways-that-boost-its-own-products-11568645345 (accessed 27 May, 2021).

Moss, D. 2019. "The Record of Weak U.S. Merger Enforcement in Big Tech." White Paper, American Antitrust Institute.

Nicas, J., and K. Collins. 2019. "How Apple's Apps Topped Rivals in the App Store it Controls." *The New York Times*, September 9. https://www.nytimes.com/interactive/2019/09/09/technology/apple-app-store-competition.html (accessed 27 May, 2021).

Nocke, V., M. Peitz, and K. Stahl. 2007. "Platform Ownership." *Journal of the European Economic Association* 5 (December), 1130–60.

Robertson, V. 2020. "Antitrust Law and Digital Markets: A Guide to the European Competition Law Experience in the Digital Economy." Working Paper. https://papers.ssrn.com/sol3/papers.cfm?abstract_id=3631002 (accessed 27 May, 2021).

Schechner, S., K. Grind, and J. West. 2020. "Searching for Video? Google Pushes YouTube Over Rivals." *The Wall Street Journal*, July 15, p. A1.

Scott Morton, F., P. Bouvier, A. Ezrachi, B. Jullien, R. Katz, G. Kimmelman, A. D. Melamed, and J. Morgenstern. 2019. "Report of the Market Structure and Antitrust Subcommittee, Digital Platforms Project." George J. Stigler Center for the Study of the Economy and the State, University of Chicago Booth School of Business.

Shapiro, C. 2019. "Protecting Competition in the American Economy: Merger Control, Tech Titans, Labor Markets." *Journal of Economic Perspectives* 33 (Summer), 69–93.

Sokol, D. 2019. "Vertical Mergers and Entrepreneurial Exit." *Florida Law Review* 70 (November), 1357–78.

Srinivasan, D. 2020. "Why Google Dominates Advertising Markets." *Stanford Technology Law Review* 24, 55–175.

Warzel, C., and R. Mac. 2018. "These Confidential Charts Show Why Facebook Bought WhatsApp." *Buzzfeed*, December 5. https://www.buzzfeednews.com/article/charliewarzel/why-*Facebook*-bought-whatsapp (accessed 3 March, 2020).

Zingales, L., and G. Rolnik. 2017. "A Way to Own Your Social-Media Data." *New York Times*, July 1, p. A23.

# Index